Indexing Concepts and Methods

LIBRARY AND INFORMATION SCIENCE

CONSULTING EDITOR: *Harold Borko*
GRADUATE SCHOOL OF LIBRARY SCIENCE
UNIVERSITY OF CALIFORNIA, LOS ANGELES

Thomas H. Mott, Jr., Susan Artandi, and Leny Struminger
Introduction to PL/I Programming for Library and Information Science

Karen Sparck Jones and Martin Kay
Linguistics and Information Science

Manfred Kochen (Ed.)
Information for Action: From Knowledge to Wisdom

Harold Borko and Charles L. Bernier
Abstracting Concepts and Methods

G. Edward Evans
Management Techniques for Librarians

James Cabeceiras
The Multimedia Library: Materials Selection and Use

F. W. Lancaster
Toward Paperless Information Systems

H. S. Heaps
Information Retrieval: Computational and Theoretical Aspects

Harold Borko and Charles L. Bernier
Indexing Concepts and Methods

INDEXING CONCEPTS AND METHODS

Harold Borko

Graduate School of Library and Information Science
University of California
Los Angeles, California

Charles L. Bernier

School of Information and Library Studies
State University of New York
Buffalo, New York

ACADEMIC PRESS New York San Francisco London 1978

A Subsidiary of Harcourt Brace Jovanovich, Publishers

ACADEMIC PRESS, INC.
111 Fifth Avenue, New York, New York 10003

United Kingdom Edition published by
ACADEMIC PRESS, INC. (LONDON) LTD.
24/28 Oval Road, London NW1 7DX

Library of Congress Cataloging in Publication Data

Borko, Harold.
Indexing concepts and methods.

(Library and information science)
Bibliography: p.
1. Indexing. I. Bernier, Charles L., joint author.
II. Title. III. Series.
Z695.9.B653 029.5 77-77229
ISBN 0-12-118660-1

PRINTED IN THE UNITED STATES OF AMERICA

Contents

Preface

This volume, like its companion, *Abstracting Concepts and Methods* (by the same authors and published in 1975), is designed as a textbook. Its purpose is to facilitate the teaching of indexing and to help indexers improve their skills. A course in indexing must prepare the student to index a monograph, a reference work, or a collection of journal articles, but a university course in indexing must do more than provide training in a given skill. A university course must also provide perspective and understanding. Students of library and information science need to understand indexing structures and indexing concepts as well as indexing methods. Future and practicing librarians need to understand the use of indexes as reference tools. Thus the largest audience for this book may well be the index user, for a knowledge of the structure of indexes will make index use easier as well as more efficient and effective.

After a brief introduction (Part I) to the nature and functions of indexing, the structure of indexes—entries, syndetic systems, and formats—are explained (Part II). Part III begins with a description of the procedures that are common to both the indexing of books and serials. Suggestions are made for the selection and paraphrasing of subjects, choosing guide words, coining modifications, and making cross-references and glosses. Following these basic procedures, the specific techniques that are used in preparing a back-of-the-book index and an index to serial publications are described. Other chapters discuss editing, typesetting, proofreading, and the use of a thesaurus in indexing. A special chapter is devoted to a review of the state-of-the-art of computer-aided indexing.

Indexes have many different aspects and forms. It is essential that the indexer, and especially the users of indexes, understand these differences and the advantages and disadvantages of each. The chapters in Part IV describe various indexes beginning with the most important subject and author indexes and continuing with citation indexes, word indexes and concordances, and a variety of special indexes, such as to musical themes and chemical formulas, and numerical and classified indexes. Indexing for personal use is not excluded since nearly everyone has files and collections of materials that need the guidance provided by indexes. The indexing procedures described can be adopted with little change to the indexing of personal files and collections.

The concluding portion of the book (Part V) begins with criteria for evaluating indexes to books, to serial literature, and to bibliographic data bases. This is followed by a chapter on indexer training and a final chapter on indexing as a profession including employment opportunities and pay scales.

It is our aim that *Indexing Concepts and Methods* will provide a basis for a well-balanced course of instruction in indexing, and it is our hope that indexing organizations and our colleagues will find it a useful vehicle for teaching and stimulating interest in indexing.

I INTRODUCTION

1 The Nature of Indexes

Without indexes we could not easily telephone, order meals at restaurants, arrange for travel, find library materials, schedule appointments, locate correspondence, find streets, or do a host of other things that we now take for granted. Social interaction, as we know it today, would be impossible without indexes. Indexes are convenient guides; they not only guide us to subjects of interest, they also provide an integrated picture—an overview—of a subject field that no other bibliographic tool can provide.

The *American Heritage Dictionary* defines an index as "an alphabetized listing of names, places, and subjects included in a printed work [which] gives for each item the page on which it may be found." More technical definitions will be found at the end of this chapter.

1.1 INDEXING GOALS AND CHARACTERISTICS

Indexing Concepts and Methods instructs in the design, structure, and kinds of indexes; how to index and edit index cards; and how to evaluate and use indexes.

The purposes of an index, as stated by Mc Colvin, are

1. To facilitate reference to the specific item;
2. To compensate as far as possible for the fact that a book can be written in one sequence, according to one plan;
3. To disclose relationships; and
4. To disclose omissions [Mc Colvin, 1958, 33–4].

To these purposes we add

5. To answer questions of discovery and foster serendipity;
6. To provide a comprehensive overview of a subject field; and
7. To give nomenclature guidance.

Indexes have been improved greatly over the years. Contemporary indexes are more accurate; they place less load on users than do earlier indexes; and there are more indexes of all kinds. Secondary publications require indexes to prevent abstracts and other surrogates from becoming piles of unused paper. Indexes are now stored in computer files and searched by correlation of subject headings. Computers aid in the preparation of concordances and the publication of indexes. Indexing is a growing field, one that is changing to meet the needs of today's scholars, scientists, and engineers—and all the other people who use indexes.

1.2 INDEXES AS GUIDANCE SYSTEMS

Indexes are guides to books, chapters in books, articles and abstracts in journals, and a host of other things. Such guidance is needed because the items are unknown; dispersed in time, in space, and among languages; or remembered imperfectly.

Guidance by indexes is required and expected in our civilization. People gain from guidance and lose without adequate guidance. "The Road Not Taken" (Frost, 1948 and 1949, 131) is a tribute to roads, an ancient guidance system, and in this case two roads without their indexes. Roads themselves are physical guidance systems that index (lead to) villages, towns, and cities. Roads need indexes (signs and maps) to show where they lead.

1.2.1 Mental and Physical Guidance Systems

Mnemonics (memory aids) are used to index memories by stacking, sequencing, associating, and repeating things to be remembered. The internal indexes of the central nervous system (CNS) differ from indexes that are shared, because the CNS can index anything with anything else. However, for shared indexes there must be rules for indexing that are followed by all.

Model railroaders delight in the guidance provided by track, flanges, switches, and turntables—the "indexes" that lead the locomotives to selected places.

The charm of mazes is that they are unindexed guidance systems that may become mentally indexed after successful wandering.

Networks of roads, highways, thruways, byways, turnpikes, avenues, streets, boulevards, courts, terraces, and the like would resemble mazes—if these routes were not well indexed by maps and street signs.

A familiar guidance system is the arrangement of books in a library—a positional indexing that some users prefer to catalogs. By this system, a browser among the shelves can see how worn the book is and how besmirched, the number of its stamp marks, its size, color, and position. All of this may convey more information more rapidly than would the card catalog. Serendipity is fostered.

Cybernetics (the science of guidance systems that function through error correction by negative feedback) includes the study of pointers as indicators (indexes). The pointer on a thermostat, for example, is set to indicate (index) the temperature desired, and the negative-feedback system then controls the room temperature. The cybernetic systems of the CNS, as described by Powers (1973), are especially fascinating in that their reference levels are set and maintained by still higher levels of control, with each level indexed by a higher level. Changing the index changes behavior, with profound implications for education, training, advertising, propaganda, cooperation, and the control of oneself and others.

Braille embossing—a system that indexes for touch—guides trained fingers to information.

Many physical guidance systems, operating by means of indicators and indexes, are themselves indicators and indexes.

1.2.2 Literature Guidance Systems

Guides to literature lead users to written works. Literature guides can refer to whole works or to the contents of a single work. Book and card catalogs, as well as classifications, guide users to whole works; indexes guide them to the contents of a work; and concordances guide them to the words in a work.

1.2.2.1 *Guides to Whole Works*

Generally, cataloging is used in libraries to guide the searcher to subjects, author names, and titles of works. The subject headings assigned tend to be broad (general), in order to guide the searcher to the subject (main theme) of the work (book, monograph, patent, report). These subject headings are used to bring like works together, not to differentiate works on the same subject. Analytics (subject indexing of the parts of a work) is rarely used in libraries because of the prohibitive cost.

Classification (a form of subject analysis) specifies the relation of one work to others in the collection by means of a notational system, for example, the Dewey Decimal Classification, the Universal Decimal Classification, and the Library of Congress Classification. These classifications logically group and arrange categories of works. Again, these classifications group categorized works as a unit and may be unaffected by the detailed contents of the works. There are also classified indexes to books and journals.

1.2.2.2 *Guides to the Contents of Works*

Users usually want much more specific information than merely the titles of books in a collection on a given broad subject area such as agriculture. For example, the user may seek data on insecticides to control a particular grain beetle. Indexes in primary and secondary works guide searchers to specific data *within* works. Organizations such as the U.S. Department of Agriculture, the Chemical Abstracts Service, and the American Psychological Association publish indexes of this type.

The various kinds of indexes—such as alphabetic subject indexes (the usual manual index), keyword indexes, correlative indexes (such as the coordinate index), and concordances—are examined in subsequent chapters.

1.3 HISTORY

In ancient times, indexes were not so numerous as they are today. Before printing, there were few books; reading was an uncommon skill. People memorized the Bible and the Koran and were able to recite long passages from them.

The first special index was made for the Bible. According to Busa

(1971), biblical concordances were probably in existence in the seventh and eighth centuries.

The word *index*, as Henry Wheatley (1879) discusses in his pioneering work *What Is an Index?* was first used by the Romans to denote a discovery, a discloser, an informer. When used in relation to literature, *index* meant a catalog, a list, an inscription, or even a title of a book. Seneca refers to an index (i.e., list) of philosophers. Cicero, when writing to Atticus, asks that he be sent two clerks to repair his books and requests that they bring along some parchment on which to make indexes. Francis J. Witty takes issue with Wheatley's interpretation and claims that the correct translation of Cicero's letter should be: "and bid them bring a bit of parchment from which title-tags (*indices*) are made. You Greeks, I believe, call them SILLYBOI [1973, 193; Witty's parentheses and italics]." Witty continues, "Although scholars might argue about the exact meaning of the diminutive *membranulam*, there is no doubt that *index* and *SILLYBOS* meant the little parchment title-tags that hung down from the papyrus roll to identify a work on a library shelf [Witty, 1973, 193]."

The English use of *index* as explained by Wheatley (1879, 8–9) is nominative rather than accusative and generally means 'table of contents' or 'literary guide.' Shakespeare often uses the word, as when Iago in *Othello* refers to "an index and obscure prologue to the history of lust and foul thoughts." In *Richard III,* Queen Margaret alludes to "The flattering index to a direful pageant." In the same play, Buckingham threatens:

> I'll sort occasion
> As index to the story we late talk'd of,
> To part the Queen's proud kindred from the King.

In about the seventeenth century, scholarly books appeared with indexes. Thus, in Speed's *History of Great Britaine* (1611) there is an "Index of Alphabetical Table containing the principal matters in this history." Scobell's *Acts and Ordinances of Parliament, 1640–1656* has "An Alphabetical Table of the most material contents of the whole book" preceded by "An index of the general titles comprised in the ensuing table."

Originally, the words *index* and *table* were used interchangeably. By the middle of the seventeenth century, the former dominates. In present English usage, the word *table* is reserved for the initial guide, in page-number order, to the contents of a book as defined by chapter headings—that is, the table of contents. The word *index* now refers to the alphabetized or classified entries usually found at the back of a book. Words such as *inventory, register, calendar, catalog, syllabus,* and *summary* are no longer synonymous with index.

William Frederick Poole is credited with the invention of the modern index to journal articles. *Poole's Index* (1882) created subject entries from keywords in the titles of the articles indexed. Not only is Poole's index a forerunner of the present-day Wilson indexes but it also anticipates the Keyword-in-Context (KWIC) concordance of Hans Peter Luhn (1960). In 1880, John Shaw Billings, of the U.S. Army Medical Library, prepared the first index catalog for medical literature. Four years earlier, Charles Ammi Cutter codified subject cataloging principles in his *Rules for a Printed Dictionary Catalog* (1876).

In the twentieth century, many changes occurred in subject indexing and cataloging. However, to detail these developments would carry us too far into the history of the subject; so it seems logical to end this brief historical review with the reference to Cutter, who ushers in the modern period of library indexing and cataloging practices.

We conclude with some current definitions from the ANSI 1968 Standard. An index is

> a systematic guide to items contained in, or concepts derived from, a collection. These items or derived concepts are represented by entries in a known or stated searchable order, such as alphabetical, chronological, or numerical.

Indexing is

> the process of analyzing the informational content of records of knowledge and expressing the informational content in the language of the indexing system. It involves:
>
> 1. selecting indexable concepts in a document; and
> 2. expressing these concepts in the language of the indexing system (as index entries); and an ordered list.

An indexing system is

> the set of prescribed procedures (manual and/or machine) for organizing the contents of records of knowledge for purposes of retrieval and dissemination.

II STRUCTURE

2 Entries

Index entries are guides rather than surrogates; that is, entries are intended to guide searchers to, rather than inform them about, the contents of a work. Entries are the principal subdivisions of an index; they generally consist of headings, modifications, and page references or locators. For some entries, a modification is unnecessary and so is omitted.

2.1 HEADINGS

Examples of five entries are

> **Smith, John William,** 19, 57, 99
> character of, 30
> honors received, 62–3

Smith, John William is an inverted heading; "character of" and "honors received" are modifications, and the numbers are page references.

Index headings have major control of the alphabetical position of entries in an index. Entries are chosen to be the best guides to the items indexed. Although it is very difficult to define "best guides," indexers and index users have little difficulty in selecting the best guides to subjects. Index headings may lead not only to subjects but also to author surnames, data, molecular formulas, patent numbers, and taxa.

In selecting the guide terms for a heading, the indexer needs to consider whether to use *(a)* the author's terminology or standard nomenclature; *(b)* an alphabetic arrangement or a classified arrangement; *(c)* a normal word order or an inverted word order.

2.1.1 Nomenclature and Terminology

Selection of subject headings involves the choice of whether or not to use the author's terminology. Decision to use the words in the text is justified by their usefulness in communicating the subject area of the text. The author has judged this usefulness and deliberately chosen the words that clearly and precisely communicate the subject matter. The indexer is generally ill-advised to change the author's words. Such change risks loss of the author's meaning. The only exceptions to use of the author's terms are *(a)* if they are in error; *(b)* if a standard nomenclature is employed in the index; and *(c)* if the indexer sees inconsistencies of which the author was not aware. Alternate terms can be used in the index as long as proper cross-references are provided. Standard index nomenclatures have been systematically developed by authors and scholars working together with indexers, lexicographers, and other nomenclature experts. These commonly accepted nomenclatures have been developed specifically to improve communication and indexing.

An enormous number of cross-references would be needed to provide adequate guidance if systematic nomenclature were not used. For example, it is reported that the average name of a pharmaceutical has seven interchangeable names. If so, then there would need to be six cross-references (on the average) for each compound name in the index. The number of cross-references might exceed the number of index entries, and the index user would be inconvenienced. It is apparent that the best solution to the problem posed by synonymy in this case is to use a standard index nomenclature derived from a set of reasonable, accepted rules. Such rules have been developed by organic chemical compound indexers working with organic chemists over the years.

Systematic organic chemical nomenclature for indexes is discussed at a later stage, to illustrate nomenclatures in general. Of the almost infinite number of organic compounds possible, there are more than 3 million known today; more are being synthesized and identified every day. Organic chemists usually use structural formulas in discussing their discipline. They write the structural formulas on paper or a blackboard and point to them (or their components) in talking about them. Organic chemists rarely use index names (especially the inverted names); in addition to the structural formulas, they often use common names (e.g., naphthalene), pet names (e.g., rabbit compound), acronyms, and initialisms (e.g., DDT). Chemists can talk indefinitely about the compound DDT without ever using its index name. Clearly, the purpose of the index name is not to aid discussion and thinking but to give the compound a unique place in an index; if not listed in the index by that name, the compound is not represented.

Because of the difficulty in learning nomenclature and naming organic compounds, some chemists have felt that ciphers and codes for organic structures were a necessary alternative to names. Among the ciphers proposed and in use are the Hayward, IUPAC (International Union of Pure and Applied Chemistry), and Wiswesser. Ciphers are intended to give a unique and unambiguous representation for each structure. Codes give representations for parts of structures; the total code for a structure may not be unambiguous or unique. Thus, more than one compound can often be represented by the same code, just as more than one compound can be represented by a molecular formula.

It is necessary to train indexers and index users in the nomenclature and terminology of a field. Subject knowledge is a prerequisite. Detailed training in nomenclature is given to indexers by on-the-job coaching. However, courses of study may be the most efficient way of learning the terminology and nomenclature of a field. Special bibliographic tools may assist in this learning process. The molecular-formula and ring indexes are outstanding examples of bibliographic tools for those who find organic nomenclature difficult and time-consuming to master and use.

2.1.2 Classification

The use of a classification system for supplying and arranging index headings has almost irresistible appeal. It is natural to believe that a carefully conceived, logical arrangement of subject headings will be spontaneously acclaimed by everyone. The illusion of universality is exceedingly difficult to dispel. However, what one person sees as logical and natural may well be perceived as illogical by others.

Three major difficulties of classification systems are

1. Fairly rapid obsolescence of the system as new terms, such as *plutonium* and *laser*, come into the language and old terms are given new meanings; for example, *bit* has acquired the meaning "binary digit"
2. The necessity of using some terms that are not quite appropriate; for example, indexing **Computers** under **Calculating machines**
3. Having to decide among multiple terms that seem equally valid, such as **Coating, Covering, Filming, Lacquering, Painting,** and **Varnishing**

No inexpensive way has yet been found for continuously updating a classification system that is being used daily by many indexers and index searchers. Perhaps the closest we have come to an ideal indexing system is that of indexing with modifications and using cross-references, both of which can be immediately altered to match the changes in language with the subjects indexed. Computer files of thesaurus terms that can be updated on-line may be used, although such files are more expensive than is the use of modifications.

2.1.3 Inversion

Multiple-word headings can be verbatim or inverted. It is generally recommended that normal word order (uninverted) be used (e.g., **Academic library,** not **Library, academic**), for this is more natural to the user. Inversion, which is both a syndetic and a classificatory device, is used to assemble entries that are similar and entries that the searcher probably should consult. The noun of a phrase may serve as an index heading, and there may be a scattering of relevant references among the index heading for the noun and those for the multiple-word terms. For example, there may be related material under: **Academic libraries, Libraries, Public libraries, School libraries,** and **Special libraries.** The indexer can reduce this scattering by establishing the following headings:

Libraries
Libraries, academic
Libraries, public
Libraries, school
Libraries, special

In all of these examples, the second word is part of the heading, not a modification. Through such inversions, index users are reminded that related material may be found under the inverted headings as well as under the more general heading, **Libraries.** All of these headings being adjacent in the index makes consultation convenient.

Another way to reduce this kind of scattering is to index material on, say, special libraries under the subject heading, **Libraries.** Then, the modifications under the heading may include the word "special," if that is the only kind of library reported in the work indexed. If more than one kind of library is involved in the study being indexed, the indexer may either specify all of the kinds of libraries in the modification or omit reference to any kind of library from the modification. The latter choice is made if the indexer believes, from study of the material indexed, that the author has used the different kinds of libraries only as examples of some general principle and could, perhaps, as well have chosen entirely different examples—that is, the specific kinds of libraries are not subjects of study; the general principle is the subject of study, and this principle applies to many kinds of libraries. However, should the text contrast or compare different kinds of libraries, or report on each separately (with or without generalization), then the indexer would use subject headings for all of the specific kinds of libraries discussed. In this last case, the indexer may choose to invert the subject headings for all of the specific kinds of libraries discussed in order to reduce scattering of related data, and may also make one entry under the general subject heading, **Libraries,** if the author's generalization extends to all libraries or to a substantial number of them.

Inversion of names is commonly used in author indexes, such as catalogs (book and card), and in telephone directories, although in Iceland the directories are reported to use uninverted names. The advantages of inversion are that identical names are not scattered by the use of one, two, or no given names or initials, for example:

Jones
Jones, J.
Jones, J. J.
Jones, John J.
Jones, John Joseph

All such names are adjacent to or near one another in an author index that uses inversion. When editing an author index, the editor, on encountering such a set of headings, will determine if all refer to the same person and will combine the names that do and leave separate those that do not.

Organic-compound names are inverted in indexes to bring index (and parent) names together. This kind of classification is useful for organic chemists. For example, DDT might be indexed as ***D*ichloro*D*iphenyl*T*richloroethane** under the *D* headings, as **1,1,1-Trichloro-2,2-bis(*p*-chlorophenyl)ethane** under *T*, or as **Benzene, 1,1′-(2,2,2-trichloroethylidene)bis[4-chloro-** under *B*. The last name is inverted to group **Benzene** derivatives. The second name is uninverted; and the first is the one from which the initialism DDT may have been derived. The first groups compounds whose names begin with **Di**, those that have two identical substituents in them; the second, under **Tri**, groups compounds that have three identical substituents in them; and the last groups **Benzene** derivatives, which organic chemists are said to prefer. From the viewpoint of the indexer and index publisher, there is no choice but to use systematic names because of the enormous number of cross-references that would otherwise be necessary.

Multiword index headings are inverted whenever clustering of related headings is desirable and whenever clean separation of related headings is found to be impossible (or too costly). Cross-references from the uninverted to the inverted names are usually unnecessary because the last word of the term suggests the heading under which to look.

2.2 MODIFICATIONS

Modifications in index entries come between the heading and the reference. In subject indexes, the modification defines the subject indexed more precisely than does the subject heading alone. In author indexes, the modification may be the title of the work or a coined statement about the work. In patent-number indexes, the modification may be the patent number. In citation indexes, the modification may be the name of the citing author and an abbreviated citing reference. A good modification enables the user to say yes or no, rather than maybe, in determining the relevance of the entry to the search.

Without modifications, there would be blocks of references under most of the headings in an index. A block of references is a group of references without verbal differentiation among them. Each reference number in a block is undifferentiated from the others as well as undifferentiated from all *potential* modifications that could be written for the heading. An example of an index heading with a block of references is

Existentialism, 23, 108, 148, 162, 273

In this set of five entries, the searcher finds it impossible to decide which reference to look up first and whether any will turn up material that is relevant to the search. Modifications reduce the risk of the searcher's looking up the entry only to find it irrelevant. In general, the more specific the modification, the smaller the risk.

Modifications can be coined for the entry or they can be selected from a standard list of words, terms, or phrases. In the latter case, the modification is called a *subheading*. Subheadings are created prior to indexing and derive from previously published indexes. Coined modifications, rather than subheadings, are used for the vast majority of all indexes. Coined modifications are as flexible as is language itself; any subject can be expressed as precisely as is necessary to differentiate it from all other entries that might be coined for the heading or, more usually, for those entries that actually exist under the heading. Only very general entries have no modifications.

Correlative indexes, also called coordinate indexes, do not permit the use of coined modifications, either in manual or in computer retrieval systems. In these systems, the index entry is a word, term, or phrase with a reference. Since modifications are not used, specificity in search is achieved by the correlation of two or more subject headings as the Boolean product (AND).

Key-Word-in-Context (KWIC) and Key-Word-out-of-Context (KWOC) concordances have neither coined modifications nor standard subheadings. In these, the subject heading word is selected automatically for the central column or for the left margin. The modification is the rest of the title—or as much of it as will fit into the line space provided on the printout.

In summary, coined modifications and standard subheadings serve

1. To define the subject more precisely
2. To enable the searcher to decide among references
3. To prevent relevant material from being overlooked because its presence has not been indicated

Indexes with modifications are easier to use than are indexes without them.

2.2.1 Subheadings

Some indexes employ subheadings to subdivide headings. Examples are **Sucrose** and **Sucrose** *(biological studies);* and **Steel** and **Steel**

manufacture. This technique increases the relevance of entries under each heading and is called splitting headings. If an index entry could be made under both headings, then the decision must be made whether to use both entries or to specify a reason for entering under only one heading. If the decision is to use only one entry, a rule is required to ensure consistency throughout the index. An example of a subject paraphrase that can be double indexed is "Molecular conformation in relation to sweetness and crystal structure of sucrose and other disaccharides." This paraphrase can logically be indexed under both **Sucrose** and **Sucrose** *(biological studies).* But the decision to use two entries in all such cases bulks the index and slows indexing.

Subheadings that split headings or substitute for coined modifications are created before the indexing is started and are based on preconceived or predicted categories into which the entries under a given heading might fall. The success of subheadings depends on the accuracy of this prediction. Creation of new subheadings during indexing is discouraged by the indexing organization, in an attempt to keep a group of indexers in harmony with an indexing authority.

In general, coined modifications produce more precise and specific entries than do standard subheadings.

2.2.2 Diction

The diction of modifications is usually that of the author of the work being indexed, in order to avoid loss of the author's meaning and to assure the searcher that the correct reference has been found.

If systematic nomenclature is used for headings, there is also some justification for using the systematic names as the first words of modifications under other headings. Such use reduces scattering among synonyms in the modifications and aids the searcher.

Subject-index entries generally do not use verbs, adverbs, or articles because these have been found to be unnecessary in expressing subjects. Prepositions, however, are used freely in good indexes, because they show the precise relations among words and because they make the modifications more specific. For example, the index entry

Methane, use in methanol manufacture, 3241

can be edited to read

Methane, in methanol manufacture, 3241

The preposition "in," can mean "use in." Many such expressions can be edited to keep only the preposition. However, if the preposition is deleted, the entry reads

> **Methane,** methanol manufacture, 3241

The searcher is then left wondering about the precise relation between the heading and the modification. Prepositions are used to make index entries unambiguous and as specific as is necessary to distinguish every modification under a heading.

Author indexes generally use the author's diction in the modification.

The molecular-formula indexes of chemistry use systematic index nomenclature (inverted names) as modifications, and the user can find the identical name in the Subject Index or Chemical Substance Index.

Patent-Number Indexes use the names of the countries in which the patent was issued as the heading and the patent number as the modification.

2.2.3 Format and Grammar

Although the words in coined modifications are usually those of the author, the syntax of the modification is almost invariably that of the indexer. The first word of the modification acts like a newpaper headline, to catch the eye of a reader skimming the column of entries. Usual, expected, and unnecessary words are not used to start modifications. For example, under the heading **Computers,** the modification "digital" is no longer needed, since most computers are now digital rather than analog; the modification "electronic" can also be omitted for the same reason. In a good index, unusual, eye-catching, and distinctive words are brought to the fore by inversion of the modification. For example:

> **Computers,** networks, user access *via,* 34

Here, "networks" has been judged by the indexer or by the index editor to have more impact than does "user" and so comes first. In another index, "user" might be considered more striking and so would come first. This might be the case, for example, in the index to a book on computer networks.

There are many other rules for the syntax and diction of modifications; only a few of the more important ones will be considered here.

The action word of the modification is normally brought to the fore if it applies to a substantive heading, for example:

Paper, printing on parchmentized, 2134

If the action word does not directly apply to the heading, it is placed later in the modification, for example:

Paper, ink spreading on, 4321

Conversely, if the heading has been derived from an action word (e.g., a gerund), the first words in the modification should refer to the thing to which the action is applied, for example:

Spreading, of ink on paper, 4321

Parallel words in modifications are placed in alphabetical order, unless there is some good reason for using some other order. An example of alphabetical order in a modification is

Shakespeare, Bacon *vs.* Marlowe as author of works of, 1423

Modifications may have a logical sequence, for example:

Copper ores, mining, grinding, screening, pulverizing and floating, 3214

Arrangement of modification words in either logical or alphabetical order helps to avoid scattering under headings; it also helps index editors to combine identical index entries and place related ones into a group.

Punctuation in modifications is simple. Commas follow the heading and the modification. There is usually no period after the reference number. In a series of modification, the comma is omitted before the conjunctions "and" and "or." An inversion is indicated by a comma or by parentheses. Quotation marks are not used because the indexer does not extract the modification verbatim from the text or title. Italics are used to indicate genera and species of biological organisms, and also to indicate Latin abbreviations, for example, *viz.* and *vs.* Periods are used after abbreviations to avoid confusion. Proper nouns are capitalized. The word that starts the heading is capitalized; the word that starts the modifications is not capitalized unless it is a proper noun. A hyphen is used to indicate carry-over of the last part of a word and between two words that, taken together, modify a noun. Modifications are indented to indicate headings omitted. Double indentation (indentation beyond that used to indicate the heading) is used to avoid repetition of modification-starting words. For example:

Information systems, automated intelligence, 645
  for automated on-the-job training, 3294
  automated or mechanized, 1001
    bibliography on, 67
    classification and, 2145
    effect on authors, 1007
    library education and, 3213
  for automatic abstracting, indexing and retrieving technical documents, 252
  automatic equipment for, 211

2.3 REFERENCES (LOCATORS)

In indexing, the term *reference* may mean either "cross-reference" or "page reference." In order to avoid ambiguity, the term *reference* will, in this volume, be used exclusively to refer to page references; the term *cross-reference* will be used when that is the intended meaning. Page numbers will be referred to either as references or as locators; both terms are in use. Since subject-index entries are made as specific as possible in order to differentiate one from another, there is normally only one or a very few page references for each heading–modification combination. When indexing a topic of continuous discussion, inclusive page numbers are used, for example, 83–95. The dash between the numbers represents the pages not listed.

Reference numbers may include mnemonic codes. For example, *P* can be used ahead of the reference number to indicate a patent; *B* can mean a book; and *R* a review. Codes help the searcher to avoid unwanted material. Another code is a letter or superscript number to indicate the fraction of the column or the part of the page that bears the subject indexed. *Chemical Abstracts* once used superscript numbers to designate ninths of the column of abstracts. Later, italic letters were used for the same purpose. The *Encyclopaedia Brittanica* has used fourths of a page, designated *a*, *b*, *c*, and *d*, to increase the accuracy of reference.

2.3.1 Serial-Number References

Serial numbers (e.g., of abstracts) are popular references; they are easily assigned and used. The principal information that serial numbers can convey is approximate guidance to the date of accession and precise data on the number of items indexed. Serial numbers are usually the pages of the work indexed; some serial numbers are those of abstracts and reports. Codes may precede the number to identify the organization publishing or distributing the report. Thus, AD (ASTIA Document) followed by a serial number (usually of six digits) refers to reports available from the Defense Documentation Center (DDC, formerly the Armed Services Technical Information Agency); PB indicates reports supplied by the Publication Board of the Department of Commerce. The NTIS (National Technical Information Service) now disseminates reports formerly handled by the Publication Board.

2.3.2 Informational References

Informational references convey more information than do serial-number references; they may include the date of publication or sometimes just the last two digits of the year. Codes are used to indicate the names of organizations publishing the reports (e.g., OAR = Office of Aerospace Research).

The Universal Decimal Classification and the Dewey Decimal Classification use code numbers that carry a great deal of data about the material indexed. These code numbers may be supplemented by a serial number in the locator. Explanation of codes and classifications is required and may appear in the introduction to the index; sometimes the explanation appears on every page of the index. Most indexers and indexing organizations prefer the simplicity of the plain serial number as reference.

2.4 PRE- AND POSTCORRELATIVE INDEXES

Indexes can also be categorized as pre- and postcorrelative. In precorrelative (the usual nonmanipulative, published) indexes, the correlation of the words in the headings and modifications provides the required selectivity. For example, the heading **Automation** is broad enough to index banking systems, libraries, machine tools, manufacturing techniques, military hardware, and so on. The index entry "**Automation,** of library circulation systems, 1234" is much more specific than is the heading **Automation**. Since correlations are made during the indexing and prior to use of the index, this is called a *pre*correlative or precoordinate index. Specificity can be shifted from the modification to the heading by taking words from the modification and adding them to the heading. For example, the heading, **Automation,** could have been **Library automation.** The modification would then have been "of circulation systems." The overall specificity would be the same for both entries.

In postcorrelative or postcoordinate indexes (the usual manipulative, computerized indexes), correlation is performed at the time of search; hence the name *post*correlative. The term *manipulative* refers to the correlation (e.g., coordination) of headings (e.g., index terms, descriptors, Uniterms) at the time of search. In contrast, *nonmanipulative* means that the headings need not be correlated, since all of the correlations have been displayed through the heading–modification combinations. In our example, the headings, **Automation, Libraries, Circulation,** and **Systems** (or **Circulation systems**) would be entered into the computerized, postcorrelative, manipulative index, and each term would be given the reference, 1234. Correlation of any set of these terms as Boolean products (AND) would show that all of the terms had been associated with the same reference number, 1234; that is, all terms had been used to index the same work. Correlation of the terms, **Automation, Libraries, Circulation,** and **Systems** in a postcorrelative index would retrieve the reference to the work numbered 1234.

Not all postcorrelative indexes are computerized. There are, for example, systems that use punched cards (Hollerith and edge-notched) and other systems that use optical-coincidence cards. Also, indexes without modifications have been printed and used for post-correlative searching by comparison of the reference numbers under two or more headings. However, the most commonly encountered form of postcorrelative indexes is computerized, and most computerized indexes are postcorrelative.

Entries for computerized, postcorrelative indexes consist of headings and document reference numbers. Direct (uninverted) files are ordered by reference numbers; inverted files assemble all reference numbers associated with a given heading. The elimination of the modifications has created difficulties in controlling the specificity of the index entries. Thus, for postcorrelative indexes and computer searching, specificity is attained by

1. Correlation of two or more terms as Boolean products
2. Correlation of one or more terms as Boolean negatives
3. Increase in the specificity of the heading by adding adjectives to the noun or gerund heading
4. Use of roles that specify the function that the heading serves
5. Use of links that prevent false correlations
6. Use of weights to indicate the "importance" of a heading in indexing a given work

Use of the Boolean product (Item 1) *A AND B* is the most common method for increasing relevance (percentage of retrieved works that are relevant to the search). Use of Boolean negation (Item 2) may result in the loss of relevant references unless used with great care. Headings that are mutually exclusive, for example, **Male** and **Female,** often cannot be used in Boolean negation because some works may be indexed by both **Male** and **Female,** and these would be excluded by the use of negation. Increase in heading specificity (Item 3) is a very effective indexing technique and one that improves search results. The use of roles (Item 4) has not been found to be universally satisfactory. The use of links (Item 5) can work if both indexer and searcher remember to use the links. The use of weights in indexing (Item 6) is mainly two-valued. More complex weighting schemes have been proposed; however, they have been little used.

These six procedures for increasing specificity when using computerized indexes have changed search strategy and results.

3 Syndetic Systems

Guidance in an index is provided by a syndetic system that includes cross-references, inversions (with comma or parentheses), glosses (notes or scope notes), and by the introduction. Guidance is directed toward the choice of terms among synonyms, related headings, what has been indexed under a heading, how the heading is organized, coverage, scope, nomenclature, and exceptions. Guidance for the indexer in alterations of cross-references is provided outside the index by inverted cross-references.

The purpose of syndetic guidance is to prevent the searcher from missing entries and to save search time. Without this kind of guidance, the indexer could not avoid scattering similar (and even identical) entries. An index without a syndetic system is inferior to an index with such a system.

The syndetic system is planned, designed, and created by the indexer. This chapter is intended to help indexers, index users, and students learn more about syndetic systems and how to use them effectively.

3.1 CROSS-REFERENCES

The major component of the syndetic system is the cross-reference. Cross-references guide searchers from where they are in the index to where they should be, or should also be, to locate relevant entries and headings. The proper use of cross-references by indexers and by searchers is essential to locating all relevant material. Cross-references are commands that are ignored only at the risk of loss of guidance through the index as a whole and to pertinent entries within it.

Cross-references may be internal (interfiled with the index entries), or external (in a thesaurus separate from the index), or both. This chapter describes commonly used cross-references, such as *see, see also*, and *see under*. Also described is a way of categorizing cross-references as general, specific, or supergeneral. An additional discussion of cross-references can be found in the chapter on thesauri (Chapter 8), which deals with external syndetic systems and includes term relations and their notations.

3.1.1 *See* Cross-References

The *see* cross-reference primarily controls scattering among synonyms. The most important and popular heading is chosen as the authorized term, and *see* cross-references are made to it from all indexed synonyms. The *see* cross-reference

Weeding see *Deacquisition*

instructs the searcher (as well as the indexer) at **Weeding** to turn to the subject heading **Deacquisition.** This *see* cross-reference means that the searcher will find no entries in the index under the heading **Weeding.** The indexer has decided that, for this index, **Deacquisition** is superior to **Weeding** as a subject heading—perhaps because it has been used more frequently than **Weeding,** or because **Weeding** was considered to be ambiguous, inelegant, or too loose an analogy. Generally, popularity of a term as reflected by frequent use among authors is the main reason for the choice of a subject heading among synonyms; the indexer wants to put the entries where most users will look first. An example of a set of *see* cross-references from a set of synonyms to one chosen term is

Corn sugar see *Glucose*
Dextrose see *Glucose*
Grape sugar see *Glucose*

For the examples in this text and for the index in the back of the book, the index heading is printed in boldface type and the referred-to term is printed in italics. The words "see" and "see also" are printed in Roman. Because typography is used to distinguish among headings, cross-references, and modifications, it has been possible to omit many commas and periods from the entries with no loss of clarity.

At the time that these *see* cross-references are made, the indexer may also create a parenthetical synonym (a kind of gloss) after the heading, to indicate what has been put under the heading, for example:

Glucose (*corn sugar; dextrose; grape sugar*)

Semicolons are commonly used between parenthetical synonyms because there may be commas within the synonymous terms, for example, *libraries, school.* Parenthetical synonyms are usually placed in alphabetical order. Other examples of *see* cross-references from synonyms are:

Aspirin see *Benzoic acid, 2-(acetyloxy)-*
ASTIA see *Armed Services Technical Information Agency*
Aurum *see Gold*
Cars see *Automobiles*
KWIC concordance see *Key-Word-in-Context concordance*
Mark Twain see *Clemens, Samuel Langhorn*
Scope notes see *Glosses*

See cross-references are sometimes used to guide searchers to antonyms. This use is neither frequent nor consistent. For example, if the indexer finds that the terms *fluidity* and *viscosity* are both used to discuss identical or similar work and that no useful distinction between the two headings can be made, then the two terms should be linked by a *see* cross-reference. Further potential examples of *see* cross-references from antonyms are

Electrical resistance see *Electrical conductivity*
Unclassified documents see *Classified documents*
Opacity see *Transparency*
Inelasticity see *Elasticity*

See cross-references are sometimes used to guide searchers from a specific to a more general term. This occurs most frequently for terms in a field adjacent to the field indexed. For example, in an index to a chemistry text, the following might appear

Calculus see *Mathematics*
Autobiography see *Biography*
Drosophila melanogaster see *Fruit flies*

By way of contrast, in an index to mathematics, this entry might appear

Organic compounds see *Chemical compounds*

See cross-references are from the specific term to the general term and *not* from the general to the specific.

Further discussion of the use of *see* cross-references, with emphasis on external syndetic systems and thesauri, occurs in Chapter 8.

3.1.2 *See also* Cross-References

The *see also* cross-reference guides searchers to related material that cannot rationally be assembled under one heading. Several relations may be recognized by *see also* cross-references. The most common is that between class (genus) and subclass (species). Examples are:

Abstracts (see also *Critical abstracts; Indicative abstracts; Informative abstracts; Modular abstracts; Special-purpose abstracts; Statistical abstracts; Tabular abstracts; Telegraphic abstracts*)
Art (see also *Painting)*
Boats (see also *Vessels)*
Libraries (see also *Special libraries*)
Painting (see also *Art*)
Ships (see also *Vessels*)
Vessels (see also *Boats; Ships*)

See also cross-references can go from the genus to the species and vice versa. They may be enclosed in parentheses to distinguish them from *see* cross-references. If the heading from which the user is referred implies or indicates the heading to which he is referred, the *see also* cross-reference may be omitted. An example is

Special libraries (see also *Libraries*)

The word, "Libraries," in the term, "Special libraries," suggests to the reader that there might be a heading, **Libraries**, and this, in some indexes, is regarded as obviating the need for a *see also* cross-reference. As another example, **Interlibrary loan** suggests the word "library" and can be used without a *see also* cross-reference.

A second relation interlocked by *see also* cross-references is between the whole and its parts. The cross-reference may be from the whole to the part or vice versa. Some examples are:

Books (see also *Pages*)
Pages (see also *Books*)
Learning (see also *Memory; Problem-solving; Reorganization*)
Lenses (see also *Cameras*)
Telescopes (see also *Lenses*)
Concrete (see also *Cement*)
Blood (see also *Erythrocytes*)

This relation is indicated by a *see also* cross-reference *only* if the searcher will actually find closely related material under both headings.

A third relation indicated by *see also* cross-references is between products and their uses. Examples are

Cornflakes (see also *Nutrition*)
Entertainment (see also *Television*)
Propaganda (see also *Motivation*)
Buildings (see also *Shelter*)
Automobiles (see also *Transportation*)
Cross-references (see also *Guidance*)

The use of *see also* cross-references to link parts with wholes and products with uses is incomplete in most indexes.

Antonyms are more frequently interlocked by *see also* than by *see* cross-references. Examples are

Fluidity (see also *Viscosity*)
Viscosity (see also *Fluidity*)
Marriage (see also *Divorce*)
Resistance (see also *Conductivity*)
Compatibility (see also *Incompatibility*)

In the last example, the reverse *see also* cross-reference would not be used because the word "incompatibility" suggests that there might be a heading **Compatibility.** This suggestibility is used to save the cost, space, and time required for entering an unnecessary *see also* cross-reference.

The cause–effect relation can be the source of *see also* cross-references, for example

Viruses (see also *Diseases*)
Pathogenic bacteria (see also *Diseases*)
Avitaminosis (see also *Diseases*)
Diseases (see also *Avitaminosis*; *Pathogenic bacteria*; *Viruses*)
Crime (see also *Suggestibility*)
Gluttony (see also *Obesity*)

Cause–effect cross-references can become misleading through changes in causes and effects with time.

There are many other kinds of relations that can be interlocked by means of *see also* cross-references. The *see also* cross-reference should be used in all cases in which the indexer believes that the searcher may otherwise miss relevant entries.

See and *see also* cross-references are generally not made between adjacent headings. The user is expected to notice the nearby heading.

Singulars and plurals are seldom interlocked by *see* cross-references because they are usually adjacent. But for very short words this may not be the case. For example, the subject heading, **Fur,** may be several pages away from the plural, **Furs,** in a large chemistry index. Between the singular and the plural there may be **Furaldehyde; Furnaces; Furnaces, blast; Furnaces, electric; Furnaces, open-hearth**; and so on. The following *see* cross-reference would then be justified

Fur see *Furs*

The use of *see also* cross-references is dependent on the judgment of the indexer and the index editor, and is stimulated by feedback from users. Systematic construction of comprehensive technical thesauri that display relations among terms is highly desirable and should prevent searchers from missing entries in indexes.

3.1.3 *See under* Cross-References

The most specific of all cross-references is the *see under*. An example is

Bergamot oil see under *Oils*

In normal indexing, the word "bergamot" can occur in any entry under the heading **Oils** because the modification can start with almost any word. For example, the entry might be

> **Oils,** apple-seed, banana, bergamot, and orange, in perfumery, 1234

Or, an action word might be deemed best to start the modification, for example

> **Oils,** determination of bergamot and other citrus, in perfumes, 1234

Examples of *see under* cross-references are

> **Self-teaching** see under *Instruction*
> **Entries** see under *Indexes*
> **Training** see under *Instruction*
> **Typesetting** see under *Composition*

See under cross-references are not used from synonyms to the chosen heading; they are used to enter species under genus names. The **Bergamot oil** cross-reference is an example. *See under* cross-references are justified only if the specific term to which the user is being referred is in an entry in the index.

3.1.4 General Cross-References

Besides categorizing cross-references as internal, external, *see, see also,* and *see under,* all cross-references can also be categorized as general, specific, and supergeneral.

The use of a general cross-reference is justified by the existence in the index of *any* entry under the heading to which the searcher is referred. Both *see* and *see also* cross-references belong in this category. Examples are

> **Abstracts** (see also *Chemical Abstracts*)
> **Buffalo** *(North American)* see *Bison bison*
> **Natrium** see *Sodium*
> **TAB** see *Technical Abstract Bulletin*
> **Vitamin B_1** see *Thiamin*

The purpose of categorizing cross-references as general, specific, or supergeneral is to save time in justifying the use of cross-references during the editing of large annual indexes. (The justification of cross-references is described in Chapter 7.) General cross-references can be justified for use by those who do not know the subject field of the index, whereas justification of specific and supergeneral cross-references is reserved for those who know the subject field. Since two-thirds of the cross-references in an index may be general, this categorization can effect considerable savings.

3.1.5 Specific Cross-References

Specific cross-references require some specific modification for their justification, for example

Bergamot oil see under *Oils*
Cornflakes (see also *Nutrition*)
Automobiles (see also *Transportation*)
Viruses (see also *Diseases*)
Calculus see *Mathematics*

It is best to have those who know the subject field of the index justify specific cross-references. The words sought may not appear in the modification because synonyms, more generic terms, and otherwise related terms can also be used to justify a specific cross-reference. Only a person who knows the subject can make the reliable decisions needed; and even the expert may have to look up the work indexed in order to justify the specific cross-reference. For example, the subject expert, seeking to justify the cross-reference

Viruses (see also *Diseases*)

may find smallpox, measles, mumps, kuru, scrapie, and the like. Although the words "virus" or "viral" may not appear in any modification under the heading **Diseases,** this specific *see also* cross-reference is nevertheless justified.

3.1.6 Supergeneral Cross-References

A supergeneral cross-reference is justified by more than one heading of the same type. An example is

Aurum see the *Gold* headings

This supergeneral cross-reference is justified by the presence in the index of such headings as **Gold; Gold, analysis; Gold, metallurgy of; Gold chloride**; and so on. Other examples of supergeneral cross-references are

> **Alloys** see alloy headings under the names of the metallic elements
> **Societies** see headings under the names of the specific societies, e.g., *American Chemical Society*

Supergeneral cross-references are justified for use in an index that has two or more headings of the type referred to. If there is only one such heading, then the supergeneral cross-reference is changed to lead the searcher directly to the existing heading.

Supergeneral cross-references may save making myriad cross-references and thus save cost, index space, and effort. But the user may not find them so reliable a guide as are *see* and *see also* cross-references.

Supergeneral cross-references are used sparingly in good indexes because they require expert knowledge on the part of the user. Also, supergeneral cross-references to headings that are scattered alphabetically may be left dangling because it could take too much time to check them and justify their use. Thus, general and specific cross-references are usually preferred in quality indexes.

3.2 INTERFILED NOTES

Notes interfiled in the index among the entries are an effective way of instructing the searcher and reminding the indexer. These notes immediately follow the heading term. An example is:

> **Abstract journals** *(abstracting organizations and services)*

This note makes it clear that abstracting organizations and services are indexed under **Abstract journals.** Other examples are

> **Finland** (including periods under Sweden and the Russian Empire)
> **Esters** (Esters of organic acids are entered under the acid headings, with the following exceptions . . . .)
> **Dyes** (Entries are arranged by the chemical-group name for the dye, method of dyeing, material dyed, and one color, in that order)

Interfiled notes are more effective than are instructions and definitions in the introduction to the index. The indexers may wish to communicate to the user how a heading is arranged, what is included under the heading, how specific examples of the heading are indexed, or what is excluded from the heading. The interfiled note is ideal for this kind of communication.

3.3 INVERSIONS

Another syndetic device for merging or making like entries adjacent is the inversion of headings and modifications. The word that controls the alphabetical position of the heading or modification is placed first and the word that normally precedes the controlling word is placed second.

3.3.1 Comma Inversions

An example of an inverted subject heading is **Libraries, public.** Author names are usually inverted, for example

Washington, George

Modifications can also be inverted, for example

Budgets, for libraries, public, 1234

The indexer (or index editor) has inverted this modification in order to assemble, under the heading **Budgets,** the budgets of various types of libraries, because users interested in budgets of one kind of library might well be interested in the budgets of other kinds of libraries or of libraries in general. The uninverted entry reads

Budgets, for public libraries, 1234

Inversions in modifications are usually made during editing because it is apparent to the index editor which modifications should be combined or made adjacent. Usually the arrangement of entries under a given heading is ad hoc, although the modifications in indexes to journals may come to have a somewhat standardized arrangement, and the indexer observes this order and follows it in coining modifications.

The inversion of headings is generally done by the indexer; however, the editor also may invert headings.

In general, uninverted headings and modifications are preferred unless this results in scattering of identical or similar material.

The preferred form is to be able to read straight from the heading into the modification; the second choice is to read back the entry by starting with the modification; the third choice is to read back the entry by starting with the part of the modification that follows the internal comma. The examples are, respectively,

Aerobics, in health maintenance, 3214
Monad symbol, history of, 1234
Statistics, medical research, misuse of, 2314

Examples of inverted headings are

Conductivity, electric
Conductivity, thermal

These two headings may have been inverted because the entries for the heading **Conductivity** dealt with the subject as a general phenomenon, characterized as either electric or thermal. The indexer or index editor has brought adjacent to **Conductivity** the headings for the specific kinds of conductivity, so that searchers will be reminded to consider all three headings and index users will find it convenient to have all related headings adjacent. Comma inversions (as well as parenthetical inversions) may be preferable to the use of *see also* cross-references in both directions. Another way of handling scattering of this nature is to use **Conductivity** as the heading and "electrical" and "thermal" in modifications under the heading, preferably at the start of the appropriate modifications. Then, as the heading grows, it can eventually be split into the three headings given above. This is the normal evolution of some subject headings. Often, the way that a heading should be split is not obvious when the heading is first formed but becomes apparent with its expansion.

3.3.2 Parenthetical Inversions

Examples of parenthetical inversions are

Bit *(binary-digit)*
Bit *(drill)*
Bit *(horse)*
Bit *(piece-of-eight)*

The words in parentheses serve as definitions and glosses. Uninverted, the headings would be

Binary-digit bit
Drill bit
Horse bit
Piece-of-eight bit

Parenthetical inversions are generally used to eliminate ambiguity and heterogeneity of headings as well as to bring like headings together. In the foregoing example, there is little likelihood of confusion among the four headings. In other cases, the indexer or editor may be unsure of the correct heading and so inverts to reduce scattering. For most indexes, it is considered best to bring the noun to the fore.

Inversions in modifications after the inversion that brings the first noun to the fore are generally pointless and best avoided. An example of a pointless inversion is

Farming, in Iowa of corn, early sweet, 1234

This could be worded better as

Farming, in Iowa of early sweet corn, 1234

3.4 INVERTED CROSS-REFERENCES

Inverted or reverse cross-references give the indexer and index editor complete control over the cross-references of an index at all times. For the cross-reference

Milk sugar see *Lactose*

the inverted cross-reference is

Lactose, milk sugar see ______

The cross-reference is alphabetized under *M* (**Milk**); the inverted cross-reference is alphabetized under *L* (**Lactose**).

The inverted cross-reference informs the indexer, and especially the index editor, that there is a *see* cross-reference at **Milk sugar** that can be used to lead the searcher to the heading **Lactose.**

The primary purpose of inverted cross-references is for use in editing. During indexing, indexers consult the inverted cross-reference file whenever they wish to change or eliminate a heading. If there are cross-references coming into the heading (as revealed by inverted cross-references), then the affected cross-references as well as inverted cross-references are changed. In the foregoing example, if the heading **Lactose** is to be changed, let us say, to the systematic organic chemical name for lactose, then the indexer changes the cross-reference as well as the inverted cross-reference by crossing out both cards but saving them to preserve the history of the heading. The crossed-out cards may be dated at the time of change and then filed in the card archives. From this time on, both lactose and milk sugar will be indexed under the systematic name for lactose; and the cross-references and inverted cross-references (a total of four) will show this.

It is important to note that inverted cross-references have nothing to do with parenthetical and comma inversions. Also, inverted cross-references are seldom published because they are of little use to the searcher; however, they are vitally important in enabling the indexer to change headings without leaving dangling cross-references.

All kinds of cross-references—*see, see also, see under*, specific general, and even supergeneral—may have inverted cross-references in order to give complete control of the index and cross-references to the indexer and index editor.

For convenience in use, inverted cross-references are usually kept in a separate file and are of a different color from the index cards and from the cross-reference cards. Separate files for all of these kinds of cards facilitate their use and prevent confusion.

The following is an example of an inverted cross-reference card:

Ongoing research
Research in progress see _____.
(72) (73) ~~74~~ (75) ~~76~~ ~~77~~ 78 79 80 81 82

The corresponding cross-reference is

Research in progress see *Ongoing research*

The numbers at the bottom of the inverted cross-reference card are the years in which the cross-reference is to be used or not used in the index. If the cross-reference is to appear in a particular year's index, that number is circled by the index editor; if the cross-reference is not to appear in that year's index, the number is crossed out.

4 Format, Standards, and Alphabetization

The structure of an index can affect its utility. Therefore, in order to improve the format and to encourage uniformity and good practice, some structural rules for the preparation of printed indexes have been devised. Common standards for all indexes are an elusive goal but one that is actively pursued by the American National Standards Institute and by international standards bodies. The United Nations UNISIST program for worldwide scientific and technical information dissemination requires standards for all phases of document handling. To achieve compatibility among the indexes of different countries, the United Nations Educational, Scientific, and Cultural Organization (UNESCO) published a draft of *Indexing Principles* (UNESCO, 1975).

The American National Standards Institute (ANSI), formerly the United States of America Standards Institute, has a committee—designated Z39—for developing standards in the field of library work, documentation, and publishing practices; its *Basic Criteria for Indexes* was published in 1959 and completely revised in 1968 and again in 1974.

The British Standards Institute has a Documentation Standards Committee and a subcommittee on Indexes and Alphabetical Arrangements. In 1964, the committee prepared a British Standard on Indexing (BS 3700:1964) *Preparation of Indexes of Books, Periodicals, and Other Publications*. This standard was revised in 1976.

The guidance for the preparation and structure of indexes presented in this book, and more specifically in this chapter, follows suggestions made in indexing manuals prepared by publishers and by abstracting and indexing services; and most important, it is based upon the published standards of both the American and British Standards Institutes.

4.1 DEFINITIONS

Technical terms that are used to discuss indexes and their components are defined in standards. The definitions in this book are based on both ANSI and BSI standards, supplemented by the way that the terms are used in this book. However, it might be well to spell out here the definitions of the two most fundamental terms—*index* and *entry*.

4.1.1 Index

As defined by ANSI (1968), "An index is a systematic guide to items contained in, or concepts derived from, a collection. These items or derived concepts are represented by entries arranged in a known or stated searchable order, such as alphabetical, chronological, or numerical."

4.1.2 Entry

The principal component of an index is the *entry*. It consists of a heading, which is most commonly a key word or phrase used to identify the subject, a modification or subheading, and a page reference or locator.

4.2 THE FUNCTIONS AND SCOPE OF AN INDEX

A good index is an objective guide to specific items in a work. The index helps the searcher to locate the items efficiently; it may also be used to browse among related entries. A good index helps to bring the language of the index and user into correlation and to indicate relations among items (ANSI, 1968, 7). To serve these purposes, an index must be complete and accurate.

4.2.1 Completeness

All indexable material must be provided with index entries as guides. ANSI standards recommend that, in addition to the basic text, the index should also cover significant items in forewords, prefaces, introductions, and appendices of books; and notes, reviews, letters to the editor, and other features of periodicals.

4.2.2 Accuracy

Incorrect or inaccurate referencing causes loss of guidance and may waste searchers' time in trying to find the correct references. Entries that accurately guide to the subject matter save the searcher from looking up fruitless entries and from missing guidance. Entries that are too broad, for example, lead the searcher to expect more than will be found; entries that are too narrow may be ignored by the searcher when they should be looked up.

4.2.3 Scattering

Poor indexes (those of low standards and quality) have extensive scattering of like entries among diverse headings and various modifications. Scattering of synonyms is especially objectionable because the indexer can control it. Scattering causes the user to have to look under many different places in the index to locate all relevant material. Scattering among modifications also leaves the searcher uncertain as to the quality of the index.

4.3 ORGANIZATION AND FORMAT

Indexes should be organized according to a logical and consistent plan. Since indexes must be in harmony with the subject matter indexed and the expectations of searchers, there must necessarily be variations in the arrangement of different indexes. Standards serve as guides and help bring some harmony and consistency to the design of indexes.

4.3.1 Single Sequence versus Multiple Sequence Indexes

Book indexes are generally arranged in a single alphabetic sequence; that is to say, most books contain only a subject index. For anthologies and reports of symposia, an author index—that is, an index to the authors of the works included in the volume—helps in finding the works of a particular author. A table of contents can, a little less conveniently, do the same.

Indexes to primary and secondary journal publications usually have multiple sequences and separate author, subject, and special indexes. These different forms are discussed in Part IV—Types of Indexes.

4.3.2 Alphabetic and Other Arrangements

Alphabetical order is the most common one for all kinds of indexes; however, for certain types of material, other sequences may be more useful. Some nonalphabetic arrangements are

1. Numerical or serial order
   - First Annual Report
   - Second Annual Report
   - Third Annual Report

   - Uranium 235
   - Uranium 236
   - Uranium 238
2. Chronological order
   - Twelfth century
   - Thirteenth century
   - Fourteenth century
3. Classified order
   - Roads
     - Interstate highways
       - Route 66
       - Route 91

Arizona
  Route 72
  Route 80
California
  Route 5
  Route 101

4.3.3 Page Layout

How the page is organized and printed is the most striking feature of an index's format.

4.3.3.1 *Type*

Although 8- to 12-point type is usual for setting text, indexes commonly use 6-point type or smaller. The volume of the index (i.e., in cubic inches) is proportional to the square of the type point size; larger type is higher as well as broader. Thus an index set in 12-point type has about four times the volume of an index set in 6-point type. The smaller type sizes are economically attractive. Since indexes are consulted rather than read, the smaller type sizes can be tolerated; however, type that is 4-point or smaller can be considered an imposition on readers, some of whom have to use magnifying lenses when consulting the index.

Typefaces are a highly visible feature of format. There are a number of beautiful faces, such as Bodoni, designed by Giambattista Bodoni 1740–1813). Rococo and sterile faces may be less legible than are the more attractive faces. The typeface used conveys an impression of the care that has gone into constructing the index. Different faces can be used effectively to label the different constituents of index entries, to differentiate cross-references from entries, and to make special nomenclatures stand out. For example, headings set in boldface speed the use of the index by enabling the searcher to ignore modifications until the right heading is found. The volume number of the reference in boldface aids in separating the abstract or page number, and so speeds search and makes it more accurate. Italics are used to indicate genus–species names of systematic biological nomenclature (e.g., *Musca domestica,* for housefly) and for certain symbols in organic chemical nomenclature (e.g., *d* and *l* to indicate stereo configuration and optical rotation of isomers). Italics are also used to indicate the entry to which the searcher is being referred by a cross-reference, the heading of which is commonly in boldface, for example, **Iron** (see also *Steel*). Parentheses can be used to differentiate *see also* cross-references from *see* cross-references.

The mixing of type sizes certainly emphasizes the larger sizes, but it also adds white space to the page and may increase the bulk of the index. The improved readability resulting from mixing type sizes has to be evaluated against the increased size and cost of the index.

In choosing a typeface, it is important to remember that type with serifs is more legible than that without serifs (Burt, 1959).

4.3.3.2 *Line Length*

Line length affects the ease of use of the index. Lines that are too long may cause the searcher to skip lines or to read the same line twice. Short lines are preferred. However, lines that are too short force the reading of several lines for each entry and waste the indentation space of the second and following lines.

4.3.3.3 *Indentations*

Indentations are a feature of the format of nearly all indexes. Only the crudest of indexes repeats heading and first words of modifications. Indentation is used in place of such repetition. Although indentations for headings and double indentations for first words of modifications are customary, more than two indentations can cause the searcher to lose track of what terms have been omitted. This difficulty occurs especially as the user turns the page. Some indexes use three, four, or even five indentations with standard subheadings. In these indexes, the searcher may forget some of the terms to be added from memory and must then go back to find all of the terms needed to read the entry correctly. To ensure consistency and to avoid confusion, indexers use rules for creating double indentations. One rule is that three or more entries are required before a double indentation is made; fewer than three entries do not justify the cost of the double indentation. This rule aids the visibility of the indentation and alerts the user to add the omitted term to the second and following modifications. The amount of space indented also affects the visibility of the indentation; the more space, the greater the visibility. However, indentations the width of only two or three characters seem to be generally adequate.

Another rule requires that prepositions after the omitted term not be dropped even though the prepositions are the same for all entries in the indentation. Retention of the starting preposition makes it easier to understand the entry. For example, "effect on" may start one double indentation, "effect of" a second, and "effect in" a third. In each of these three double indentations, the prepositions *on*, *of*, and *in* are retained for all of the entries under each double indentation.

4.3.3.4 *Headlines and Continued Headings*

To aid the searcher in reaching the correct page of the index rapidly, the index format should include a *headline* that is, a printing of the first entry heading at the top of the page. A *running head* differs from a headline in that the *same* running head—usually the title of a major section (e.g., chapter title or part title) of the book—is repeated on consecutive pages. In an index to a secondary publication, the running head may include the name and volume number of the index and so facilitate accurate reference. Another format device that aids the searcher is the *continued heading*. This is used whenever an entry breaks from one column to another or from one page to another. When such a break occurs, the heading is repeated at the top of the column or page.

4.3.3.5 *Special Symbols, Codes, and Abbreviations*

Indexes for some disciplines require the use of special characters. For example, chemists are used to seeing H_2SO_4; H2SO4 appears odd. The use of all capital letters may confound different things: Co stands for cobalt; CO for carbon monoxide. Mathematicians need integral and summation signs. Electronic component designers and engineers have developed their own sets of symbols that can be used in indexes. Dr. Hans Selye (1966) has invented symbolic statements for representing biological experiments and their results. Symbols of this kind can and should be used in indexes. Without them, indexes may appear to be strange and unfamiliar to engineers, scholars, and scientists.

In contrast to the accepted use of special symbols in indexes, the use of codes has always been a debatable indexing practice. Codes require indexer and user alike to memorize the codes or to use a table to identify their meaning. For the indexer, this is not a major problem; it is a part of indexing to remember codes. For occasional users, codes will probably be unfamiliar and thus require time to look up and interpret. Examples of codes used in indexes are: *P* for patent, *B* for book, and *R* for review. These codes are mnemonic; other codes, such as those for journal titles, are not consistently mnemonic because the constituents are too numerous and the mnemonic codes are used up long before all constituents have been coded. Consultation of translation tables is the only way to find the answer, and such consultation wastes the time of indexers as well as of users. For ease of use, the number of different code symbols used in an index should be limited to four or five.

Abbreviations can easily be made mnemonic. There are hundreds of abbreviations that can be recognized immediately by most readers. Examples are abbr., cf., contin., i.e., N.Y., *viz.*, etc. An excessively long list of abbreviations may become a millstone around the necks of abstractors, indexers, editors, proofreaders, and, most important of all, the users of a journal and its indexes. Abbreviations are desirable because they save space and reading time. However, there is much to be said for limiting the list of abbreviations to those commonly used by the searchers anticipated for the index. Abbreviations should be used consistently to avoid their becoming time-wasting puzzles for index users.

4.3.4 Paper

Paper quality affects the use of indexes. Indexes receive much more use than does the material indexed. Since indexes may be separately published and rebound (sometimes several times in the life of the volume), unusually large margins on the index pages may be desirable so that print is not removed during the trimming that follows rebinding.

Durability of the paper on which indexes are printed is also of concern. Paper of low acidity has increased durability; it does not age rapidly or become brown, yellow, or brittle. Rag (cotton fiber) content of paper also increases its durability. Gloss interferes with the visibility of the type. A page that is off-white or ivory in color is said to be less of a strain to read than is white paper. Opacity is desirable because visibility of the printing on the reverse side of the page is a distraction and reduces legibility. Although thin paper makes the index smaller and lighter, it is usually less opaque than is thicker paper; there has to be a trade-off between opacity and bulk of the index. The ideal paper should be off-white, resistant to tearing, and opaque yet thin; and it should slide easily over adjacent pages to avoid crumpling when the index is closed. Printers are usually helpful in selecting the best paper for the least cost.

4.4 CHARACTERIZATION OF INDEXES

The *Basic Criteria for Indexes* (ANSI, 1968) provides a scheme for characterizing by (*a*) search objectives; (*b*) arrangement; (*c*) heading; and (*d*) by access points or structure. The introductory sentence "Indexes must respond to search objectives" means that indexes must be designed to aid the searcher in finding relevant information. Properly designed indexes take into account the kind of material indexed and the needs of searchers. The title of the index indicates its general search objectives; one would not expect to find guidance to names of authors in a subject index, nor to find references to contemporary poetry in the subject index of *Chemical Abstracts*. The index designer tries to eliminate previously encountered difficulties and to meet current requests and needs by varying the structure of the index. For example, if chemists have had difficulty in naming organic compounds, a formula index and a ring index can be built. In subject fields in which there is a renowned classification, this is ideal for organizing the index entries, rather than alphabetizing them. An example is the U. S. Patent-Office Classification.

4.4.1 Characterization by Search Objective

Basic Criteria for Indexes (ANSI, 1968) describes three kinds of searches: synthetical, analytical, and hierarchical.

4.4.1.1 *Synthetical Searches*

Synthetical searches correlate heading terms by Boolean logic (product, sum, negation). Such correlative indexes use headings but not modifications. Specificity is attained by the correlation of two or more headings during search, by means of the Boolean product. By way of contrast, precorrelative indexes use subject headings plus modifications and references. The index entries fully specify the subject (concept or topic) being indexed, and the search is performed by reading all of the entries under the relevant headings. With precorrelative indexes, searching is either analytical or hierarchical; with some difficulty, synthetical search is also possible, but it is hardly neccessary.

4.4.1.2 *Analytical Searches*

In analytical searches, one looks for guidance by means of highly specific entries; therefore each index entry should be maximally specific. In the few indexes that do permit posting-up (entry under a generic as well as under a specific heading), broad as well as specific subjects have separate entries. Thus, **Oranges** may be one heading and **Fruit** (or **Citrus fruit**) another heading in the index. However, if the author generalizes, it is the indexer's responsibility to index under a general subject heading. For example, if the author studies oranges and reports that his results apply to all fruit, it is the indexer's responsibility to index both under **Fruit** and under **Oranges**. If the specific subject being studied is only exemplary and many other specific subjects could have been reported just as well, then the indexer usually omits the specific subject heading (as being a common example) and indexes *only* under the general heading. An example would be an experimental study relating to mammals, in which the author has used guinea pigs but reports that his results apply to *all* mammals. The index would have an entry under **Mammals** and not under **Guinea pigs.** The indexer may not generalize a subject beyond what is reported in the author's work, except in indexes that employ posting-up. Thus, if the study is about oranges and the author does not generalize to include all fruit or all citrus fruit, the indexer may *not* use **Fruit** as a subject heading.

If specific entries are indented under broader headings, an hierarchical index is created.

4.4.1.3 *Hierarchical Searches*

An hierarchical search employs the permanent semantic relations of entries in a classified index. A general term is used to collect more specific subject headings under it. The modifications, as usual, define each subject indexed more specifically than does the heading alone. If an hierarchical arrangement is accepted as standard for the index, then the headings must be carefully classified under terms that are more general than the subject headings. Searchers must know the hierarchical relations that obtain in a classified index and must use this knowledge. Hierarchical searches are facilitated by a well-classified thesaurus and an alphabetical list of thesaurus terms that guides users to the appropriate categories in the thesaurus. Most searchers may have to consult the alphabetical before the classified arrangement.

4.4.2 Characterization by Arrangement

> The arrangement of an index may be alphabetical, as in the familiar book index, or an index to a periodical; numerical, as in a report-number or contract-number index; chronological; hierarchical, as used in taxonomy; arbitrarily systematic, as in an index to a coded collection; or a combination of these. The various arrangements are used by the index designer to make searches more complete than otherwise would be possible, to facilitate search, and to reduce scattering among related entries [ANSI, 1968, 11].

Once the kind and purpose of the index is established, the order of the entries is predetermined—or almost so. For example, it is difficult to picture a patent-number index being in other than numerical order. An index to organisms (animal, plant, micro-) might best be hierarchical according to taxa: classes, phyla, families, genera, species, and subspecies. And it is difficult to imagine an author index in other than alphabetical order by the last name of the first author. The arrangement that is accepted as standard is controlled largely by the subject matter, rarely by the index designer.

4.4.3 Characterization by Heading

Indexes are characterized by the type of entry headings and the subject field of the index, for example, "Subject Index to *Chemical Abstracts*." Index headings may consist of names of people, titles of books and journal articles, chemical formulas, patent numbers, codes for musical themes, and so on—the wide range of possibilities is indicative of the variety of indexes that can be designed.

4.4.4 Characterization by Access Points

"The structure of an index may provide only one access point to items or concepts, or it may provide multiple access points [ANSI, 1968, 11]." A patent-number index is an example of a single access point index—because multiple approaches are impossible. By way of contrast, subject indexes invariably provide multiple access to indexed subjects, because nearly all subjects require two or more index entries for adequate guidance to them. Multiple access can also be provided through *see also* cross-references that join subject headings having various relations to one another.

4.5 ALPHABETIZATION

Widespread familiarity with alphabetic and numerical order makes alpha numerical indexes practical and convenient. Because of the simplicity of the concept, one might assume that alphabetizing an index and searching in an alphabetical index are simple procedures; such is not the case. When punctuation marks, different typefaces, foreign letters, digits occurring in strings of letters, headings, references, modifications, inversions, and abbreviations are all taken into account, the processes of ordering and searching for entries become complex—very complex at times. Searchers untrained in strict alphabetization can use alphabetical indexes because they can get near the entry and then skim headings until the desired one is found. The indexer needs to follow stringent alphabetizing rules.

Indexing the names of people and places may present unexpected problems. For this reason some of the rules for alphabetizing names are discussed and illustrated here. Even the rules themselves may cause difficulty, because in a complex index arrangement some of the rules seem to be contradictory. An entire chapter could be devoted to filing rules, but to do so does not seem appropriate. Instead, only some of the more common alphabetization problems are touched upon. Obviously, there is no substitute for the knowledge and judgment of the indexer.

4.5.1 Some General Conventions and Aids

Alphabetization is either letter by letter or word by word. For single words, all alphabetization is letter by letter. In letter-by-letter alphabetization, spaces between words are ignored and the string of symbols is alphabetized as one long word. The differences between the two kinds of alphabetization are shown by the following two lists.

Letter-by-letter alphabetization	Word-by-word alphabetization
1. portable	3. Port Authority
2. portal	5. port duty
3. Port Authority	8. port of call
4. portcullis	10. port wine
5. port duty	1. portable
6. porter	2. portal
7. portland cement	4. portcullis
8. port of call	6. porter
9. portrait	7. portland cement
10. port wine	9. portrait

Letter-by-letter alphabetization is preferred for subject indexes.

An indexing board may be used to make the alphabetization of cards more efficient. This device has 24 open-top boxes (six columns and four rows). The boxes are labeled with the letters of the alphabet, the last box being "XYZ," and the alphabetizer soon learns to toss index cards into the appropriate boxes rapidly and accurately. The same board can be used to arrange cards numerically by rotating the board through 180° and labeling the opposite sides of 10 of the boxes with numbers.

An even faster device is the flapboard. This is a long, narrow board with flaps of cardboard, metal, or plastic hinged to the board at ¼- to ½-in. intervals. On one side the flaps are labeled with the letters of the alphabet, on the other with numbers. These boards are used by lifting a flap with the index finger of the left hand and inserting the top index card from a small deck of cards held in the right hand. After the initial pass through the flapboard the deck of cards from behind each flap can be placed into final order by hand.

4.5.2 Names of People

Full names are preferred if there is time, money, and space. Card catalogs in libraries provide the full names by the use of reference sources. Many indexes use only the surname (family name) and initials, in order to save space and cost. When the same surname and initials are encountered, the index editor expands the initials. If the full names are the same, the editor differentiates by adding, in parentheses, (*a*) the person's birth date; (*b*) the place where the person works or lives; (*c*) the name of the organization with which the person is associated; or (*d*) the person's profession, for example, **Miller, James Edward** (educator). An exception to the use of the full name is made if the person is widely and professionally known by initials, for example, **Lawrence, D. H.** (not **Lawrence, David Herbert**).

Pseudonyms are used in the index when the person is widely known by that name or the actual name is generally unknown. Examples are **Stalin** and **El Greco. Clemens, Samuel L.** (pseud. *Mark Twain*) may be used, or **Mark Twain,** or even **Twain, Mark,** because this author is widely known under both actual name and pseudonym.

Married women are indexed under the most familiar form of their names, for example, **Sutherland, Joan** (*Mrs. Richard Bonynge*); **Roosevelt, Eleanor** (*Mrs. Franklin D.*); **Browning, Elizabeth Barrett; Besant, Annie** (*Annie Wood*); and **Wainright, Alice** (*Mrs. Robert Graham,* afterward *Mrs. Arthur Randolph*). When names have changed, the best known name is used as index heading, and cross-references and parenthetical synonyms are provided for the lesser-known names.

Compound surnames, whether hyphenated or not, are indexed under the name as written, for example, **Lloyd George, David;** and **Mendes-France, Pierre.** *See* cross-references are made from the second half of the surnames.

For surnames with prefixes, the indexer may follow *Webster's Biographical Dictionary* or some similar work and indicate this in the introduction to the index.

Surnames with particles such as *de, la, van,* and *von* are indexed, by tradition and by the preference of the individual. *Webster's Biographical Dictionary* can be used as a guide, and *see* cross-references may be used in some cases. Some indexes alphabetize by the particle if the individual lives in an English-speaking country; if the person lives in the country where the particle is in common use, then the particle is omitted in alphabetization.

The prefixes *Mc* and *M'* are treated as abbreviations for *Mac* and alphabetized accordingly, for example, **McAdoo, James,** would precede **MacAllister, Donald.** *Mc* and *M'* are *not* changed to *Mac* in the index.

Saint, St., Sainte and *Ste.* are commonly accepted as a part of the name, and all are alphabetized as though spelled *Saint.* Again, *St., Ste.,* and *Sainte* should not be changed to *Saint* in the index. The preference of the person should be respected. Canonized saints are indexed by the inverted name, for example **Francis, Saint.**

In some countries, for example, China, the family name is placed first. But Chinese living in the United States may invert their names to correspond to American custom. The telephone directory can be used as a guide to the desires of the person.

4.5.3 Place Names

When names of places, such as countries, cities, mountains, and lakes, have been changed, both old and new names may be carried in the work being indexed. To avoid scattering, the indexer may choose to index by the one name and use a *see* cross-reference from the other. Parenthetical synonyms are also helpful, for example, **Ethiopia** (*Abyssinia*). In historical works, both the earlier and later names may be used in the index, with *see also* cross-references going both ways, for example, **Palestine** (see also *Israel*); and **Israel** (see also *Palestine*).

Names of places are often spelled differently in various countries. For English-language works, the English spelling is normally used, for example, **Cologne** (not **Köln**), **Copenhagen** (not **Köbenhavn**), **Prague** (not **Praha**), and **Vienna** (not **Wien**).

Names beginning with geographic features, such as *Cape, Lake, Mount,* and *Sea,* are inverted and then alphabetized, for example **Banff, Lake; Everest, Mount; Japan, Sea of;** and **Mendocino, Cape.** However, should the first element be an integral part of the complete name as normally used, then the name should remain uninverted and be alphabetized that way, for example, **Cape of Good Hope** and **Lake of the Woods.** The names of some cities and towns begin with a geographic feature. Such names should remain uninverted and be so alphabetized, for example, **Mount Vernon, N. Y.,** and **Lake Forest, Ill.**

Non-English articles that start place names are usually alphabetized, for example, **El Paso, LaPorte,** and **Los Angeles.** When the English article begins a name, it is inverted, for example, **Hague, The;** and **Ohio State University, The.**

Names of places that start with the word *Saint* or its abbreviation, *St.*, are indexed as *Saint,* that is, the abbreviation is spelled out, for example, **Saint Louis, Mo.** (not **St. Louis, Mo.**). Other variations of *Saint,* such as **San Francisco, Calif.**; and **Santa Monica, Calif.**, are alphabetized letter by letter.

The names of places that are divided geographically are inverted, for example, **Berlin, East; Berlin, West; Korea, North;** and **Korea, South.** But names established by long use are not inverted, for example, **North Carolina, South Carolina,** and **West Virginia.**

4.5.4 Some Alphabetizing Dilemmas

To be effective, an index must be arranged in strict alphabetical order. The conventions described in the previous sections discuss the alphabetic arrangement of personal and place names. These alphabetization rules are based on the use of the English alphabet. However, not all names and subject headings are in English; many are written in a non-Latin alphabet, and many include special characters and punctuation marks. More complex alphabetization rules have been proposed for the arrangement of these symbols.*

Words from languages that do not use the English (Latin) alphabet (e.g., Russian, Hebrew, Greek, and Chinese) are first transliterated and then alphabetized. The system for transliteration is specified in the introduction to the index.

Accent marks and *diacritical marks*, such as those commonly found in French, Spanish, and German, are generally ignored in alphabetizing. For example, *ö* (the letter *o* with an umlaut) is treated as if it were *o*. Similarly, *â* is treated as *a*, and so on. The accent marks do not affect the alphabetical order. In some indexes, *ö* is alphabetized as *oe*, to assemble names in which *ö* both has and has not been transliterated as *oe*. An example is: **Möller,** and **Moeller.**

Apostrophes are also ignored by most indexers. Thus:

Webster, James
Websterman, Henry
Webster's Dictionary

This method of alphabetization is consistent with the letter-by-letter procedure discussed earlier.

Some indexers, while ignoring the apostrophe, treat the term as the possessive case and place it immediately after the last example of the same word without an apostrophe. This is the procedure recommended by Knight (1969, 42), and he gives the following example:

Cox, Percival
Cox, Terence
Cox's Orange Pippins
Coxe, Henry

For works in mathematics and science, it may be necessary to

*Many of the examples and suggested procedures in this section are based on Knight (1969) ed.

alphabetize *digits, numbers, symbols,* and *other special characters.* The general rule is to spell out the symbol and then alphabetize the spelled-out word, for example, 3 = three; 79 = seventy-nine; $ = dollar; % = percentage, + = plus; β weight = beta weight; and $\phi\beta\kappa$ = phi beta kappa.

Names of organizations may include an *ampersand* (&) or a *preposition.* Knight (1969, 46–7) recommends BSI usage, which ignores the ampersand and encloses in parentheses (and thus ignores) *prepositions, conjunctions,* and *articles,* as follows:

Bourne Bros.
Bourne & Co. Ltd.
Bourne, Biggs & Co.
Bourne & Hollingsworth
Bulletin (d') Hygiène
Bulletin (de l') Institut Pasteur
Bulletin Météorologique
Bulletin (du) Photoclub de Nice
Society (of) Indexers
Society (for the) Promotion of Christian Knowledge
Society (of) Radiographers
Society (for) Visiting Scientists

An alternative is to alphabetize all words, including the ampersand, which would be alphabetized as *and.*

Sometimes nonalphabetical orders, such as chronological, classified, and serial arrangements, need to be used in an index. Knight (1969, 44) suggests that monarchs be listed by country and chronologically:

Henry IV, King of England
Henry VIII, King of England
Henry IV, King of France

As was pointed out in a previous section (4.3.2) uranium isotopes and organizational reports are best listed in numerical order. Obviously, there are no hard and fast rules, and the indexer must decide what procedures to follow. The only universal rule is that, once a rule has been adopted, it should be followed consistently. Our preference, and thus recommendation, is that the indexer follow a strict letter-by-letter rule while ignoring the apostrophe as well as any accent marks. A comma normally stops alphabetization until all material to the left of the comma has been put into order. After this, the material to the right of the comma is taken up.

III INDEXING AND EDITING PROCEDURES

5 Common Indexing Procedures

Nearly all indexing procedures are the same for both monographs and serials, and so to avoid duplicate descriptions, these common procedures (such as subject selection, paraphrasing, coining modifications, etc.) are described in this chapter. Procedures unique to the indexing of monographs, and those specific to the indexing of serials, are described in Chapter 6. Both chapters emphasize the preparation of subject indexes, for these are the most important and the most used indexes. In general, the same or similar procedures could be applied to the creation of other types of indexes. Where special indexing techniques are required, these will be indicated.

5.1 SELECTING SUBJECTS

Subjects are the principal ideas represented, discussed, or otherwise treated in a discourse or creative work. Clearly not all the ideas expressed in a work can be considered subjects—some may be concepts that are simply mentioned, others may be used only as examples. A subject is a main focus of the work and not a peripheral theme. The first task for the subject indexer is to select from among all the ideas, topics, and concepts expressed by the author only those that are the subjects of a work, for only these are to be included in a subject index.

The distinction between subject, concept, and word indexes is emphasized throughout this book and is explained again, in more detail, in Chapter 10, Section 1.1.

5.1.1 Maximum Specificity

"Indexing to the maximum specificity" means indexing a subject as specifically as it is reported by the author. For example, if the author reports on the hazards of winter driving, the subject indexed is *not* so broad as "Climate in relation to vehicular traffic." The subject reported is "Hazards of winter driving," and that is what the indexer indexes. The indexer determines whether or not "hazards" is too general; perhaps by "hazards" the author means only "collision hazards." Perhaps "driving" applies only to driving automobiles; and perhaps "winter" applies only to driving on icy streets. If so, for maximum specificity the subject should be paraphrased as "Collision hazards of driving automobiles on icy streets."

5.1.2 Generalizations

Authors generalize their findings; thus is progress made in science. Authors also generalize in titles because titles must be brief to be remembered and understandable. Title generalization for brevity alone is called unwarranted generalization by indexers, that is, it does not warrant indexing. (Some titles carry warranted generalization.) The subject indexer understands this tendency and uses the title only as a general guide; it is up to the indexer to identify the maximum specificity. If the author reports on specific subjects and then generalizes from them, the indexer must also index the generalization—that is, a warranted generalization. Both specific and general subjects, as reported, must be selected for indexing. A single work may discuss several specific subjects, perhaps on several levels of generalization. All of these subjects need to be selected for indexing, otherwise guidance to the work will be incomplete.

5.2 PARAPHRASING SUBJECTS

Indexers select words from the material indexed to provide broad guides; then they paraphrase subjects specifically in order to index them. The words used in the paraphrases then become parts of the index entries. "Collision hazards of driving automobiles on icy streets" is an example of a subject paraphrase mentioned earlier in this chapter. Proper paraphrasing requires that a subject be recorded in a proper form and at the correct level of specificity.

5.2.1 Diction of Paraphrases

Subject paraphrases (verbalizations of subjects, or subjects embodied in words) have no verbs, adverbs, articles, or pronouns. Subject paraphrases start with a capital letter, but they do not end with a period because they are not sentences. Examples of subject paraphrases are

Use of card catalogs by freshmen
Multifactorial analysis of anxiety
Equation relating energy, mass, and speed of light

Every word selected for indexing is given one paraphrase; there is only one paraphrase for a subject. Omission of a relevant subject paraphrase will mean at least some lack of guidance to the work being indexed.

In concept indexing, concepts are paraphrased in the same way; so are topics in topic indexing. For word indexes, words are provided with verbatim context.

The number of paraphrases needed depends entirely upon what the author reports; it is the author of the document who determines the number as well as the kind of subjects reported and not the indexer.

5.2.2 Specificity of Paraphrases

Paraphrasing should conform to the maximum specificity authorized by the author. Even generalizations should be paraphrased to the maximum specificity and should not go beyond what the author reports. It is obvious that no paraphrase of reasonable length can be as specific as the work from which the paraphrase was derived. The reasons that paraphrases can be effective and yet not lengthy include

1. Differentiation among index entries need be only among those entries actually present and not among all possible entries.
2. Omission of data (especially quantitative data) promotes brevity; that is, indexes are indicative, not informative.
3. Omission of verbs, adverbs, articles, and pronouns shortens the paraphrases.

5.3 SELECTING GUIDE WORDS

Once a broad subject word has been selected from the work being indexed and the subject has been paraphrased, the next step is to select the words from the paraphrase that best lead the index user to the subject paraphrased. These guide words will become the subject headings in the index unless (rarely) they are translated into standard subject headings. Translation is the topic considered in the next major section, 5.4.

For topic and concept indexes, guide words are selected from paraphrases in the same way. For word indexes, the word itself becomes the guide word.

5.3.1 The Best Words as Guides

Experienced indexers and even beginners find little difficulty in selecting the best words from text and from subject paraphrases to provide guides to the text and paraphrases. However, it is difficult to define "best words" or to prescribe a method of selection. As a demonstration, take the paraphrase "Review on sword manufacture." Most indexers select "sword" as the best word leading to this paraphrase because it is more specific than "manufacture." "Review" is not selected because the subject is not a study of reviews. Of course "on" is not selected. For the subject paraphrase "Characteristics of technical reviews," "reviews" would be selected. The author is reporting a study of reviews, not of "characteristics" per se nor of "technical" things in general. The best word is the one that leads most specifically to the subject reported by the author.

Terms that are too broad for an index to works in one subject area may not be too broad for an index to works in another subject area. For example, "manufacture," "formation," and "synthesis" might be ideal subject guide words in an index to a work on poetry; but they are hopelessly inclusive for an index to works on chemistry. When translated into standard subject headings, broad terms accumulate entries under them that are too heterogeneous. For example, "bit" as a subject heading might accumulate under it guides to works on drills, binary digits, horse bridles, pieces-of-eight, soldering irons, devices to make watermarks in paper, etc. Searchers are inconvenienced by heterogeneity. Also, the too numerous entries under broad terms inconvenience users, who must skim or read all of the modifications under these large headings.

Many subject paraphrases require two or more guide words. Conjunctions in the paraphrase almost certainly indicate two or more guide words. Take the paraphrase "Atherosclerosis and coronary heart disease from sucrose." Obvious guide words (subject headings) are "atherosclerosis," "coronary heart disease" (or "heart disease," or even "disease"), and "sucrose." Specific actions, operations, and processes generally require guide words. In the subject paraphrase "Tempering of swords," both "tempering" and "swords" are good guide words. In creating this subject paraphrase, the indexer may start with either "tempering" or "swords" as indicating broad subject areas reported by the author and then, from either word, coin the same paraphrase.

For a string of operations in conjunction, many guide words may be needed, for example, for the subject paraphrase "Ploughing, discing, harrowing, planting, fertilizing, and irrigating in wheat culture," the required guide words are "ploughing," "discing," "harrowing," "planting," "fertilizing," "irrigating," and "wheat." "Culture" would not be a suitable guide word, being too broad.

5.3.2 Multiple-Word Headings as Guides

Two or more words commonly used together in speech and writing are not separated in choosing guide words. For example, "United States," "hydraulic ram," "heat of activation," and "free energy" would all be dealt with as whole terms and *not* separated into their component words. The dictionary is a good guide to terms and phrases that should not be split.

Whether "coronary heart disease" should be taken as a unit or separated into its components in the selection of guide words depends on a number of factors, including *(a)* the subject area of the entire index; *(b)* the degree of specificity of subject heading desired; *(c)* the modifications under the heading; and *(d)* the "commonness" of the term or phrase. If the entire index is to works on heart disease, then "coronary heart disease" would obviously be the term selected. If the index is to works on diets, then "heart disease" or even "disease" might be the better choice. Scattering and potential scattering in the index determine the specificity of the subject heading desired; the more words taken from the modification and put into the heading, the greater the specificity of the heading. But, the more words in the heading, the greater the potential for scattering among headings in the index and the greater the necessity for cross-references or inversions.

5.4 TRANSLATING GUIDE WORDS

Guide words selected from the subject paraphrases are translated into standard subject headings, if necessary, in order to avoid the scattering of identical or related entries in the index. Scattering loads the searcher; translation reduces this load. The standard subject headings may be found in other published indexes for the same subject area, in word lists, and in thesauri. New standard headings may, if necessary, be created by the indexer. In general, the words of the author, rather than standard terminology, are preferred, because these have been chosen with care to communicate precisely with others who work in the subject area. This means that the indexer should try to avoid translation except among grammatical forms and synonyms.

5.4.1 Grammatical Form

The most frequent translation is to another grammatical form. Either the singular or the plural form may be used, but not both in the same index unless the singular has a different meaning from the plural, for example, *wood* and *woods*. The choice is generally based on common use (cf. Chapter 4). Since verbs are not used as subject headings, they are translated into gerunds. Adverbs are translated into equivalent nouns or phrases; the same is true for adjectives. This makes all subject headings consist of nouns, gerunds, or noun phrases.

Inversions are another common translation, for example, **Voltaic cells** into **Cells, voltaic.** Inversion is used to reduce scattering and to bring related headings into proximity.

5.4.2 Synonyms

In quality indexes, scattering among synonyms is unacceptable. Such scattering is prevented by translating the term in the subject paraphrase into a synonymous standard term. Another way of reducing scattering is to use cross-references to guide the searcher from the synonym to the chosen subject heading. However, there are enormous numbers of synonyms in some fields, for example, in organic chemistry. Rather than making cross-references from all synonyms to a standard heading, it is better to use a standard nomenclature throughout. Organic-compound nomenclature was developed to avoid myriad cross-references and to prevent scattering.

When translation is necessary, experienced indexers will translate into standard subject headings as they paraphrase; very few guide words are translated after they have been selected from the subject paraphrases. Beginners prefer to make translation a separate operation, for this makes learning simpler and emphasizes the desirability of using the author's words.

5.5 COINING MODIFICATIONS

Once the subject guide word has been selected and, if necessary, translated into a standard subject heading, the words remaining in the subject paraphrase are often useful in coining the modification. For example, the subject paraphrase "Review on sword manufacture" would be given the subject-index entry

Swords, manufacture of, review on, 1234

The subject heading is **Swords,** and the modification, "manufacture of, review on," is derived entirely from the paraphrase, except for the preposition "of." The modification need not necessarily be derived from the paraphrase; it may, for example, be desirable to make it more specific than the paraphrase. In this case, additional words will be added to the modification.

Modifications (modifying phrases, subheadings) make the heading more specific, much as an adjective modifies a noun. The heading–modification combination is made to fit the subject being indexed as precisely as is necessary to differentiate all entries under the heading. The more precisely the indexer indicates what will be found when the reference is looked up, the less fruitless looking up will be imposed on the searcher. Modifications prevent blocks of undifferentiated references from accumulating under headings, and improve guidance.

Repetition and circumlocutions are inappropriate in index entries. The heading–modification combination is coined to the maximum specificity authorized by the author—even for indexing generalizations. Since index entries are indicative (rather than informative), modifications do not carry data, especially numerical data. This makes the entries shorter, saves reading time, reduces the cost of the index, and avoids the possibility of the indexer's skipping data while coining the modification.

In addition to these general rules for coining modifications, there follow a few rules applying in more specific instances.

5.5.1 Guide Words

Words that are used to start modifications are generally those that apply directly to the heading, adjectives and prepositions excepted. Examples are

> **Sanding,** of mahogany before shellacking, 1234
> **Mahogany,** sanding before shellacking, 1234
> **Shellacking,** mahogany sanding before, 1234

Unusual, unique, and eye-catching words are used to start modifications, so that the attention of the searcher is immediately attracted while skimming the index. Most modifications are used by searchers to *exclude* references rather than to *include* them. Unique starting words facilitate this use.

Adjectives at the start of modifications are avoided, because they divide the heading into compartments that may be difficult to keep complete and their use may create scattering. However, exceptional or unique adjectives may start modifications, as, for example,

> **Parallel-access computers,** in self-organizing systems, 1234

5.5.2 Conjunctions and Prepositions

Items connected by conjunctions *(and, or)* in modifications are put into alphabetical order unless a logical order is preferable. An example of logical order in an index entry is

> **Farming**, plowing, planting, cultivating, and harvesting in, 1234

Separate modifications need not be written for each of the items under **Farming** for this one reference. To do so would bulk the index and irritate the searcher, who might refer repeatedly to the same work or page.

Prepositions are used freely and precisely in modifications; they show exact relations among words of the entries, they enable the searcher to decide whether or not to look up the reference, and they shorten the modification. All prepositions are alphabetized, letter by letter, except those starting modifications. To omit prepositions would cause ambiguity and confusion.

5.5.3 Nomenclature

Names, for example of drugs, used in modifications are those of the author unless a standard nomenclature has been adopted for the index. Some indexes require that the first word of modifications be the standard index name, rather than the name used by the author, in order to reduce scattering. If the standard name is not placed first in the modification, then the author's term should be used, because it helps to assure the searcher that the correct reference has been found. Also, the author may have had a specific reason in not using standard nomenclature, and that purpose will be lost if all names are translated into standard names when creating the modification.

5.5.4 Specificity

Modifications are usually made a little more specific than they need to be, because at the time of indexing the indexer does not know what other entries will appear under the heading and so is not in a position to differentiate one modification precisely from all other modifications under the heading. This differentiation is left to the index editor, who finds it easier to delete excess specificity than add specificity by looking up the indexed material. The degree of specificity necessary is immediately apparent to the index editor.

The editor also may decide to retain some excess specificity, because entries in cumulative indexes may require it and because it is easier to delete excess specificity in editing than to add it.

5.6 MAKING INDEX CARDS

Index entries are first made on cards to permit alphabetization of the entries. Index entries are typed or written onto cards or are dictated for transcription onto cards. It has been found that 3- × 5-in. cards are the most satisfactory because they are easily typed and handled, large enough, and easily filed in standard equipment. Twenty-pound rag-content paper, cut into 3- × 5-in. slips, has been found to be as durable as the cardboard index cards and takes up only half the filing space. The slips of paper feed into a typewriter more easily than do the cardboard cards. Another alternative is to type the index entries on a continuous roll of cards, perforated for easy separation. This avoids the necessity of feeding each card, individually, into the typewriter. These continuous card forms are more expensive, but they are very convenient.

The heading is typed or written across the top of the cards. Modifications are placed across the middle of the cards, and the reference is placed in the lower left. One entry is made per card; it is time-consuming to have to find out whether a card already exists for a particular heading and then add another modification or reference to it. When the cards are made, they are initially maintained in page order for convenience in checking and teaching. Afterwards, the cards are alphabetized so that cards with identical headings and modifications are grouped. Modifications are alphabetized under their proper heading—always ignoring the first preposition. References are never identical; they are placed in numerical order if the headings and modifications are identical.

Some compositors set type from cards; others require that the cards be retyped onto sheets. Retyping introduces errors that must be removed by checking.

Since dictation of subject-index entries increases the speed of indexing by a factor of 2 to 4 it is recommended especially for indexing very large publications such as abstracting and indexing services. For the price of a dictating machine, a transcribing machine, and the salary of one transcriber, indexing output can be increased as if two or three indexers had been added to the staff. Considering the cost of hiring or training indexers, this is quite a bargain (Bernier and Langham, 1955). The most effective equipment uses magnetic recording, has instant start and stop, provides immediate erasure of errors, has high fidelity of consonants, and has a locking device to prevent accidental erasure.

The indexer "marks" the copy being indexed, by underlining subject headings or writing them in the margin of the page while simultaneously dictating the heading. The indexer then coins a modification and dictates it—without writing it on the marked copy, so as to save time. If the marked copy is given to the transcriber (the typist who makes the cards), the references need not be dictated nor words spelled out, for these can be seen on the copy. When completed, the cards are checked by the indexer, at least until the transcriber is trained; the cards and copy then go to the checker, who corrects errors both of the indexer and of the transcriber.

5.7 MAKING CROSS-REFERENCES AND GLOSSES

It is the indexer's responsibility to provide guidance in the index by means of cross-references and glosses. Also, indexers add informational material to index introductions. The most important *see* cross-references are those from synonyms to the chosen subject headings; for example,

Vitamin B_1 see *Thiamin*

Some specific headings are referred to more general headings by *see* cross-references. *See also* cross-references tie together related headings, such as genus to species, product to use, cause to effect, a word to its antonym, etc. An example is

Fluidity (see also *Viscosity*)

See cross-references eliminate scattering; *see also* cross-references point out possible scattering to the searcher by refering to related terms. Cross-references are written onto the marked copy by the indexer and are written or typed onto cards, or dictated.

Glosses inform the searcher as to what has been put under the heading, how the heading is organized, and exceptions to the indexing. Some glosses provide definitions; others give specifications. Parenthetical synonyms let the user (and the indexer) know what synonyms have been combined under the heading of choice. An example is

Thiamin (Vitamin B_1)

Cross-references external to the index, for example, those in a thesaurus, place a greater load on the searcher than do cross-references interfiled among the printed index entries because the user must remember to consult the external list of cross-references and because the external cross-references may not all be justified.

6 Indexing Monographs and Serials

Features common to the indexing of monographs and serials were presented in the preceding chapter; the differences are presented in this chapter.

One major difference is that most monographs provide a new synthesis of previously published material; whereas most serials contain new material. Thus, monographs are subject indexed according to material emphasized by the author; serials are indexed mainly by novel, new, or original material. For monographs, the presentation is new; for serials the content is new. The monograph indexer seeks emphasized subjects; the serial indexer looks principally for new subjects. Another major difference is that nearly all monographs are complete in themselves, whereas serials are continuing works. Indexing methods will vary to accommodate the content and form of the specific work being indexed.

6.1 SPECIAL ASPECTS OF MONOGRAPH INDEXING

Procedural differences in indexing monographs can be traced to the fact that book indexers work alone and are responsible for every aspect of the task, including planning, indexing, checking, typing, checking proof, and proofreading. Serial indexers usually work as part of a team. They work for organizations that provide office facilities, reference materials, dictating equipment, transcribers, typists, and, most important, continuing consultation with other indexers. Because of this difference, more formal guidance is needed for those learning to index books; the novice serial indexer will be part of an organization and receive coaching from senior colleagues.

6.1.1 Planning the Index

Before indexing begins, a number of decisions need to be made about the size and style of the index. Some publishers have a preferred format for the index, perhaps to make it consistent with other works in a series. The design of monograph indexes should be discussed with the publisher before indexing begins, and all limitations clearly understood. The indexer is an expert on indexing, design of indexes, and the effect of an index's characteristics on its use. The publisher is expert in the techniques and economics of publication. By combining their talents, the indexer and publisher can produce the best index that is economically feasible. The interests of the index user should be paramount in all decisions about indexes.

Book indexing is done from page proofs so that the correct page numbers can be entered on the index cards as references (locators), and usually the task does not begin until the page proofs are ready. Some monograph indexers like to read the complete manuscript to get an overall picture before starting to index; others prefer to index as they read. As indexers become proficient, they develop individual styles.

6.1.1.1 *Size*

The size of most monograph indexes is a compromise between what the indexer knows is ideal and what the publisher believes to be economically feasible. As soon as possible after accepting the indexing assignment, the indexer should determine whether the publisher has set restrictions on the number of entries or the number of pages. It is in the mutual interest of author and publisher that the index be complete enough to serve adequately the needs of the reader. It is also of mutual interest that costs not be escalated unnecessarily by excessive detail. Thus, specifications of the index should be clearly understood by both the indexer and the publisher before indexing starts. It is exceedingly difficult to modify a completed index to make it fit into a specified number of pages. It is also very difficult to remove entries from a completed index and still maintain its consistency and integrity. If planned in advance, size reduction can be accomplished by combining modifications, that is, by sacrificing specificity—putting more load onto index users by having them look up more references, not all of which may be relevant.

6.1.1.2 *Format*

A major feature of format is the arrangement of modifications (subheadings) in either entry-per-line or paragraph style. The former is the more common, especially in engineering and scientific indexes. The entry-per-line style is

1. Easy to skim and read
2. Convenient for returning to a remembered entry
3. Necessary for the use of subheadings and sub-subheadings

However, entry-per-line style does take more space than does paragraph style; there is more white space in the right margin (see Figure 6.1).

Paragraph style is commonly used in history and social science texts. Some paragraph style indexes arrange the modifications by page number, rather than alphabetically by the first nonpreposition in the modification. That is, the modifications serve as a list of contents under a given heading.

Another feature of format relates to alphabetization conventions. The two commonly used methods of alphabetization are letter by letter and word by word. These methods were discussed in Chapter 4. If the publisher does not specify the convention to be used, it is recommended that letter-by-letter alphabetization be adopted for subject indexes and word-by-word for name indexes, in accordance with ANSI standards.

A third feature has to do with the number of indexes that are prepared. In a unified or combined index, all entries are arranged in a single sequence, usually but not necessarily alphabetically. A divided index consists of two or more independent sequences of index entries, for example, by subject, name, or title, or by a chronologically ordered index of events. The use of a single index, as in a dictionary catalog,

Back of the Book Index

Entry-per-line style	Paragraph style
Image storage, 203 Implicit search, 121–122 Index Medicus, 83, 296, 316 Index sequential technique, 110 Index variables, 181 Indexer consistency (and inconsistency), 84, 171, 175 Indexing, 72, 76, 80–83, 91, 95, 159, 245, 256, 257, 307, 347 (see also: Author indexing; Automatic indexing) alphabetic subject, 91 book, 83 computer-aided, 86, 95 coordinate, 172, 176, 178–179 depth, 80 evaluation, 171–190, 11, 51 (see also: Cranfield indexing evaluation studies) prescriptive, 117 Indexing and classification systems, comparison, 290 Indexing languages, 71, 72, 92 Indexing methods and schemes, 81, 171, 279 Indexing services (see Abstracting and indexing services) Indexing terminology, comparisons, 56	Immediacy of need, 212 Immediate access, 275 Impermanence (of subjects), 37 Implementation, 11, 69, 291 ff., 317 ff of arithmetic, 92 Imprecision (in labeling), 37 Inadequacy (in conventional tools), see Difficulties, Problem areas Inclusion relation, 341 Index: as part of file item, 391; by card catalog, 24; change with time, 25; coordinate, 46 ff.; file, 76, 155 ff., 268; for file access ability, 111, 391; for mechanical location, 157, 190, 289, 317, 360, 412; mechanical aids for indexing, 98; process of, 47, 110, 124, 130; record, 158; registers, in computer, 289; research in indexing, 19, 40f., 130; speeds, 267; use of dictionary in indexing, 63 Index Medicus, 82 Index Searcher (of CCC), 150 Indicators, see Role indicators Individual: differences (in catalogers) 37; requests, 247; responsibilities, 231 Industry, 39 Inference, 362 Inflexional natural languages, 261

Figure 6.1 *Examples of entry-per-line and paragraph style index entries. [Entry-per-line style reprinted by permission from* Annual Review of Information Science and Technology, *Vol. 1 (New York: Wiley, 1966); paragraph style reprinted by permission from J. Becker and R. M. Hayes* Information Storage and Retrieval *(New York: Wiley, 1964).*]

provides more efficient access, for it saves searchers from having to refer to several indexes.

6.1.1.3 *Sections Needing Indexing*

The main text of a work is generally preceded by various introductory sections and followed by appendixes and other material at the back of the book. In addition, the body of the work may include nontextual material, such as tables, photographs, graphs, and charts. Decisions must be made as to whether these parts should be indexed. The choice is influenced by the nature of the work (reference or other) and by the subject. The general rule is that, if the material is novel, it should be indexed no matter where it appears. More specific guidance follows.

The dedication, acknowledgments, introduction, foreword, preface, table of contents, list of illustrations, and the like are generally not indexed. However, if any of these items carry new material integral to the work, they are indexed.

Appendixes, glossaries, bibliographies, references, and indexes are normally found at the back of monographs. Appendixes should be indexed only if they contain novel material that is not included in the body of the text. When an appendix comprises the full text of a document, it is indexed if it was discussed in the text or if it contains new and relevant material; otherwise, it is not indexed. Bibliographies, references, and glossaries are not indexed in detail, since references to their contents are carried in the text; however, the index should guide to these items as units. Index entries that refer to items in a bibliography or glossary should so indicate, for example, "367 *bib*." or "345 *glos*."

Notes (whether appearing at the foot of the page, end of the chapter, or as back matter) should not be indexed if they document statements made in the text, since the statements will, presumably, have their own entries. These are called reference notes. Notes that continue or amplify discussion in the text should be indexed if they contain relevant material not included in the text. Some indexers consider it useful to code the reference to indicate that a note has been indexed, for example, "175*n*."

The captions (legends) of charts, graphs, maps, photographs, tables, and the like are usually indexed so as to help the searcher locate illustrative material as well as textual references. Usually, the modification of the entry indicates the character of the material; or the reference may contain a code, for example, "134 *map*."

6.1.2 The Index Cards

Let us assume that the indexer has made all the necessary preparations, has received page proofs, and is now ready to begin indexing. How does one proceed? Indexing consists of

1. Identifying the subjects or other indexable items in the text that are novel and are emphasized in the theme of the work and that should become candidates for index entries
2. Selecting the heading term that will provide reliable guidance to the subject or other indexable item
3. Modifying the heading with words or phrases (or a subheading) that make the heading more specific and thus enables the searcher to be more selective
4. Recording the page reference following the modification
5. Coining *see* and *see also* cross-references to connect related headings

As the indexer creates entries, these are recorded on the 3- × 5-in. index cards, one entry per card, as recommended earlier. Each card contains

1. A subject heading beginning in the upper left corner
2. A modification in the center
3. A reference or locator in the lower left corner

Cross-reference cards may also be created. These contain the subject heading and the desired *see* or *see also* cross-reference.

As each card is completed, it is placed at the back of the pack, so that the cards at this stage are arranged by page number. The cross-reference cards are located at the point where they were written.

6.1.2.1 *Checking and Verifying*

When the indexer has finished reading and marking the page proofs and has prepared cards for all entries and cross-references, the cards must be checked with the proofs for completeness and accuracy. To determine completeness, the indexer must scan the entire work one last time. As the proofs are scanned, one looks for any unmarked items that on first reading seemed to be peripheral but which in retrospect are subjects and should be indexed. Particular attention should be paid to finding any names that may have been overlooked. Each item added calls for the preparation of a new index entry or cross-reference card.

To check for accuracy, the indexer must compare the marked proofs with the index cards, checking for correctness of heading and modification, and noting the spelling of all proper nouns. As a separate process, page references should be checked against the pages to ensure accuracy. If the indexer has marked galleys instead of page proofs, the page references are added later when the page proofs arrive. The page numbers on the cards are then checked in the way described.

The indexer should ask the publisher about all significant changes and additions that the author may have made in page proof. The addition of a few lines may cause a change in some page numbers; it may also require an added entry. The searcher expects the index to be accurate, and the indexer is responsible for the completeness and accuracy of the index.

6.1.2.2 *Sorting by Subject Heading*

The subject heading is recorded on the top of the index card. So, the first grouping of the cards is by alphabetization of their subject headings. The modifications and references on the cards are ignored for the moment.

As the indexer alphabetizes the cards by their subject headings, he or she may notice inconsistencies in nomenclature, terms that can be combined, or subject headings that should be divided. Changes that will improve the quality of the index should be made at the time they are discovered or devised.

At the conclusion of this operation, the index cards should be grouped by subject headings and the groups placed alphabetically into boxes or drawers. Then the cards are alphabetized by modifications and arranged numerically by references.

6.1.3 Typing the Index

If possible, arrangements should be made for the publisher and compositor to accept and set type from the edited index cards. If such arrangements cannot be made, the index must be typed onto 8½- × 11-in. sheets. Entries are typed double space and in a single column. Lightly penciled vertical rules are used to indicate the margins. The lines of type are spaced to contain the maximum number of characters (generally 36) of the printed index line.

Entry-per-line or paragraph style may be used. Headings are capitalized and begin at the left margin. If there is no modification, the reference follows the comma after the heading. For entries with modifications, commas come before and after the modification. Modifications of the second and following entries are indented two spaces from the left margin to indicate that the heading has been omitted. Modifications are all lower case, except for proper names, acronyms, initialisms, and symbols that have capitals.

See also cross-references start the heading and, if more than one, they are arranged in alphabetical order, in parentheses after the heading. An example is

> **Abstracts** (see also *Critical abstracts; Extracts; Indicative abstracts; Informative abstracts; Modular abstracts; Special-purpose abstracts; Statistical abstracts; Tabular abstracts; Telegraphic abstracts)*

The first modification immediately follows the closing parenthesis in order to save space. The second and following modifications are indented as indicated earlier. In this book, headings are boldface, and the headings to which the searcher is referred in *see* or *see also* cross-references are italic, to make them distinctive. Multiple headings in *see also* cross-references are separated by semicolons because some headings have commas in them to indicate inversion.

See cross-references have no entries following them; they are complete in themselves. An example is

> **Deacquisition** see *Weeding*

Index entries that are too long to fit on one printed line are run over onto the next line after indenting six spaces. Entries run over onto the next page have the heading repeated and put in italics and parentheses to refresh the memory of the searcher.

Three modifications starting with the same word (not a preposition) are required to make a double indentation. However, immediately after the heading, it takes four or more modifications starting with the same word to make a double indentation; only the last two modifications are indented.

6.2 SPECIAL ASPECTS OF SERIAL INDEXING

Guidance into the primary literature is provided by indexes to journals in which articles appear and by the secondary services in which articles are abstracted and indexed. Issues of such journals nearly always contain tables of contents, their entries consisting of titles of the articles, names of the authors, and numbers of the pages on which the articles start; arranged in page-number order. The articles are selected and arranged for publication by the editor, who also may prepare the table of contents.

Subject and author indexes are usually prepared for a volume of issues, generally at the end of each year. These indexes are most likely to be prepared by the editor of the publication or by an associate. The subjects reported in the article are identified, and guidance to them is provided by index entries. Titles of articles in science journals usually give a good general indication of the subjects covered; sometimes a KWIC title index is provided instead of a subject index. If the index to an annual volume of a journal is small, no special effort may be made to control terminology or prevent scattering of related entries. The effort invested in preparing the index for a primary journal may be minimal because the searcher is expected to skim the headings to locate any scattered references. Helpfully, the introduction to such an index should alert the searcher to this kind of scattering and to his responsibility to check for it.

In discussing the indexing of primary journals, we might usefully discuss the origin of such journals. Primary journals are produced by a variety of publishers. Those produced by *commercial publishers* may strive to edify or educate the general public or a specific group of individuals. Those produced by *scientific* and *professional societies* are often under the society mandate to keep the membership informed and to provide a forum for members. Such journals may be sent to all who belong to the organization. Primary journals are also produced by *industries* to carry news of new products, trade, etc., and also the results of research done in the industry. Some publishers consider the publications of industries to be ephemeral, throwaway material that rapidly outlives its usefulness. However, special librarians may see beyond the publisher's notion of the usefulness of such serials and may keep and prepare indexes to those serials that have research and archival value as well as immediate usefulness to the organization that supports the special library.

By far the most important guides to the primary literature are the secondary publications produced by abstracting–indexing services. Here, it is not just a single journal that is indexed but all (or a selected group of) journals covering a specified subject. Because of the volume of the primary literature and its rapid growth during the past century, the secondary services have also expanded and increased in number at the same rate. Many of the organizations publishing indexed abstracts are now very large, employ trained indexers educated in the field of the secondary service, and produce indexes of the highest quality.

One unique aspect to the indexing of serial literature results from the fact that serials, by definition, are expected to appear over an indefinite period of time. Consequently, the indexing system developed and used for serials should be flexible enough to be effective over the life of the serial. The system should be dynamic and should, as usual, employ the vocabulary of the material being indexed in order to provide guidance to this material. In addition to appearing regularly, the index to a serial is sometimes cumulated periodically. Language changes over the years of publication, and so the index must be hospitable to changes in terminology and nomenclature.

Indexing procedures are, for the most part, common to the indexing of both monographs and serials. Subjects must be identified and paraphrased, guide words must be selected and if necessary translated into standard terminology, and modifications must be prepared to make the headings as specific as required. The differences are in the working arrangements.

Since serial indexers will probably be employed by an abstracting and indexing service, they will not be concerned about the size and arrangement of the index; these are decisions of earlier indexers and of management. The work to be indexed will be assigned, and some assistance will be provided for card checking and typing. The indexer of serials concentrates on the task of creating the index entries; if advice is needed, it will be available from colleagues.

7 Editing, Typesetting, and Proofreading

Editing the alphabetized index cards prepares them for being set in type. The index editor deletes headings that are not to be printed, rearranges entries and modifications to reduce scattering, corrects errors that become visible only when the cards have been alphabetized, makes double indentations, corrects the cross-reference and inverted cross reference systems and applies them to the index cards, increases or decreases specificity of some modifications, and adds items to the introduction of the index. Editing is nearly always done by an indexer.

Editing improves the quality of the index and is essentially the same for monographs and serials. However, because of differences in the size of the task, the procedures and techniques used in editing may differ. This chapter includes details of the manual procedures used in editing quality indexes for large abstracting and indexing services, such as the Chemical Abstracts Service. In recent years, computerized techniques have been used in producing this and other large indexes. However, editing remains, for the most part a manual operation, although computer aids can be provided. For editing smaller indexes, and specifically back-of-the-book indexes, the editing procedures can be simplified.

Typesetting may introduce errors into the index; therefore the galleys and page proofs must be checked and edited to maintain quality. When necessary, errata sheets should be prepared.

7.1 EDITING OF LARGE SERIAL INDEXES

Editing involves alphabetized index entries on cards, cross-reference cards, and inverted cross-reference cards. The editor is responsible for readying the index cards (including cross-references) for the printer.

7.1.1 General Procedures

If several editors work on an index, the cards are logged out to keep track of them. The log is a permanent record of who did which cards and when they were checked out and in. Only complete headings are logged out, along with the corresponding cross-references and inverted cross-references. After being logged out, the small decks of corresponding index cards, cross-references, and inverted cross-references are placed on the desk in front of the editor. The usual arrangement for right-handed editors is to keep the deck of cross-reference cards on the left, the inverted cross-reference cards in the center, and the regular index cards on the right.

The editor reads the top index card and checks to see if there is a cross-reference that would transfer this card to another heading. If there is, the editor crosses out the incorrect heading on the card, writes in the correct heading, and puts the card into the transfer box, first checking to make sure that the modification is unaffected by the change. If the top card is not to be transferred, the editor checks the top inverted cross-reference card to see if the index card justifies the use of the corresponding cross-reference. If so, the editor circles the volume number printed on the inverted cross-reference card to ensure that the corresponding cross-reference will be used. If none of the index cards with the same heading justifies the use of the cross-reference, the volume number is crossed out; this causes the cross-reference to be omitted for this volume of the index.

For example, the editor may find a subject-index card that reads

> **Abstracts,** indexing of, 1234

and a *see* cross-reference that reads

> **Abstracts,** indexing of—see *Indexing*

The editor then corrects the index card to read

> **Indexing,** of abstracts, 1234

puts the changed card into the transfer box, marks the cross-reference with the volume number in the lower left corner, and circles the number to keep it from being printed. The circled volume number protects the cross-reference, which is now justified for use in the index, from being discarded.

As another example, the editor may find an inverted cross-reference that reads

> **Abstracts.** Precis see ______

and also an index entry under the heading **Abstracts.** Any entry under the heading **Abstracts** justifies this cross-reference

> **Precis** see *Abstracts*

so the volume number on the inverted cross-reference is circled to ensure that its corresponding cross-reference is used in the index. For subject headings that have more than one entry (card), the second and following cards require that the heading(s) be crossed out to prevent them from being printed.

During the editing of headings, the editor may find that three or more cards may start with the same modification words (excluding prepositions). In these cases, the editor indicates a double indentation by crossing off the identical words on the second and following cards and marking those cards with an *X* to indicate to the printer that four spaces (the usual number) are to be used to make the double indentation. Note that the first prepositions of the subsequent modifications are not crossed off.

Rather than combining identical modifications, it is more usual for the editor to look up both entries on the marked copy to see if they can be differentiated by making each more specific through additional words.

The modifications under a heading can nearly always be rearranged to bring similar or identical ones together or adjacent. Rearrangement, done by inverting the words in modifications or by adding words, reduces scattering of like entries and reduces the likelihood that the searcher will miss relevant material. Sets of related modifications are difficult to miss.

Some modifications may be judged more specific than is necessary for adequate differentiation from the other modifications under the heading. By comparing it with the other modifications under the heading, the editor can usually see precisely how to cut the modification that is too long and yet retain adequate specificity for differentiation—even in a cumulative index. Modifications that on the other hand lack adequate specificity are also easy to detect—usually because they are identical with other modifications under the heading. The editor looks up all identical modifications in the marked copy (or original work, if necessary) and adds words to differentiate each from the other. As emphasized earlier, blocks of undifferentiated references load and discourage the searcher. At the time of indexing, the indexer cannot predict accurately the amount of specificity that will be required to differentiate all modifications under a heading. The index editor does not need to predict, he or she can see exactly how much specificity is needed. Thus, adjusting the specificity of modifications is best left to the editor.

Index editors find that singleton cards (unique headings) are more apt to be incorrect than are several cards with the same heading on them. Often a cross-reference card will indicate what the correct heading should be, and the singleton is then transferred to the correct heading. If there is no cross-reference to show where the singleton might be transferred, the editor tries to think of possible headings that should have been used. Sometimes the heading on the singleton is misspelled. Sometimes it is an entry that does not lead to a subject in the work indexed; if so, the card can be removed from the index.

Errors other than those in singletons occur. An example is in the entry

Thiamin, polynephritis from deficiency of, 1234

The editor knew that "nephritis" related to inflamation of the kidneys, of which there are only two; the "poly" was therefore suspect. He also knew of the link between polyneuritis and deficiency of Vitamin B_1

(thiamin). Examination of the original work from which the indexed abstract was derived yielded "polyneuritis" instead of "polynephritis." Another error produced the strange entry

Ice Cream, CaO-flavored, 1234

The editor remembered that calcium oxide (CaO) was used to dispose of the bodies of victims in popular murder mysteries and wondered what kind of devilment was being reported. The abstract from which this index entry was derived had "lime-flavored ice cream." The transcriber had been instructed to translate "lime" in modifications into "CaO", lime (quicklime) being the common name for CaO. Thus, the strange entry was corrected to read

Ice cream, lime-flavored, 1234

When all of the entries under a given heading are assembled by alphabetizing for editing, certain kinds of errors and possibilities for improvement become much more apparent than they were on the isolated cards. Together, the cards of the heading establish a pattern, and the editor can readily spot deviations from the pattern. Misspellings, for example, are more apparent as are modifications that should be assembled and, perhaps, indented—even though this may entail considerable change of wording.

Editors develop what seems like a sixth sense for detecting missing entries. Not infrequently, they look up one entry to correct an error or to add specificity to the modification and discover an entry that has been missed. The omission is apparent because the heading has not been marked on the marked copy.

7.1.2 Large Headings

Large headings (those that have many cards) take more time to edit than do small headings. Editors cannot remember all of the modifications in their first editing of the index cards; several readings are needed to correct errors, make double indentations, reorganize the cards, add specificity where needed, and combine identical cards. For a large heading, as many as five or six readings may be needed, because even experienced editors cannot find all changes in large headings. These are changes that indexers cannot anticipate because, at the time the individual cards are made and checked, there is no way of knowing what other entries will be placed under that heading. The editor sees all the entries under the heading as a unit, and potential improvements are immediately obvious.

However, because the editing of large headings takes more time, an abstracting and indexing service may use what is called a "first survey" approach to editing. The editing is not completed as the editor proceeds through the alphabet of cards. Decks of cards representing large headings (¼ in. or more in thickness) are bundled, labeled "not edited," and left (still in alphabetical order) for later handling. The cross-references and inverted cross-references are applied to these large headings, but the individual cards are not edited. Only after the first survey has been completed are the large headings and problem entries edited. Cards are shipped to the typesetter as soon as the first survey is completed. This method allows the system of cross-references to be applied to all the cards before any are shipped to the printer and avoids the need to transfer index entries on galley proof. It also speeds editing.

7.1.3 Use of the Inverted Cross-References

Before index cards can be sent to the printer, the cross-references that are justified for the index must be run into the index cards. The inverted cross-references are used to identify the unjustified cross-references that are to be discarded.

During the first survey, the inverted cross-reference cards have been marked by circling the volume number if the cross-reference is justified and is to be used in the index being edited. If the cross-reference is *not* to be used, the inverted cross-reference has been marked by *crossing out* the volume number. After the first survey, the inverted cross-reference cards (1/xf cards) are sorted into three piles: (1) those on which the volume number has been crossed out, (2) those on which the volume number has been circled, and (3) those with nothing done to them. Group (3) is returned to the appropriate editors for marking. Group (2) is returned to the files in fireproof safes for use in editing the next index. Group (1) (the cross-outs) is realphabetized to put them into the same alphabetical order as their corresponding cross-references. Cross-outs are realphabetized rather than the circled 1/xf cards because there are fewer of the former. Realphabetization is done to facilitate applying the 1/xf cards to their corresponding cross-references. Then the 1/xf cards with the volume numbers crossed out are applied to the corresponding cross-reference cards (usually by clerical staff). The corresponding cross-references are marked with a large *X* if there is only one cross-reference on the card. If there is more than one cross-reference on the card, the unwanted ones are simply crossed out by drawing a line through them. If the cross-reference card has a circled volume number on it, this card is protected and nothing is crossed out. The cross-reference cards are all left in the deck; none are thrown away. Editors run the justified cross-references into the index cards just before the cards are checked for alphabetical order and sent to the printer. While running in the justified cross-references, editors (*a*) look for any possible errors that may have occurred; (*b*) discard the unwanted cross-references unless they are justified by late entries and changes; (*c*) cross off unwanted headings; and (*d*) possibly make a few necessary double indentations among the modifications starting the headings. Should the editors find *see* cross-references with entries under them or *see also* cross-references without entries, these have to be corrected. In the latter case, the *see also* cross-reference is changed into a temporary *see* cross-reference.

7.1.4 Miscellaneous Functions

Index editors have so many specific tasks that the correct alphabetical ordering of the cards may be overlooked. When the editing has been completed, it is advisable to make a final check for the correct alphabetical order of the edited cards. This should be done just before the cards are sent to the printer. Changing proof is costly.

In some organizations, the index cards are stamped with consecutive numbers and microfilmed. Should the cards be lost during shipment, the microfilm can be developed to provide copies of the lost index entries. Without this precaution, the loss, and the delay, would be very serious.

Cards are usually tied to prevent disorder and loss. Each bundle usually makes one galley. Cards with centered holes near the bottom edge facilitate the tying. Also, the printer can put a ring through the holes and fasten the ring so that the keyboard operator can turn over the cards as they are set. The printer is normally notified of coming shipments of cards and provided with a self-addressed postal card to let the publisher know that the shipment has been received.

7.2 EDITING OF SMALL INDEXES

The editing procedures for large, continuing indexes can be modified for small and for one-time indexes. But, in all indexes, editing is an essential procedure that follows the preliminary alphabetization of the index cards.

For one-time indexes of fewer than 1000 entries, the inverted cross-reference system can be dispensed with because the indexer can remember most of the cross-references and can check *all* of them in the edited cards, with little additional effort to see if they are justified by entries at the heading to which they refer. Cross-references need not be divided into general and specific because the *one* editor does all of the checking for their justification in the index. Editing procedures include

1. Crossing off unnecessary headings
2. Organizing modifications into an ad hoc, logical order
3. Making double indentations
4. Eliminating blocks of undifferentiated references by adding modifications or by adding specificity to existing modifications
5. Limiting the specificity of some modifications
6. Justifying all cross-references so that none are dangling
7. Eliminating scattering among headings by combining some headings and making cross-references among others
8. Reducing scattering among modifications
9. Watching for, and eliminating, circular (elliptical) cross-references
10. Noting errors in meaning and correcting them
11. Watching for errors in format, spelling, and punctuation, and eliminating these errors
12. Adding missing entries (the most difficult of all)
13. Making a final check for alphabetical order

The editing of small indexes should not be attempted until all of the index cards have been made. The picture seen by the index editor is quite different from that seen by the indexer during indexing. The alphabetized cards give the index editor an accurate overview of the entire index—something that the indexer does not (and cannot) have. The index editor can make changes in the entries not possible for the indexer because the index editor sees the total picture.

As small serial indexes grow, become periodic, and are made a permanent addition to an organization, and especially as the number of indexers increases, it is of vital importance for the index editor(s) to convert the procedures to those used for editing large indexes, as described earlier in this chapter. Failure to make this conversion will lower the quality of the indexes and make them much more costly to produce.

7.3 PRINTING

Whenever possible, indexes should be typeset directly from the index cards. Retyping the cards is expensive and may introduce new errors. Furthermore, the printer can be instructed to do certain uniform things that would otherwise require hours of card-typing and editing time, for example, to put commas before and after modifications, to indent all modifications after the first one exactly two em spaces, and to set all headings (written at the tops of cards) and volume numbers in boldface.

Typographers can also help to design published indexes. They can be helpful in selecting attractive typefaces that are the most legible for the small sizes of type used in indexes. Printers can advise about the format, such as leading between lines, that will provide greatest ease of use and about the opacity and durability of paper. Since subject indexes wear out before the other bound volumes in libraries, paper durability is important; so is a page format with extra-wide margins so that pages can be trimmed repeatedly during rebinding without loss of printed matter.

In selecting the kind of composition to be used, an important factor is the ease with which corrections can be made; another is the number and variety of type sorts available. Setting chemical indexes requires over a thousand type sorts.

In selecting a printer, publishers are well advised to see if the printer can give the desired priority to the index and to do so at a reasonable price.

7.4 PROOF CHECKING AND PROOFREADING

Mistakes and errors can be made at *any* stage during the publication of an index. Errors of authors, reviewers, editors, indexers, index editors, alphabetizers, printers, proof checkers, and proofreaders can all be found in a finished index. Procedures are necessary to reduce these errors to an acceptable minimum.

Proof checking means comparing the printed material against the original material to discover and remove those errors that the proofreader cannot be expected to find. Examples are incorrect references, misspelled proper names, and some punctuation. However, checking for every conceivable error may prove too costly, so it is usually limited to those errors that proofreaders cannot be expected to find.

The proofreader is responsible for the correctness of the entire index—content, completeness, format, spelling, typography, order, etc. Most of the changes are made on galley proof—those long sheets returned by the printer. Page proofs are often checked only to make sure that all of the changes on the galleys have been made correctly and that the type at the start and end of pages has not been pied. Extensive changes in page proof are very costly, especially if they affect several pages.

Once the corrections on the page proofs have been made on the type, the pages are ready for printing, collating, binding, and shipment to the subscribers or purchasers from a mailing list provided to the printer.

7.5 ERRATA

Despite care on the part of the indexers and index editors, errors do creep into published indexes. It has been said that if an error, no matter how improbable, can be made, somebody someday will make it. Publication of an abstract–index journal is a continual uphill fight against error, although indexers and index editors who are highly trained and experienced make fewer and less serious errors than do those with less training and experience.

Errors can appear anywhere in an index (Bernier, 1964). Incorrect references are especially serious, since not only is guidance lost but so also is the time of users in finding (or trying to find) the correct references. Equally serious is the omission of valid entries, such omissions are almost invisible except during reindexing or when indexable material is found by chance. When errors of omission are found after the index has been printed, they should be recorded in the errata.

Entries in subject indexes that do not lead to the subjects indicated are in error. This type of error is discovered by the user who looks up the entry only to find nothing of interest in the referenced abstract or paper. Although this error is quite visible, the searcher may not consider it to be an error. Yet such entries waste search time.

Modifications may be incorrect. The most serious error is that of omitted words. This error is similar to that of omitted entries, but less serious in its consequences because the searcher may find some clues to the omission in the rest of the words in the entry. Even in the best indexes, there will be scattering of like material among modifications. Users have come to expect this kind of scattering and they reduce it by reading all modifications under all the headings consulted.

Errors in spelling can occur in all parts of an index—introduction, headings, and modifications. They are obvious and usually cause more amusement than damage.

All detected errors should be brought to the attention of the index publisher, who should then publish errata. If the discovery is made before the index is distributed, then a tipped-in sheet can be used as correction at the end of the index; this, however, is expensive. If discovery comes after distribution of the index, errata can be published in subsequent indexes to issues of the journal. Depending on the possible seriousness of the consequences of the errors, separate errata sheets can be sent to all subscribers.

The actual use of these errata has been a matter of concern to the authors of this book. How should errata be brought to the attention of users? Who should apply the errata to the correction of indexes? Librarians? Purchasers? Users? It may be true that most lists of index errata are ignored and never used. Should one find or suspect an error in an index, it may save time to look for an errata sheet. This is especially true if the reference seems to be incorrect. No large index can be expected to be error-free. Errata sheets are necessary and should be used.

Errors and mistakes occur even in the best indexes. Users probably discover the greatest number of errors and should take the responsibility for reporting these to the publishers. Editors and publishers try to maintain the quality of their indexes and appreciate being informed of any errors.

8 Thesauri

Efficiency in the use of a thesaurus can be increased by knowledge of its structure and the principles underlying its development.

A thesaurus is an organized list of terms from a specialized vocabulary arranged to facilitate the selection of synonyms and of words that are otherwise related. For reference retrieval systems, the thesaurus is used to bring the vocabulary of the searcher into coincidence with that of the index.

For a thesaurus, it is necessary to specify

1. The objectives
2. The subject area
3. The terms to be included
4. The relations among the terms
5. The display of terms
6. The procedures for updating by editing, correcting, reorganizing, adding and deleting terms

The following publications are recommended as guides in planning and constructing a thesaurus: Aitchison and Gilchrist (1972), ANSI (1974), Bernier and Heumann (1957), Bernier (1976), Lancaster (1972), and Soergel (1974).

8.1 THESAURUS DESIGN AND TERM SELECTION

Thesauri that are components of reference retrieval systems must conform to the goals of the systems, must be related to the system content, and must be designed to serve as a retrieval device for a designated category of users. M. Wolff-Terroine writes

> Thus, a medical thesaurus, although it covers the same field, will differ according to whether it is intended for use by doctors or nurses. This affects not only the choice of concepts, but also the way in which these concepts are linked together (hierarchically or by category). Thus a given concept may be represented by a certain term in a thesaurus compiled for one particular group of users and another term in a thesaurus compiled for a different group. In addition these terms may be organized differently:
>
> (a) in a thesaurus for chemists
> term: sucrose
> generic term: disaccharides
> (b) in a thesaurus for the food industry
> term: sugar
> generic term: sweetener
>
> [Wolff-Terroine 1975, 506]

Thesaurus design is complex and may be approached from several directions. Harold Wooster (1970) describes two approaches and, in his usual whimsical style, characterizes these as the stalagmitic and the stalactitic. More precisely, these two approaches for the selection of terms in a thesaurus are (*a*) terms derived from a relevant set of documents; and (*b*) terms derived from a consolidation of existing thesauri. A third, closely related approach, is through the development of microthesauri (Bernier, 1976); and a fourth approach is a compromise, which uses indexers to select terms and lexicographers to organize them (Bernier and Heumann, 1957).

The *stalagmitic approach* is one that begins "down on the floor of the cave among the documents, slowly building toward the ceiling [Wooster, 1970]." Less whimsically, this can be described as the empirical or *original-indexing approach*. A representative sample of documents is collected and indexed, by means of a free vocabulary consisting of the most appropriate terms with no controls or restrictions. After completion of this initial task, the designers of the thesaurus (usually a committee of subject experts) review, organize, and structure the proposed terms. If the documents have been truly representative and the indexing satisfactory, then all of the index terms of concern to the information system will have been included. This is the idea and the ideal of the stalagmitic approach to thesaurus construction. In practice, the ideal is never fully achieved; the thesaurus based upon a sample of documents is never complete enough, nor are all problems identified.

The *stalactitic approach*—let us call it the consolidation approach—is what Wooster (1970) puckishly describes as being "much more fun—one convenes groups of experts who hang up on the roof of the cave, twittering and chirping among themselves but as far away from the actual documents as they can get." Although the imagery is vivid, the denotation is needlessly negative. This procedure has also been characterized as the committee approach to thesaurus building, a label which also has a somewhat pejorative connotation. More important, the description is not sufficiently precise, for both the original-indexing approach and the consolidation approach usually employ committees.

In the consolidation approach, committees of experts are convened and are assigned responsibility for preparing a consolidated list of terms that can be used in indexing a given discipline or subdiscipline. The committee members do not work from documents; instead, they use previously compiled lists of terms. The committee strives for completeness. It will be recalled that the original-indexing approach often leads to incomplete lists of terms. In the consolidation approach, terms can be added even though no document has, as yet, been indexed by that term.

The task of compiling a comprehensive thesaurus is monumental. For example, about 300 panelists were involved in making the Engineers Joint Council (EJC) *Thesaurus of Engineering and Scientific Terms*.

> Some 350 subject-indexing vocabularies, thesauri, glossaries, and other specialized lists were collected. . . . This extensive data bank contained some one and one-quarter million line entries, listing more than 150,000 separate terms and how they had been used or treated by the sources [EJC, 1967, 1].
> After editing, "when all the steps were completed, 23,364 separate main entries had been established—17,818 descriptors, and 5,554 USE references [EJC, 1967, 22]."

Obviously, the quality of the result is dependent upon the effort put in, and the EJC thesaurus is one of the best in the field.

Rules for constructing microthesauri are reported by Bernier (1976) in the *Encyclopedia of Library and Information Science*. Essentially, this is a special application of the consolidation approach. The first and perhaps most essential task in the construction of a microthesaurus is to define the subfield sufficiently precisely and narrowly so that only 100 to 500 terms are needed. Names of experts in the field are selected from reports, papers, and recommendations of other experts. Terms in the subject field are selected from reports, papers, and indexes, and alphabetized and categorized in a draft of the thesaurus to be edited by experts in 1 day to create Draft 2—usually the final draft after approval of copies mailed to the experts.

There are advantages and disadvantages to all of the above approaches to the construction of a thesaurus. The choice is usually dictated by the size of the effort, the time and money available, and the state of the existing vocabularies in the field. Once the scope of the thesaurus has been determined, one may begin "on the floor of the cave," grubbing among the documents and compiling individual lists of terms. Eventually one may "hang from the roof," conferring, comparing, and completing the list with the help of experts and all the subject knowledge at one's command. Professional indexers select the terms from works being indexed for the system. Lexicographers organize the terms into related categories, combining synonyms under the term of choice, and so on.

J. F. Blagden, of the British Institute of Management, reviewed the literature on thesaurus compilation methods before making a thesaurus of management terms. He concluded that

> From the numerous approaches that have been discovered in the literature, it would appear that there is no one method that can be used exclusively in the construction of a thesaurus. The investigator [Blagden] proposed therefore to use an amalgam of all these different approaches [Blagden, 1968, 355].

His amalgam comprised

1. Selecting terms from three years of *Management Abstracts*
2. Supplementing these terms by terms selected from other listings in consultation with specialists
3. Experimentally using the vocabulary for indexing and retrieval
4. Evaluating: keeping records of the number of postings (entries) for each term, and modifying the vocabulary as necessary

Term selection is important, both when constructing a new thesaurus and when maintaining or updating an existing one. It is a continuing process because new terms continue to come into the language, old terms continue to fall into disuse, and a few terms acquire new meanings or shades of meaning. What criteria can be used when selecting terms for inclusion in a thesaurus?

In Project LEX (Heald, 1966) it was proposed that thesaurus terms be selected according to their "usefulness in communication, indexing, and retrieval" and that the utility of terms be estimated by

1. The relative frequency of the term's occurrence in the literature of the field
2. The relative frequency of the term's use in the operating system
3. Relations to descriptors already in the system
4. Scientific or technical precision and acceptability

Later, when the EJC adopted the Project LEX procedures for thesaurus construction, an additional restriction was added to facilitate computerization (Speight, 1967, 14).

5. A maximum of 36 characters per term

The Guidelines for the Establishment and Development of Monolingual Thesauri, prepared by the joint UNESCO-ISO/TC 46 Task Group, and published by UNESCO, aims "to facilitate the preparation and development of thesauri regardless of whether they are administered mechanically or manually. The Guidelines were, therefore, prepared as an attempt to lay the basis for compatibility, both at present and in the future, of thesauri that are being elaborated simultaneously in most of the disciplines of science, basic as well as applied [UNESCO, 1973]." Subject headings (descriptors) are selected through the four steps: "collection, verification, evaluation, and choice." The Guidelines list sources for term collection and favor the use of internationally agreed nomenclatures. It is recommended that the proliferation of unrelated specific names be avoided and that such names be listed separately from the main part of the thesaurus. ". . . the authenticity of selected descriptors should be verified by consulting dictionaries, other indexing or standardized vocabularies, current usage in the literature and especially the opinion of subject specialists. Obsolete terminology should not be included, unless only as forbidden terms." The utility of candidate descriptors is evaluated by their frequency in the literature or in existing stocks of information; anticipated incidence in retrieval inquiries, relation to descriptors already accepted; appropriateness and authenticity as current terminology in the discipline, and effectiveness and expediency in connoting and denoting the particular concept. It is stated that none of these factors should be considered independently and that "attention should be paid to areas of peripheral interest where the exhaustiveness and specificity required of the descriptors are not the same as for the core subject." As to choice of descriptors, it is recommended that, "In all cases, descriptors should be selected for inclusion in the thesaurus on the basis of their estimated effectiveness for retrieval purposes and their measurable significance in the material to be indexed [UNESCO, 1973, 30–33]." Although the emphasis may differ, the UNESCO criteria for selection of descriptors are similar to the guidelines proposed in the Department of Defense (DoD) manual (Heald, 1966). Again, the effectiveness and practicality of these guidelines is determined by actual use.

8.2 TERM RELATIONS AND NOTATIONS

One of the more important functions of a thesaurus is to display relations among terms of the vocabulary and thus help the user to select the most appropriate terms when indexing a document or formulating a search request.

The UNESCO guidelines for thesaurus development (UNESCO, 1973, 10–11) describe three types of term interrelations: preferential, hierarchical, and affinitive. All three have the property of reciprocity; so that if A is a broader term than B, then B is a narrower term than A. *Preferential relations* refer from a nonallowed term to an authorized one. *Hierarchical relations* are of the genus–species or whole–part type applicable in most subject fields; terms are labeled as being broader or narrower than related terms, that is, the hierarchical relation among terms is indicated. *Affinitive relations* refer from one authorized term to another authorized, nonhierarchical, related term.

Richard S. Angell, formerly of the Library of Congress, has made a detailed analysis of term relations (Angell, 1968). He studied 10 thesaural lists to identify the kinds of term relations used, then reduced the many examples to a few basic relations that could be expressed formally. A slightly modified version of his table is reproduced in Table 8.1.

Angell describes three types of relations (*a*) *Preferential*; (*b*) *Affinitive*; and (*c*) *Hierarchical*. Under the preferential relation there are three statements; for the affinitive relation, there are two, and for the hierarchical relation, one statement. These statements prescribe the relations between the words in natural language and words in the thesaurus; that is, how words in text are to be converted into subject headings used in controlled indexing.

Table 8.1
Classification of Thesaurus Descriptor Relations

Type of relationship	Statement number	Formal statement
A. Preferential	1	A is not authorized; see B instead
	2	A is not authorized; see B and C instead
	3	A is not authorized; see B or C or . . . *n* instead
B. Affinitive	4	A is permitted; B is also required
	5	A is permitted; consider using B or C or . . . *n* as well
C. Hierarchical	6	A is permitted; consider using B or C or . . . *n* instead

SOURCE: Adapted from Angell (1968). [*Reprinted by permission of R. S. Angell, The Library of Congress, Washington, D. C., 1977.*]

8.2.1 Preferential Relations

Statement No. 1: A is not authorized for assignment; see B instead.

The term, *A*, is not authorized in the index language; the term, *B*, is used instead. However, Term A appears in the thesaurus to guide users to Term *B*. This is a statement of the preferential relation, that is, *B* is preferred to *A*, but this same formula can be used in different contexts to indicate different relations among terms.

(a) Synonyms:

Hallways see *Corridors*

(b) Antonyms:

Instability see *Stability*

(c) Spelling variants:

Colour see *Color*

(d) Abbreviations:

Adrenocorticotropic hormone see *ACTH*

(e) Specific to general:

The general term is in the authorized vocabulary; the specific term is not:

> **FORTRAN** see *Programming languages*

This rule does not apply if both the specific term, *FORTRAN*, and the general term, *Programming Languages*, are in the authorized vocabulary. If both terms are authorized, indexing should be to maximum specificity with appropriate cross references.

Statement No. 2: A is not authorized; see B and C instead.

The user is instructed to assign Terms *B* and *C* instead of *A*. This form of construction is used only in post-coordinate index systems. An example is:

> **Pulmonary embolism** see *Embolism* and *Lungs*

Statement No. 3: A is not authorized; see B or C or . . . n instead.

This form is used only when the collection contains no works on the general topic but only works on one or more of its elements. When a work of a general nature is to be added to the collection, the general term should be added to the vocabulary, and Statement No. 3 would no longer be applicable. When the rule is in effect and Term *A* is not authorized, the indexer is directed to assign Term *B* or *C* or *n*, according to the content of the document—which is what the indexer normally does. This statement is used to refer from the general to the specific and to distinguish homographs.

(a) General to specific:

The general term is not admissible at this time; only specific terms can be used.

> **Programming Languages** see *FORTRAN*; *ALGOL*; *COBOL*; *PL/1*

(b) Homographs (ambiguous terms):

> **Lead** see *Electrical connections; Metallic lead*

8.2.2 Affinitive Relations

Statement No. 4: A is permitted; B is also required.

For certain permitted index terms, additional affinitively related terms must also be used to specify fully the concept. This formulation is used only in the API and EURATOM thesauri.

Acetylation see (in addition) *Acetic acid* and *Chemical reaction*

Statement No. 5: A is permitted; consider using B or C or . . . n as well.

This formulation describes the affinitive relation among subject headings. It advises the indexer and searcher to consider specifying a related term, in addition to the previously selected subject heading.

Reading difficulty RT *Reading failures*
RT *Learning disabilities*

8.2.3 Hierarchical Relations

Statement No. 6: A is permitted; consider using B or C or . . . n instead.

This is the general statement of hierarchical relations. The indexer and searcher are instructed to consider using either a broader or a narrower term instead of Subject-heading *A*.

(a) Broader term:

Geometry BT *Mathematics*

(b) Narrower term:

Geometry NT *Plane geometry*
Geometry NT *Analytic geometry*

A much more elaborate analysis of the relations that can be displayed in a thesaurus has been devised by Soergel (1974, 178). For example, under the heading "Related Terms" there are included the subdivisions (*a*) related reflexive (RT–RF); (*b*) related to (RT–TO); (*c*) related from (RT–RF); (*d*) similar in meaning (RT–SI); (*e*) empirically connected (RT–EC); (*f*) check also to (RT–CT); and (*g*) check also from (RT–CF). These examples illustrate the kinds of relations that can be built into a thesaurus. The *check also* cross-reference, for example, is made not to a specific subject heading but to a class of subject headings, in order to indicate that further specification can be obtained by use of the subject headings in related classes. Supergeneral cross-references are of this nature. The following is an example:

Diseases (Check also *RT part of body and causes of disease*)

This cross-reference informs the indexer that in indexing a document about cancer, for example, one should check also to see whether it deals with cancer of a specific part of the body, such as the lung; if so, one should use the term **Lung** in indexing. The same holds for the causes of cancer, such as smoking.

In most thesauri, it is not advisable to include all of these fine distinctions; only distinctions necessary for indexing and searching should be made part of the thesaurus structure. In the example about indexing cancer, the trained indexer does not need this kind of instruction, but the new searcher may.

Two commonly used cross-referencing and notational systems have been developed by the National Library of Medicine for medical subject headings (MeSH) and by the Committee on Scientific and Technical Information, COSATI, for science and technology. The syndetic structure is the same for both systems, but the notations differ.

MeSH	*COSATI*
see	use
x (seen from)	UF (use for)
see under	BT (broader term)
see also specific	NT (narrower term)
see also related	RT (related term)

COSATI notation is being adopted for many thesauri in the sciences and social sciences. It is a simple mnemonic system of proven value. Figure 8.1 is an example of a set of thesaurus entries with their notations.

8.3 DISPLAY

The structure of a thesaurus is not self-evident. Users may need some instruction on the organization of the thesaurus and how to consult it. This is especially true if there are a number of arrangements. The basic structure of the thesaurus may need to be described and possibly illustrated by a sample entry and explanatory notes in which the hierarchical structure of the vocabulary, the system of cross-referencing, and all of the notations and special symbols employed are explained.

8.3.1 Alphabetic

The main thesaurus display is an alphabetic listing of all subject headings and cross-references. Generally, only one level of generic

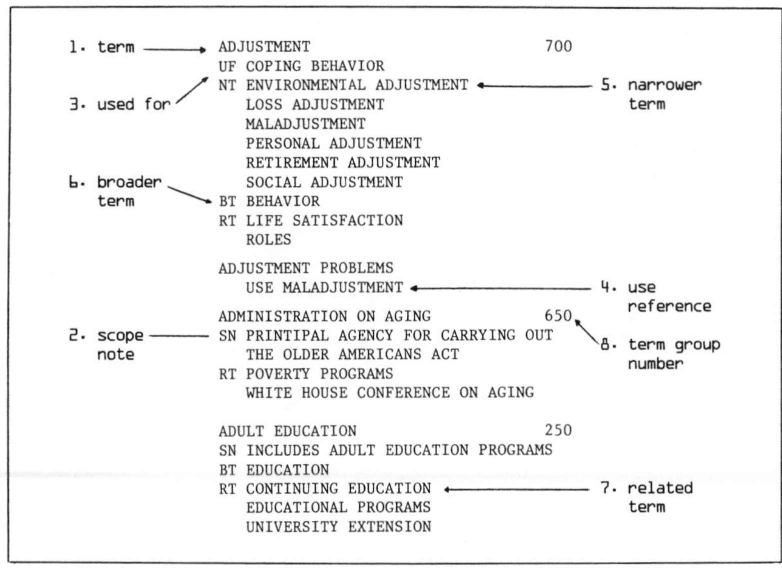

Figure 8.1 *Examples of thesaurus entries and notations.*

1. Term: the word or phrase selected as an index term.
2. SN {scope note}: included to define the content of a given term more specifically, or to differentiate between homonyms.
3. UF {used for}: The preferred term is used instead of this term.
4. USE {use reference}: Use the term indicated instead of the term looked up.
5. NT {narrower term}: This term is narrower in concept and may be consulted if more specific information is desired.
6. BT {broader term}: This is generically broader than the given term and may be consulted if more general information is desired.
7. RT {related term}: This term is related to a given term in some way but is not broader or narrower; it alerts the user to other terms that may be of interest.
8. Term Group Number: represents a broad subject grouping into which the term has been placed.

[*Reprinted with permission from* Thesaurus of the National Clearinghouse on Aging, *1975.*]

structure is shown in the alphabetic display—that is, one BT up and one NT down—plus RT terms. The ANSI recommends that "Whenever a term for which there are narrower terms in the vocabulary appears in the thesaurus display as either a narrower term or a related term, it should be followed by an unambiguous symbol (such as a hyphen) to indicate that it is not the narrowest concept of its class [ANSI, 1974, 14]." The following example illustrates the use of the hyphen in an alphabetic display:

Adhesives
UF Binders
Cements
Glues
BT Bonding materials
NT Adhesive tapes
-Pressure-sensitive adhesives
Rubber adhesives
RT Cohesion
Epoxy resin
-Fasteners
Joints
-Sealers

8.3.2 Hierarchical

Because the alphabetic listing does not display the complete hierarchy, another display is used to show the full range of genus–species relations; it begins with the broadest term followed by narrower terms, through various levels of indentation. For example:

Vertebrates
. Mammals
.. Whales
... Sperm whales

and:

Analysis (mathematical)
. Functional analysis
. Real variables
.. Calculus
... Differential calculus
... Integral calculus
.... Convergent integrals
.... Divergent integrals

8.3.3 Categorized

Some subject fields have many subfields; examples are education, engineering, and gerontology. Thesauri for these fields may provide an additional categorized term display, in which appropriate terms are listed alphabetically within their subject group. A searcher using the

Thesaurus of Engineering and Scientific Terms could look up the subject category 0502, **Information sciences,** and find an alphabetic listing of all terms that are used to index works in this category:

0502
Information sciences
  Abbreviations
  Abstracting
  Abstracts
  Alphabets
  Aperture cards
  Archives
  Atlases
  Authors
  Automatic abstracting
  Automatic indexing
  Bibliographies
  etc.

8.3.4 Permuted

Thesauri that utilize multiword terms generally provide a permuted display of the vocabulary so that each word in the term is an entry point. It is a KWIC index of the words in the vocabulary. The user is advised to refer first to the permuted display in order to obtain the proper word order for a multiword term. Is the correct form *Indexing concepts and methods?* Or *Concepts and methods of indexing?* Or *Methods and concepts of indexing?* The permuted display will provide the proper order regardless of how the term is searched. The permuted arrangement generally suggests more specific terms or concepts than the user originally perceived. For example:

Automatic	indexing
Coordinate	indexing
KWIC	indexing
	Indexing theory

8.3.5 Graphic

An alphabetically arranged index is a list, a single sequence of items, also called a linear array. The sequencing is controlled alphabetically so that **Apple** is preceded by **Applause** and followed by **Appliance. Oranges** and **Pears** are a fair alphabetical distance apart from each other, and *see also* cross-references are required to advise the user that **Fruit** is a broader term.

Although there are many advantages to displaying the terms in a thesaurus alphabetically, other displays—graphic displays—can also be used. Graphic displays are two-dimensional; subject headings are arranged on the plane of paper so as to show the relations among the headings and not just their alphabetic similarity. Figure 8.2 is a page from the *EURATOM Thesaurus* (EURATOM, 1967) showing the relations between biology and other subjects. Note that the lines have different densities. The density or width of the line indicates the strength of the relation between the two subject headings. Thus, *radiobiology* is more closely related to *radiosensitivity* than it is to general *biology*.

Another type of graphic display is illustrated by Figure 8.3, the BIOSIS (Biosciences Information Service) subject profile of *aquatic biology*. It is explained that the purpose of the display is "to facilitate searches of *Biological Abstracts* and *Bio-Research Index* in this field." The segmented divisions in the profile illustrate the broad fields and grouping of headings important to each subdivision, while the outer circle lists the frequently related, broader, cross-referenced terms.

Graphic displays supplement, but do not supplant, the more conventional alphabetic index listings.

8.4 MAINTENANCE

Language is dynamic; new words are constantly being added, old words acquire new meanings, and some words disappear from common use. Thus, the thesaurus, the vocabulary of the information retrieval system, must itself be dynamic and responsive to change. Furthermore, no thesaurus is complete at the time it is compiled. Terms that may have been overlooked during construction need to be added, and errors that have crept into the work need to be corrected. For all these reasons, procedures must be available for updating and maintaining the thesaurus.

Computers can also be used to aid in the compilation and maintenance of thesauri. The work of the Educational Resources Information Center (ERIC) in this connection is especially noteworthy. The computer programs and procedures that have been developed are highly specialized and are not described in this book. Nevertheless, anyone faced with the task of compiling a thesaurus should be aware of the existence of these computer aids and should, if possible, use them.

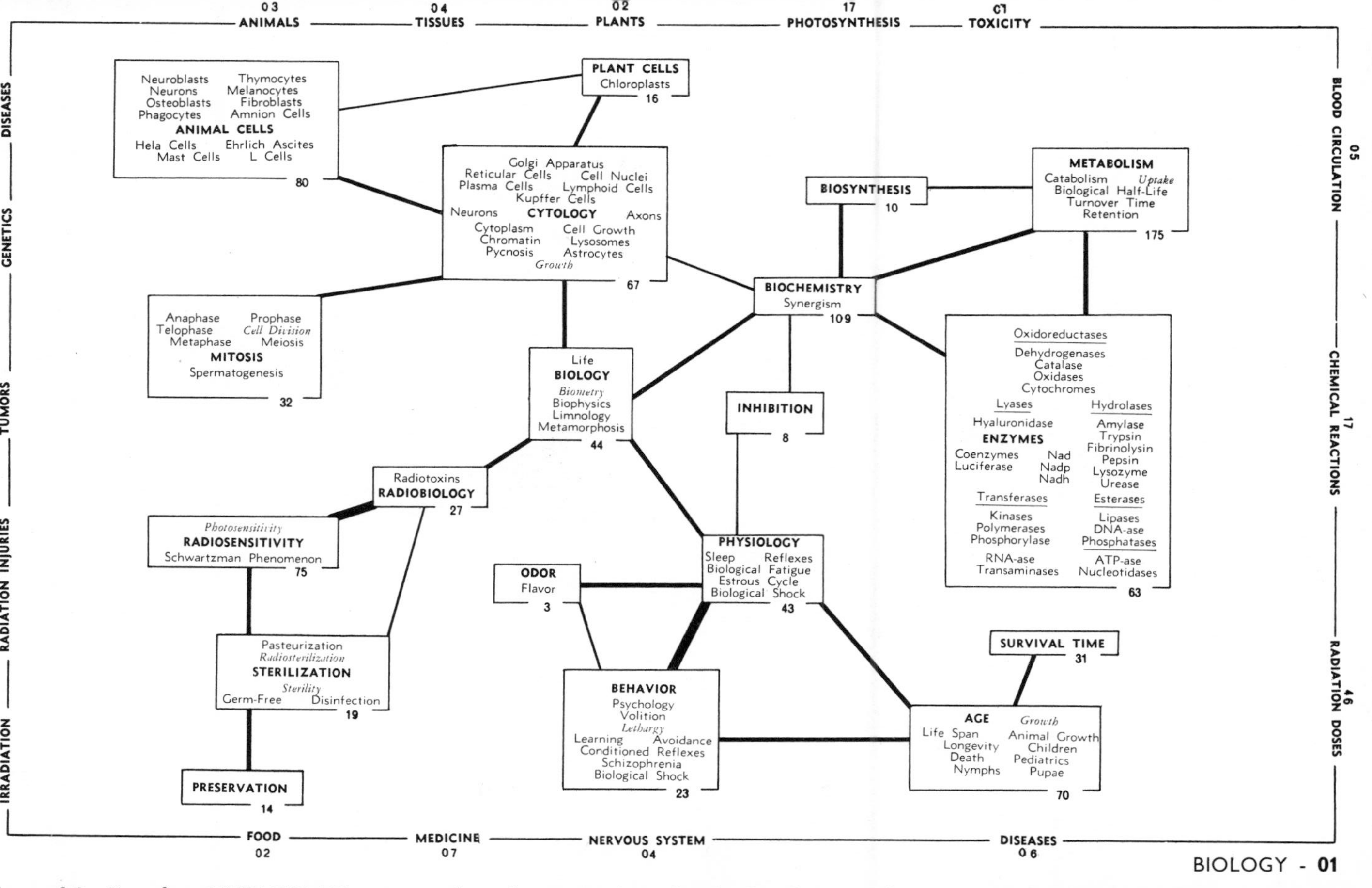

Figure 8.2 *Page from* EURATOM Thesaurus. *Three-dimensional graphic display showing relations among headings.* [*Reproduced from the 2nd ed. Part Two, EUR 500e, by permission. EURATOM—C. I. D., 1972.*]

AQUATIC BIOLOGY

SUBJECT PROFILE

SCOPE OF AQUATIC BIOLOGY RESEARCH IN BIOLOGICAL ABSTRACTS AND BIORESEARCH INDEX.

• BIOSIS 1971 COVERAGE OF AQUATIC BIOLOGY INCLUDES 14,737 REPORTS SELECTED FROM SOME 7600 JOURNALS ORIGINATING IN 100 COUNTRIES. • THIS SUBJECT PROFILE DEFINES THE SCOPE OF CURRENT PUBLISHED RESEARCH IN MAJOR AREAS OF AQUATIC BIOLOGY TO FACILITATE SEARCHES OF BIOLOGICAL ABSTRACTS AND BIORESEARCH INDEX IN THIS FIELD. IT SHOULD BE USED WITH THE GUIDE TO THE INDEXES AND THE SUBJECT CLASSIFICATION OUTLINE, BOTH AVAILABLE UPON REQUEST FROM BIOSIS. • SEGMENTED DIVISIONS ARE ACCORDING TO BROAD FIELDS AND ALSO GENERAL GROUPINGS FOR THOSE HEADINGS IMPORTANT TO EACH SUBDIVISION. THE OUTER CIRCLE LISTS THOSE HEADINGS TO WHICH THESE REPORTS ARE FREQUENTLY CROSS-REFERENCED.

RELATED AREAS

See Biosystematic Index for related taxonomic studies.

METHODS, MATERIALS, APPARATUS, GENERAL
MEDICAL & CLINICAL MICROBIOLOGY (includes Veterinary)
ECOLOGY (Bioclimatology, Biometeorology)
PLANT PHYSIOLOGY, BIOCHEMISTRY, BIOPHYSICS
ECOLOGY (Plant, Animal)
BACTERIOLOGY, GENERAL, SYSTEMATIC
BEHAVIORAL BIOLOGY
FORESTRY, FOREST PRODUCTS
RADIATION BIOLOGY
METABOLISM
SANITARY ENTOMOLOGY*
ENZYMES
CHEMOTHERAPY
MATHEMATICAL BIOLOGY; STATISTICAL METHODS
PHARMACOLOGY
NUTRITION (Diet)
PALEOZOOLOGY
BODY SYSTEMS
BIOPHYSICS
PUBLIC HEALTH MICROBIOLOGY*
SUBTERRANEAN BIORESEARCH*
ENDOCRINE SYSTEM
MICROORGANISMS, GENERAL (includes Protista)
PUBLIC HEALTH
NERVOUS SYSTEM
TOXICOLOGY
GENERAL BIOLOGY, (INFORMATION, DOCUMENTATION, RETRIEVAL, COMPUTER APPLICATIONS)
BIOCHEMISTRY

PLANT

ECONOMIC BOTANY
PLANT PHYSIOLOGY, BIOCHEMISTRY, BIOPHYSICS
PEST CONTROL, GENERAL; PESTICIDES; HERBICIDES
SOIL SCIENCE (Irrigation, Underground Waters)
AGRONOMY
PLANT ECOLOGY
PHYTOPATHOLOGY
BOTANY, GENERAL; SYSTEMATIC

MICROBIAL

MORPHOLOGY, CYTOLOGY OF BACTERIA
FOOD, INDUSTRIAL MICROBIOLOGY
MICROBIOLOGICAL APPARATUS, METHODS, MEDIA
BACTERIOLOGY, GENERAL, SYSTEMATIC
PHYSIOLOGY, BIOCHEMISTRY OF BACTERIA
VIROLOGY

BIOMEDICAL

NUTRITION
IMMUNOHEMATOLOGY (includes Blood Groups) (under Immunology)
TOXICOLOGY
PHARMACOLOGY
NEOPLASMS, NEOPLASTIC AGENTS
BODY SYSTEMS
METABOLISM
PUBLIC HEALTH
PHYSIOLOGY, GENERAL

GENERAL

METHODS, MATERIALS, APPARATUS, GENERAL
DEVELOPMENTAL BIOLOGY • EMBRYOLOGY MORPHOGENESIS
ECOLOGY (Oceanography, Limnology, Wildlife Management-Aquatic and Terrestrial)
CIRCADIAN RHYTHM, OTHER PERIODIC CYCLES
AEROSPACE AND UNDERWATER BIOLOGICAL EFFECTS
CYTOLOGY, CYTOCHEMISTRY
EVOLUTION
BIOCHEMISTRY
GENETICS, CYTOGENETICS
GENERAL BIOLOGY
BIOPHYSICS
RADIATION BIOLOGY
FOOD TECHNOLOGY (Non-toxic studies)

ANIMAL

ANATOMY, HISTOLOGY GENERAL, COMPARATIVE
BEHAVIORAL BIOLOGY
TEMPERATURE: ITS MEASUREMENT, EFFECTS, REGULATION
PALEOZOOLOGY
INVERTEBRATA, MORPHOLOGY, PHYSIOLOGY, PATHOLOGY
ECONOMIC ENTOMOLOGY (Animal Pests; Biological Control; Chemical and Physical Control, General, Apparatus; Integrated Control)
PARASITOLOGY (includes Ecto- and Endoparasites)
ANIMAL ECOLOGY, Wildlife Management (Aquatic)
DEVELOPMENTAL BIOLOGY • EMBRYOLOGY
ANIMAL DISTRIBUTION*
CHORDATA AND INVERTEBRATA, GENERAL, SYSTEMATIC ZOOLOGY

AQUATIC BIOLOGY

*CROSS HEADING ONLY

3-720

BIOSCIENCES INFORMATION SERVICE, 2100 ARCH ST., PHILA., PA. 19103, U.S.A.

Figure 8.3 Subject profile showing broad fields, grouping of headings, and cross-referenced terms from Biological Abstracts. *[Reproduced by permission of Biosciences Information Service of* Biological Abstracts.*]*

Chai Kim (1973) considers the thesaurus updating problem from a communications point of view. He hypothesizes that communication is a linear process (one way only) if the updating is done either by indexers or by searchers alone. The updating process is cybernetic (two-way including feedback) if the thesaurus is updated by both indexers and searchers. In a survey to test his hypothesis, he found that

> Most of the retrieval thesauri adopted today in operating information storage and retrieval systems are not updated at all. Where updating is done, it is carried out by indexers alone, which indicates that the use of a retrieval thesaurus allows a linear process of communication between authors and readers, allowing for no feedback [Kim, 1973, 155].

Kim further suggests that since meaning is defined "as the reciprocal and reversible relationship between concepts and words" a theory of thesaurus making and updating must "account for the conversion of what is read or written into knowledge and the conversion of knowledge into what is read or written." However, we do not have such a theory as yet. Thus, our procedures will have to be ad hoc and empirical, but always keeping in mind the fact that both indexers and searchers should be able to nominate new terms whenever an appropriate term needed to express a concept cannot be found in the thesaurus.

The following types of changes are involved in updating a thesaurus (Soergel, 1974, 458):

1. Introduction of a new subject heading
2. Elimination of a subject heading
3. Subdivision of an existing subject heading into a number of more specific subject headings
4. Changes in the definition or use of a subject heading, especially changing the delineation between two subject headings, which changes the definition of both
5. Addition or elimination of an hierarchical relation, especially assigning a subject heading to another category in the hierarchy
6. Addition or deletion of syndetic relations

Procedures for nominating new terms, or for proposing changes, vary with the size and complexity of the responsible organization. The ANSI *Guidelines for Thesaurus Structure, Construction and Use* include a thesaurus term review form (Figure 8.4) together with a recommendation that whenever an indexer–searcher is unable to provide or find guidance for a given subject with an appropriate term in the thesaurus, a new term should be proposed. The form provides

THESAURUS TERM REVIEW	DATE SUBMITTED DAY | MO | YR	NUMBER

SUBJECT TERM

ACTION REQUIRED

ADD AS A NEW TERM POSTABLE ☐ NONPOSTABLE ☐	CHANGE TERM TO POSTABLE ☐ NONPOSTABLE ☐	SPELLING FROM
CROSS-REFERENCE ADD ☐ DELETE ☐ REFERENCES SHOWN BELOW	DELETE TERM DELETE ONLY ☐	DELETE & TRANSFER ☐ POSTINGS TO ____

SOURCE DATA

ACCESSION NO.	SUGGESTED BY

TERM USED IN LIEU OF REQUESTED TERM

AMPLIFYING INFORMATION

SOURCE NOTE

DEFINITION

CROSS-REFERENCE STRUCTURE

USE	USED FOR (UF)
BROADER TERMS (BT)	NARROWER TERMS (NT)

RELATED TERMS (RT)

COMMENTS	SUBMITTED BY
	TITLE

REVIEW AUTHORITY

REVIEW COMMENTS

ACTION APPROVED ☐ DISAPPROVED ☐	REVIEWER (Signature)	DATE DAY | MO | YR

Figure 8.4 *Thesaurus Term Review Form.* [*This Review Form is reproduced with permission from American National Standards Institute; copies may be purchased from the ANSI at 1430 Broadway, New York, New York 10018.*]

space for the definition of the term, scope notes (glosses), syndetic relations, and additional comments. ANSI further recommends that all requests for thesaural changes be collected and reviewed by an official thesaurus editorial board or a lexicographer.

The criteria for accepting new terms and new relations into the indexing language are the same as were used in constructing the original thesaurus, that is, use by authors and indexers, and a belief that the new term will come into general use.

A new term cannot be used for searching the part of the collection indexed before the term was introduced into the indexing. There are two ways for dealing with this problem:

1. To reindex all documents already in the file. In an operating system, this is rarely economical and not usually considered.
2. To set a cutoff date when the term can be used for indexing and searching. For documents processed prior to that date, the term is not to be used. If this cutoff procedure is adopted, then a search request would have to be translated into two sets of search terms—one for use before the introduction of the new term, the second for use with the more current parts of the file.

If a term is dropped, the updating problem is not so great. All documents that have been indexed by the obsolete term are retrieved from the collection; the old term is removed from the documents or from the indexing worksheets, and the documents are reexamined to determine whether or not substitute headings should be assigned.

Terminology control in the thesaurus affects the effectiveness of the document retrieval system. It is costly to make changes, yet the language must reflect current use. These are the horns of the dilemma. Management must strive to achieve a cost-effective solution.

9 Computer-Aided Indexing

Automatic text analysis became a subject for serious research in the late 1950s and a major focus of activity within the then emerging field of information science. Many streams converged to create this strong new current. First there was the desire to provide faster and more complete access to the scientific and engineering literature and "to control the information explosion." A second factor was the availability of computers and the recognition that these machines were symbol manipulators capable of processing words as well as numbers. A third influence was the emergence of a new field of study called computational linguistics, that is, the application of computer analysis to the structure and meaning of language, led by such men as Noam Chomsky (1956, 1957) and Zellig Harris (1962). Still a fourth thrust was the research and advances in the fields of artificial intelligence and self-organizing systems ("thinking machines"). The National Science Foundation supported these efforts to nurture the development of information science. Studies on automatic indexing blossomed during this period, as did studies on automatic abstracting, machine translation, and various other information-processing and retrieval activities.

Other chapters discuss computer-produced KWIC indexes and citation indexes. In this chapter we examine some of the techniques and developments for text processing and indexing. The literature on automatic indexing is voluminous. Two excellent state-of-the-art reviews have been prepared by Stevens (1970) and Sparck-Jones (1974a, b). In addition, there is the series *Annual Review of Information Science and Technology*, as well as a number of relevant books (*Machine Indexing*, 1961; Borko, 1967; Salton, 1971). This chapter will not be yet another review of the literature; our concern is with the methods, principles, and prospects of automatic indexing.

9.1 AUTOMATIC INDEXING METHODS

The differences between word indexing and subject indexing are crucial for evaluating machine-indexing techniques. Word indexing has also been called *derived indexing*, as contrasted with subject indexing, which is *assigned indexing*. Word indexes are derived from the words used by the authors of a work, and they guide to words and their contexts; subject headings are assigned and modifications coined (usually by a human indexer) using words (generally those of the author) that best lead to the subject matter of the work and not to extraneous material. Subjects are expressed in words, of course, but subject indexes are quite different from word indexes.

The foundation on which automated language analysis rests is that ideas are communicated by words (written or spoken) and by their arrangement. Stemming from this fundamental axiom is the hypothesis that the subject of a document can be derived by a mechanical analysis of the words in a document and by their arrangement in a text. In the current state of the art, fully automatic machine indexing is derived or word indexing. However, subject indexing may be approximated (*a*) by using some human intervention, as in machine-aided indexing; and (*b*) possibly by use of advanced linguistic techniques, including automatic syntactic and semantic analysis.

For computational purposes, a word is defined as a sequence of symbols, either alphabetic, numeric, or punctuative, separated by spaces on both sides. Assuming that the words are in machine-readable code, the computer can be programmed to process these words in a variety of ways. Programs can count the number of words in a document and calculate the mean number of words in the average sentence of the document. Programs can count the number of times a given word appears in a document or in the entire data base and can print lists of words, ordered alphabetically or by frequency of occurrence.

Truncation (removal of prefixes and suffixes from the stems of words) makes it possible to count all appearances of the same stem as one word type. For example, programs can combine the counts of the stem *index* with the counts of *indexes*, *indexer*, *indexers*, and *indexing*. Programs can also count the number of times that the word *indexing* is preceded by the word *automatic*, and can search titles and abstracts for a selected word or phrase and obtain a list of all documents in which these terms occur. An almost unlimited number of kinds of counts can be made; the problem is to select only those word counts that prove useful in automating the assignment of index headings or in determining the subject of a document—if, indeed, word counts alone can do this. The solution of this problem has been a major concern of researchers. Three basic methods of automatic indexing have been studied (*a*) statistical analysis of text; (*b*) syntactic analysis; and (*c*) semantic and discourse analysis.

9.1.1 Statistical or Frequency Analysis

One hypothesis underlying the statistical method of indexing is that the more times a word is used in a document, the more likely it is that the word is an indicator of the subject matter. Based upon this hypothesis, a computer program lists all of the words in a document; the words are grouped by number of occurrences and arranged alphabetically within each frequency. Function words (such as articles, conjunctions, prepositions, and pronouns) are usually excluded. Words having the same stem can be counted either as the same or as different words.

Counting words is basic to all techniques of machine indexing and was first suggested by Luhn (1957). At the simplest and most unsophisticated level, the computer is programmed to select as index terms all words on the list that have been used more than a specified minimum number of times in the work being indexed. The application of this rule may result in the selection of large numbers of index terms, most of which will provide poor guidance to subjects reported by the author. This result is not surprising because indexing is much more complicated than merely selecting all words used more than a minimum number of times. Certainly, human indexers do not use as a criterion for index selection the number of times a term is used in the text, and authors try to avoid word repetition. Thus, word counts cannot be used as a sole basis for selection. If the cutoff number of words is set too high, for example, 10 to 12 repetitions, then many useful index headings will be eliminated; if it is set too low, for example, 1 or 2 repetitions, many terms useless as subject guides will be included.

Machine Indexing (1961), Stevens (1970), and Borko (1967) describe a number of research studies aimed at providing more effective procedures for automatically selecting index terms. Some of the more pertinent suggestions are:

1. *Weighting by location:* For example, a word appearing in the title might be assigned a greater weight than a word appearing in the body of the work.
2. *Relative frequency weighting:* This is based upon the relation between the number of times the word is used in the document being indexed and the number of times the same word appears in a sample of other documents.
3. *Use of noun phrases:* Only nouns and adjective–noun phrases are used as index terms, and these are selected from the title or abstract.
4. *Use of thesaurus:* In addition to combining words of the same stem, a thesaurus is used to combine synonyms and otherwise related words. In this way, the count of some word types is increased, as is the separation between "good" and "poor" index terms.
5. *Use of association factors:* By means of statistical association and correlation techniques, the degree of term relatedness, that is, the likelihood that two terms will appear in the same document, is computed and used for selecting index terms.
6. *Maximum-depth indexing:* This procedure indexes a document by all of its content words and weights these words, if desired, by the number of occurrences in the document. In this way, the problem of selecting terms is avoided.

9.1.2 Syntactic and Semantic Analysis

All of the foregoing techniques of statistical analysis were developed by the mid-1960s and formed the basis for most automatic-indexing studies. The potential benefits of syntactic and semantic analysis were recognized, but there was little contact between linguists and information scientists (Sparck-Jones and Kay, 1973). Statistical analysis identifies frequently used words and, by hypothesis, significant content words. Syntactical analysis identifies the role of the word in the sentence, that is, its grammatical class (e.g., whether the word *work* is used as a noun or as a verb) and the relation among the words in the sentence (*dog bites man* versus *man bites dog*). Semantic analysis helps to establish the paradigmatic or class relations among terms so as to associate words with simple concepts.

The linguistic model proposed by Chomsky distinguishes between surface and deep structure of language—a sentence being a particular surface structure. For instance, the two sentences "Mary went home with John" and "Mary and John went home together" have different surface structures but the same deep structure. By means of transformational grammar, a sentence can be changed; it can go through a series of transformations that will exhibit its deep structure. It is Chomsky's view that a purely syntactic transformation can provide a semantic interpretation of the sentence. As is probably obvious, this type of sentence parsing, especially in automatic text analysis, is complex. Sparck-Jones concludes her discussion of syntactic indexing by saying,

> It must be allowed that syntactic descriptions may be of value in specific contexts, but there is no hard evidence to the effect that they are generally of value . . . . However, it may be that the correct way of providing syntactic information in document descriptions has not yet been discovered, and that when it has, it may be worth writing, or attempting to write, programs to provide it automatically [Sparck-Jones, 1974a, 3,9].

The goal of semantic analysis as applied to document processing is to identify the subjects and content-bearing words of the document or surrogate text. A number of procedures have been studied, including (*a*) keyword normalization, that is, stripping words of prefixes and suffixes; (*b*) dictionary or thesaurus reference, in which the extracted word is looked up in a thesaurus; and (*c*) various classification techniques aimed at grouping related words. The value of these techniques of semantic analysis for automatic indexing is, at best, unproven; much more experimentation is needed.

9.2 BOOK INDEXING BY COMPUTER

A word index to a book's contents is a concordance, and concordances can be easily produced by computer (see Chapter 12). In a concordance, all of the words used by an author in a given work are indexed; no selectivity is exercised, with the usual exception of a list of excluded words. In contrast, words in a subject index are carefully selected, and only those words that relate to the subject of the work are chosen to be index headings. The task of automatic subject indexing is to provide an index that guides to all of the subjects in the work, and only to those subjects.

In the chapter on the manual indexing of monographs, we explained that, even without precise rules, the experienced indexer has little difficulty in recognizing subjects and in preparing useful index entries to them. We also stressed the importance of intelligence and education, and that an indexer must be familiar with the subject matter of the document so as to be able to identify novel and emphasized subjects that need to be indexed. If indexing and selection of terms is to be done by computer, then the computer program must be constructed with operational definitions, rules for identifying and selecting novel and emphasized subjects, and procedures for identifying and selecting index terms that lead to these subjects. Two principles for automatically selecting index headings have been proposed: specification and inclusion of useful terms, and specification and exclusion of useless terms (Borko, 1970).

Indexing by term inclusion requires an operational definition of index terms that can provide guidance to subjects in the document. In addition, a program or set of programs consistent with this definition must be devised to enable the computer to select useful index headings from among all of the words appearing in the text.

Indexing by term exclusion avoids the difficult problem of defining useful index terms and instead seeks to provide an operational definition of those words, or classes of words, that are not valuable as index terms. By the process of exclusion, all words in the document that are not excluded become index terms.

Lynch uses similar principles, which he labels *derived* and *assigned*, in presenting a four-way categorization of printed alphabetic subject indexes (1971, 98).

To illustrate the procedures involved in implementing these opposing principles of inclusion and exclusion, two experiments will be described briefly, with emphasis on the methods used and the results obtained.

9.2.1 Indexing by Term Inclusion

The principle of inclusion was used by Dr. Susan Artandi (1963). Her experiment was designed to index by computer a chapter on halogens in J. W. Mellor's *Modern Inorganic Chemistry*. Good index terms were defined as words commonly used in textbooks containing information about halogens. Artandi did not attempt to select index terms automatically. Hers was to be a subject index in which subject headings were assigned, not derived from the text. The index terms were selected from five standard textbooks on inorganic chemistry. A thesaurus was prepared of all of these index terms plus synonyms and related terms, which were to be indexed under the same subject heading. The automatic indexing consisted of searching the chapter in Mellor and locating those passages in which the preselected terms appeared. This was no trivial task, for problems involving synonyms, homographs, word order, word endings, etc., all had to be solved.

Artandi's experiment demonstrates that it is possible to index a chapter (or a book) automatically by using as input to the computer program a set of manually preselected terms. Good index headings are operationally defined as subject headings previously used in standard works on a similar subject, and programs are written to enable the computer to identify passages in the text that are related to the preselected subject headings. While this method avoids the problem of devising procedures for the automatic selection of only good index terms, it has the unfortunate limitation of not being able to index novel ideas expressed by new terms. Also, this procedure does not differentiate between terms used to describe subjects and terms used to describe concepts or topics. Indexing by inclusion is limited to indexing by previously used subject headings.

In evaluating this technique, we can say (*a*) that an index produced by computer is similar in form to the usual back-of-the-book index; (*b*) that the use of preselected terms ensures useful guidance, provided that the headings chosen are those used by the author of the document indexed to report novel and emphasized subjects; and (*c*) that, on the negative side, the method cannot guarantee that all novel and emphasized subjects will be indexed, nor that guidance to nonsubjects (e.g., concepts and topics) will be excluded.

9.2.2 Indexing by Term Exclusion

Recognizing the limitations of basing automatic indexing on the principle of inclusion, Borko (1970) experimented with selection of index headings from the text and elimination of useless headings by means of derived indexing based on the principle of exclusion. The experimental text was the book *Automated Language Processing*, which was available in machine-readable code.

As described earlier, it is a relatively simple matter to program the computer to prepare a list of the different words in a text, along with the pages on which the words appear. But a subject index must be selective, so it is necessary to develop a set of algorithms that will enable the computer to eliminate all words in the running text that should not be used as index headings. Two word exclusion lists were prepared. The first was a relatively small list of 500 function words. By eliminating these high-frequency (common) words, the number of terms in the data base was reduced to approximately half, representing a considerable saving in processing time and storage. The remaining words were processed by a program that combined, for counting, all words having the same stem. This list was sorted alphabetically and printed. It still contained many words that, while not function words, were also not useful index headings, for example, such words as *alternative, analogous, assert, available*, which did not lead to subjects. The initial experimental task was to identify these words manually, put them on a second delete list, and develop a programming algorithm that would recognize and eliminate them automatically. Unfortunately, it was found that there was virtually no agreement among subject specialists as to which words should be deleted. With human experts disagreeing, it was clearly impossible to write a program that would recognize and eliminate nonuseful index terms. Working only from the computer-derived list of words, the experts involved in the experiment found it as difficult to specify what constitutes a poor index term as it was to define a good index term. The fault was laid to the fact that index entries are generally multiple-word terms, and the usefulness of single words could not be evaluated.

A computer program was then written to select word pairs, rather than individual words, from the text. A *word pair* is defined as two consecutive content words, with the function words, if any, removed. On the basis of his knowledge of the subject matter and the frequency of word-pair occurrence, the experimenter was able to identify meaningful word pairs. But again, it proved impossible to develop an algorithm that would enable the computer to identify and eliminate all useless word pairs and select only the useful ones. Final selection had to be made manually, and the useful multiple-word index terms were keypunched and prepared for input into (i.e., inclusion in) the indexing program. The computer produced an index that resembled a concordance more than a subject index; underneath each index term was a list of all locations, by page and paragraph number, in which the word pair occurred. *See* and *see also* cross-references were prepared manually and keypunched to become part of the index (see Figure 9.1). The resulting index led searchers to word pairs that indicated

AUTOMATA

14 5 14 6 15 3 31 1 34 5 37 3 61 1

61 2 62 2 62 3 67 1 241 2 287 1 330 5

366 1 367 1

AUTOMATED ANALYSIS SEE ALSO AUTOMATIC ANALYSIS

AUTOMATED ANALYSIS

1 2 6 4 7 4 99 3 120 2 120 4 204 1

211 1 248 1 250 1 288 1 316 4

AUTOMATED BILINGUAL DICTIONARY

294 3 294 4 294 5 316 4

AUTOMATED CLASSIFICATION SEE ALSO CLASSIFICATION AUTOMATIC

AUTOMATED CLASSIFICATION SEE ALSO DOCUMENT CLASSIFICATION

AUTOMATED CLASSIFICATION SEE CLASSIFICATION AUTOMATED

AUTOMATED CONTEXT ANALYSIS

6 4 120 2 211 1 288 1

Figure 9.1 *Sample entries from an automatic subject index. [Reprinted by permission from* Information Storage and Retrieval *(now* Information Processing and Management) *Vol. 6.; and from Harold Borko,* Experiments in Book Indexing, *1970, by permission of Pergamon Press, Ltd.*]

concepts and topics as well as subjects; that is, the semiautomatically produced index was not a true subject index.

9.3 COMPUTER-AIDED INDEX PRODUCTION

As used in this work, the term *automatic indexing* means the mechanized selection of index headings from a natural language text that has not been specially edited. As pointed out in the previous section, fully automatic subject indexing has not yet been achieved. However, if index terms are selected manually, the computer can play a significant role in the production of book and journal indexes. A number of investigators have developed procedures to aid the human indexer by automating the clerical tasks associated with producing an index once the subject headings have been selected.

9.3.1 Computer-Aided Indexing of Books

While teaching indexing at the Columbia University School of Library Science, Theodore Hines and Jessica Harris designed a computer system for producing a book index (1970). First, an indexer marks the text to identify the subject headings. The indexer must style the entries carefully so that they will file correctly. Then, a keyboard operator keys the entries from the marked manuscript onto punched cards, in the order of the text references. After keying, the cards are read into the computer and filed by a special sorting routine. This program alphabetizes the entries, consolidates page references, and subordinates modifiers under the appropriate subjects. For example:

TUNGSTEN 27–32
TUNGSTEN 44
TUNGSTEN/MINING 211
TUNGSTEN/REFINING 38

becomes

Tungsten	27–32, 44
mining	211
refining	38

"Page references may be right-justified, with or without leading dots, or be left ragged right [Hines and Harris, 1970, 52]." Such programs, as the authors point out, deal only with the mechanical and clerical operations of book indexing; the identification and phrasing of the indexable subjects remain the province of the human indexer.

Peter Rooney, a professional indexer, has designed an indexing system called TOPIC—Text Organization with Parameters for Indexing by Computer.

> As the name implies, the *text* of a book or periodical to be indexed is put into a logical *organization* by a trained TOPIC indexer, using a conventional marking and editing system to indicate topics to be indexed and the relationships between them. Style *parameters* are chosen to suit the indexing task at hand. The data are prepared for the TOPIC program, and the mechanics of *indexing*

> (alphabetizing, sequencing, checking, styling, and printing) are accomplished on an IBM 360 series *computer* [Rooney, 1974].

An innovative, patented text-editing and indexing system, called PRINSTAMATIC, was designed by Vincent J. Ryan and Vinton A. Dearing. Whereas, in the present procedures of book production, work on the index cannot be started until text composition has been completed, with PRINSTAMATIC, indexing is concurrent with manuscript writing or editing; the index is compiled in successive stages while the book is being composed. A detailed description of this system has been published (Ryan and Dearing, 1974), and with the permission of the authors and the publisher, a summarized description of the indexing system and illustrations are reproduced here.

The first task of the indexer or author using this system is to underline or otherwise identify on a duplicate copy of the manuscript the subject headings and heading–modification combinations to be indexed and to number the items consecutively (i.e., serially) in the manuscript margin. If a subject runs over a number of manuscript pages, the indexer indicates where it begins and where it ends. This is done within the numbering system by putting the same number at the beginning and end of the portion involved; each time the number is recorded, it is accompanied by a hyphen that indicates that at the first appearance of the number the item begins and at the second the item ends. For example, if an item ranges over more than one page, as does "Boulder Dam: name controversy" in Figure 9.2, its identifying number, 355, is written as "355-" in the manuscript margin where the item begins and as "-355" where the item ends. Cross-references are also indicated in the margins of the manuscript, as required. No numbers are assigned to these because they may apply to entries throughout the manuscript.

After the index entries have been identified on the manuscript, the indexer prepares a separate list of them (see Figure 9.3). The entries need not be listed in the order of their appearance in the text; they may be scrambled, as long as the identifying numbers are correct. New entries may be added and old ones deleted. Although it may seem repetitious and unnecessary for the indexer to prepare this list, since the entries are already indicated on the manuscript, the fact is that some of the heading–modification combinations on the manuscript will be incomplete or not in the correct form, that is, they will not always be in the exact words or identical order of the text. Sometimes the entry may not even exist in the text. Moreover, it is necessary to distinguish headings from modifications, much as one would when

351 begin before a year or more of preliminary work. Wilbur
elected to symbolize the start of the project by driving a
silver spike for the short railroad line which was to con-
352 nect the dam site with the Union Pacific Railroad in Las
353 H.H. as engineer — Vegas. On 17 September 1930 Wilbur drove the spike and
" " " " (see also Compact) — declared, "I have the honor to name this dam after a
354- H.H., dam named for — great engineer who really started this greatest project of
Hoover Dam: see Boulder Dam — all times, the Hoover Dam."[35] Shock reverberated
355- Boulder Dam: name controversy — throughout California, Nevada, and wherever the friends
B.D.: see also Johnson, Hiram — of the Boulder Canyon project were to be found. The
356 Sacramento Bee castigated Wilbur for his "unapproach-
able gall," and leveled the accusation that he had ignored
facts. "He made a consummate ass of himself," and he
"assumed the prerogative of Mussolini."[36]

On the day Wilbur renamed the dam the San Francisco
357 News carried comment on the recent primary election.
They predicted that governor-elect James Rolph and Con-
gressman Phil D. Swing were the men who would most
likely be Senate candidates in 1932. The News further
identified Swing for its readers as a popular young veteran,
an aggressive and experienced lawmaker, and "the real
Father of B.D.: see Swing — father of Boulder Dam."[37]
" " " : see B.D.

Examining Wilbur's act from a legal rather than an
emotional stance, Swing was convinced that the original
name given to the project would stand. Congress had the
legislative prerogative and it had recognized the project

Figure 9.2a *A sample of manuscript indexing with terms underlined and numbered.* [*Figures 9.2a and 9.2b are reprinted by permission from* Information Storage and Retrieval, *Vol. 10, Ryan and Dearing and from* Computerized Text Editing and Processing with Built-In Indexing, *1974, by permission of Pergamon Press, Ltd.*]

using conventional index cards. Cross-references need to be indicated and worded correctly. Proper names have to be inverted and listed in full. These and other adjustments are made by the indexer when preparing the list of index entries. This step may be considered comparable to creating the index cards prior to alphabetizing them.

It is usually desirable to check the list of index entries before it is keypunched or otherwise fed into the computer. It is necessary to distinguish headings from modifications; to bracket words and phrases that would interfere with alphabetization (such as introductory articles, conjunctions, prepositions, and some pronouns); and occasion-

as Boulder Dam. There had already been two attempts
358 to change the name in Congress. Representative Edward Taylor had introduced a bill to change the dam name to
359 Hoover in May 1929. Senator Reed Smoot of Utah had introduced a similar measure in January 1930. Both bills had been assigned to the respective Irrigation committees and never reported out.[40]

Privately Swing was very disappointed at the turn of events. "It looks as if those of us who worked for the great Boulder Dam are going to be shoved out of the picture by changing the name and credit for the work."[41] The following sincere, originally punctuated letter could not help but restore his good humor:

> My, Dear, Mr, Swing,
> I do not comprehend his legal right? and I hope ever man and woman in Nevada, Arizona and California will unanimously demand the name to remain known to the entire United States as the Swing, Johnson, Bolder Dam.[42]

–354 H.H., dam named for
–355 B.D.: name controversy
Swing was justifiably pleased when a second amendment by Colorado Representative Taylor to change the name of the dam officially was rejected by the House on 12 December 1930.[43]

In October 1930 Arizona filed a complaint in the Supreme Court against all other Colorado River basin
360 states and Ray Lyman Wilbur. Arizona alleged that the
361 Boulder Canyon Project Act was unconstitutional, that

Figure 9.2b

ally to indicate nonprint letters, for alphabetizing such entries as "Mc" and "St.," which would then appear as "M«a»c," and "S«ain»t." However, if the keypuncher is an experienced indexer, this checking step can be assigned to the keypuncher. In any event, the indexer or author or both will have an opportunity to check the computer printout.

The checking of the list completes the indexing of the manuscript. The author and indexer now have an opportunity to review and discuss the list of index entries, a step that may be of considerable help to both of them. Omissions from either the manuscript or the entry list can be identified, and errors noted and corrected.

The indexed manuscript and list of index entries are submitted to

351 Wilbur, Ray Lyman

352 Union Pacific Railroad

353 Hoover, Herbert: as engineer

" " : " " : (see also Compact)

354- " " : dam named for

Hoover Dam: see Boulder Dam

355- Boulder Dam: name controversy

" " : see also Johnson, Hiram

356 Sacramento Bee, The

357 San Francisco News

Father of Boulder Dam: see Swing, Philip David

" " " " : " Boulder Dam

358 Taylor, Edward

359 Smoot, Reed

-354 Hoover, Herbert: dam named for

-355 Boulder Dam: name controversy

360 Wilbur, Ray Lyman

361 Boulder Canyon Project Act

Figure 9.3 *Index list prepared by author from marked manuscript.*

the publisher while the master manuscript is still being edited. The list is processed by a computer program that alphabetizes the entries, coordinates and arranges the component parts of the entries, eliminates redundancies, places cross-references in the proper places, and provides appropriate punctuation. The assembled index is printed in upper- and lowercase letters, with bold and italic typefaces as required, and with either a hanging (indentation) or run-on (paragraph style) format. This is the index as it will appear in final form, except that lines are double-spaced for easy proofreading and correction, and entry-identifying numbers (now following the entries) are listed instead of the final book-page numbers (see Figure 9.4).

As the master manuscript is marked for typesetting, the entry numbers are transferred to it from the indexed manuscript. Then, as soon as book pages are typeset and made up, the entry numbers are extracted together with the corresponding page numbers and formed into a computer-produced "concurrence table." When the existing index data base and the indexing program are rerun, the concurrence

```
Boulder Canyon Project Act, 361

Boulder Dam: name controversy, 355--355. See also John
     son, Hiram

Father of Boulder Dam. See Boulder Dam; Swing, Philip
     David

Hoover Dam. See Boulder Dam

Hoover, Herbert: as engineer, 353 (see also Compact);
     dam named for, 354--354

Sacramento Bee, The, 356

San Francisco News, 357

Smoot, Reed, 359

Taylor, Edward, 358

Union Pacific Railroad, 352

Wilbur, Ray Lyman, 351, 360
```

Figure 9.4 *Index printout.*

table is fed in and, under program control, as the final index is assembled, the book-page numbers are attached to the entries instead of the entry serial numbers. For example, the entry numbers of "Boulder Dam: name controversy," 355- and -355, are fed in (they were in the existing data base already), but under application of concurrence conversion, the page numbers 132–133 are printed out. In this way, with computer-operated typesetting equipment, the index is typeset, including the final pagination, within minutes from the time the book pages are ready. The index does not then delay production.

9.3.2 Computer-Aided Indexing of Journals

The principles involved in creating subject indexes are the same whether the material being indexed is a book or a collection of journal articles; however, some of the production techniques differ. A number of investigators have developed computer support systems to aid in the production of journal indexes.

Louise Schultz, Systems Development Director of BIOSIS (BioSciences Information Services) of *Biological Abstracts,* considers the role of data processing (*a*) to produce published indexes; (*b*) to support manual indexing; and (*c*) to control indexing vocabularies (Schultz, 1976).

Regarding the automatic or semiautomatic production of indexes, she states that while some progress has been made in enabling a computer "to analyze the individual occurrences, the statistical significance of co-occurrences, and the role of interrelationships among individual character strings . . . we do not seem to be in immediate threat of eliminating human indexing."

Schultz also points out that computer support for the indexing functions involves a price—namely, the cost of putting the full text into computer-readable form, the actual computer processing of the text, and the establishment and maintenance of complex authority files and dictionaries far more vigorous than needed in systems not using computer support. Although no costs were given, it can safely be assumed that the costs are considerable. The sophistication of computer-support techniques is not limited; however, application is limited primarily by cost as compared to the cost of the less-sophisticated techniques. In contrast, the degree to which computerization can replace the intellectual aspects of indexing and index production is limited not only by cost but also by our own inability to model the behavior of indexers and index users.

The Postgraduate School of Librarianship and Information Science of the University of Sheffield, England, has developed and implemented computer-aided production of "articulated subject indexes" (ASIs) (Lynch and Petrie, 1972). The ASI techniques have been used for the subject indexes of *World Textile Abstracts* and *Rubber and Plastics Research Association Abstracts (RAPRA Abstracts).* Chemical Abstracts Service is evaluating the extension of methods used in the production of ASIs. The ASI uses indexer-coined subject paraphrases in which subject headings are indicated by the indexer through the symbols < and > before and after each heading term. An example of a marked paraphrase is "<Silicosis> in <copper> <miners>." The marked paraphrases are then fed into a computer, which processes them to create a modification for each marked heading term, for example,

Silicosis, in copper miners, 1234
Copper, miners, silicosis in, 1234
Miners, silicosis in copper, 1234

The subject headings and modifications come exclusively from the coined paraphrases. The modifications for each subject heading are created by computer rearrangement of the paraphrase (minus the heading) by means of an algorithm of six rules, which control the order of the words in modifications: If the heading starts the subject paraphrase, the order of the rest of the words remains unchanged. If the heading is part of a noun phrase, the rest of the phrase starts the modification, then come the words following the subject heading, and finally the words preceding the heading. If the heading is followed by "of," the words after the heading start the modification and the words preceding the heading follow. If "of" precedes the heading, the noun phrase plus "of" start the modification, these words are followed by the words after the heading, and finally come the rest of the words at the start of the paraphrase—up to the noun phrase that started the modification. If a noun phrase in the paraphrase occurs with the subject heading more frequently than do other words, it is placed first in the modifications. This rule helps to assemble related modifications under the heading. If the foregoing rule fails because different words occur with equal frequency, then the order of the words in the paraphrase is used also in the modification.

The index entries so produced simulate those created by human indexers working without computer assistance; however, human indexers are considerably more flexible, as they can employ word orders based on the unusualness of the modification-starting word or on the ineffectiveness of the word in differentiating among closely related modifications. Also, words not in the subject paraphrase can be employed by human indexers, if needed, to give adequate specificity and to improve the accuracy of the entry in representing the subject being indexed. However, the ASIs are of much higher quality than are unedited KWIC and KWOC concordances because (*a*) subjects are selected from text as well as from title; (*b*) all subjects are selected; (*c*) the paraphrases more specifically represent subjects than do titles; (*d*) the specificity of the paraphrase is under indexer control; and (*e*) the subject headings are indexer-coined and indexer-selected. This human effort reduces scattering among synonyms and modifications, reduces missed entries from about 60% to a relatively small number, and helps avoid index entries that do not lead to subjects reported by the author.

The major cause of delay in the publication of high-quality manually produced subject indexes is the editing of the alphabetized index cards. The editing cannot begin until all of the cards in the first of the *A*s have been alphabetized, and it cannot be completed until all of the cross-references have been justified and run into the rest of the cards. The purpose of editing is to remove a large number of errors, eliminate serious scattering that becomes visible only after the cards are assembled, delete unwanted headings, make double indentations in modifications, justify the use of all cross-references, improve the choice of synonyms for headings, add specificity to modifications where needed, delete unnecessary specificity from modifications, combine identical modifications, reword modifications to make them clearer, and carry out a number of other operations. In the production of ASIs by computer assistance, editing is bypassed; the few existing cross-references are justified manually (a relatively slow process). The speed of production of ASIs should be compared to the speed of production of unedited, manually produced subject indexes. For the average nonorganic abstract in *Chemical Abstracts*, the time required to index with dictation equipment (Bernier and Langham, 1955) and to check the index cards is 4 to 5 min each; for organic abstracts it is 9 to 10 min each. The coining and recording of subject paraphrases and the designating of subject headings in them during ASI processing should take approximately the same amount of time and thus not be the cause of appreciable delay in issuance of either kind of index. The cost of ASI and manual indexing procedures should be closely comparable if both editing and justification of cross-references are bypassed. But bypassing these two procedures appreciably reduces the quality of the index produced—a reduction in quality that is felt by index users in the form of additional load (missed entries, wasted time, and frustration) in the use of the index.

The use of subject-paraphrase input and its articulation as described by Armitage and Lynch (1968) for "articulated subject indexing" has been tried at *Chemical Abstracts* (Cohen, Dayton, and Salvador, 1976). The coding error of 24% for the paraphrases is close to the 20% error found by card checkers (Bernier, 1968) in the subject indexing of *CA* by dictation (Bernier and Langham, 1955). These two percentages would be additive for articulated indexing to give a total of about 44% of error. The anticipated reduction in effort in formulating and dictating "multiple permutations" and the reduction in keying cost remain to be quantified.

9.3.3 Computer-Aided Indexing of Bibliographies

The British National Bibliography has developed a computer-aided system to provide subject index data for UK/MARC records and to produce a subject index for the National Bibliography. The system is called PRECIS (Preserved Context Index System). A number of articles have been published describing this system (see especially Austin, 1974a, b; Austin and Digger, 1977; and Bakewell, 1975).

Only the conceptual basis of the system will be outlined here. The indexing is done manually through the exercise of human judgment. The indexer examines a document, decides what it is about, and records (*a*) a string of terms that paraphrases the subject; (*b*) the accession number of the document; (*c*) the PRECIS instruction codes and role operators to ensure that correct index entries are generated; (*d*) Reference Indicator Numbers (RINs), which instruct the computer to extract, from a computer-stored thesaurus, the *see* and *see also* references appropriate to the terms in the string; and (*e*) a Subject Indicator Number (SIN), which identifies the location at which the indexing data will be stored for future use. The computer implements the indexer's decision, generates the index entries and references, sorts these alphabetically, and generates a magnetic tape that can be used for searching or for phototypesetting.

The PRECIS system uses a two-line entry format shown diagrammatically as

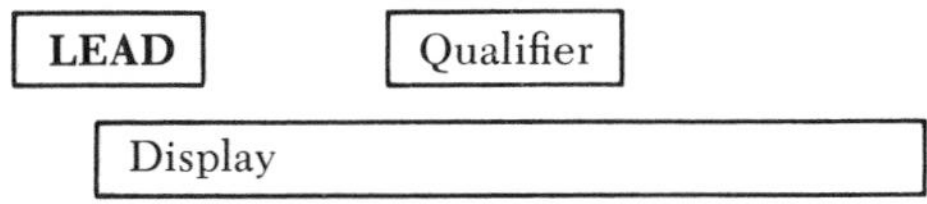

The "lead" is analogous to the subject heading; it is the primary filing element and is printed in boldface. The "qualifier" is a modification or subheading that defines the lead term broadly. The "display" is also a modification that defines the lead term more specifically.

The qualifier and display portions of the format are not necessarily occupied in all index entries. Their use depends upon whether the subjects indexed have contexts broader or narrower than the lead term, and this is indicated by the "role operators" assigned to the terms by the indexer.

The input string of terms must be recorded in context-dependent order, which is a kind of PRECIS indexing grammar. The indexer expresses the relation by responding to such questions as:

1. Which terms are related?
2. How are they related?
3. Which terms provide a wider context?
4. Which terms provide a narrower context?

An example from Austin and Digger (1977) illustrates the process. The imaginary document to be indexed concerns the training of personnel in India's cotton industries. The string of terms chosen by the indexer to characterize the subject of the document is: **India, Cotton industries, Personnel, Training**. Note that a good deal of human judgment has been exercised in selecting this string, for, as Austin points out, "cotton industries" is recorded as a single concept while "personnel training" is broken into two separate concepts.

The next task for the indexer is to answer the questions on how the terms are related and to record the role indicators selected from the PRECIS manual. (To simplify the explanation, we will ignore the reference and subject indicator numbers.) After the information has been recorded in machine-readable form, the computer takes over and prepares the index entries. These are printed in the index, in the PRECIS entry format, as follows:

India
  Cotton industries. Personnel. Training
Cotton industries. India
  Personnel. Training
Personnel. Cotton industries. India
  Training
Training. Personnel. Cotton industries. India

Bakewell (1975) conducted a small study to evaluate the effectiveness of PRECIS indexing. In this experiment, an experienced PRECIS team from the British Library Bibliographic Services Division's Subject Systems office indexed in depth 584 periodical articles on management, and they supplied copies of this printed index to 25 students at the Liverpool Polytechnic's Department of Library and Information Studies. Bakewell and his associate prepared a list of 100 questions from a data base that represented "typical" inquiries of the sort handled by a management information service. Each searcher was asked to try to answer four questions by using the PRECIS index and to record the results and the time taken.

Of the 100 questions searched, 83 answers were obtained, and 62 of these (approximately 75%) took less than 2 min to locate. Analysis was done of the 17 items not located. Seven failures were due to inadequate searching, 2 to the ambiguity of the question, and only 8 to inaccurate or incomplete indexing. Student response to the PRECIS index was favorable.

Bakewell's conclusion about the relevance of the PRECIS system to book indexing is worth quoting: "The indexes are not perfect—I detected a number of omissions—but they are very good and do illustrate the feasibility of PRECIS as a system for producing book indexes—provided enough space has been allotted to the task [Bakewell, 1975, 162]!"

9.4 AUTOMATIC INDEXING FOR INFORMATION RETRIEVAL

The manual indexing of documents for input into computer-based information storage and retrieval systems contributes greatly to the cost of such systems. Machine processing of text and the production of word indexes is relatively inexpensive. The question needing investigation is whether machine indexes provide retrieval equivalent to that of manually prepared subject indexes. The justification of any indexing technique lies in its retrieval effectiveness—measured by recall and precision.

This question is even more meaningful today than it was a few years ago, for many bibliographic data bases can now be searched on-line, and retrieval services are being offered by the System Development Corporation/ORBIT and the Lockheed Corporation/DIALOG search services, and by BRS (Bibliographic Retrieval Services). Most of the data bases are manually indexed, but the services provide capabilities for searching the words in the title or the abstract of the documents. The fact that these programs are provided and are used is pragmatic evidence that natural language search is useful. The degree, or level, of effectiveness is still open to question. Research is needed to determine the relative retrieval effectiveness of existing procedures and to devise new techniques for improving on-line searching.

In *Dynamic Information and Library Processing* (1975), Gerard Salton summarizes and synthesizes many of the experiments by himself and others to develop techniques for modifying derived index terms—to make them more general (for greater recall), or more specific (for higher precision).

9.4.1 Techniques for Improving Recall

High recall is a high percentage of relevant documents that a term, or a combination of terms, can retrieve. One way of increasing recall is to add to the query terms related as Boolean OR. This can be done automatically in a number of ways.

1. *By synonym dictionary or thesaurus:* A simple look-up process enables terms in the query to be expanded to include synonyms and otherwise related terms.
2. *By word truncation:* Various computer text-processing techniques have been developed for removing prefixes and suffixes. Combining words with the same stem increases the number of terms in the query on which matches can be made.
3. *By substituting universal symbols:* A universal symbol is one that stands for any character. It may be substituted in a search term when one is not sure of the correct spelling or if one wishes to retrieve all forms of that term. For example, if it is desired to retrieve all works written by Smith or Smyth, one can search the author field with SM*TH. Similarly, a universal symbol such as $ can represent any number of characters, for example, $BIOLOG$ would retrieve microbiology, psychobiological, etc.
4. *By associative indexing:* This method is more complex than the others, but it allows for a more general and a more controlled term expansion. By means of a computable, statistical algorithm, the co-occurrence of two terms in the same document is calculated and recorded as an *association value*. That is, if Term A and Term B co-occur in a large number of documents, these two terms have a high association value.

It is also possible to calculate higher-order associations, for example, if Term A is associated with Term B in one document, and B is associated with C in another document, then a second-order association exists between A and C. To be more concrete, *Vitamin C* and *acorbic acid* are synonymous and are unlikely to occur in the same document. Authors will choose one or the other. However, it may be that *Vitamin C* will co-occur with *scurvy* and that *ascorbic acid* will also co-occur with *scurvy*. Using the simple logic that if A is related to B and B is related to C then A is related to C, we can calculate a second-order association coefficient between *Vitamin C* and *ascorbic acid.* It has been demonstrated that terms linked by second-order associations are more likely to be semantically related than are first-order association terms.

9.4.2 Techniques for Improving Precision

Recall is increased by adding to and generalizing the terms in the query. Precision is improved by using very specific terms or by combining words into phrases. There are a number of statistical and syntactical procedures for automatically generating phrases; however, the computer programs that will combine selected words into content-identifying phrases with any degree of reliability are complicated, expensive to operate, and difficult to implement. Salton (1975) points out that, in an interactive computer system, one can use a primitive phrase-generating algorithm and allow the human indexer or searcher to review intermediate results and select the best phrases for searching.

9.4.3 Comparison of Controlled and Automatic Indexing

Indexing quality can be evaluated by measuring how effective the index tags are in retrieving relevant documents. The Cranfield experiments (Cleverdon, 1967) compared three different manual-indexing techniques: single terms derived from text, a controlled vocabulary of single terms, and concepts or multiword terms. Each of these basic index languages was tested by a variety of recall and precision-improving techniques. Cleverdon concluded that the controlled Uniterm index language gave the best retrieval performance; the use of phrases tended to be overspecific.

Salton made some comparisons between MEDLARS, which is a controlled manual indexing system and the SMART automatic indexing and retrieval system. He concludes that, "In any case, the tests show again that relatively simple automatic text analysis systems do not produce in a document retrieval environment search results inferior to the controlled indexing performed conventionally [Salton, 1975, 105]."

9.5 COMMENTS ON COMPUTER-AIDED INDEXING

Automatic subject indexing must be accomplished by entering the words of a work into a computer, identifying the subjects of the work, selecting from the work only those words and phrases that guide the user to the subject, and coining index entries complete with modifications. A limited number of methods have been explored for analyzing and processing works to achieve automatic subject indexing. These methods of text analysis involve the use of statistics, syntactics, and, to a lesser extent, semantics. The application of these procedures to indexing is still experimental. Subject indexing is a difficult text-processing problem, because it involves more than selecting words or word pairs from text and attaching page numbers to them. Experimentation continues, and some progress is being made.

In this chapter we have chosen to examine first the experiments on automating the preparation of a back-of-the-book index—although less experimental work has been done on book indexing than on journal indexing. Results to date indicate that the outlook for machine-aided book indexing is more promising than for fully automatic indexing.

In the realm of computer-aided book indexing, three significant directions have been identified. These are:

1. New books about previously reported subjects such as, for example, textbooks, can be indexed automatically once the index terms to be used as concept headings have been preselected by examining the indexes in several books on those subjects.
2. Index headings can be derived from the text being indexed (rather than preselected from the indexes of external works) if the text is computer searched for multiple-word phrases rather than for single words; however, this increases the cost of processing considerably. Even so, the selection of subject headings requires some human intervention aided by computer-produced lists of multiword terms and their frequency of occurrence. This form of computer-aided indexing produces indexes that resemble concordances of word phrases more than a true subject index.
3. Perhaps the most promising method of computer-aided indexing available today is through the integration of manual indexing with computerized text processing in book production. The intellectual part of indexing is done manually while the manuscript is being written or edited. The computer then arranges and organizes the entries, alphabetizes the headings, arranges the modifications in order, and changes the references of the entries from the equivalent of manuscript-page numbers (i.e., item numbers) into book-page numbers. Automation does what automation can do best—that part of the task that can be specified and done by following rules. This use of computer-aided indexing may reduce the time and labor required for book production and thus cut production costs.

Experiments on the automatic indexing of journal articles and documents have as their goal to derive document identification terms for subsequent retrieval from a computer data base. These systems do not attempt to create true subject indexes for the documents; they derive word tags as document identifiers and match these with the words used in retrieval requests.

Results obtained from automatic indexing within a computer-based information storage and retrieval system appear to be about the same as when the documents have been manually indexed by a controlled vocabulary. It should be pointed out that these results were obtained on a relatively small experimental data base, and, while these experiments were carefully controlled and are undoubtedly accurate, the results have not yet been validated on a large operating system. Also, the results have shown only that automatic indexing is effective within an automated retrieval system. This conclusion should not be generalized to draw conclusions about the effectiveness of automatic indexing for manual retrieval systems in which searchers make use of printed indexes and abstracts.

Obviously, we need a great deal more experimentation on automatic and computer-aided indexing for both books and journal articles. Current available results are encouraging, but there are still a lot of unanswered questions.

IV TYPES OF INDEXES

10 Subject and Author Indexes

Of all indexes, subject and author are the most familiar. In this chapter we distinguish among subject, concept, topic, and word indexes; and between personal-author and corporate-author indexes.

10.1 SUBJECT INDEXES

The term *subject index* is commonly applied to all those not clearly identifiable as author, title, or special indexes, or those with some other obvious nonsubject orientation. Such inaccuracy causes problems both for the indexer and for the user. The different indexes should be clearly differentiated and labeled. In this book we distinguish among subject, concept, topic, and word indexes. The distinctions are important, although not commonly made.

10.1.1 Subjects, Concepts, Topics, and Words

Subjects are the foci of a work, the central themes toward which the attention and efforts of the author have been directed. They are those aspects of a work that contain novel ideas, explanations, or interpretations. And they should all be indexed.

Not all items about which an author writes are subjects; previous research may be reviewed, subjects may require introduction through other concepts, passing thoughts may be expressed, and examples may be used for illustration only. Such items are *concepts*; they aid in understanding the report, but they are not subjects and they need not be subject indexed. For example, an author may review the relation between sucrose and heart disease in order to introduce and show the importance of current research on the possible harmful effects resulting from the depletion of chromium from the body through excess sucrose. The relation between sucrose and heart disease is a concept; it is well known and need not be subject indexed. The relation between sucrose and the possible detrimental effects of chromium depletion is the subject of the research study and should be subject indexed. Many concepts, nearly all of them old and familiar, must be presented in order to make the writing on a subject clear and rational. However, indexing these concepts will increase the size of the index, will lead the searcher to known material, and will make it more difficult to find the new and significant subjects that have been reported.

Many writings are divided into *topics*—often with subtitles. Indexing these topics (or their subtitles) creates an index to topics. Sometimes these topics are subjects, in which case they should be subject indexed. Usually, they are too broad for subject indexing; often they are concepts that serve to introduce, justify, prove, and amplify the subject studied and reported. Thus, a topic index is different from a concept index and from a subject index.

A *word index* is still another type of index. Obviously, the thoughts of an author are expressed in words, but not all words—not even all content words, as distinguished from conjunctions, prepositions, and other function words—lead to the subjects, concepts, or topics presented in a work. An index to all the words in a book is a concordance, or word index, not a subject index. With the advent of computers and the techniques of language data processing, many new word indexes have been created, such as KWIC, KWOC, and Permuterm. These indexes are of value; they are also quick and inexpensive to prepare, and they serve useful functions including current awareness alerting.

But they are not subject indexes, for the words they contain lead to both subjects and nonsubjects.

In addition to these considerations, it can be seen that word indexes are the most bulky; concept indexes are the next most bulky; topic indexes the next most; and subject indexes the least bulky. For guidance to subjects, subject indexes are much more efficient than are the other three kinds of indexes. Users of subject indexes do not waste time consulting concepts, topics, and words in which they have no interest. This does not mean that indexes to concepts, topics, and words are of no value; it simply means that such indexes are different in function from subject indexes. It is important to know and observe this difference.

10.1.2 Subject Indexes

The most important and most used kind of index is introduced here through an analysis of the format and structure of sample entries derived from the index of *Abstracting Concepts and Methods* (Borko and Bernier, 1975).

Abbreviation(s)
 in abstracts, 10–11, 69
 journal-title, 12, 62
Abstracting
 American National Standards Institute standards for, 47–48
 assignment and article selection for, 141–145
Abstracting organizations and services
  see *Abstract journals*
Abstract journals *(abstracting organizations and services)*, 3–5, 131–159
 abstractor employment by, 197
Abstracts (see also *Critical abstracts; Extracts; Indicative abstracts; Informative abstracts; Modular abstracts; Special-purpose abstracts; Statistical abstracts; Tabular abstracts; Telegraphic abstracts)*
 abbreviations and symbols in, 10–11, 69
 editing of, see *Editing*
 identifier lists in, 67

We see that the subject heading **Abbreviation(s)** has a parenthetical plural to indicate that both the study of the process of abbreviation and the study of the product of the process (the abbreviations) can be indexed under this heading. **Abbreviation(s)** and other headings are flush to the left margin and printed in boldface, to make them more rapidly identifiable and to indicate the omission of the heading from all following indented entries. The first modification, “in abstracts,” limits the scope of the heading to the study of abbreviations in abstracts. Being a modification, it is indented. The references, "10–11, 69," indicate that two index entries have been combined under the same modification. The first reference is a compound one to consecutive pages; the second leads to a specific subject—the study of abbreviations as exceptions to the use of words of the author in abstracts. These two entries could have been differentiated from each other by using, for the second entry, "as exceptions to use of the author's words in abstracts."

The first cross-reference in the sample is "**Abstracting organizations and services** see *Abstract journals*" To most abstracting organizations, this *see* cross-reference would have been considered unnecessary because it is adjacent to the heading to which it refers. Differentiation between "**Abstracting organizations and services**" and "**Abstract journals**" was believed, for this index, to be unnecessary. The decision to separate or not to separate a heading into two headings is based on the anticipated convenience to the searcher. If differentiation among the entries under two different headings is difficult, it is better to combine the headings; if differentiation is simple, that is, if the entries under the two headings are quite different, then two headings should be used.

In the next heading, "**Abstract journals** *(abstracting organizations and services)*," the material in italics is a gloss that shows what has been combined under the heading.

There is, in the sample, a set of *see also* cross-references, under the general heading "**Abstracts**" to the headings for the specific kinds of abstracts discussed in the book, for example, to *Critical abstracts*. The headings to which one is referred by *see* and *see also* cross-references are printed in italic type to differentiate them clearly from the subject headings that the searcher has consulted. Semicolons are used between this set of nine *see also* cross-references because in some cases inverted headings, which require the use of commas, are referred to; semicolons are needed to separate the headings from one another.

One of the modifications under the heading **Abstracts** is the *see* cross-reference "editing of, see *Editing*" Including this *see* cross-reference among the *see also* cross-references at the start of the heading would be incorrect because there is nothing about editing as a subject under the heading **Abstracts**.

Some subject indexes have no modifications or only a few of them; this places an undue load on the user, who must look up all of the entries to see if any are relevant. The structural features of indexes are discussed in Part II of this book.

10.2 AUTHOR INDEXES

There are personal-author indexes and corporate-author indexes (indexes to the names of organizations in which the work was done). Sometimes both kinds are combined into one "author index." A subject, concept, or topic index may be combined with the author index to give a one-alphabet product that is simply called an index. Dictionary catalogs used in libraries are of this kind. Dictionary catalogs save searchers from having to use several indexes; however they include many extraneous entries unrelated to the search of the moment. Author indexes have long been the second most popular kind of index. For example, the "main entry" on each card in a card catalog is the surname of the first author of the work.

Name indexes differ from, and should be distinguished from, author indexes. An author index is an index to the authors of various items in the work being indexed—such as an anthology or a journal. A name index is an index to the names of people cited or otherwise referred to in a work. Such names are, in effect, subjects and can become headings in a subject index. However, when many names are cited in a work, as is often the case in a textbook or a scientific treatise, a separate name index may be desirable. Author indexes (personal and corporate) are used primarily to guide searchers to subjects rather than to the names of authors per se. Authors tend to specialize and so become concentrators of data and knowledge in a few subject areas. However, entries in an author index seldom provide complete guidance to specific subject areas because there may be other authors and groups working in the same area, and only a few of them will be known. After the names of authors working in a subject area have been identified along with their key papers, citation indexes (discussed in Chapter 11) can prove useful in expanding the search.

10.2.1 Personal-Author Indexes

Author names are stable and easily remembered. Name changes, through marriage and by law, do not significantly affect the ease of finding names in author indexes that provide cross-references from earlier to later names.

Author indexes (meaning "personal-author indexes") have, as their primary function, guidance to subjects and to specific works. They also show what authors are doing, whether they have changed their subject fields, and just how active they are.

Author indexes without modifications (i.e., indexes whose entries consist of author names followed by blocks of reference numbers) force searchers to look up many reference numbers to find recalled works. Load is shifted from the indexer and index-publisher onto the user. In order to avoid blocks of undifferentiated reference numbers, author indexers usually employ as modifications the titles of the articles. Titles adequately differentiate among author-index entries because authors seldom publish a second work with the same title. Indexer-coined modifications in author indexes are rare. The use of the full reference (author name(s), title, journal name, volume number, issue number, inclusive pagination, series number, and year) creates more of a bibliography than an author index and is not recommended.

Headings in author indexes are unambiguous; that is, all entries under a given heading refer to only one author, and all entries are, or should be, unique. Initials of personal-author names adequately distinguish names in nearly all cases. In the very few cases in which the surnames and initials are identical, different authors are differentiated by the inclusion of additional data, such as the life dates of the author or the place (organization, city, or country) where the work was done. Examples are, **J. J. Jones (1894–1922)** and **J. J. Jones (1901–1960)**; **S. S. Smith (Australia)** and **S. S. Smith (Canada)**. Identical undifferentiated author names, although rare, are a source of confusion and irritation for users.

Author names are not repeated after the first entry. Indentation is used to indicate omission of the author's name in second and subsequent entries. This is done to save reading time and space (index bulk), and to make the index standard.

The better author indexes have *see* or *see also* cross-references to variant spellings, for example, **Müller**, **Mueller**, and **Muller**. Also, there are *see* cross-references from parts of names to whole names, for example, from **Government Services** to **United States Government Services** in a telephone directory. The best author indexes have *see* cross-references from pseudonyms to the actual names—or the reverse. For example:

Twain, Mark see *Clemens, Samuel Langhorne*

10.2.2 Corporate-Author Indexes

The names of organizations (usually universities or corporations) are used as headings in corporate-author indexes. Organizations specialize in subject fields, as do people, thus these indexes can be used to locate published works in a particular field. In some cases, the only name remembered to be associated with a work is the name of the group or organization where the work was done, for example, the RAND Corporation. Even for searches to discover published works whose existence is not known, the corporate-author index may be of help because of the tendency of organizations to specialize. The names of organizations doing work in a given subject area can be found in a subject index or in a permuted title concordance.

The modifications in corporate-author indexes, generally the titles of papers and reports, prevent blocks of undifferentiated references under headings.

Books do not need author indexes; guidance to author names in anthologies and other collections of works is usually provided by a table of contents. Book-form bibliographies with entries arranged by author name do not need author indexes, although they may use cross-references from the names of second (and subsequent) authors to the names of first authors. Published proceedings of symposia may have author indexes for contributors. The following is a sample heading from the author index of a book bibliography:

Crane, E. J,*(see also *Bernier, C. L.*)
CA Today—The Production of *Chemical Abstracts*, 1272
Procedures in the development of chemical nomenclature, 3609
and **C. L. Bernier**. Indexing and Index Searching, 1605
and **C. C. Langham**. On-the-Job Training at Chemical Abstracts Service, 3271

An example of entries without modifications in an author index to an abstract journal is

Abdian, A. G., 2063
Abysheva, M. E., 2442
Ackerman, H. J., 2379, 2443, 2455
Adler, L. S., 2382
Albert, L. N., 2282.

The omission of modifications is common in indexes to issues of an abstract journal; however, this saving for the publisher puts an unnecessary load on the searcher, who must look up all the references to ascertain which reference is the one sought.

The telephone directory is an example of an "author" index. In the

* The letter *J* in Crane's name is not an initial and therefore does not take a period.

"white pages," all headings are the names of individuals or organizations. The modifications are the addresses, each of which consists of the street number and street name plus, for large communities, the name of the suburb, district, or neighboring community. The reference is the 7-digit telephone number or the 2-letter–5-digit number. Some entries are weighted by being printed in capitals and by the use of larger type. There is a note, for example, directing searchers from **Government Services** to city, county, state, and United States Government listings. Entries for some of the government listings are double-indexed, that is, found both under **Government Services** and under the names of the units of government. There are *see* cross-references, for example:

> **Federal**, for United States Government departments and agencies not listed below see *United States Government*

And there are supergeneral cross-references that lead the user to a class of entries, for example, "**Mac**, see Mc." Subdivisions of an organization are classified under the heading of the main organization, for example:

DU PONT DE NEMOURS E I & CO INC

Buffalo Explosives Div.
191 Reading Rd West Falls 652-8801
Buffalo Film Dept River Rd Ton 876-4420
Buffalo Refinish Svce Whse
1696 Walden ave Chktg 896-7979

[*Reproduced from the* Buffalo Telephone Directory, 1977–8, *p. 274, by permission of the New York Telephone Co. and the E. I. Du Pont de Nemours & Co.*]

11 Citation Indexes

A citation index provides the means for locating earlier references and more recent works that refer to earlier works.

The headings in a citation index are the names of authors of the earlier works. The modifications are the rest of the bibliographic references of the earlier works; and the index reference is the bibliographic citation for the later work. For legal citations, the heading is a cited case number; the modification, the rest of the citation; and the index references, the later cases that cite the earlier case.

The citation index enables a researcher to obtain answers to such questions as:

What developments in a specific subject have taken place since Article A was published?

What recent articles has the author of Article A published?

What new research workers are in the field pioneered by the author of Article A and who now refer to Article A?

How many works have referred to Article A?
Who has referred to Article A?

Since citation indexes are not produced by indexers, only the structure and use of these indexes is discussed here.

11.1 SHEPARD'S CITATIONS

English common law operates on the principle of *stare decisis et non quieta movere* (to stand by decisions and not to disturb settled matters). This is the doctrine or policy of following rules and principles laid down in previous judicial decisions. Since later decisions may reverse or modify earlier decisions, it is legally important to find *all* later decisions that affect an earlier decision. *Shepard's Citations* enables searchers to find all later decisions. This reference tool was started in 1873. Figure 11.1 is an example of a fictional Shepard's citation reproduced from the article by Weinstock in the *Encyclopedia of Library and Information Science* (Weinstock 1971, 17). "101 Mass. 210" is the code for one cited case reported in *Massachusetts Law Reports*, page 210. The cases that cite 101 Mass. 210 are indented below this heading as a list of modifications that end with "35 HLR 76," which is decoded as, "*Harvard Law Review*, volume 35, page 76." The lowercase letter codes that start the modifications mean "a" for affirmed, "q" for questioned, and "o" for overruled. It is interesting to note the economy of symbols in *Shepard's Citations* as well as the effectiveness of guidance.

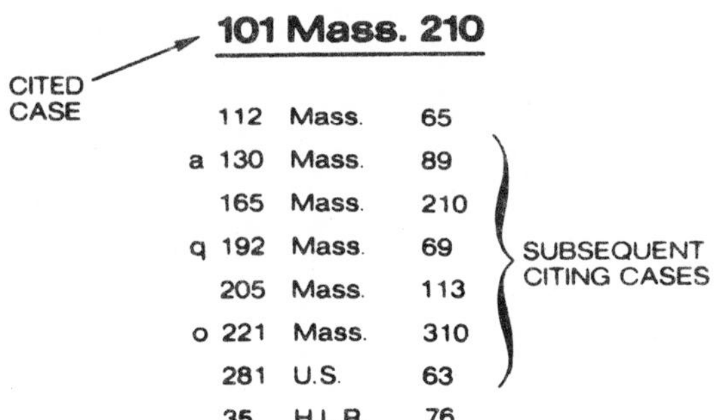

***Figure 11.1** A typical* Shepard's Citations *entry. [Reprinted from the* Encyclopedia of Library and Information Science, *1971, Vol. 5, p. 17, by courtesy of Marcel Dekker, Inc.*]

11.2 THE SCIENCE CITATION INDEX

Just as *Shepard's Citations* serves the legal field, so the *Science Citation Index* serves the scientific field.* The *Science Citation Index* (SCI), published by the Institute for Scientific Information, is one of the best-known and most commonly used of citation indexes. More than 2000 journals are searched for references to be used in the SCI. The author's last name and initials, the source (of cited reference), and the volume number and beginning page number of each article or other work (called the source item) are keypunched along with the titles of cited articles. Separate sets of punched cards are prepared for each source item. The cards are verified and the data transferred to magnetic tape. Additional editing is done by computer program and the citation data are then formatted and prepared for photo-offset printing.

A major advantage of the citation index is that it is produced by computer processing with very little expensive intellectual effort. Human indexers are *not* needed to select subjects from the articles, paraphrase the subjects, or create subject-index entries. The references in the source article have all been found, evaluated, and verified by the author of the article. The keypunching of these data is according to clear rules; it is a clerical task requiring accuracy and attention to detail but no knowledge of indexing or of subject content. This is a major advantage.

Some disadvantages should also be pointed out. The very fact that the citations are unedited causes problems. In the SCI only the last name and initials are used, but Charles Robert Williams may sometimes list himself as C. R. Williams and sometimes as Charles Williams. In the citation index, two listings will be created, "CR Williams" and "C Williams," and scattering will occur. Should there be both a Charles Robert Williams and a Charles Richard Williams, the citations will be combined under the heading CR Williams. Another disadvantage that occurs is the listing of citations with the wrong volume number or year. In principle, such errors could be corrected by careful checking, but editorial control is expensive and perhaps not cost effective for the publisher.

There is another class of error that is more fundamental and intrinsic to the nature of the citation index; the document cited may be partially or wholly irrelevant to the citing article. When authors refer to mate-

* The *Social Science Citation Index* covers the social sciences. It is similar in structure to the *Science Citation Index*.

rial unrelated to the current search, then the searcher is led to irrelevant material.

11.2.1 Structure

The *Science Citation Index* consists of three parts (*a*) the *Citation Index;* (*b*) the *Source Index;* and (*c*) the *Permuterm Subject Index.*

Entries in the *Citation Index* portion (CI) of the SCI are alphabetically by the earlier author. In Figure 11.2, A. E. Broadus is shown to be the author of two articles: the first in "*Clin. Res.* **17,** 65 (1969)," the second in "*J. Clin Invest.* **49,** 2222 (1970)." The author name is the index heading, and the two bibliographic references constitute two modifications. The initial index reference under the first modification is "FRANKLIN TJ NATURE-BIOL 246 119 73"; the last index reference under the second modification is "WOO YT ARCH BIOCH 154

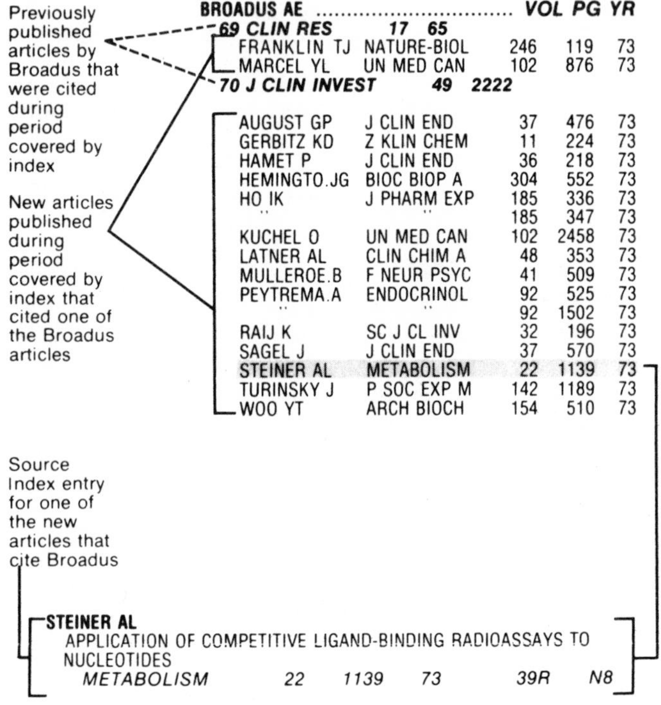

BROADUS AE .... ***VOL PG YR***

69 CLIN RES 17 65

		VOL	PG	YR
FRANKLIN TJ	NATURE-BIOL	246	119	73
MARCEL YL	UN MED CAN	102	876	73

70 J CLIN INVEST 49 2222

		VOL	PG	YR
AUGUST GP	J CLIN END	37	476	73
GERBITZ KD	Z KLIN CHEM	11	224	73
HAMET P	J CLIN END	36	218	73
HEMINGTO.JG	BIOC BIOP A	304	552	73
HO IK	J PHARM EXP	185	336	73
"	"	185	347	73
KUCHEL O	UN MED CAN	102	2458	73
LATNER AL	CLIN CHIM A	48	353	73
MULLEROE.B	F NEUR PSYC	41	509	73
PEYTREMA.A	ENDOCRINOL	92	525	73
"	"	92	1502	73
RAIJ K	SC J CL INV	32	196	73
SAGEL J	J CLIN END	37	570	73
STEINER AL	METABOLISM	22	1139	73
TURINSKY J	P SOC EXP M	142	1189	73
WOO YT	ARCH BIOCH	154	510	73

STEINER AL
APPLICATION OF COMPETITIVE LIGAND-BINDING RADIOASSAYS TO NUCLEOTIDES
METABOLISM 22 1139 73 39R N8

Figure 11.2 *A typical entry in the* SCI Citation Index. [*Reprinted by permission of the Institute for Scientific Information.*]

510 73." This means that T. J. Franklin referred to the first article of Broadus in *Nature-Biol.* **246,** 119 (1973); and Y. T. Woo referred to the second article of Broadus in *Arch. Bioch.* **154,** 510 (1973). The user of the *Citation Index* discovers that 18 articles or documents refer to 2 of Broadus's works; the names of the authors of these 18 articles or works are given, as are the names of the journals in which they appear, together with their volume, page, and year numbers. The titles of the works citing Broadus can be found in the *Source Index*, which is discussed in the next section.

The searcher is led, by the CI, from works of Broadus that are closely related to the current interests of the searcher to later works (selected from more than 2000 journals) that have cited Broadus. Thus, the searcher has been led *forward* in time to subject-related material. Authors cite and refer to works of other authors nearly always because of a *subject* relation between the two works. In this way, the CI functions as a subject index by means of which the searcher is able to trace closely related subjects.

The *Source Index* (SI) of the SCI (see Figure 11.3) gives the searcher additional bibliographic data; the co-author, language of the citing article, title of the article, number of references, and journal issue number. From these additional data, especially the article title, the searcher can often determine whether or not to look up the reference. From the SI, the user can turn to the primary literature or to surrogates, such as abstract journals.

Searchers who do not know of earlier works in a field of interest may first turn to the *Permuterm Subject Index* of the SCI (see Figure 11.4) for aid in locating published works by means of title-word pairs. This index might be more accurately described as a concordance, rather than a subject index. It is computer-produced from every word (that is, every word not on an exclusion list) in the titles of all earlier and later works included in the *Source Index*. For a title with *N* selected words,

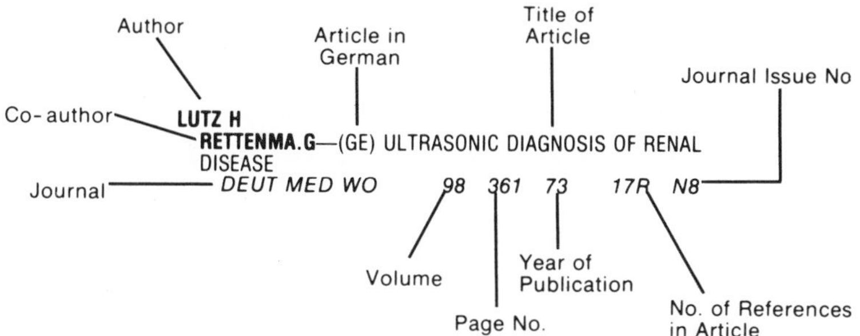

Figure 11.3 A typical entry in the SCI Source Index. [*Reprinted by permission of the Institute for Scientific Information.*]

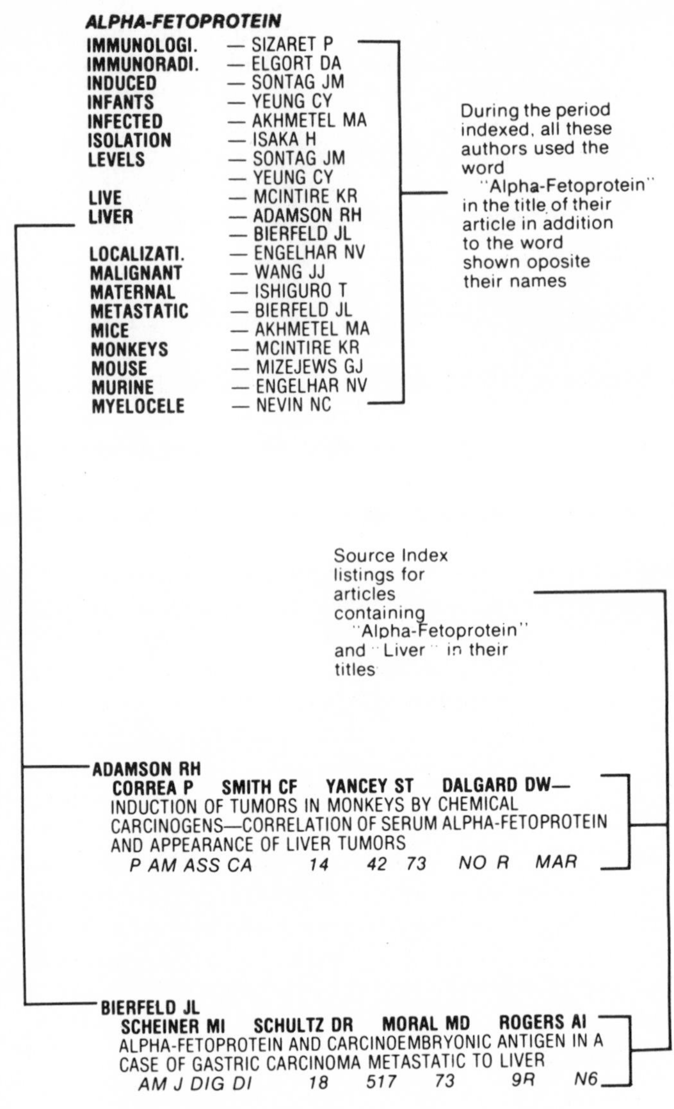

ALPHA-FETOPROTEIN
IMMUNOLOGI. — SIZARET P
IMMUNORADI. — ELGORT DA
INDUCED — SONTAG JM
INFANTS — YEUNG CY
INFECTED — AKHMETEL MA
ISOLATION — ISAKA H
LEVELS — SONTAG JM
— YEUNG CY
LIVE — MCINTIRE KR
LIVER — ADAMSON RH
— BIERFELD JL
LOCALIZATI. — ENGELHAR NV
MALIGNANT — WANG JJ
MATERNAL — ISHIGURO T
METASTATIC — BIERFELD JL
MICE — AKHMETEL MA
MONKEYS — MCINTIRE KR
MOUSE — MIZEJEWS GJ
MURINE — ENGELHAR NV
MYELOCELE — NEVIN NC
During the period indexed, all these authors used the word "Alpha-Fetoprotein" in the title of their article in addition to the word shown oposite their names
Source Index listings for articles containing "Alpha-Fetoprotein" and "Liver" in their titles
ADAMSON RH
CORREA P SMITH CF YANCEY ST DALGARD DW—
INDUCTION OF TUMORS IN MONKEYS BY CHEMICAL CARCINOGENS—CORRELATION OF SERUM ALPHA-FETOPROTEIN AND APPEARANCE OF LIVER TUMORS
P AM ASS CA 14 42 73 NO R MAR
BIERFELD JL
SCHEINER MI SCHULTZ DR MORAL MD ROGERS AI
ALPHA-FETOPROTEIN AND CARCINOEMBRYONIC ANTIGEN IN A CASE OF GASTRIC CARCINOMA METASTATIC TO LIVER
AM J DIG DI 18 517 73 9R N6

Figure 11.4 *A typical entry in* SCI Permuterm Subject Index. [*Reprinted by permission of the Institute for Scientific Information.*]

$N(N-1)$ pairs of words will be formed. Thus, the *Permuterm Subject Index* is a two-term permuted index of titles in which all pairs of selected terms are published. Every pair of terms is permuted (a,b and b,a)—which gives the concordance its name. Permutation indexing is discussed in greater detail in Chapter 12.

After some title words have been identified, either by means of the *Permuterm Subject Index* or by other indexes, the user is directed to the Source Index and thence to the CI for guidance to more recent works.

11.2.2 Use

After the initial search has been completed or is well under way, a more extensive bibliography can be compiled by a process called cycling. In this process, the searcher uses the references (footnotes, bibliographies, etc.) found in the primary literature located through the CI and the SI. The relevant references are cycled through the CI and the SI to find additional relevant works. From the bibliographic data in the new references one can go backward in time to earlier works and from the CI and the SI one can go forward in time. Cycling continues until the searcher is satisfied that all relevant works have been found.

It is important to note that citation indexes are not meant to be a substitute for subject and author indexes; citation indexes *complement* subject and author indexes. Since authors refer to other works because of the close relation between subjects, citation indexes actually function as subject indexes. Subjects are located through citations and references, rather than through subject headings, descriptors, or hierarchical codes (Garfield, 1974). Thus, heading–modification combination KNOWLES WS CHEM-TECH 2 590 72 is not only bibliographic data, it is also a multifaceted subject entry that leads the searcher to subjects related to *asymmetric hydrogenation, phosphines, catalysts,* etc. Authors refer to Knowles's article because their own works deal with one or more of these subjects. Searchers seeking data on asymmetric hydrogenation may find relevant references under the CI entry for Knowles. It is also important to note that the CI entries under **Knowles** do not uniquely stand for asymmetric hydrogenation; they may lead the searcher to works on phosphines, catalysts, etc. The character of the work located through the CI can best be determined by consulting the SI, as explained earlier. In some cases, the original work may have to be consulted in order to determine relevance. Citation indexes are unaffected by changing terminology and nomenclature.

Spencer (1967) found that citation indexes were faster and more efficient than conventional indexes for searchers who have searches of less than 6 hr. In his comparison of the *Science Citation Index, Chemical Abstracts,* and *Index Medicus* for the preparation of a drug bibliography, he found that most of the references were obtained in the first 3 hr; even more important, of the three indexes, *Science Citation Index* yielded the highest percentage of unique references.

Citation indexes may provide the best access to the interdisciplinary (multidisciplinary) literature. An article about educational programs for children with cerebral palsy may be of interest to researchers in neurology, psychology, education, rehabilitation, and other fields. The CI cuts across discipline lines.

Citations and citation indexes have additional uses—as a tool for historical research, as a measuring tool for science, as a means of automatic content analysis, and as a way of evaluating journals, papers, authors, departments, and candidates for appointment, promotion, and tenure. They provide a useful measurement of the impact of a work. The use of citation indexes for these purposes is still new; hence we are cautioned that "the mere ranking by numbers of citations or the numbers of papers published is no way to arrive at objective criteria of importance [Garfield, 1963, 290]." Yet it has been found that, of 14 reasonable measures of rank for departments of chemical engineering, the number of references to works from the departments by engineers other than the authors is the best measure (Bernier, Gill, and Hunt, 1975). The total number of references and even the number of references to one's own work outrank most of the other 13 measures used in this study.

Figure 11.5, a diagram of a citation network, illustrates the use of SCI data in the study of the history of science.

> By examining the interconnecting links of scientific events shown in the citation network, it is possible to observe historical and sociological processes at work. It is also easy to identify the nodal publications in the citation network, that is, those that are cited most by others, those that have the most impact. From [Figure 11.5] it would be quite reasonable to conclude that whoever published paper number 2 had considerable impact on research involving nucleic-acid staining. It is at this point that the *SCI* begins to serve as an objective sociometric tool; it begins to show who has truly influenced the course of science [Garfield, 1970, 670].

The use of the number of references to evaluate journals, measure research activity, and determine research performance has been proposed by a number of authors (Garfield, 1972, 1973; Margolis, 1967).

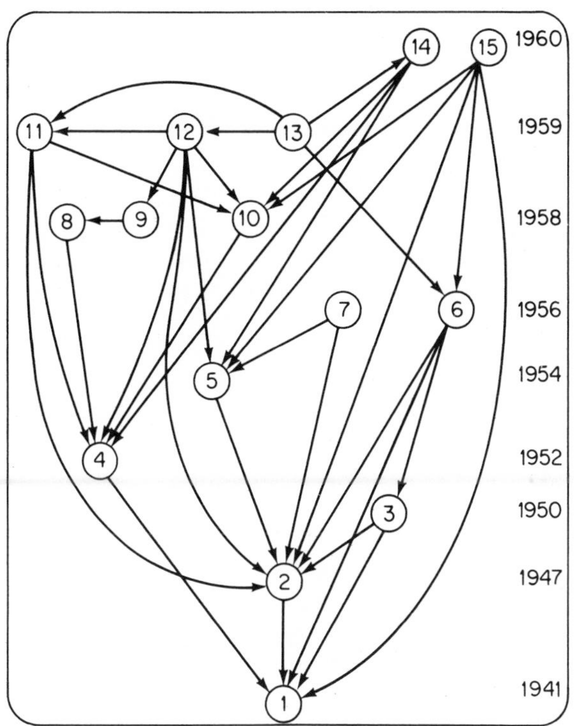

Figure 11.5 *Citation network of 15 articles on nucleic acids. [Reproduced from* Nature, *Vol. 227, p. 670 (Aug. 15, 1970), by permission of* Nature *and Eugene Garfield.]*

An analysis of journal references based on the 2000 or more journals covered by the SCI is summarized in Figure 11.6. A core of only 152 journals accounts for about one-half of all references. From this, it might be assumed that a multidisciplinary journal collection can have only a few hundred titles. The relation between the number of references to a journal and its "importance" needs study. Since references are to the papers in a journal rather than to the journal itself, Margolis states that "The value of a scientific paper can be measured by the influence it has on others, and citation indexing provides, as a by-product, a measure of the impact of articles, authors, and journals [1967, 1, 214]." Both Garfield and Margolis stress that impact is not the same as the quality, importance, or significance of a work. De Solla Price (1963, 41) shows that scientists whose work is judged to be of high quality usually have large numbers of publications, and these papers are usually referred to more frequently than are a random sample of papers. One would expect that better papers would be cited

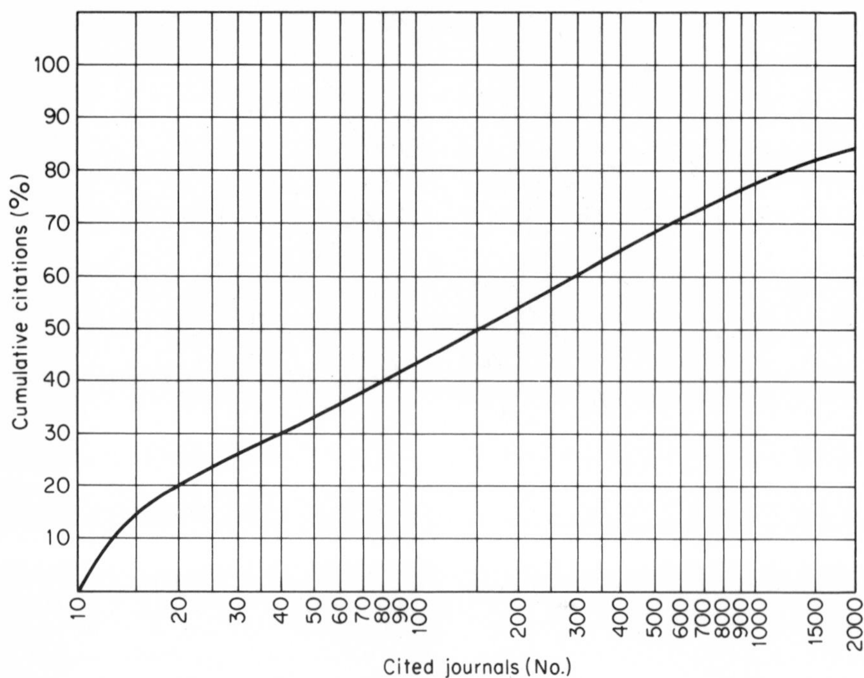

Figure 11.6 Distribution of citations among cited journals. [*Reproduced from* Science, *Vol. 155, pp. 1213–19, 10 March 1967, by permission of J. Margolis and* Science, *copyright 1967 by the American Association for the Advancement of Science.*]

and referenced more frequently than others. However, the best papers are not necessarily the ones to which references are made most frequently. In fact, articles that are in error may be cited by authors who have discovered this error and refer to this finding in another article on the same or a similar subject, thus increasing the citation count of the erroneous article. The Institute for Scientific Information has prepared a bibliography on citation indexes and their uses.

12 Word Indexes and Concordances

Word indexes guide the searcher to the words used by the author of a document—but not necessarily to the subjects of the work. The distinction between word indexes and subject indexes has been made throughout this book. Subject indexes are guides to new and significant subjects reported by the author, not to all concepts and topics mentioned in the work. Subject indexes are selective, and the terminology is controlled so as to minimize scattering. Word indexes are not selective nor is the vocabulary controlled. However, they have their own unique qualities and uses.

Two types of word indexes are described—those derived from the titles of articles and those derived from the full text. Among the former are KWIC (Keyword in Context) indexes, KWOC (Keyword out of Context) indexes, and permuted (term-pair or revolved) indexes. Full-text word indexes with partial context are commonly called concordances.

12.1 KEYWORD IN CONTEXT AND KEYWORD OUT OF CONTEXT INDEXES

The acronym KWIC was coined by H. P. Luhn in his now classic paper *Keyword in Context Index for Technical Literature (KWIC Index)* (Luhn, 1959). The concept of permutation indexing is much older, dating back more than 100 years. German libraries of that period used the term, *Schlagwort,* meaning catchword or keyword (literally 'favorite expression') to describe the alphabetized expressions used in their cataloging (Lewis, 1964). It has also been pointed out that Crestadoro's great work *The Art of Making Catalogues in Libraries*, published in London in 1856, referred to the concept of permutation indexing. Even if one were to consider only machine-produced indexes, two other works preceded Luhn's. Mary Veilleux had been operating a permuted title–word indexing system at the Central Intelligence Agency (CIA) since 1952 and first reported this fact in 1961 at the American University's Third Institute on Information Storage and Retrieval (Veilleux, 1961). Herbert Ohlman and his colleagues at the System Development Corporation also developed a permutation index and distributed machine-produced copies of this index at the 1958 International Conference on Scientific Information in Washington, D.C. (Citron, Hart, and Ohlman, 1958).

It is worth noting that although Luhn and Ohlman lived on opposite sides of the continental United States and worked independently, they both came up with the same idea at about the same time; they both demonstrated the idea by indexing the same set of documents, namely, the papers for the International Conference on Scientific Information, and they distributed their reports at the same meeting. Clearly, this was an idea whose time had come.

The citing of historical precedents is in no way intended to take credit away from Luhn. On the contrary, the purpose is to show that the method has withstood the test of time. And, although the identity of the inventor may be in doubt, no one can dispute the fact that the popularizer was Hans Peter Luhn; it is he who deserves the credit for making KWIC a common term and a popular form of index.

12.1.1 Description

KWIC indexing is based on three principles (*a*) that titles are generally informative; (*b*) that words extracted from the title can be used effectively to guide the searcher to an article or a paper likely to contain desired information; and (*c*) that although the meaning of an individual word viewed in isolation may be ambiguous or too general, the context surrounding the word helps to define and explain its meaning.

Each line in a KWIC index consists of three parts: the keyword (which is the heading), the context (which functions as a modification), and the code (which is the reference). KWIC indexes have every significant word in the title alphabetized, so that each word becomes an index heading and each word is placed adjacent to the same sequence among keywords and its contexts derived from other titles. As an illustration, let us examine the following article title of a recent article by Abraham Bookstein and Gary Fouty published in *Information Processing and Management* 1976, Vol. 12, No. 2, 111–116. The title of the article is "A Mathematical Model for Estimating the Effectiveness of Bigram Coding."

12.1.1.1 *Keyword*

The first task the designer of a KWIC index faces is to identify the keywords. The general solution to this problem has been to prepare, in advance of indexing, a stoplist of words that are not to be heading terms and to exclude these words from the indexing process. All other words are keywords. Articles, conjunctions, prepositions, and pronouns are generally on stoplists, as are many other common words. Organizations that publish KWIC indexes prepare their own stoplists (of as many as 1000 words) according to their special needs. Returning to the example, it is clear that the words *a, for, the,* and *of* would be on the stoplist and all others would be keywords.

12.1.1.2 *Context*

Context for keywords, is provided by the other words of the title. The words in the sample title would be revolved (permuted) as follows:

```
 BIGRAM CODING / A  MATHEMATICAL MODEL FOR ESTIMATING
G/A  MATHEMATICAL   MODEL FOR ESTIMATING THE EFFECTIV
MATICAL MODEL FOR   ESTIMATING THE EFFECTIVENESS OF B
   OR ESTIMATING    THE EFFECTIVENESS OF BIGRAM CODING /
   EFFECTIVENESS    OF BIGRAM CODING / A MATHEMATICAL MO
  VENESS OF BIGRAM  CODING / A MATHEMATICAL MODEL FOR
```

This particular title has six keywords (which is about average), although numbers vary among disciplines. The keywords of titles are printed so as to form an alphabetized column on the page. An extra space is used to the left of keywords to make it easy for the searcher to identify them. Words at the beginning and end of the line may be truncated or omitted, which increases the difficulty in reading the line. But a symbol, in this particular example a virgule (/), is used to indicate the end of the title.

Some keywords have multiple meanings, as do "model" and "coding" in our sample title; however, keywords in KWIC indexes are not isolated; they are adjacent to other words in the title, and this context serves as an index modification that fairly well defines the meaning of the keyword.

12.1.1.3 *Reference*

The third part of the index line is the reference. The reference may be a code—a set of identifying symbols tying the line in the KWIC index to the complete bibliographic citation that always accompanies (usually following) the index entry. The references used vary from simple document-accession numbers (serial numbers) to the so-called Luhn code, which is systematically derived from the first author's name, the publication date, and the words in the title. This 11-character identification code has the following components:

$$X_1X_2X_3X_4X_5X_6\text{—}Y_1Y_2\text{—}Z_1Z_2Z_3$$

$X_1X_2X_3X_4$ = the first 4 letters of the first author's last name
X_5X_6 = the initials of the author's first and middle names (If the author has no middle initial, X_6 is left blank.)
Y_1Y_2 = the last 2 digits of the year of publication
$Z_1Z_2Z_3$ = the initial letters of the first 3 words of the title that are not common function words (i.e., not articles and prepositions)

Thus, the code for the sample article is

BOOKA —76—MME.

This code is more informative than is an accession number, and it can be produced automatically by means of a computer-program algorithm used at the same time that the KWIC index is being produced. Other codes are also in use, as shown in Figures 12.1 through 12.6.

12.1.2 Advantages and Disadvantages

KWIC indexes are currently being produced by organizations in the United States and abroad. The fact that this type of index is so widespread is indicative of its acceptance by publishers and users. But to use a KWIC index successfully, one must understand its strengths and weaknesses.

12.1.2.1 *Advantages*

The major advantage of KWIC indexes is that they are quickly produced. The acronym KWIC, pronounced "quick," serves as a particularly apt designation of this type of index from the viewpoint of the publisher. The preparation of a permuted index requires only that the document reference be converted into machine-readable form so that the computer can process the data. Elimination of the need for indexers specializing in the subject field, omission of editing, and the use of computer processing, allows guides to newly published articles to be distributed more rapidly than is possible by other systems. For these reasons, KWIC indexes also cost much less to produce than do conventional subject indexes. Early publication and low cost are the two most important advantages of KWIC indexing.

Other advantages that have been claimed for KWIC indexes are (*a*) that the indexing vocabulary is always current and has the actual words of the author; and (*b*) that more access points are provided than in many other printed subject indexes.

12.1.2.2 *Disadvantages*

A question raised at the very onset of KWIC indexing concerns the adequacy of titles alone as a source of indexing terms. A number of investigators have studied the adequacy of journal article titles in different fields. Much of this literature is summarized in the state-of-the-art report by Mary Stevens (1970). Depending on the subject field, anywhere from about 34 to 86% of the terms assigned by human indexers can be derived from title words. On the lower end of the spectrum is the study by Bernier and Crane (1962), who reported that for nonorganic chemistry articles covered by *Chemical Abstracts* only 34% of the entries could be derived from the titles. For organic chemistry, the percentage would be considerably lower. On the high end is a study by Montgomery and Swanson (1962), who used as their test corpus the September 1960 issue of *Index Medicus,* found that, for 4770 items, 85.8% of the titles contained either the assigned subject-heading term or a synonym of it; only 11% contained no such term. For the remaining titles the investigators were unable to decide. In a study of the titles in 10 periodical indexes, Lane (1964) concluded that "in science and engineering the titles of articles usually describe or at least imply the contents of the articles. In non-technical fields, titles reveal the contents less frequently; and in a general index, such as the *Reader's Guide*, titles are indicative less than half the time."

Better titles would result in better KWIC indexes. Four approaches have been used to make titles more useful for KWIC indexes. Titles have been supplemented by keywords derived from the article. However, since a skilled indexer or editor must read the work and add keywords, index preparation becomes more time-consuming and costly than without supplementation. A second approach uses a supplementary or added title, which follows the author's title and is also entered into the KWIC indexing system. This procedure, too, requires skilled editing.

A third, quite different, approach is to encourage authors to write more specific titles. Fortunately this seems to be occurring. More specific titles may be on the increase partly because of the existence of KWIC indexes. Authors want their papers to be used. A greater awareness of KWIC indexes may persuade authors to include more keywords (and more specific keywords) in their titles because of the consequent better chances of their articles being retrieved. A trend in this direction has been noted (Tukey, 1962). As summed up by Brandenberg (1963), "The title must permute or perish."

Some effort has been made to instruct authors to write better and more permutable titles. At the 1963 meeting of the American Documentation Institute (now the American Society for Information Science), those who submitted papers were told, along with other instructions, that "the title must be composed with care and must contain at least six significant words."

The lack of terminology control in the unedited KWIC index to titles is a serious deficiency. Similar entries may be scattered throughout the index owing to the use of synonyms, words otherwise related, and neologisms as keywords. The searcher is forced to prepare a list of all the terms that the different authors may have used and then to search under all of these terms. If the searcher misses synonyms and other related terms, he will miss relevant material.

The fourth approach toward improving KWIC indexes is to compensate for the lack of a controlled vocabulary, but this cannot be done inexpensively. Kennedy (1962) suggested that subject scatter can be reduced by cross-references; and Campbell (1963) has proposed the use of *see* and *see also* cross-references and the classification of keywords. Fischer (1966) reports that it is difficult to use a KWIC index with cross-references, but that some of this difficulty can possibly be eliminated by a variety of typefaces. The use of a thesaurus has also been proposed, but, as Fischer again points out, there are conflicting opinions on the need for a thesaurus when using a KWIC index. The user of such an index must be prepared to search for relevant materials under different keywords.

The disadvantages and problems of format of the KWIC index are discussed in the next section. On consideration, Stevens concludes, "The consensus seems to be that of qualified praise, especially for the early announcement and dissemination applications. The KWIC index is recognized as responding to a definite need, as having merit for fields in which more-conventional indexes do not exist as well as for current-awareness searching [Stevens, 1970, 67]." Bernier has pointed out that for questions of recall in which a specific, remembered work is to be retrieved, a concordance or KWIC index is ideal, provided that the searcher remembers the author's name or one significant word in the title. For questions of discovery and of reasonable inference, concordances are much more difficult to use than are quality subject indexes.

12.1.3 Variations and User Reactions

Not all users are enthusiastic about the form of the KWIC index. A number of suggestions have been made for its improvement. The need to make the title more informative and more specific of the document's contents has already been mentioned, as has the use of an improved stoplist to prevent insignificant terms from appearing as index headings. Postediting of a deck of punched cards used in the production of KWIC indexes is a rapid way of removing some entries not leading to subjects reported and for locating additional words to be added to the stoplist.

12.1.3.1 *Line Length*

One of the most common complaints about KWIC indexes concerns the length of the index line. KWIC indexes commonly use either a 2-column, 60-character line (as in Figure 12.1) or a 1-column line of about 100 characters (as in Figure 12.2), not including the reference. Line length controls the context that can be displayed, the amount of white or wasted space on the page, and title truncation.

The 2-column, 60-character line seems to be the most popular. Experience has shown that this format is cost-effective for the

```
ED PROGESTERONE 7-ALPHA              AND DEHYDROEPI ANDROSTERON     65843
Y LABELED R AND S ALPHA              BENZYL ALCOHCL DERIVATIVES     66123
OSPECIFICALLY LABELED R              BENZYL ALCOHOLS AND S ALPH     68996
YL ALCOHOLS AND S ALPHA              BENZYL ALCOHOLS STEREOCHEM     68996
PI ANDROSTERONE 7-ALPHA              BY PORCINE FETAL AND MATER     65843
C PREDNISOLONE WITH 1 2              CORTISOL IN VARIOUS PROTEI     65827
TER PULSE LABELING WITH              DI AMINO PIMELIC-ACID AUTO     68581
INTESTINAL TRANSPORT OF              DIGITOXIN IN-VITRO INCOMPA     68235
HEOPHYLLINE METAB-DRUGS              LEUCINE PRO INSULIN MEMBRA     65959
M CATION PUMPS MEMBRANE              OUABAIN/ CHARACTERISTICS O     64683
LE IN THE FASTING STATE              PALMITATE IODINE-125 ALBUM     67533
OF PREGNENOLONE 7-ALPHA              PROGESTERONE 7-ALPHA TRITI     65843
T 5 SYNTHESIS OF 13S 13              SCCULERINE AND 13R 13 TRIT     68996
D SCOULERINE AND 13R 13              SCCULERINE FROM STEREOSPEC     68996
/ IN-VIVO METABOLISM OF              TESTOSTERONE IN ADULT MALE     65957
IN RAT LIVER BLOOD LUNG              TESTOSTERONE 5-ALPHA DI HY     65934
FEULGEN CYTO PHOTOMETRY              THYMIDINE AUTO RADIOGRAPHY     67558
IN ANTI NEOPLASTIC-DRUG              THYMIDINE AUTO RADIOGRAPHY     67740
NG LATE PREGNANCY WOMEN              THYMIDINE INCORPORATION 2N     66712
IN B-1 STERIGMATOCYSTIN              THYMIDINE INCORPORATION/ D     67576
DIOGRAPHY RADIOACTIVITY              THYMIDINE INCORPORATION/ S     65389
 OF THE TECHNIQUE MOUSE              THYMIDINE MILLIPORE FILTER     64717
NS TRITURUS-VIRIDESCENS              THYMIDINE/ DNA REPLICATION     65238
B-DRUGS CARTILAGE SERUM              THYMIDINE/ RESPONSE OF ISO     66025
TAB-DRUGS DNA SYNTHESIS              THYMIDINE/ THE DIFFERENTIA     65956
AL SEROTONIN CONTENT ON              TRYPTOPHAN UPTAKE RAT CATR     68281
N PENICILLIUM-CYCLOPIUM              TRYPTOPHAN/ STERIC COURSE      69018
HESIS AND LABELING WITH              TYROSINE BRAIN HEART INTES     65892
UTININ EDTA METAB-DRUGS              URIDINE POLY ACRYLAMIDE GE     64728
E HAMSTER CELL CULTURES              URIDINE/ SOME REGULARITIES     65255
PIS-ALBA PULSE LABELING              URIDINE/ STIMULATION OF PR     69108
 INDOLE COMPOUNDS AFTER              5 HYDROXY TRYPTAMINE RAT S     64665
DROXY IAA/ STUDY ON THE              5 HYDROXY TRYPTAMINE TRANS     64665
ILIZING ON THE YIELD OF  TRITICALE AND OF SPRING WHEAT NITROG     64240
ONAL VALUE OF WHEAT AND              AS EVALUATED BY WEANLING M     67923
RONOMICAL PRACTICES FOR              PART 1 THE EFFECT OF THE S     64240
IONS OF LEAF CELLS OF A              TRITICUM-VULGARE SECALE-CE     66526
STUCEAE PHALARIDEAE AND  TRITICEAE AGROSTIS-SPP CALAMAGROSTIS     64903
LUTENIN SUBUNITS IN THE  TRITICINAE BY SODIUM DODECYL SULFATE     64895
COSIDES GLUCOSYL ESTERS  TRITIUM /METABOLISM OF GIBBERELLINS      68927
EGRADATION OF CARBON-14            AND CHLORINE-36 LABELED GAMM     69734
NZOMORPHAN ID-1229 WITH            ANIMAL/ LABELING OF A NEW AN     68376
RATS OXYGEN CONSUMPTION            CARBCN-14 COLD ADAPTATION NO     64787
 OF CHRONIC EXPOSURE TO            PART 1 EFFECTS ON ADULT RATS     67559
TRA UTERINE EXPOSURE TO            RAT EMBRYO FETUS POST NATAL      69587
ENT STATUS OF DEUTERIUM            TARGETS FOR CANCER THERAPY B     67730
E RAT CHOLESTEROGENESIS  TRITON AND PHENC BARBITAL TREATMENT/     66140
 PHENOXY ANALOGS IN THE            HYPER LIPIDEMIC RAT MODEL CLO     68233
RE OF MIXED MICELLES OF            X-100 AND DI MYRISTOYLPHOSPHA     64565
ARIOUS DETERGENTS HUMAN            X-100 LUBROL WX NONIDET DEOXY     67860
TIGATED WITH THE USE OF            X-100 PYRUVATE DEHYDROGENASE      67870
AERIAL APPLICATION OF N  TRITYL MORPHOLINE TO IRRIGATION CANA     69381
COLD ACCLIMATION IN THE  TROCHLEAR NUCLEUS OF LIZARDS SCELOPO     69814
 CENTRAL CALIFORNIA USA  TROCHOPHORE SHELL CLEAVAGE/ SPAWNING     66956
-PIG RODENT TICKS MITES  TROMBICULIDAE LAELAPIDAE IXODIDAE MA     69353
IGGER MITES ACARIFORMES                ON BATS IN KIANGSU PRO     67043
CE OF HALACARIDAE ACARI  TROMBIDIFORMES IN THE OLIGOTROPHIC L     67042
-RECORD/ BUTTERFLIES IN  TROMS AND FINNMARK NORWAY LASIOMMATA     67134
 MONKEYS OF THE KOSHIMA  TROOP /SIGNALS FCUND IN THE GROOMING     64413
```

```
IC ACTIVITY THE ROLE OF              AS AN ACTIVATCR IODINE-125 A   64928
ES SPECIFICITIES PEPSIN              CATHEPSIN D L LEUCYL-BETA NA   66149
YBEAN TRYPSIN INHIBITOR              CHYMOTRYPSIN ADHESIVENESS/ C   65218
R IODATE LYSOZYME RNASE              CHYMCTRYPSIN GLYCC PROTEIN P   64487
SUCCINATE DEHYDROGENASE              CHYMCTRYPSIN NUCLEOTIDE PH F   68608
 GLUCOSE OXIDASE SYSTEM              CHYMCTRYPSIN PRONASE IODINE-   64640
C-2.7.5.1 TUBER SLICING              CHYMCTRYPSIN PRONASE ISOZYME   68860
 NAJA-MELANOLEUCA MOUSE              CHYMOTRYPSIN/ SNAKE VENCM TO   69865
INSOLUBLE AT NEUTRAL PH              CHYMCTRYPSIN/ THE PRIMARY ST   67527
IS OUCHTERLONY ANALYSIS              CLEAVAGE IMMUNO DIFFUSION/ M   67564
NASE PER IODATE PRONASE              DIGESTION GLIAL CELL SEPHARO   65324
S SEDIMENTATION PRONASE              HYALURONIDASE RNASE NEURAMIN   67638
 THE REDUCED PANCREATIC              INHIBITOR DI SULFIDE BOND FO   64475
NE 38 OF THE PANCREATIC              INHIBITOR KINETICS THERMODYN   64474
ER KIDNEY CELLS SOYBEAN              INHIBITOR TRYPSIN CHYMOTRYPS   65218
OUSE PERITONEAL SOYBEAN              INHIBITOR TURKEY OVO MUCOID    64725
F THE BOVINE PANCREATIC              INHIBITCR/ COMPLETE TYROSINE   64589
DATION MOLECULAR WEIGHT              MAGNESIUM ION UTP ITP KINETI   68571
S IN CULTURE EFFECTS OF              CN THE THYROTROPIN RECEPTOR    66078
OLYSIS PEPSIN BROMELAIN              PH WATER ABSORPTICN GEL ELEC   66250
EROL PHCSPHATE RESIDUES              PHENCL MURAMIC-ACID POLY RIB   68565
 COMPONENT ALPHA-1 ANTI              PLASMA PROTEINS PHOSPHO GLUC   66472
ROMBOPLASTIN FACTOR-VII              PLASMIN/ THE ACTIVATION OF H   64667
ALGAE UPTAKE EXTRACTION              PRONASE/ PHYSIOLOGICAL VARIA   68989
IATUS VERTEBRATE MAMMAL              PROTEASE SECRETOGOGUE/ RELAT   66853
ORTRIX THROMBIN PLASMIN              REPTILASE SNAKE VENOM FIBRIN   64660
 SITES PRE IMMUNE SERUM              TREATMENT IODINE-125 IMMUNO    66623
M-SATIVUM AUXIN INDUCED              TREATMENT/ DISTRIBUTION OF T   68781
TRALIZATION TEST PAPAIN              TREATMENT/ RESTORATION OF SP   67641
LECULAR WEIGHT SUBUNITS              TYRCSINE UMP ATP MANGANESE I   68574
TIC ENZYMES PRONASE AND              WITH SPECIAL REFERENCE TO TH   65389
 MEMBRANE PERTURBATIONS  TRYPSINIZATION LYSC LECITHIN TREATME   64639
GLOBULIN G SODIUM AZIDE                 NEURAMINIDASE BIVALEN   66734
CHROISM/ EFFECT OF CELL                 ON NUCLEAR PROTEINS O   65267
S ENDOPLASMIC RETICULUM  TRYPSINIZED ERYTHROCYTES MEMBRANE FU   68787
ATE AFFINITIES OF THEIR  TRYPSINS RHODEUS-AMARUS TINCA-TINCA    66138
E METAB-DRUGS 5 HYDROXY  TRYPTAMINE /EFFECT OF DI PHENYL HYDA   68387
TORIA IN-VIVO 5 HYDROXY             /EFFECT OF 5 HYDROXY TRYP   66886
ION SEROTONIN 5 HYDROXY             /EFFECTS OF PAPAVERINE CH   68160
-DEPRESS-DRUG 5 HYDROXY             /IS THERE A CATECHOLAMINE   68489
ASE INHIBITOR 5 HYDROXY             /LACK OF EFFECT OF INCREA   68281
INE SEROTONIN 5 HYDROXY             /NEURO PHARMACOLOGICAL ST   68421
NT-STIM-DRUGS 5 HYDROXY             /SIMULTANEOUS ADMINISTRAT   68455
BETA CARBOLINE N METHYL             /THE ALKALOIDS OF NECTAND   68091
N AND ZYMOSAN 5 HYDROXY             ADENINE NUCLEOTIDES CELL-   66659
THE UPTAKE OF 5 HYDROXY             AND DOPAMINE IN HUMAN PLA   68226
RATS TRYPTOPHAN ISOMERS             CENT-STIM-DRUGS METAB-DRU   68449
E PRESENCE OF 5 HYDROXY             DOPAMINE AND ACETYL CHOLI   66978
SE TRYPTAMINE 5 HYDROXY             DCPAMINE DI THIO THREITOL   67869
 FINDINGS RAT 5 HYDROXY             DOPAMINE NOREPINEPHRINE E   68479
IR NMR SPECTRA N ACETYL             ELEAGNINE HARMAN BETA PHE   68092
RUG SEROTONIN 5 HYDROXY             ENDO TOXIN/ PHARMACOLOGY    68142
MMATORY DRUGS 5 HYDROXY             HISTAMINE BRADY KININ ACE   68204
ELS SEROTONIN 5 HYDROXY             HYPOTHALAMIC HYPOPHYSEAL    66007
CENTRATION OF 5 METHOXY             IN RAT BRAIN AND ITS EFFE   68461
AMINE PARA TYRAMINE AND             IN RAT BRAIN PARGYLINE ME   67865
DRENALINE AND 5 HYDROXY             IN THE AWAKE RABBIT APO M   68422
EPHRINE/ 5 7 DI HYDROXY             INDUCED CHANGES IN THE PO   67808
-CAROLINENSIS 5 HYDROXY             LIGHT REGIME SLEEP ACTIVI   67849
```

Figure 12.1 *Sample page of a 2-column, 60-character KWIC index:* Biological Abstracts. [*Reprinted by permission from* BioSciences Information Service of Biological Abstracts, *Vol. 60, 1975, p. E307.*]

```
               THE COMIT SYSTEM FOR MECHANICAL TRANSLATION                                                     ICIP59   183
                  ENGLISH-JAPANESE MACHINE TRANSLATION                                                     ICIP59   194
                       SYMPOSIUM ON MACHINE TRANSLATION                                                     ICIP59   218
              A NEW ALGORITHM FOR ALGEBRAIC TRANSLATION                                                     PACM59    22
                          SYMBOLIC LANGUAGE TRANSLATION                                                     WJCC59   288
    THREE LEVELS OF LINGUISTIC ANALYSIS IN MACHINE TRANSLATION                                              JACM591   24
               THE SHARE 709 SYSTEM, INPUT-OUTPUT TRANSLATION                                               JACM592  141
                      ALGORITHMS FOR FORMULA TRANSLATION                                                    TCJ2592   53
                    SOVIET RESEARCH IN MACHINE TRANSLATION                                                  NSMT60     2
                           RESEARCH IN MACHINE TRANSLATION                                                  NSMT60   160
  THE HIGH-SPEEC GENERAL-PURPOSE COMPUTERS IN MACHINE TRANSLATION                                           NSMT60   485
     SYSTEM CESIGN OF A COMPUTER FOR RUSSIAN-ENGLISH TRANSLATION                                            NSMT60   491
                       THE OUTLOOK FOR MACHINE TRANSLATION                                                  WJCC60   203
     MAN-TO-MACHINE COMMUNICATION AND AUTOMATIC CODE TRANSLATION                                            WJCC60   329
                         SEQUENTIAL FORMULA TRANSLATION                                                     CACM602   76
                RECURSIVE PROCESSES AND ALGOL TRANSLATION                                                   CACM611   10
                 A PROGRESS REPORT ON MACHINE TRANSLATION                                                   ICC 6115  11
A PRELIMINARY APPRCACH TO JAPANESE-ENGLISH AUTOMATIC TRANSLATION                                            MTL 611     7
        INTRINSIC MACHINE ACDRESSING IN AUTOMATIC TRANSLATION                                               MTL 611   283
                  MULTIPLE MEANING IN MACHINE TRANSLATION                                                   MTL 612  405
                       SYNTAX IN UNIVERSAL TRANSLATION                                                      MTL 612  593
                          MACHINE LANGUAGE TRANSLATION                                                      DIP 62   444
      THE USE OF COMPUTERS IN RESEARCH CN MACHINE TRANSLATION                                               IFIP62   301
       SYMPCSIUM ON MCDERN TECHNIQUES OF LANGUAGE TRANSLATION                                               IFIP62   326
            A GRCWING TREE FOR DESCRIPTOR LANGUAGE TRANSLATION                                              ROME62   153
NTERPRETER FCR USING IN NUMERICAL ORIENTED LANGUAGES TRANSLATION                              COMPILER-I ROME62   539
  EUPHRATES, A COMPARISON BETWEEN HUMAN AND MACHINE TRANSLATION                               TIGRIS AND MTP 58    279
SEGMENTATION PROBLEM IN SPEECH ANALYSIS AND LANGUAGE TRANSLATION                        AN APPROACH TO THE MTL 612  703
AND DEVELOPMENT IN INFORMATION RETRIEVAL AND MACHINE TRANSLATION                THE ROLE OF USAF RESEARCH WJCC59    66
   ARITHMETIC CATA, AND ITS APPLICATION TO THESAURIC TRANSLATION              A REDUCTION METHOD FOR NCN- ICIP59   321
MING SYSTEM FOR EXPERIMENTAL RUSSIAN-ENGLISH MACHINE TRANSLATION   /TRIAL TRANSLATOR, AN AUTOMATIC PROGRAM EJCC58   138
                            A NEW THEORY OF TRANSLATION ANC ITS APPLICATION                             NSMT60   363
              THE ANALOGY BETWEEN MECHANICAL TRANSLATION ANC LIBRARY RETRIEVAL                          ICSI582  917
                                    MACHINE TRANSLATION ANC-OR AN INTERNATIONAL LANGUAGE                IFIP62   323
ACTIC ANALYSIS         CURRENT RESEARCH ON AUTOMATIC TRANSLATION AT HARVARD UNIVERSITY AND PREDICTIVE SYNT NSMT60   173
                           RESEARCH IN MACHINE TRANSLATION AT RAMO-WOOLDRIDGE                            NSMT60    26
                         RESEARCH ON AUTOMATIC TRANSLATION AT THE HARVARD COMPUTATION LABORATORY        ICIP59   163
                                            TRANSLATION BETWEEN ALGEBRAIC CODING LANGUAGES              PACM58    29
                          HUMAN TRANSLATION AND TRANSLATION BY MACHINE, I                               MTL 611  221
                          HUMAN TRANSLATION AND TRANSLATION BY MACHINE, II                              MTL 612  507
                                      MIMIC, A TRANSLATION FOR ENGLISH CODING                           NSMT60   451
                                   INPUT-OUTPUT TRANSLATION IN THE SHARE 709 SYSTEM                     PACM58    18
                                      AUTOMATIC TRANSLATION IN THE USSR                                 MTP 58   351
ANGLO-RUSSIAN SCHEME                          MACHINE TRANSLATION METHODS ANC THEIR APPLICATION TO AN   ICIP59   199
LANGUAGE                                   SEQUENTIAL TRANSLATION OF A PROBLEM-CRIENTED PROGRAMMING     ROME62   263
                          AN ALGORITHM FOR THE TRANSLATION OF ALGOL STATEMENTS                          IFIP62   498
AMS, RESEARCH REPORT AND DESIGN FOR FUTURE LANGUA/   TRANSLATION OF ARTIFICIAL LANGUAGES BY COMPILER PROGR PACM59    75
                                            ON TRANSLATION OF BOOLEAN EXPRESSIONS                       CACM627  384

364                    COMPUTER LITERATURE BIBLIOGRAPHY 1946-1963                                                364
```

Figure 12.2 *Sample page of a 1-column, 100-character KWIC index.* [*Reprinted from* U. S. Bureau of Standards, Computer Literature Bibliography, *1965, p. 364.*]

publisher because it results in a densely printed page with very little wasted space while still providing adequate context and retaining enough words of the title to avoid misleading the user. Of course, shifting the title so as to place each keyword in the alphabetized column of a 60-character line causes some beginning and ending words of long titles to be omitted. Generally the user can compensate for omitted words, but sometimes the wrong impression can be conveyed. Stevens (1970, 63) illustrates this difficulty with the example (perhaps apocryphal) of the KWIC-index line:

EROTIC TENDENCIES AMONG TRAPPIST MONKS

Here, the first nine letters of "atherosclerotic" had been amputated.

A longer printout line would eliminate most of such difficulties. Youden (1963, 331) analyzed the titles in computer science literature and concluded that 30% of the titles would be truncated in a 60-character-line format, whereas only 2% would be truncated in a 103-character line. However, it must be pointed out that with the 103-character line there are fewer lines per page, thus the index has more pages and costs more to produce. Ideally, the decision about line length should be based on a cost–performance–benefit analysis that includes the mean cost of the use of the index and the value of users' time.

12.1.3.2 *Scanning Aids*

A second common complaint by users of KWIC indexes is the practice of printing identical keywords (headings) down the alphabetized column (as in Figure 12.2). It is alleged that the practice is unaesthetic and that it makes the scanning of long blocks of index terms difficult. By slightly more sophisticated programming, some KWIC indexes have eliminated this repetition of heading words (see Figure 12.1).

12.1.3.3 *KWOC Indexes*

A way to avoid truncation is to print the entire title and to repeat the keyword out of context, listing it in a column at the left. This forms a KWOC (Keyword Out of Context) index (see Figure 12.3). The KWOC format preserves the title verbatim; however, it does not provide the convenient adjacent context that the KWIC format does.

The permuted (KWIC, KWOC, revolved, rotated, term-pair) index is far from perfect from the searcher's viewpoint, but from the producer's viewpoint it offers a way of providing prompt guides to words in titles without the use of indexers and index editors and with only the help of keypunchers, a computer, and an available program. Some KWIC and KWOC indexes are in use, and presumably they are cost-effective.

12.2 CONCORDANCES

Whereas the KWIC index (actually a title concordance) is generally limited to the words in a title, the concordance (as the term has been used over the years) is an index to all of the words in a single text or in the multivolume works of a single author. One definition of *concordance* is an alphabetical index to the principal words in a book or in all the works of a single author, together with their contexts. The context is the passage, phrase, sentence, or line, in which the word occurs. Busa, in his article on concordances in the *Encyclopedia of Library and Information Science*, elaborates on this definition and explains that "all the sentences which concord in containing one and the same given word are transcribed one after the other in text sequence, so that, for instance, the sentences of the Bible in which the word "Emmanuel" appears are all grouped together, the same being done for all the different words appearing in the Bible [Busa 1971, 593]."

Note that by this definition a concordance is an alphabetical index to only the *principal* words in a book. The reason for limiting the concordance to principal words is a practical one. Where the average sentence contains 10 words, a full concordance would average 10 times longer than the original work, for each sentence would be repeated for every word it contained. The omission from the concordance heading of such common words as articles, conjunctions, prepositions, and pronouns reduces the size of the headings list. However, the determination of which words are unimportant and thus to be omitted will differ for, say, the biblical scholar and the linguist. A complete concordance contains, without exception, all of the words in their contexts.

The method of preparing concordances by computer is similar to that used for KWIC indexes. The major difference is in the amount of context used. In KWIC indexes the context is the title in which the word occurs. For the concordance, the context may be the passage, phrase, sentence, or line; or it may, for example, be limited to the three words before and after the keyword—but without going beyond the beginning or end of the sentence. Sufficient context should be

THOMAS MAY, MAN OF LETTERS, 1595-1650. CHESAG-30-TMM

GOETHE'S ESTIMATE OF THE GREEK AND LATIN WRITERS AS REVEALED BY HIS WORKS, LETTERS, DIARIES, AND CONVERSATIONS. KELLWJ-14-GEG

PHINEAS FLETCHER, MAN OF LETTERS, SCIENCE AND DIVINITY. LANGAB-37-PFM

THE LETTERS OF LADY GREGORY TO JOHN QUINN. MURPDA-62-LLG

UNPUBLISHED LETTERS OF FRENCH ACTRESSES, 1798-1861. MLLE. RAUCOURT, MME. FREDERICK LEMAITRE AND RACHEL. SEDGCH-50-ULF

THOMAS HOLCROFT, RADICAL AND MAN OF LETTERS. STALVR-34-THR

ANTHONY MUNDY, A STUDY IN THE ELIZABEYHAN PROFESSION OF LETTERS. TURNJC-28-AMS

JOHN GALSWORTHY'S LETTERS TO LEON LION. WILSAB-62-JGL

LETTRES

L'AVENTURE DE POESIE CHEZ JEAN GIRAUDOUX, HOMME DE LETTRES. HAMLFG-56-LDP

LEVEL-OF-LIFE

AN ANALYSIS OF FOUR OF THE LEVEL-OF-LIFE CHARACTERS IN SHAKESPEARE'S TRAGEDIES. DRUHRA-52-AFL

LEWES

GEORGE HENRY LEWES AS PLAYWRIGHT AND DRAMATIC CRITIC. HIRSEW-51-GHL

GEORGE HENRY LEWES. A VICTORIAN LITERARY CRITIC. KAMIAR-52-GHL

LEWIS

SINCLAIR LEWIS. AMERICAN SOCIAL CRITIC. GREBSN-54-SLA

THE AUDEN GROUP AND THE GROUP THEATRE. THE DRAMATIC THEORIES AND PRACTICES OF RUPERT DOONE, W.H. AUDEN, CHRISTOPHER ISHERWOOD, LOUIS MACNEICE, STEPHEN SPENDER, AND CECIL DAY LEWIS. HAZAFE-64-AGG

LEXICOGRAPHICAL

A LEXICOGRAPHICAL STUDY OF THE EARLY FRENCH FARCES. ANDRNI-42-LSE

LIBRARY-MUSEUM

THE LIBRARY-MUSEUM OF MUSIC AND DANCE. A STUDY OF NEEDS AND RESOURCES, LEADING TO SUGGESTIONS FOR AN EDUCATIONAL PROGRAM. MOORAP-38-LMD

LIBRETTI

THE LIBRETTI OF THE RESTORATION OPERA IN ENGLISH. A STUDY IN THEATRICAL GENRES. HAUNFE-54-LRO

THE MEILAC-HALEVY LIBRETTI FOR OFFENBACH. OLANJH-64-MLO

LIBRETTO

PSYCHOLOGICAL MELODRAMA IN MODERN OPERA WITH TRANSLATIONS OF TWO REPRESENTATIVE WORKS, ERWARTUNG AND WOZZECK, AND AN ORIGINAL LIBRETTO, CAPTAIN MARK. DACEEW-52-PMM

INCORRUPTABLE HADLEYBURG. A MUSICAL PLAY ADAPTED FROM MARK TWAIN'S STORY, 'THE MAN THAT CORRUPTED HADLEYBURG.' LIBRETTO AND MUSIC. DUBORE-64-IHM

A COMPARATIVE ANALYSIS OF SELECTED EUROPEAN OPERA LIBRETTO ADAPTATIONS OF THE ROMEO AND JULIET LEGEND. PARKCE-53-CAS

A SINGING TRANSLATION IN ENGLISH OF GIAMBATTISTA CASTI'S LIBRETTO FOR GIOVANNI PAISIELLO'S OPERA, IL RE TEODORO IN VENEZIA (KING THEODORE IN VENICE). SCHOAP-63-STE

DRAMA AND LIBRETTO. A STUDY OF FOUR LIBRETTO-ADAPTATIONS OF TWO OF SHAKESPEARE'S PLAYS. SEYMJL-40-DLS

STUDIES IN THE LIBRETTO. OTELLO, DER ROSENKAVALIER. A PROLEGOMENA TO A POETICS OF OPERA. WEISUW-54-SLO

THE LIBRETTO IN CONTEMPORARY AMERICAN MUSICAL COMEDY. WORKWI-54-LCA

LIBRETTO-ADAPTATIONS

DRAMA AND LIBRETTO. A STUDY OF FOUR LIBRETTO-ADAPTATIONS OF TWO OF SHAKESPEARE'S PLAYS. SEYMJL-40-DLS

LIBRETTOS

THE DEVELOPMENT OF THE LEADING FEMININE CHARACTER IN SELECTED LIBRETTOS OF AMERICAN MUSICALS FROM 1900 TO 1960. KLEIES-62-DLF

SOCIAL CRITICISM IN THE ORIGINAL THEATRE LIBRETTOS OF MARC BLITZSTEIN. TALLPM-65-SCO

```
LEXINGTON
     A HISTORY OF THE LEXINGTON (KY.) THEATER FROM 1887
       TO 1900.                                        ARNOJC-56-HLK

     THE HISTORY OF THE LEXINGTON (KY.) THEATRE FROM THE
       BEGINNING TO 1860.                              CRUMMT-56-HLK

     THE THEATRE IN THE FRONTIER CITIES OF LEXINGTON,
       KENTUCKY, AND CINCINNATI, OHIO, 1797-1835.
                                                       LANGHE-53-TFC

LEXIQUE
     LEXIQUE DE JEAN ROTROU.                           JADEME-32-LDJ

LIBERAL
     THE EVOLUTION OF LIBERAL THEORY AND PRACTICE IN THE
       FRENCH THEATRE (1680-1757).                     BORGEB-34-ELT

     DEFINITION OF THE PHILOSOPHY UNDERLYING THE RECOGNITION
       AND TEACHING OF THEATRE AS A FINE ART IN THE LIBERAL
       ARTS AND GRADUATE CURRICULA AT THE STATE UNIVERSITY
       OF IOWA.                                        DAVEPW-51-DPU

     AN INVESTIGATION OF THE EDUCATIONAL THEATRE PROGRAMS
       IN THE LIBERAL ARTS COLLEGES SPONSORED BY THE
       REFORMED CHURCH IN AMERICA.                     ENGLTC-64-IET

     AN HISTORICAL, ANALYTICAL AND INTERPRETATIVE STUDY OF
       EDUCATIONAL THEATRE PROGRAMS IN MICHIGAN PROTESTANT
       CHURCH-RELATED LIBERAL ARTS COLLEGES.           HARTHL-56-HAI

LIBERTAD
     A CRITICAL EDITION OF LA FAMOSA COMEDIA DEL CERCO Y
       LIBERTAD DE SEBILLA POR EL REY DON FERNANDO EL
       SANTO. (MS. OF 1595).                           BABCJC-35-CEL

LIBRARY
     A CÁLENDAR OF THE WILLIAM DEAN HOWELLS COLLECTION IN
       THE LIBRARY OF HARVARD UNIVERSITY.              BALLRH-53-CWD

     LA RESURRECTION NOSTRE SEIGNEUR JAESUCRIST FROM
       MANUSCRIPT 1131 OF THE SAINTE GENEVIEVE LIBRARY IN
       PARIS, A CRITICAL EDITION.                      BURKJF-57-LRN

     AN ANALYTICAL BIBLIOGRAPHY OF THE FRENCH DRAMA AND
       THEATRE COLLECTION IN RUSH RHEES LIBRARY OF THE
       UNIVERSITY OF ROCHESTER, EIGHTEENTH CENTURY D-Z.
                                                       GRUBBK-43-ABF

     A STUDY OF AMERICAN VERSE, 1890-1899, BASED UPON THE
       VOLUMES FROM THAT PERIOD CONTAINED IN THE HARRIS
       COLLECTION OF AMERICAN POETRY AND PLAYS IN THE
       BROWN UNIVERSITY LIBRARY.                       KINDCT-53-SAV

     AN ANALYTICAL BIBLIOGRAPHY OF THE FRENCH DRAMA AND
       THEATRE COLLECTION IN RUSH RHEES LIBRARY OF THE
       UNIVERSITY OF ROCHESTER, SEVENTEENTH CENTURY--
       EIGHTEENTH CENTURY, A-C.                        VONWEA-43-ABF

LICENSING
     AN INQUIRY INTO THE OPERATIVE PRINCIPLES APPLICABLE
       TO THE LICENSING OF MOTION PICTURES IN NEW YORK
       STATE.                                          BECKSA-59-IIO

     PLAYS ABOUT THE THEATRE IN ENGLAND FROM THE REHEARSAL
       IN 1671 TO THE LICENSING ACT IN 1737.           SMITDF-34-PAT

LIFE
     THE ATTITUDE OF HEINRICH VON KLEIST TOWARD THE PROBLEMS
       OF LIFE.                                        BLANJC-15-AHV

     SENECA'S PHILOSOPHY OF LIFE. TRAGEDIES COMPARED WITH
       PROSE.                                          BYRNLE-01-SPL

     THOMAS HEYWOOD. A STUDY IN THE ELIZABETHAN DRAMA OF
       EVERYDAY LIFE.                                  CROMOT-26-THS

     THE DRAMATIC TECHNIQUE OF THOMAS MIDDLETON IN HIS
       COMEDIES OF LONDON LIFE.                        DUNKWD-25-DTT

     THE SEVENTEENTH CENTURY WIT AND FOP. A STUDY OF
       RESTORATION COMEDY IN ITS RELATION TO LIFE OF
       FASHION.                                        FERGTE-30-SCW

     IS AMERICAN RADIO DEMOCRATIC. A STUDY OF THE AMERICAN
       SYSTEM OF RADIO REGULATION, CONTROL, AND OPERATION
       AS RELATED TO THE DEMOCRATIC WAY OF LIFE WITH
       EMPHASIS UPON ITS EDUCATIONAL ASPECTS.          FROSTS-38-IAR

     LONDON LIFE IN THE ELIZABETHAN DRAMA FROM 1590 TO 1630.
                                                       HALEHL-34-LLE

     EXPERIMENTAL PRODUCTION OF THREE ORIGINAL PLAYS
       INTERPRETATIVE OF THE FARM LIFE OF THE MIDWEST.
                                                       LEEWMA-41-EPT

     SOCIAL AND PRIVATE LIFE AT ROME IN THE TIME OF PLAUTUS
       AND TERENCE.                                    LEFFGW-18-SPL

     WE WEAR THE MASK. LIFE AND CHARACTER OF THE NEGRO IN
       AMERICAN DRAMA.                                 LINNED-49-WWM

     AN INVESTIGATION OF THE THEME OF THE NEGATION OF LIFE
       IN AMERICAN DRAMA FROM WORLD WAR II TO 1958.
                                                       LOGAWB-61-ITN

     ENGLISH LIFE IN LONDON PANTOMIMES, 1806-1836.
                                                       MAYEDA-62-ELL

     PUPPETS IN AMERICAN LIFE, 1524-1915.              MCPHPA-40-PAL

     THE LIFE OF THE CHILD AS STUDIED PRIMARILY IN THE FRENCH
       DRAMA BEFORE 1550.                              OWENAL-29-LCS

     ON LUCHA POR LA VIDA, THE STRUGGLE FOR LIFE IN THE
       THREE PLAYS OF MIGUEL DE UNAMUNO.               PEPPWH-65-LPL
```

Figure 12.3 *Sample page of a KWOC index. [Reprinted by permission of Kent State University Press from Frederic M. Litto,* American Dissertations on the Drama and the Theatre: Bibliography, *1969, p. 138.]*

provided to enable the searcher to judge whether or not to look up the entry or to infer the use or meaning of the word in question.

12.2.1 Biblical Concordances

Concordances have a long history and were, in all likelihood, the first reference retrieval devices used by medieval scholars. Biblical concordances were probably in existence in the seventh and eighth centuries, A.D. (Busa, 1971). These concordances provided guidance to the words of the Bible and were used by clergy, laity, and all who wished to study this work. A very famous thirteenth-century concordance to the Bible was prepared by Cardinal Hugo (Hugo de St. Caro), who died in 1262.

The organization of a biblical concordance (Ellison, 1957) can be seen in the following excerpt:

GOLD
land of Havilah, where there is g. Gen. 2.11
and the g. of that land is good 2.12
in cattle, in silver and in g. 13.02

The context lines are arranged in order according to the books, chapters, and verses of the Bible. Variations in the structure and context of concordances can be observed. Differences among the various translations of the Bible can be seen by examining the concordances to those translations. For example:

MYRRH
My beloved is to me a bag of m. Sol. 1.13

and

MYRRH
Song. 1.13 A bundle of myrrh (is) my well beloved.

The position and abbreviation of the reference ("Sol." versus "Song." for the "Song of Solomon") differ; the chapter and verse numbers (1.13) of course are the same. In the King James Version of the Bible, the corresponding entry is:

A bundle of myrrh is my well-beloved unto me

It is interesting to note that myrrh came in bundles in the earlier version, in bags in the later. Also, "beloved" became "well beloved."

Early concordances were prepared manually, but all recent concordances have been produced by computer. The pioneer in this application of computers to language data processing (as contrasted with numerical data processing) is Father Roberto Busa. Father Busa began in 1949 compiling a concordance to the works of St. Thomas Aquinas, using punched card equipment. The task was completed in 1951.*

The advantages of the computer in terms of speed and economy are staggering. One estimate is that

> it would take 50 scholars 40 years (2,000 man-years) to index manually the 13 million or so words of St. Thomas Aquinas' complete works. IBM punched-card machines would produce the indexes and concordances much more accurately and would take ten scholars about 4 years (40 man-years). Large scale data processing techniques would reduce the time to about 25 percent of that required for the punched-card method, and would enable the ten scholars to do the job in less than a year (10 man-years) [Tasman, 1958, 11].

Tasman, like Busa, is a pioneer in language data processing. He is best known for his work in preparing a concordance to the Dead Sea Scrolls—a monumental and challenging task. The first of these scrolls was discovered in the early summer of 1947 by a Jordanian shepherd boy who followed a stray goat into a cave near the Dead Sea. Altogether, some 400 scrolls were found—or, more accurately, some 40,000 fragments representing about 400 scrolls. These small fragments were found on the floors of the caves; and the phrases, words, and even characters on each fragment had to be identified and fitted into the proper scroll, much like putting together a jigsaw puzzle—or, rather, like putting together 400 jigsaw puzzles whose 40,000 pieces were all mixed together and many of the pieces missing.

As an aid to the scholars who were trying to restore the text to its original form, insofar as this was possible, specialized word lists and concordances were prepared. With these aids, it was possible to study systematically the ways in which words were used and to consider every possible use of each fragment.

The story of the preparation of this unique concordance is fascinating and is briefly described by Tasman (1958). Each word of text had to be keypunched, then stored on magnetic tape for processing by an IBM 705 computer. Numerous technical problems were solved, not the least of which was to learn to work with the Hebrew alphabet which, among other characteristics, has no vowels and is written from

**Sancti Thomas Aquinatis Hymnorum Ritualium Varia Specimina Concordantiarum. A First Example of Word Index Automatically Compiled and Printed by IBM Punched Card Machines.* Bocca, Milan, 1951.

potestate facta dicendi, positis ferocibus animis pacem sibi ab Romanis	bellique	ius aduersus Sidicinos petierunt: quae se eo iustius petere, quod et	8	1	8
quod ad Sidicinos attineat, nihil intercedi quo minus Samniti populo pacis	bellique	liberum arbitrium sit. foedere icto cum domum reuertissent	8	2	3
et apud Romanos ab nocturni periculi memoria. sed ante omnia obsidionis	bellique	mala fames utrimque exercitum urgebat, Gallos pestilentia etiam,	5	48	1
staretur. patribus id tempus rei publicae uisum est ut per ueteres et expertos	bellique	peritos imperatores res publica gereretur; itaque moram fieri	27	6	10
relictum, stirpem genti Fabiae dubiisque rebus populi Romani saepe domi	bellique	uel maximum futurum auxilium. cum haec accepta clades est, iam	2	50	11
tamen, uelut eam sortitis, Africae cura erat, seu quia ibi summam rerum	bellique	uerti cernebant seu ut Scipioni gratificarentur, in quem tum omnis	30	3	1
bellum opus essent; nauibus, armis, iuuentute ⟨nos⟩ nostra, sicut prioribus	bellis,	ad omnia paratos fore. ne praestaremus, per uos stetit, qui de	45	23	6
deum benignitate et rem publicam esse gratiae referendae. Scipionem,	bellis	adsuetum, ad seditionum procellas rudem, sollicitum habebat res ne	28	25	8
iam aetates continua bella Macedonas; ipso quoque regnante et naualibus	bellis	aduersus Rhodios Attalumque et terrestribus aduersus Romanos	33	3	3
"iuuenem flagrantem cupidine regni uiamque unam ad id cernentem si ex	bellis	bella serendo succinctus armis legionibusque uiuat, uelut materiam	21	10	4
di tulissent uinciri. interim ad Veios terror multiplex fuit tribus in unum	bellis	conlatis. namque eodem quo antea modo circa munimenta cum	5	13	9
perculit decemuiros ut senatum, simul duobus circumstantibus urbem	bellis,	consulerent. citari iubent in curiam patres, haud ignari quanta	3	38	6
fauente populo Romano regnum adeptum; aequatis iis postea trium regum	bellis	deinceps omnibus eum functum officiis. uictoria uero populi Romani	45	14	2
quidem elephanti militem Romanum deterrebant, adsuetum iam ab Africis	bellis	et uitare impetum beluae et ex transuerso aut pilis incessere aut, si	37	42	5
a Volscis fuisse, quam pestem adhaerentem lateri suo tot super alia aliis	bellis	exhauriri nequisse. quae relata patribus magis tempus quam causam	6	10	9
id quod probabant exsequi potuerunt. maior pars senatus, multis saepe	bellis	expertam populi Romani clementiam haud diffidentes sibi quoque	26	14	2
ut me consulem esse obliuiscar. eodem iure imperii quo bella gessi,	bellis	feliciter gestis, Samnio atque Etruria subactis, uictoria et pace parta	10	37	8
capi. tantumque praedae fore quantum non omnibus in unum conlatis ante	bellis	fuisset, ne quam inde aut militum iram ex malignitate praedae	5	20	2
ab iuuenta finitimis Thracum atque Illyriorum et circa omnium accolarum	bellis,	hic, ut aliam omnem uitam sileam, is est, qui cum ad inferendum	36	17	6
bellis uicti uicerimus. uetera omitto, Porsennam Gallos Samnites: a Punicis	bellis	incipiam. quot classes, quot duces, quot exercitus priore bello amissi	26	41	10
plebem: si leniter ducta res sine populari strepitu ad consules redisset, aut	bellis	interpositis aut moderatione consulum in imperiis exercendis posse in	3	41	6
Alexandri est, quem sorore huius ortum in alio tractu orbis, inuictum	bellis,	iuuenem fortuna morbo exstinxit. ceterum Romani, etsi defectio	8	3	7
qui pugnarent, occisum. sed gens nata instaurandis reparandisque	bellis	Magone ad conquisitionem militum a fratre misso breui repleuit	24	42	6
arte atque usu belli. iam inde a puero patris contubernio Romanis quoque	bellis,	non finitumis tantum adsuetum, missum a patre in expeditiones	42	11	7
multitudinem in Macedoniam traduxerat, quietusque aliquamdiu a	bellis	omni cura in augendas regni opes intentus fuerat. rediere deinde	39	24	4
tumultum augebat, cicatrices acceptas Veienti Gallico aliisque deinceps	bellis	ostentans: se militantem, se restituentem euersos penates, multiplici	6	14	7
L. Genucio Ser. Cornelio consulibus ab externis ferme	bellis	otium fuit. Soram atque Albam coloniae deductae. Albam in Aequos	10	1	1
arguens, si semel nefas ducerent captam ex hostibus in aerario exhausto	bellis	pecuniam esse, auctor erat stipendii ex ea pecunia militi numerandi ut	5	20	5
impelli posse, ut totiens infeliciter temptata arma caperent: multis saepe	bellis,	pestilentia postremo amissa iuuentute fractos spiritus esse; arte	2	35	8
est, quos leuitas ingeniorum ad cognoscendas hostium res in omnibus	bellis	praebet. Philippus aliquid et ad caritatem suorum et ut promptius pro	31	33	11
annos; ne plus obsit nobis, quod uno bello cessauimus, quam quod duobus	bellis	pro uobis pugnauimus. Philippum, Antiochum, Persea tamquam tris	45	24	8
is est quo adiuncto duplicent uires suas, quem secernere ab se consilia	bellis	propriis ponendis sumendisque nolint, cur non omnia aequantur?,cur	8	4	3
Horatiusque ante idus Maias decemuiros abisse magistratu insimulent,	bellis	quae immineant perfectis, re publica in tranquillum redacta, senatu	3	40	11
animum dumtaxat uobis fidelem ac bonum praestitit, sed omnibus interfuit	bellis,	quae in Graecia gessistis, terrestribus naualibus, omni genere	37	53	9
quod iustissimae irae uestrae negastis. Rhodii ⟨et in hoc⟩ et in omnibus	bellis,	quae in illa ora gessistis, quam forti fidelique uos opera adiuuerimus,	37	54	28
Macedonicum quoque bellum uti res publica uellet, aliis ex aliis orientibus	bellis	quid aliud quam publicatam pro beneficio tamquam ob noxiam suam	31	13	4
et aliarum Graeciae ciuitatium instituta mores iuraque noscere. ab externis	bellis	quietus annus fuit, quietior insequens P. Curiatio et Sex. Quinctilio	3	32	1
proelioque uno debellatum est. fusis Auruncis, uictor tot intra paucos dies	bellis	Romanus promissa consulis fidemque senatus exspectabat, cum	2	27	1
responsum ignosci adulescentibus posse, senibus non posse qui bella ex	bellis	sererent. actum tamen est de pace, impetrataque foret si, quod	2	18	11
plebis, uiam antiquam criminandi patres ingressus, incusauerat bella ex	bellis	seri ne pace unquam frui plebs posset. aegre eam rem passi patres	31	6	5

et progeniem ediderat, cuius magna pars matura militiae esset, et leuibus	bellis	Thracum accolarum, quae exercerent magis quam fatigarent, sub	42	52	2
Tusculo exercitus Romam est reductus. quanto magis prosperis eo anno	bellis	tranquilla omnia foris erant, tanto in urbe uis patrum in dies	6	34	1
ferum prohibet. ea fato quodam data nobis sors est ut magnis omnibus	bellis	uicti uicerimus. uetera omitto, Porsennam Gallos Samnites: a Punicis	26	41	9
uirtuti eorum iuuentaeque urbis per trecentos sexaginta annos omnibus	bellis	uictricis quaecumque reliqua esset fortuna. digredientibus qui spem	5	40	1
omnes tribus, quia uerso in Africam bello omnibus aliis in praesentia leuari	bellis	uolebant. P. Sempronius pace facta ad consulatum Romam decessit.	29	12	16
inierunt. eo anno Tarquinienses noui hostes exorti. qui quia multis simul	bellis,	Volscorum ad Anxur, ubi praesidium obsidebatur, Aequorum ad	5	16	2
eo deduci antiquamque frequentiam recipere uastam ac desertam	bellis	urbem paterentur, omnium neminem praeter Aristomachum mouit.	24	3	11
conscriptis ipsi, a pueris eruditi artibus militiae, tot subacti atque durati	bellis.	auxilia Romanis Lydos et Phrygas et Numidas esse, sibi Thracas	42	52	11
decuit cum adempta sunt nobis arma, incensae naues, interdictum externis	bellis;	illo enim uolnere concidimus. nec est cur uos otio uestro consultum	30	44	7
Africam traiecisset perculsis Carthaginiensibus, Syphace impedito finitimis	bellis;	quem certum habere, si spatium ad sua ut uelit componenda detur,	29	4	8
fecit, ut non modo praedandi causa quisquam ex agro Romano exiret	belliue	inferendi memoria patribus aut plebi esset, sed ultro Fidenates, qui	4	21	7
Castoris aedis eodem anno idibus Quintilibus dedicata est; uota erat Latino	bello	⟨a⟩ Postumio dictatore; filius eius duumuir ad id ipsum creatus	2	42	5
exercitus in animo est, neminem digniorem esse ex sociis uestris, qui	bello	a uobis parta possideat quam me dicere ausim. at enim magnificum	37	53	27
aedem C. Seruilius duumuir dedicauit: uota erat sex annis ante Gallico	bello	ab L. Furio Purpurione praetore, ab eodem postea consule locata.	34	53	7
seu furoris sui seu erroris uenia. et ceteras Graeciae ciuitates defecisse eo	bello	ab optime meritis Romanis; sed quia post fugam regis, cuius fiducia	36	22	2
quae creati erant, comitia consularia habita, quia neuter consulum potuerat	bello	abesse. creati consules L. Postumius Ti. Minucius. hos consules Piso	9	44	2
in praesentia dare possim, fidele consilium est. abi, nuntia meis uerbis,	bello	absistat, pacis condicionem nullam recuset." nihil ea mouerunt regem,	37	36	8
rebus constantiae erat; reparandum exercitum Syphacemque hortandum ne	bello	absisteret censebat. haec sententia quia Hasdrubal praesens	30	7	7
partem utramque fouendo incerta respondisset, una denuntiatione, ut	bello	abstinerent, donec Romam ad senatum legatos misissent, finem	38	32	4
curam esse. sed res haudquaquam erat populo facilis et liberis cultoribus	bello	absumptis et inopia seruitiorum et pecore direpto uillisque dirutis aut	28	11	9
Cn. Fuluio, Scipionibus meis, tot tam praeclaris imperatoribus uno	bello	absumptis superstes est populus Romanus, eritque mille aliis nunc	28	28	12
semirutae ac fumantis sociae urbis cum uenisset, paucis uix qui sepelirent	bello	absumptos relictis aeque raptim ac uenerat transgressus ponte	31	24	3
atque iniuria est — loquar? auspiciis hanc urbem conditam esse, auspiciis	bello	ac pace domi militiaeque omnia geri, quis est qui ignoret? penes quos	6	41	4
animus in regno auito reciperando, non condendae urbis consilium, non	bello	ac pace firmandae. ab illo enim profecto uiribus datis tantum ualuit ut	1	15	6
nihil maius praestiteris quam si hic tibi dies satis documenti dederit ut	bello	ac pace pati legitima imperia possis." cum se nihil morari magistrum	8	35	8
designati consules Romam accersiti magistratum inierunt, senatumque de	bello	ac prouinciis suis praetorumque et de exercitibus quibus quique	24	43	9
rei bene gerendae sed absentem etiam gestae obstare [et in ducendo	bello]	ac sedulo tempus terere quo diutius in magistratu sit solusque et	22	25	4
incurrere ea gens in Macedoniam solita erat, ubi regem occupatum externo	bello	ac sine praesidio esse regnum sensisset. ad frangendas igitur ⟨uires	26	25	7
uiris ambitio obstabat. itaque ne penes ipsos culpa esset cladis forte Gallico	bello	acceptae, cognitionem de postulatis Gallorum ad populum reiciunt;	5	36	10
facta dictis aequando, memorasset, nudasse pectus insigne cicatricibus	bello	acceptis et identidem Capitolium spectans Iouem deosque alios	6	20	9
alii Tarenti, alii in Campania mortuum tradunt; ita quod nullo ante	bello	acciderat, duo consules sine memorando proelio interfecti uelut orbam	27	33	7
speciem duarum⟩ clarissimarum urbium excidio, ac celeberrimis uiris uictos	bello	accusatores in urbem adducentis. de re publica tamen primum ac de	26	27	17
est ad indictum multo ante sociorum concilium. ibi de Aetolico finiendo	bello	actum ne causa aut Romanis aut Attalo intrandi Graeciam esset. sed	27	30	10
Saguntum ad Hannibalem atque inde Carthaginem si non absisteretur	bello	ad ducem ipsum in poenam foederis rupti deposcendum. dum ea	21	6	8
ceperant: hinc Etruriae principum ex omnibus populis coniurationem de	bello	ad fanum Voltumnae factam mercatores adferebant. nouus quoque	6	2	2
tribuni, denuntiando impedituros se dilectum, ut Quinctius consul de	bello	ad populum ferret. omnes centuriae iussere. in eo quoque plebs	4	30	15
caecata mens subito terrore, nudatis omnibus praesidiis patefactisque	bello	ad Pydnam refugit. consul plurimum et praesidii et spei cernens in	44	6	17
legibus antiquis et libertate stabiliri, non fessam miseranda seruitute	bello	adfligi; inter tyrannorum et ducis Romani certamina praemium	26	32	3
adeo infestam nobis ut illa gente incolumi stare Saguntum non posset, ita	bello	adflixit ut non modo nobis sed — absit uerbo inuidia — ne posteris	28	39	11

Figure 12.4 *Sample page of a concordance using KWIC format.* [*Reprinted from David W. Packard,* A Concordance to Livy, *Vol. 1, 1968, p. 582, by permission of Harvard University Press.*]

```
  SIZE THAT I HAVE A KIND OF ALACRITY IN SINKING;   WIV 3.05. 13P
  SPLITTING ROCKS COW'R'D IN THE SINKING SANDS,     2H6 3.02. 97
  AND SORE BLOWS | FOR SINKING UNDER THEM.          COR 2.01.253
  LEAKY | THAT WE MUST LEAVE THEE TO THY SINKING,   ANT 3.13. 64
  THEN WHO FEARS SINKING WHERE SUCH TREASURE LIES?  LUC      280
SINKING-RIPE              1 FREQ  0.0001 REL FR     1 V      0 P
  AND LEFT THE SHIP, THEN SINKING-RIPE, TO US.      ERR 1.01. 77
SINKS                     6 FREQ  0.0006 REL FR     6 V      0 P
  WHILST MY GROSS FLESH SINKS DOWNWARD, HERE TO     R2  5.05.112
  WHY SINKS THAT CAULDRON?                          MAC 4.01.106
  I THINK OUR COUNTRY SINKS BENEATH THE YOKE:           4.03. 39
  IS OUT OF BREATH, | AND SINKS MOST LAMENTABLY.    ANT 3.10. 25
  BUT NOW MY HEAVY CONSCIENCE SINKS MY KNEE, | AS   CYM 5.05.413
  WITH TWO ALONE | SINKS DOWN TO DEATH, OPPRESS'D   SON      45. 8
SINN'D                    6 FREQ  0.0006 REL FR     5 V      1 P
  O SWEET-SUGGESTING LOVE, IF THOU HAST SINN'D,     TGV 2.06.  7
  YET SINN'D I NOT, | BUT IN MISTAKING.             ADO 5.01.274
  I HAVE THEN SINN'D AGAINST HIS EXPERIENCE AND     AWW 2.05. 10P
  IF YOU FIRST SINN'D WITH US, AND THAT WITH US     WT  1.02. 84
  I AM A MAN | MORE SINN'D AGAINST THAN SINNING.    LR  3.02. 60
  AND DOUBTING LEST HE HAD ERR'D OR SINN'D, | TO    PER 1.03. 21
SINNER                    4 FREQ  0.0004 REL FR     3 V      1 P
  MADE SUCH A SINNER OF HIS MEMORY | TO CREDIT HIS  TMP 1.02.101
  I CROSS ME FOR A SINNER.                          ERR 2.02.188
  I WILL BE SO MUCH A SINNER TO BE A DOUBLE-DEALER  TN  5.01. 34P
  HERE'S THAT WHICH IS TOO WEAK TO BE A SINNER,     TIM 1.02. 58
SINNERS'                  1 FREQ  0.0001 REL FR     1 V      0 P
  LIKE DAMNED GUILTY DEEDS TO SINNERS' MINDS:       ROM 3.02.111
SINNERS                   3 FREQ  0.0003 REL FR     2 V      1 P
  O LORD, HAVE MERCY ON US, WRETCHED SINNERS!       1H6 1.04. 70
  FORBEAR TO JUDGE, FOR WE ARE SINNERS ALL.         2H6 3.03. 31
  WHY WOULDST THOU BE A BREEDER OF SINNERS?         HAM 3.01.121P
SINNING                   1 FREQ  0.0001 REL FR     1 V      0 P
  I AM A MAN | MORE SINN'D AGAINST THAN SINNING.    LR  3.02. 60
SINON                     7 FREQ  0.0008 REL FR     7 V      0 P
  COULD, | AND, LIKE A SINON, TAKE ANOTHER TROY.    3H6 3.02.190
  TELL US WHAT SINON HATH BEWITCH'D OUR EARS, | OR  TIT 5.03. 85
  THIS MILD IMAGE DREW | FOR PERJUR'D SINON, WHOSE  LUC     1521
  "FOR EVEN AS SUBTILE SINON HERE IS PAINTED, | SO          1541
  TO SEE THOSE BORROWED TEARS THAT SINON SHEEDS!            1549
  FOR SINON IN HIS FIRE DOTH QUAKE WITH COLD,               1556
  SHE TEARS THE SENSELESS SINON WITH HER NAILS,             1564
SINON'S                   3 FREQ  0.0003 REL FR     3 V      0 P
  AND SINON'S WEEPING | DID SCANDAL MANY A HOLY     CYM 3.04. 59
  SAYING, SOME SHAPE IN SINON'S WAS ABUS'D:         LUC     1529
  PRIAM'S TRUST FALSE SINON'S TEARS DOTH FLATTER,           1560
SINOW (ALSO SINEW, ETC.)
SINOW                     2 FREQ  0.0002 REL FR     2 V      0 P
  SO SHALT THOU SINOW BOTH THESE LANDS TOGETHER,    3H6 2.06. 91
  CROWNS | THE SINOW AND THE FOREHAND OF OUR HOST,  TRO 1.03.143
SINOWS                    1 FREQ  0.0001 REL FR     1 V      0 P
  AND YOU, MY SINOWS, GROW NOT INSTANT OLD, | BUT   HAM 1.05. 94
SINOWY                    4 FREQ  0.0004 REL FR     4 V      0 P
  TIRES | THE SINOWY VIGOR OF THE TRAVELLER.        LLL 4.03.304
```

```
SIPP'D                          1 FREQ  0.0001 REL FR      1 V      0 P
  I NONE THESE TWO DAYS -- | SIPP'D SOME WATER.        TNK 3.02. 27
SIPPING                         1 FREQ  0.0001 REL FR      1 V      0 P
  A CHALICE FOR THE NONCE, WHEREON BUT SIPPING,        HAM 4.07.160
SIR (ALSO ZIR)
/SIR                           22 FREQ  0.0024 REL FR     17 V      5 P
  /SIR, THIS IS THE HOUSE, PLEASE IT YOU THAT I        SHR 4.04.  1
  /PARDON /ME, /SIR, /IT /WAS /A /BLACK                TIT 3.02. 66
  /BUT /THERE /IS, /SIR, /AN /AERY /OF /CHILDREN,      HAM 2.02.339P
  HAVE REFORM'D THAT INDIFFERENTLY WITH US, /SIR.          3.02. 37P
  /SIR, /IN /THIS /AUDIENCE, | LET MY DISCLAIMING          5.02.240
  /O, /SIR, /ARE /YOU /COME?                           LR  1.04.257
  /THOU, /SAPIENT /SIR, /SIT /HERE.                        3.06. 22
  /HOW /DO /YOU, /SIR?                                     3.06. 33
  /AY, /SIR, /SHE /TOOK /THEM, /READ /THEM /IN /MY         4.03. 11
  /WELL, /SIR, /THE /POOR /DISTRESSED /LEAR'S /I'          4.03. 38
  /WHY, /GOOD /SIR?                                        4.03. 41
  /WELL, /SIR, /I'LL /BRING /YOU /TO /OUR /MASTER          4.03. 50
  /GOOD /SIR --                                            4.06.197
  /NO, /SIR, YOU MUST NOT KNEEL.                           4.07. 58
  /HOLDS /IT /TRUE, /SIR, /THAT /THE /DUKE /OF             4.07. 84P
  /MOST /CERTAIN, /SIR.                                    4.07. 86P
  /FARE /YOU /WELL, /SIR.                                  4.07. 94P
  /SIR, /YOU /SPEAK /NOBLY.                                5.01. 28
  /KENT, /SIR, /THE /BANISH'D /KENT, /WHO /IN              5.03.220
  LIEUTENANT -- SIR -- MONTANO -- /SIR -- | HELP,      OTH 2.03.159
  I SEE, /SIR, YOU ARE EATEN UP WITH PASSION:              3.03.391
  WHY, SO I CAN, /SIR, BUT I WILL NOT NOW.                 3.04. 86
SIR                          2591 FREQ  0.2928 REL FR   1278 V   1313 P
  CERTAINLY, SIR, I CAN.                               TMP 1.02. 41
  SIR, ARE NOT YOU MY FATHER?                              1.02. 55
  SIR, MOST HEEDFULLY.                                     1.02. 78
  O, GOOD SIR, I DO.                                       1.02. 88
  YOUR TALE, SIR, WOULD CURE DEAFNESS.                     1.02.106
  AND NOW I PRAY YOU, SIR, | FOR STILL 'TIS                1.02.175
  ALL HAIL, GREAT MASTER, GRAVE SIR, HAIL!                 1.02.189
  I DO NOT, SIR.                                           1.02.256
  NO, SIR.                                                 1.02.260
  SIR, IN ARGIER.                                          1.02.261
  AY, SIR.                                                 1.02.268
  'TIS A VILLAIN, SIR, | I DO NOT LOVE TO LOOK ON,         1.02.309
  BELIEVE ME, SIR, | IT CARRIES A BRAVE FORM.              1.02.411
  NO WONDER, SIR, | BUT CERTAINLY A MAID.                  1.02.428
  A WORD, GOOD SIR, | I FEAR YOU HAVE DONE                 1.02.443
  SOFT, SIR, ONE WORD MORE.                                1.02.450
  SIR, HAVE PITY, | I'LL BE HIS SURETY.                    1.02.475
  COMFORT, | MY FATHER'S OF A BETTER NATURE, SIR,          1.02.497
  BESEECH YOU, SIR, BE MERRY:                              2.01.  1
  THEN WISELY, GOOD SIR, WEIGH | OUR SORROW WITH           2.01.  8
  SIR --                                                   2.01. 14
  THIS TUNIS, SIR, WAS CARTHAGE.                           2.01. 84P
  SIR, WE WERE TALKING THAT OUR GARMENTS SEEM NOW          2.01. 97P
  IS NOT, SIR, MY DOUBLET AS FRESH AS THE FIRST            2.01.103P
  SIR, HE MAY LIVE.                                        2.01.114
```

```
  THAT DID BUT LATELY FOIL THE SINOWY CHARLES,       AYL 2.02. 14
  MILO HIS ADDITION YIELD | TO SINOWY AJAX.          TRO 2.03.248
  WHOSE SINOWY NECK IN BATTLE NE'ER DID BOW, | WHO   VEN       99
SIN'S                5 FREQ  0.0005 REL FR           5 V      0 P
  THY SIN'S NOT ACCIDENTAL, BUT A TRADE.             MM  3.01.148
  DAYS, | TO SIN'S REBUKE AND MY CREATOR'S PRAISE,   3H6 4.06. 44
  TO KILL, I GRANT, IS SIN'S EXTREMEST GUST, | BUT   TIM 3.05. 54
  TO MY SICK SOUL, AS SIN'S TRUE NATURE IS, | EACH   HAM 4.05. 17
  BASE WATCH OF WOES, SIN'S PACK-HORSE, VIRTUE'S     LUC      928
/SINS                3 FREQ  0.0003 REL FR           3 V      0 P
  /INDEED | /WHERE /ALL /MY /SINS /ARE /WRIT, /AND   R2  4.01.275
  RECEIVE THE SENTENCE OF THE LAW FOR /SINS | SUCH   2H6 2.03.  3
  /DEAR /BLOOD /SHED /FOR /OUR /GRIEVOUS /SINS,      R3  1.04.190
SINS                38 FREQ  0.0043 REL FR           31 V     7 P
  O, FORGIVE ME MY SINS!                             TMP 3.02.130P
  MAKES HIM RUN THROUGH ALL TH' SINS:                TGV 5.04.112
  HEAVEN FORGIVE MY SINS AT THE DAY OF JUDGMENT!     WIV 3.03.212P
  HEAVEN FORGIVE OUR SINS!                               5.05. 31P
  BUT THOSE AS SLEEP AND THINK NOT ON THEIR SINS,        5.05. 53
  THE TEMPTER, OR THE TEMPTED, WHO SINS MOST, HA?    MM  2.02.163
  OUR COMPELL'D SINS | STAND MORE FOR NUMBER THAN        2.04. 57
  DOTH WARRANT, | LET ALL MY SINS LACK MERCY!        ADO 4.01.180
  YOU MUST BE PURGED TOO, YOUR SINS ARE RACK'D,      LLL 5.02.818
  THE SINS OF THE FATHER ARE TO BE LAID UPON THE     MV  3.05.  1P
  SO THE SINS OF MY MOTHER SHOULD BE VISITED UPON        3.05. 14P
  IF THE SINS OF YOUR YOUTH ARE FORGIVEN YOU,        WT  3.03.120P
  SOME SINS DO BEAR THEIR PRIVILEGE ON EARTH,        JN  1.01.261
  THY SINS ARE VISITED IN THIS POOR CHILD, | THE         2.01.179
  BE MOWBRAY'S SINS SO HEAVY IN HIS BOSOM | THAT     R2  1.02. 50
  THEN MURTHERS, TREASONS, AND DETESTED SINS,            3.02. 44
  MORE SINS FOR THIS FORGIVENESS PROSPER MAY.            5.03. 84
  THE OLDEST SINS THE NEWEST KIND OF WAYS?           2H4 4.05.126
  OUR CHILDREN, AND OUR SINS LAY ON THE KING!        H5  4.01.232
  O, GOD FORGIVE MY SINS, AND PARDON THEE!           3H6 5.06. 60
  O, LET THEM KEEP IT TILL THY SINS BE RIPE, | AND   R3  1.03.218
  ALL SEVERAL SINS, ALL US'D IN EACH DEGREE,             5.03.198
  BUT CARDINAL SINS AND HOLLOW HEARTS I FEAR YE.     H8  3.01.104
  PRODUCE THE GRAND SUM OF HIS SINS, THE ARTICLES        3.02.293
  YOU CANNOT MAKE GROSS SINS LOOK CLEAR;             TIM 3.05. 38
  IN THY ORISONS | BE ALL MY SINS REMEMB'RED.        HAM 3.01. 89
  /GOD FORGIVE US OUR SINS!                          OTH 2.03.112P
  WHEN DEVILS WILL THE BLACKEST SINS PUT ON,             2.03.351
  THINK ON THY SINS.                                     5.02. 40
  PORTENDS | (UNLESS MY SINS ABUSE MY DIVINATION)    CYM 4.02.351
  FEW LOVE TO HEAR THE SINS THEY LOVE TO ACT;        PER 1.01. 92
  WICKED, ALL MY SINS | COULD NEVER PLUCK UPON ME.   TNK 2.03.  6
  WHAT SINS HAVE I COMMITTED, CHASTE DIANA, | THAT       4.02. 58
  WINS | LOSES A NOBLE COUSIN FOR THY SINS.              4.02.156
  BY THINE INCLINATION | TO ALL SINS PAST, AND ALL   LUC      923
  EXCUSING /THY SINS MORE THAN /THY SINS ARE;        SON    35. 8
  EXCUSING /THY SINS MORE THAN /THY SINS ARE;             35. 8
  O, IN WHAT SWEETS DOST THOU THY SINS ENCLOSE!            95. 4
SIP                  3 FREQ  0.0003 REL FR           2 V      1 P
  NEVER GET HER SO MUCH AS SIP ON A CUP WITH THE     WIV 2.02. 75P
  WILL DEIGN TO SIP OR TOUCH ONE DROP OF IT.         SHR 5.02.145
  TOOK TO QUENCH IT | SHE WOULD TO EACH ONE SIP.     WT  4.04. 62

  SIR, YOU MAY THANK YOURSELF FOR THIS GREAT LOSS,        2.01.124
  IT IS FOUL WEATHER IN US ALL, GOOD SIR, | WHEN          2.01.142
  I WOULD WITH SUCH PERFECTION GOVERN, SIR, | T'          2.01.168
  AND -- DO YOU MARK ME, SIR?                             2.01.170
  PLEASE YOU, SIR, | DO NOT OMIT THE HEAVY OFFER          2.01.193
  THUS, SIR:                                              2.01.231
  AY, SIR;                                                2.01.276
  PUT | THIS ANCIENT MORSEL, THIS SIR PRUDENCE,           2.01.286
  UPON MINE HONOR, SIR, I HEARD A HUMMING | (AND          2.01.317
  I SHAK'D YOU, SIR, AND CRIED.                           2.01.319
  BY'R LAKIN, I CAN GO NO FURTHER, SIR, | MY OLD          3.03.  1
  FAITH, SIR, YOU NEED NOT FEAR.                          3.03. 43
  I' TH' NAME OF SOMETHING HOLY, SIR, WHY STAND           3.03. 94
  I WARRANT YOU, SIR, | THE WHITE COLD VIRGIN SNOW        4.01. 54
  BE CHEERFUL, SIR,                                       4.01.147
  SIR, I AM VEX'D;                                        4.01.158
  I TOLD YOU, SIR, THEY WERE RED-HOT WITH DRINKING        4.01.171
  ALL PRISONERS, SIR, | IN THE LINE-GROVE WHICH           5.01.  9
  BUT CHIEFLY | HIM THAT YOU TERM'D, SIR, "THE            5.01. 15
  MINE WOULD, SIR, WERE I HUMAN.                          5.01. 20
  I'LL FETCH THEM, SIR.                                   5.01. 32
  AND A LOYAL SIR | TO HIM THOU FOLLOW'ST!                5.01. 69
  BEHOLD, SIR KING, | THE WRONGED DUKE OF MILAN,          5.01.106
  FOR YOU, MOST WICKED SIR, WHOM TO CALL BROTHER          5.01.130
  I AM WOE FOR'T, SIR.                                    5.01.139
  WELCOME, SIR:                                           5.01.165
  SIR, SHE IS MORTAL;                                     5.01.188
  THERE, SIR, STOP.                                       5.01.198
  O, LOOK, SIR, LOOK, SIR, HERE IS MORE OF US.            5.01.216
  O, LOOK, SIR, LOOK, SIR, HERE IS MORE OF US.            5.01.216
  SIR, ALL THIS SERVICE | HAVE I DONE SINCE I WENT        5.01.225
  IF I DID THINK, SIR, I WERE WELL AWAKE, | I'LD          5.01.229
  SIR, MY LIEGE, | DO NOT INFEST YOUR MIND WITH           5.01.245
  HOW FARES MY GRACIOUS SIR?                              5.01.253
  SIR, I INVITE YOUR HIGHNESS AND YOUR TRAIN | TO         5.01.301
  SIR PROTEUS! 'SAVE YOU! SAW YOU MY MASTER?          TGV 1.01. 70
  AY, SIR;                                                1.01. 96P
  NAY, SIR, LESS THAN A POUND SHALL SERVE ME FOR          1.01.105P
  YOU MISTOOK, SIR:                                       1.01.113P
  WHY, SIR, HOW DO YOU BEAR WITH ME?                      1.01.122P
  MARRY, SIR, THE LETTER, VERY ORDERLY, HAVING            1.01.123P
  WELL, SIR, HERE IS FOR YOUR PAINS.                      1.01.131P
  TRULY, SIR, I THINK YOU'LL HARDLY WIN HER.              1.01.133P
  SIR, I COULD PERCEIVE NOTHING AT ALL FROM HER;          1.01.136P
  AND SO, SIR, I'LL COMMEND YOU TO MY MASTER.             1.01.146P
  WHAT THINK'ST THOU OF THE FAIR SIR EGLAMOUR?            1.02.  9
  SIR VALENTINE'S PAGE;                                   1.02. 38
  SIR PROTEUS, YOUR /FATHER CALLS FOR YOU:                1.03. 88
  SIR, YOUR GLOVE.                                        2.01.  1
  SHE IS NOT WITHIN HEARING, SIR.                         2.01.  8P
  WHY, SIR, WHO BADE YOU CALL HER?                        2.01.  9P
  YOUR WORSHIP, SIR, OR ELSE I MISTOOK.                   2.01. 10P
  GO TO, SIR; TELL ME, DO YOU KNOW MADAM SILVIA?          2.01. 14P
  YOU HAVE LEARN'D, LIKE SIR PROTEUS, TO WREATHE          2.01. 19P
  WHY, SIR, I KNOW HER NOT.                               2.01. 45P
  IS SHE NOT HARD-FAVOR'D, SIR?                           2.01. 48P
```

Figure 12.5 *Sample page of a concordance using KWOC format.* [*Reprinted from Marvon Spevack (Ed.),* A Complete and Systematic Concordance to the Works of Shakespeare, *1970, p. 2915, by permission of Georg Olms Verlag*]

Sins(*cont*)
Can never seek, once dead in sins and lost; Par Lost 3.233
So many Laws argue so many sins Par Lost 12.283
Long time shall dwell and prosper, but when sins Par Lost 12.316
The Law that is against thee, and the sins Par Lost 12.416
Or work Redemption for mankind, whose sins Par Reg 1.266

Sinuous
Streaking the ground with sinuous trace; not all Par Lost 7.481

Sin-worn
With the rank vapours of this Sin-worn mould. Mask 17
Bridgewater ms 'sin-worne'
Trinity ms 'sin-worne'
1637 'Sin-worne'

Sion
Rose out of *Chaos*: Or if *Sion* Hill Par Lost 1.10
ms 'Sion'
Jehovah thundring out of *Sion*, thron'd Par Lost 1.386
ms 'Sion'
In *Sion* also not unsung, where stood Par Lost 1.442
ms 'Sion'
Infected *Sions* daughters with like heat, Par Lost 1.453
ms 'Sions'
Thee *Sion* and the flowrie Brooks beneath Par Lost 3.30
Over Mount *Sion*, and, though that were large, Par Lost 3.530
With *Sion*'s songs, to all true tasts excelling. Par Reg 4.347
On *Sion* my holi' hill. A firm decree Psalm 2, 13
In Sion do appear. Psalm 84, 28
Sions *fair* Gates the Lord loves more Psalm 87, 5
Be said of Sion *last* Psalm 87, 18

Sip
But this will cure all streight, one sip of this Mask 811

Sips
And every Herb that sips the dew; Penseroso 172

Sir
Sir, what ill chance hath brought thee to this place Par Reg 1.321
Thy age, like ours, O Soul of Sir *John Cheek*, Sonnet 11, 12

Sire
Thick clouds and dark doth Heav'ns all-ruling Sire Par Lost 2.264
Dear Daughter, since thou claim'st me for thy Sire, Par Lost 2.817
His mother bad, and thus bespake her Sire. Par Lost 2.849
Which to our general Sire gave prospect large Par Lost 4.144
What day the genial Angel to our Sire Par Lost 4.712
Mean while our Primitive great Sire, to meet Par Lost 5.350
Unanimous, as sons of one great Sire Par Lost 6.95
So spake our Sire, and by his count'nance seemd Par Lost 8.39
Nor are thy lips ungraceful, Sire of men, Par Lost 8.218
So spake the Godlike Power, and thus our Sire. Par Lost 8.249
Rowling in dust and gore. To which our Sire Par Lost 11.460

Sit(*cont*)
The Signal to ascend, sit lingring here Par Lost 2.56
Sit unpolluted, and th' Ethereal mould Par Lost 2.139
What sit we then projecting peace and Warr? Par Lost 2.329
And Heav'ns high Arbitrator sit secure Par Lost 2.359
Attempting, or to sit in darkness here Par Lost 2.377
To sit in hateful Office here confin'd, Par Lost 2.859
Here shalt thou sit incarnate, here shalt Reign Par Lost 3.315
To sit and taste, till this meridian heat Par Lost 5.369
For while I sit with thee, I seem in Heav'n, Par Lost 8.210
To sit indulgent, and with him partake Par Lost 9.3
With Gods to sit the highest, am now constraind Par Lost 9.164
There sit not, and reproach us as unclean, Par Lost 9.1098
O Son, why sit we here each other viewing Par Lost 10.235
Appointed to sit there, had left thir charge, Par Lost 10.421
Thou shouldst be great and sit on *David*'s Throne, Par Reg 1.240
With honour, only deign to sit and eat. Par Reg 2.336
What doubts the Son of God to sit and eat? Par Reg 2.368
What doubt'st thou Son of God? sit down and eat. Par Reg 2.377
While Virtue, Valour, Wisdom sit in want. Par Reg 2.431
To sit upon thy Father *David*'s Throne; Par Reg 3.153
But tedious wast of time to sit and hear Par Reg 4.123
Know therefore when my season comes to sit Par Reg 4.146
There I am wont to sit, when any chance Samson 4
But to sit idle on the houshold hearth, Samson 566
Or seven, though one should musing sit; Samson 1017
Not to sit idle with so great a gift Samson 1500
Of sort, might sit in order to behold, Samson 1608
May sit i' th center, and enjoy bright day, Mask 382
Would sit, and hearken even to extasie, Mask 625
Comus. Nay Lady sit; if I but wave this wand, Mask 659
Where I may sit and rightly spell, Penseroso 170
That sit upon the nine enfolded Sphears, Arcades 64
To sit the midst of Trinal Unity, Nativity 11
While Birds of Calm sit brooding on the charmed wave. Nativity 68
And Mercy set between, Nativity 144
1673 'Mercy will sit between'
Bright-harnest Angels sit in order serviceable. Nativity 244
There doth my soul in holy vision sit Passion 41
Attir'd with Stars, we shall for ever sit, On Time 21
Sit not thou still O God of *strength* Psalm 83, 3

Sits
Sits Arbitress, and neerer to the Earth Par Lost 1.785
Forc't Halleluiah's; while he Lordly sits Par Lost 2.243
High honourd sits? Go therfore mighty Powers, Par Lost 2.456
For him who sits above and laughs the while Par Lost 2.731
Before mine eyes in opposition sits Par Lost 2.803
Hee rules a moment; *Chaos* Umpire sits, Par Lost 2.907

At length a Reverend Sire among them came, Par Lost 11.719
Thir order: last the Sire, and his three Sons Par Lost 11.736
The ancient Sire descends with all his Train: Par Lost 11.862
A Virgin is his Mother, but his Sire Par Lost 12.368
As at the Worlds great period; and our Sire Par Lost 12.467
His Mother then is mortal, but his Sire, Par Reg 1.86
By matchless Deeds express thy matchless Sire. Par Reg 1.233
But see here comes thy reverend Sire Samson 326
With thee; say reverend Sire, we thirst to hear. Samson 1456
Next *Camus*, reverend Sire, went footing slow, Lycidas 103
  1638 'sire'
  Trinity ms 'sire'
Immortal Nectar to her Kingly Sire: Vacation 39

Sirens
My Mother *Circe* with the Sirens three, Mask 253
And the Songs of *Sirens* sweet, Mask 878
  Bridgewater ms 'sirens'
To the celestial *Sirens* harmony, Arcades 63
  Trinity ms 'sirens'
Blest pair of *Sirens*, pledges of Heav'ns joy, Musick 1

Sirocco
Sirocco, and *Libecchio*, Thus began Par Lost 10.706

Sirs
End Green. Why is it harder Sirs then Gordon, Sonnet 11, 8
  Trinity ms 'sirs' ←'Sirs'

Sisera
Smote *Sisera* sleeping through the Temples nail'd. Samson 990
To Sisera, and as *is told* Psalm 83, 35

Sister
Wisdom thy Sister, and with her didst play Par Lost 7.10
But O that haples virgin our lost sister Mask 350
I do not think my sister so to seek, Mask 366
Of our unowned sister. *Eld. Bro.* I do not, brother, Mask 407
Inferr, as if I thought my sisters state Mask 408
My sister is not so defenceless left Mask 414
2. *Bro.* Heav'n keep my sister, agen agen and neer, Mask 486
Of my most honour'd Lady, your dear sister. Mask 564
Com Lady while Heaven lends us grace, Mask 938
  Bridgewater ms 'come sister'
With two sister Graces more Allegro 15
Prince *Memnons* sister might beseem, Penseroso 18

Sisters
Atlantick Sisters, and the *Spartan* Twins Par Lost 10.674
Begin then, Sisters of the sacred well, Lycidas 15
Sleek *Panope* with all her sisters play'd. Lycidas 99
Amongst her spangled sisters bright Psalm 136, 34
Sphear-born harmonious Sisters, Voice, and Vers, Musick 2
  Trinity ms 'sisters'

Sit
For while they sit contriving, shall the rest, Par Lost 2.54
From the pure Empyrean where he sits Par Lost 3.57
Sits on the Bloom extracting liquid sweet. Par Lost 5.25
Had not th' Almightie Father where he sits Par Lost 6.671
Where now he sits at the right hand of bliss. Par Lost 6.892
Chor. His manacles remark him, there he sits. Samson 1309
And sits as safe as in a Senat house, Mask 389
  Bridgewater ms 'sitts'
We cannot free the Lady that sits here Mask 818
  Trinity ms 'sits' ←'remaines'
  Bridgewater ms 'sitts'
Wherwith she sits on diamond rocks Mask 881
  Bridgewater ms 'sitts'
But night sits monarch yet in the mid sky. Mask 957
  Bridgewater ms 'sitts'
  Trinity ms 'sitts' ←'raignes'
Sadly sits th' *Assyrian* Queen; Mask 1002
  line not in Bridgewater ms
I will bring you where she sits, Arcades 91
Now sits not girt with Tapers holy shine, Nativity 202
To him that sits theron Musick 8
  Trinity ms 'sitts' ←'sits'
The God that sits at marriage feast; Winchester 18

Sitst
Amidst the glorious brightness where thou sit'st Par Lost 3.376
Amid the Suns bright circle where thou sitst, Par Lost 4.578
Unspeakable, who sitst above these Heavens Par Lost 5.156

Sittest
Listen where thou art sitting Mask 860
  Trinity ms 'art sitting' ←'sit'st'
Whilst thou bright Saint high sit'st in glory, Winchester 61
That sitt'st between the Cherubs *bright* Psalm 80, 5

Sittim
Israel in *Sittim* on thir march from *Nile* Par Lost 1.413
  ms 'Sittim'

Sitting
Thus sitting, thus consulting, thus in Arms? Par Lost 2.164
For you, there sitting where ye durst not soare; Par Lost 4.829
Earth sitting still, when she alone receaves Par Lost 8.89
As sitting Queen ador'd on Beauties Throne, Par Reg 2.212
Thy right by sitting still or thus retiring? Par Reg 3.164
Will be for thee no sitting, or not long Par Reg 4.107
And view him sitting in the house, enobl'd Samson 1491
Amidst the flowry-kirtl'd *Naiades* Mask 254
  Trinity ms 'amidst' ←'sitting amidst'
Lingering, and sitting by a new made grave, Mask 472
  Bridgewater ms 'sittinge'
Listen where thou art sitting Mask 860
Thy rapt soul sitting in thine eyes: Penseroso 40
Sitting like a Goddes bright, Arcades 18
  Trinity ms 'sitting' ←'seated'

***Figure 12.6** Sample page of a concordance using KWOC format. [Reprinted by permission of the Oxford University Press from William Ingram and Kathleen H. Swain,* A Concordance to Milton's English Poetry, *Oxford University Press, 1972.]*

right to left. The problems were solved, and the resulting concordance—perhaps the most unusual concordance ever prepared—provided scholars with a valuable research tool for the literary analysis and textual criticism of what has been hailed as the greatest manuscript discovery of all time.

12.2.2 Literary Concordances

In addition to the Bible, concordances have been prepared for many other important works. It is fair to say that without the computer most of these tasks would never have been undertaken. The results clearly demonstrate that computers have applications both for the humanities and for the sciences.

An early example of a computer-processed concordance is *A Concordance to the Poems of Matthew Arnold* by S. M. Parrish, published by Cornell University Press in 1959. In the production of this work, many technical problems had to be solved. Parrish's work was followed, in 1968, by Packard's monumental four-volume *Concordance to Livy,* published by Harvard University Press (see Figure 12.4). Note the resemblance of this concordance to a KWIC index. Note also the quality of the printing. Advanced computer typesetting techniques were used in preparing this publication. Marvin Spevack's *Complete and Systematic Concordance to the Works of Shakespeare,* published by Olms in 1970, is in a KWOC format (see Figure 12.5), as is the excellent *Concordance to Milton's English Poetry* by Ingram and Swain, published by Oxford University Press in 1972 (see Figure 12.6).

Many other nonbiblical concordances have been prepared, and more will be. Now that computer processing has been simplified, it is to be hoped that literary scholars will make greater use of computers and of computer-produced concordances as research tools. Librarians as well as library users should certainly become better acquainted with concordances and their potential applications.

12.2.3 Uses

Concordances are designed to guide researchers to particular words and their contexts. For this purpose, they are unexcelled. While the concordance itself sheds no new light on the text, it does provide the scholar with a means of finding remembered passages, as well as with a most valuable research tool for linguistic research literary analysis—especially by facilitating comparison of closely related passages.

The following are some of the ways in which concordances can be used:

1. To locate a partly or completely remembered passage: If even a single word is recalled, it can be looked up and the source of the complete quotation identified.
2. To assemble subject matter: The clergyman, for example, when preparing a sermon on charity, can find in the biblical concordance, all verses in which this word appears and then select appropriate passages.
3. To compare and analyze word meaning: For the lexicographer and linguist studying polysemy (multimeaning), the concordance is an essential tool. Some words have many different meanings and are used in many different contexts. For example, to *work* hard, to be out of *work*, to *work* one's passage, an earth*work* dam, a clock*work* toy, etc.—all of the various uses will be included in the concordance, usually without separation according to meaning. This is in contrast to subject indexes, in which sets of related entries are separated by meaning, usually through the use of glosses. For example: **Lead** (*metal*), **Lead** (*graphite*), **Lead** (*ore*), **Lead** (*electrical*), and **Lead** (*guidance*).
4. To discover homographs: Concordances can help find different uses of the same word, for example, "*lead*," in such contexts as: a *lead* weight, a *lead* pencil, *lead* ore, an electrical *lead*, and to *lead.*
5. To compare and analyze word usage: Concordances enable the scholar to examine differences and similarities in word use among different authors, as well as in the earlier and later writings of a single author. Such linguistic analysis also aids in the identification of authorship.

13 Special Indexes

In addition to the more common subject, author, and word indexes, there are many special indexes providing unique guidance to unusual items. The examples that have been selected to illustrate the class of special indexes are thematic, ring, molecular-formula, taxonomic, group, numerical, and classified.

13.1 THEMATIC INDEXES

Musicians, composers, and music lovers also need indexes. One of the more interesting special indexes in the field of music is the thematic index, which guides searchers to themes, tunes, and melodies that they remember but cannot name. Most thematic indexes are devoted to the works of one composer, for example, *Melodic Index to the Works of Johann Sebastian Bach* (Payne, 1938). This work indexes and tabulates all of the themes of Bach according to their melodic design.

The index enables the searcher to locate a Bach composition by the pattern of its first three intervals, with repeated notes ignored. The line formed by the composition's first four notes of different pitch, excluding ornaments, creates the pattern used in finding the composition. These patterns are categorized as for those themes in which:

The direction of the line is unchanged:

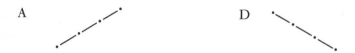

The direction is changed once:

The direction is changed twice:

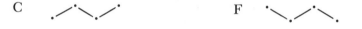

Subdivisions of these six general categories give 842 types. The melodic designs are all in the treble clef and in the key of C. There are 363 themes.

Finding charts under A, B, ...F may contain as many as seven subcategories based on the starting note (A through G); thus each category may contain as many as seven groups. There are special subdivisions for categories B, E, C, and F. Each group or subdivision has the themes arranged by the increasing size of their intervals. The Thematic Index, in the same order as the charts, lists the themes in full and in Bach's tonality. An example of a finding chart is

In the thematic index, this is represented as follows

Cantata 54. Widerstehe doche der Sünde

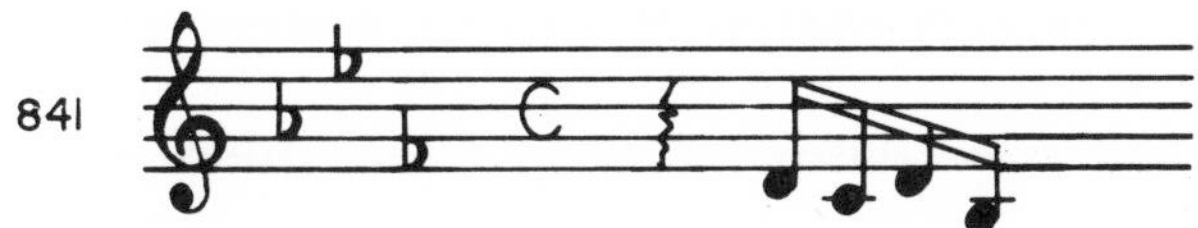

[Theme direction lines, Finding Chart, and Thematic Index excerpt reproduced with permission of May De Forest (Payne) McAll, 517 E. Ridge Valley Drive, Miami, Florida 33157 from Melodic Index to the Works of Johann Sebastian Bach. *Schirmer, New York, 1938.]*

A Dictionary of Musical Themes (Barlow and Morgenstern, 1948) carries 10,000 themes. For use of this work, the searcher plays the theme in the key of C major or C minor, then writes the letter names of the notes in the order in which they are played. The resulting note sequence is sought in the index, which leads the user to the name of the original work and the name of its composer.

Thematic indexes vary in their approach to indexing of musical themes. Still other approaches are possible, and computers are being used to develop new guides to musical themes.

13.2 THE RING INDEX TO CHEMICAL ABSTRACTS

Chemical compounds (usually organic compounds—those containing carbon) form molecules of, or containing, rings. One of the most important ring compounds is benzene,

```
     H H
     C–C
    //   \\
  HC       CH
    \     /
     C=C
     H H
```

with a molecular formula C_6H_6. With the exception of the simpler examples, ring compounds are difficult for chemists to name. Especially difficult have been those compounds in which the rings contain elements other than carbon and those compounds that have many fused rings. A large number of common or trivial names have been used to name ring compounds. The multiplicity of these names burdens the memories of chemists and makes recall difficult.

A relatively simple solution was found to the problem of naming ring compounds and indexing them so that they could be readily searched in indexes. The solution was the ring index. In using the ring index, the chemist counts the number of rings that are directly attached to one another and turns to that part of the index. Next, the number of atoms in each ring are ranked by ring size, the smallest ring is first. Thus, 5,6 indicates a two-ring compound that has one ring of 5 atoms and another of 6 atoms. The number 5,6 is located in the ring index under that part of the index dealing with 2-ring systems. Under the set of index entries located at 5,6, the arrangement is by kinds of atoms in the smallest ring. Carbon (C) comes first in the symbol string, and the rest of the chemical elements follow in alphabetical order by symbol. Thus Ag (silver) comes with the *A*s and not with *S*s. Hydrogen (H) is not normally an atom in the ring, nor are other univalent elements. Except for the digit 1, the numbers of each element follow the symbol for the element as a subscript. This is the same as in the molecular formula, except that all of the atoms are *in* the ring and not *attached to it*. The following is an example from a ring index

2-RING SYSTEMS
6,6
  $C_2H_4-C_2N_4$
    [1,2,4,5]Tetrazino[1,2-alpha][1,2,4,5]tetrazine
  C_6-C_6
    Bicyclo[3.3.1]nonane
    Bicyclo[2.2.2]octane
    Naphthalene
    Spiro[5.5]undecane
  Si_6-Si_6
    Bicyclo[3.3.1]nonasilane
    Bicyclo[2.2.2]octasilane

In this coined example from a ring index, the heading is "2-Ring systems." The overall modification is "6,6" which means that all of the 2-ring systems entered have six atoms in each ring. When rings are fused (have one or more atoms in common), the fused atoms are counted in each of the rings. As a subheading under the modification 6,6 is "$C_2N_4-C_2N_4$." This indicates that the first ring has two carbon atoms and four nitrogen atoms; the second ring has the same. As the reference, there is the name of a specific ring, "[1,2,4,5]Tetrazino[1,2-alpha][1,2,4,5]tetrazine." In this case, the reference can *also* be considered to be a part of the modification. The reference, as explained in the introduction to the index, is to the subject index or to the chemical-substance index, in which the searcher will find this ring name, possibly together with substituents to the ring, and possibly with a modification. The purpose in turning from the ring index to the subject index is to discover the substituents of the rings and the modifications in order to determine if the entries are relevant to the current search. The references in the indexes then lead to the works indexed.

The next entry under the modification 6,6 is "C_6–C_6." Under this there are four entries, the third of which is "Naphthalene" (moth balls), $C_{10}H_8$,

```
     H H
     C C
   //\ /\\
  HC C CH
   |  ||  |
  HC C CH
   \\/ \//
     C C
     H H
```

From the ring index, the searcher turns to the subject or chemical-substance index to find, for example, the word "naphthalene." In the subject or chemical-substance index, the searcher finds modifications that precisely tie "naphthalene" to the subject being indexed. There, the user will also find the reference number leading to the abstract.

13.3 MOLECULAR-FORMULA INDEXES

About 80% of the names of organic compounds assigned by authors (chemists) are translated by the nomenclature experts of *Chemical Abstracts* into inverted index names. Many chemist authors either do not know or choose not to use the index names (inverted or uninverted). Use of names other than the index names may, at times, be desirable in order to emphasize a common name or to show relations among compounds discussed in a work. In an increasing number of cases, index names differ greatly from common names. The index names are absolutely necessary in an index, both to avoid scattering in the index and to avoid myriad *see* cross-references from synonyms to the index name. It is important to note that names of chemical compounds given by authors may be just as useful as, and in many cases more useful (outside of an index) than are the systematic names given for the purposes of indexing.

Because of difficulty in naming chemical (usually organic) compounds, chemists in about the year 1918 devised formula indexes for *Chemical Abstracts*. These ingenious devices enable chemists who do not know systematic nomenclature to find the names of compounds in indexes. Since learning to name compounds is a slow and costly process, it is to the credit of formula indexes that they save the time and money of chemists and of organizations employing chemists.

Chemical compounds have definite kinds and numbers of atoms in them. The kinds and numbers of atoms can be determined and calculated from the structural formula or index name. The kinds of atoms can be specified in the molecular formula by the symbols for the elements. The numbers can be specified by subscript numbers following the symbols. Thus, methane (natural gas, fuel gas, carbon hydride, hydrogen carbide, fire damp, marsh gas, etc.) has a structural formula:

```
  H
H C H
  H
```

Methane has one carbon atom and four hydrogen atoms. The molecular formula is CH_4. In molecular formulas the order of the symbols for the chemical elements is specified as C, H, with the rest of the symbols following in alphabetical order. This is for the Hill system. For the Richter system, the order is: C, H, O, N, Cl, Br, I, F, S, and P, followed by the remaining elements in alphabetical order according to their symbols. Thus, potassium would be alphabetized in either system under *K* rather than under *P*, and iron under Fe rather than under *I*.

Different chemical compounds having the same molecular formula are called isomers. From the existence of isomers, it can be seen that the formula index may not lead users to only one compound name. There are many molecular formulas under which are found several isomers. This is somewhat unfortunate for the person who does not know nomenclature. However, the formula index usually leads the searcher to only a very small number of names of isomers, in contrast to the subject index or the chemical-substance index, which leads to enormous numbers of compound names. In the formula index, it is relatively easy to learn enough about nomenclature to select the correct name from the small set of names found under a single molecular formula.

The entries in the formula index (the molecular-formula index) are listed in order of the symbol for the first element, then of the symbols within that set of formulas, then by the number of atoms of the first element in the molecule. Within this defined set of formulas having the same number of atoms of the first element, the formulas are then arranged by the symbol for the second element, and within this set by the number of atoms of the second element in the molecule. This arrangement continues until all of the symbols and their numbers are taken into account. Under a given formula, the systematic index names of the isomers are alphabetized. The systematic names are used so that the searcher can easily turn from the formula index to the subject or substance index and find the same name—which is a great convenience. Through the use of the formula index, the user is able to find the index name with relatively little difficulty.

In subject or substance indexes, the user is usually given a modification or a set of modifying phrases that relate the compound studied to the subject studied in the abstract or article. This convenience enables the searcher to separate rapidly and fairly accurately the relevant index entries from those that are irrelevant for the current search. In turn, this accurate separation saves the user time by enabling him to avoid looking up irrelevant references.

Formula indexes are published by the Chemical Abstracts Service and by *Chemisches Zentralblatt* and its successor. Any chemist can prepare his own formula index for the chemical compounds in which he is interested. His formula index could be designed to include modifications under the names of compounds as subject headings, to save further reference to a substance index or subject index.

The following is an example from a formula index:

$C_{12}H_{22}O_{11}$
  Isomaltose, 4567
  Lactose, see also *Subject Index*
    beta, 5674
    polymer of, 6754
  Maltose, see also *Subject Index*
    alpha, 4576
    beta, 4576
    polymer of, 6754
  Mannose, 4-*O*-*beta*-D-glycopyranosyl-, 6645
  Melibiose, 5674, 5746, 5764, 6457
  Sophorose, 5674, 6457, 6475, 7456
  Sucrose, see also *Subject Index*
    compound with strontium hydroxide, 7456
    polymer with vinyl chloride, 7465
  Trehalose, 456, 675, 7645, 7654
  Turanose, 7546

In this coined example from a formula index, the heading for all of the entries is "$C_{12}H_{22}O_{11}$." This molecular formula (formula of a molecule) represents *all* chemical compounds that contain 12 atoms of carbon, 22 atoms of hydrogen, and 11 atoms of oxygen, and that have been indexed for this index. The names of the chemical compounds having this molecular formula appear as modifications under the formula. Since all of these compounds have the same molecular formula, they are all isomers. The first isomer is "Isomaltose," which means 'isomer of maltose.' The reference (4567) is to the work dealing with isomaltose. The next entry is a *see also* cross-reference from "Lactose" to the subject index. It leads the user from the formula index to the heading **Lactose** in the subject index. The modifications under **Lactose** will tell the searcher what has been studied about lactose and enable him to decide which entries to look up. The next entry is the modification "Lactose, beta." The entry is double indented to indicate omission of the word *Lactose*. The following entry indicates that a polymer of lactose is being studied in the work referred to by "6754." The next entry is a *see also* cross-reference from "Maltose" to the subject index. All of the entries under this heading are sugars.

Besides being interested in specific, individual compounds, chemists are also interested in all compounds having certain structural features in common. One example would be all compounds having a nitro group and a pyridine ring. Another would be all compounds having an ethyl group (C_2H_5-) attached to rings having five or more atoms, at least one of which is oxygen. Classes of compounds may have properties in common. Examples of properties are biological, physical, chemical, pharmaceutical, and electrical. Subject, substance, and formula indexes bring relatively few kinds of names of compounds together; group or structural-class indexes would bring all kinds of names of compounds together if all names were entered into the index and if the index functioned properly.

A number of group indexes have been developed; some are in successful operation (Bernier, 1957, 1961).

There are a number of systems for coding structural formulas that are much more flexible in search than are those systems that rely on standard groups, rings, and chains. One such system was devised by Edward H. Sussenguth, Jr., of the Computation Laboratory of Harvard University (Sussenguth, 1965). In this system, any set or combination of sets of groups, rings, or chains—or their fragments—can be discovered. That is, in addition to all compounds containing the nitro group, this system can find all compounds in which the nitrogen atom is attached to one or more oxygen atoms and to a chain of two carbon atoms. Compounds in which fragments of rings (attached or unattached) are identical can also be discovered, as another example. Systems with this much flexibility should be able to meet most, if not all, of the needs of organic chemists in their searches of the literature for related chemical compounds.

Another system is that of D. J. Gluck of Du Pont (Gluck, 1965). This system, which also permits substructure searching, is being developed and used by the Chemical Abstracts Service.

13.4 TAXONOMIC INDEXES

Special indexes, called taxonomic indexes, have been designed to guide biologists and others interested in various life forms. *Biological Abstracts* has two such indexes: the *Biosystematic Index* and the *Generic Index.* Taxonomic indexes lead searchers directly to works related to taxa specified by the searcher. This is a great convenience in studying specific forms of life—plant and animal, large and small. Researchers and other scholars may be interested in viruses, bacteria, and fungi as well as in plants and animals.

The *Biosystematic Index* lists taxonomic categories that lead to subject headings and to serial numbers of abstracts found in *Biological Abstracts.* An example of an entry in this index is

PRIMATES HOMINIDAE SERODIAG 9184

In this entry, which is found under the class CHORDATA, it is seen that entries related to man ("Hominidae") are indexed as a subheading under "Primates." "Serodiag" is given in the list of abbreviations preceding the index as meaning. "Medical and Clinical Microbiology (Includes Veterinary)—Serodiagnoses."

The *Generic Index* alphabetically lists up to 20 genera in an abstract. An abbreviated subject heading (keyword), to which the paper relates, and a reference number appear with the name of the species. An example of an entry is

HOMO-SAPIENS PSYCH GEN 10730.

In this entry, man ("Homo-sapiens") is the organism and "PSYCH GEN" refers to "Psychiatry-General; Medical Psychology and Sociology," according to the list of abbreviations.

Taxonomic indexes can be used as guides to all works in which organisms play an important role as subjects under study or concerning which subjects are studied. Comparative studies of taxa (e.g., biochemical relations among different organisms) provide especially fitting entries for a taxonomic index. Studies on the biology and biophysics of taxa are also appropriately served by such an index.

The following is an example from a taxonomic index:

Ectoprocta		
	Paleozoology	1234
Brachiopoda		
	Paleozoology	2341
Mollusca		
cephalopoda	Enzymes	3241
"	Paleozoology	2341
gastropoda	Ecology	1324
"	Immunology	1423

In this coined example from a taxonomic index, the first heading (subject heading) is "Ectoprocta." The modification, "Paleozoology," defines the relation of the subject studied to the heading. The reference is "1234." The next heading is "Brachiopoda," and its modification is the same as for the first entry. Under "Mollusca" are subsumed "cephalopoda" and "gastropoda." These taxonomic relationships are useful in bringing related works to the attention of the searcher.

13.5 NUMERICAL INDEXES

Numbers can be used to guide searchers to works. An example is the patent-number index. For the searcher who has been given only a patent number, this index is indispensable. A patent number is an ideal reference, provided that one has a patent-number index available, because it is unambiguous and unique; its presence or absence in an index can be determined rapidly and accurately. The *Numerical Patent Index* of *Chemical Abstracts*, for example, groups patents by the name of the country in which the patent was issued. Thus, patent numbers are gouped under, for example, "Austrian," "Belgian," "USSR," and "United States." Within each of these groupings, the patent numbers are listed in increasing numerical order. Following each number is the serial number of the abstract published for the patent. The abstracts are published in serial-number order. There may be separate listings, under the name of each country, of patent applications and of additions to existing patents.

The following is a coined example of a patent-number index:

Country and number	Document number
Austria	
324,512	234,469
Belgium	
800,027	230,312
Britain	
159,624	236,610
159,731	236,608
Czechoslovakia	
150,991	231,420
151,084	231,000
France	
2,158,700	236,542
France-Addition	
2,168,932	232,313
France-Application	
2,169,945	236,798

The name of the country and the status of the patent constitute the heading in each case. Under that comes the number of the patent. On the same line is the reference (locator), which guides the searcher to the patent or its surrogate in the collection indexed.

Another numerical index is the patent concordance. It has been found very difficult to determine if a patent has been issued in another country. The patent concordance eliminates this difficulty.

The following is a coined example of a patent concordance:

U.S. patent number	Corresponding patent	Reference number (locator)
1,475,093	S. Afr. 7,608,659	76 126,782
1,475,111	Ger. 2,344,361	76 126,555
1,475,150	Fre. 2,165,290	77 107,432

The U.S. patent numbers, listed in numerical order, correspond, respectively, to patents of the Republic of South Africa, of Germany, and of France. All can be located through the corresponding reference number, which leads to the original patent or a surrogate.

bles function as indexes for numerical data. From the independent variables (those controlled by the searcher), tables function as guides to the controlled variables (those controlled by, or dependent on, the independent variables). For example, a table for the vapor pressure of mercury at different temperatures guides the user from the temperature of the mercury to its vapor pressure at that temperature. Also, the same table can guide the searcher to the temperature at which mercury has a specified vapor pressure. This last is the reverse of the first guidance. In vapor-pressure and similar tables, the temperature (or other independent variable) may be listed in a column to the left of the page. The temperature intervals used may be large, say, 10, 20, 30, 40, 50, etc. degrees Celsius. Interpolation of temperatures between these large intervals is aided by the use of smaller intervals (say, 2-degree intervals) as column heads across the page. The following is an example of a segment of a table for vapor pressure:

Temp. (°C)	0	2	4	6	8
100	.2729	.3032	.3366	.3731	.4132
110	.4572	.5052	.5576	.6150	.6776

Tables such as these compress a large amount of data into a small space and are very handy for finding the desired data. These tables are, effectively, indexes to data. The labels for the numbers in the table are carried in the captions of the tables, as are the instructions for use of the tables. For this reason, tables of data have been popular and widely used in handbooks or "handy-books."

13.6 CLASSIFIED INDEXES

Entries in an index do not need to be in alphabetical order. In a classified index, entries are arranged according to some classification scheme. Combinations of alphabetical and classified indexes are possible. For example, the major headings may be arranged in classified order; the entries under them may be in alphabetical order. Alternatively, the major headings may be alphabetized and the subheadings or the entries under them may be placed in a classified order.

The advantage of classified order is that like things are brought together—not all like things, but usually enough to justify the classified order—whereas alphabetization tends to scatter related items. As the searcher skims or scans a category of items, his attention is directed to closely related items in the index. The same effect occurs in a supermarket in which, for example, the cereals are in one section, the meats in another, and the fruits and vegetables in yet another. This type of display is effective in bringing a new member of the category to the attention of the shopper.

In alphabetical subject indexes, classification is achieved in part by the syndetic system—mainly by cross-references. Synonyms are put into the same class by means of *see* cross-references. An example is "**Vitamin B_2**, see *Riboflavin.*" The term most frequently used in the literature of the field is, let us say, *riboflavin*. This cross-reference recognizes this fact and classifies vitamin B_2 and riboflavin as being the same substance. The *see also* cross-reference is used most often to bring attention to two headings that are related as genus is to species—or the reverse. An example is "**Poems** (see also *Ballads*)" or "**Ballads** (see also *Poems*)." Other relations that may be shown by cross-references include: whole–part, cause–effect, product–use, and the reverse of all of these. The cross-reference system brings related index headings to the attention of the searcher without the necessity of replicating entries that can be classified in several ways. In effect, the cross-reference system functions as a classification scheme distributed alphabetically throughout the index.

Sometimes cross-references are published independently of the index because of the delay, difficulty, and cost in justifying the cross-references that are valid for the index and in interfiling and printing them. Cross-references printed in a separate list are always arranged alphabetically. In addition, they may also be given another arrangement—according to some classification scheme. An example of the latter is to be found in *Medical Subject Headings (MeSH)*. The classified listing brings all related subject headings together into logical groups. For example, all similar drugs are grouped, as are all similar diseases.

The index in which the entries themselves are classified, rather than being arranged alphabetically, is usually supplemented by an alphabetical guide to the classification scheme—an index to the classification scheme. This added alphabetical guide has been found to be necessary because what may be logical to the classifier may appear illogical or unexpected to the user. For example, in one classified index, **Blood** was classified under **Tissue**. This classification, while quite correct, might be unexpected to someone who was not a physiologist or physician. The classification of **Sodium** under **Alkali metals** might be unexpected by those who are not chemists. The use of an index to a classification scheme has seemed more cumbersome than is the use of an alphabetical index directly—especially if the classification scheme is interfiled (also alphabetically), in the form of cross-references and notes.

Several examples of classified indexes are available. In *Meteorological & Geoastrophysical Abstracts*, the abstracts are numbered according to the Universal Decimal Classification (UDC) system under such general headings as **Forecasting** and **Upper air temperature**. Thus, the arrangement of the abstracts themselves becomes an index in which one can find a single abstract or a set of very closely related abstracts—provided that one understands the UDC. In addition to this index, there are author and subject indexes that can be used by those unaquainted with the UDC.

The subject index to Volume 5 of *Geological Abstracts* for 1957 is classified. The major categories are (1) Mineralogy, (2) Petrology, (3) Surficial geology, (4) Structural and aereal geology, (5) Stratigraphy and historical geology, (6) Paleontology, (7) Geophysics, (8) Economic geology, and (9) Miscellaneous (history of geology, biography, bibliography, tables, glossaries, education). There are also subclasses, such as those under Category 8: (*a*) Metals, (*b*) Coal, (*c*) Oil and gas, general, (*d*) Oil and gas, regional and local, (*e*) Oil and gas developments, (*f*) Ground water, (*g*) Other mineral deposits, (*h*) engineering geology, and (*i*) Mineral economics. Under each subclass are listed the issue and volume numbers of *Geological Abstracts* in which the index item appears, followed by the page numbers of the abstracts in those issues. Then come the last names of authors followed by words selected from the title, in turn followed by the geographical location of the study—for example, "Sampson and Hriskevich (cobalt-arsenic minerals, Cobalt, Ontario)."

The principal index to *Mathematical Reviews* is the table of contents that classifies the contents of each issue into 61 categories. Abstracts are placed into these categories and then numbered serially. There is also an author index and a "key index," which lists titles, parts of titles, or key words alphabetically by the first word for general subjects of abstracts.

Another classified index is the HAIC (*H*etero-*A*tom-*i*n-*C*ontext) index of *Chemical Abstracts*. The HAIC index supplements the formula index by grouping chemical compounds by the chemical elements other than by the carbon and hydrogen in them. This is a classified index because it brings together the molecular formulas of compounds alike in kinds of atoms. The HAIC index aids chemists who may be interested in all compounds that have a specified element in them.

Molecular formulas, such as $AgGaSe_2$, are listed in this index in alphabetical order by each of the symbols in the formula. Thus, "Ag" is alphabetized under *A* (for "Ag") rather than under *S* (for "Silver"). The molecular formula is spaced so that the alphabetized chemical element stands out. For further emphasis, the alphabetized element is printed in boldface type, for example, **Ag** $GaSe_2$. There is no reference number. The existence of this entry in the HAIC index indicates to the searcher that the same compound will appear in the formula index for the same volume of *Chemical Abstracts*. This same molecular formula is also listed in the HAIC index under, "Ag **Ga** Se_2" and under "AgGa $\mathbf{Se_2}$." Note that the molecular formula is always retained in each entry in the same order as is found in the molecular-formula index. In this example, the formula, $AgGaSe_2$, is also listed with other silver-compound formulas, gallium-compound formulas, and selenium-compound formulas. Within a set of compound formulas the entries are listed by the numbers of the elements being grouped. Thus, formulas with one "Ag" atom precede those with 2 Ag atoms, and these precede those with 3 Ag atoms, and so on. This index was abandoned in 1969 for apparent lack of interest by chemists.

Many of these special indexes in this section lead to unexpected items. Such indexes can best be discovered by examining the last issue of a relevant periodical for a given year or by seeking cumulative indexes. Some special indexes are experimental and appear for only a year or so, then are abandoned because of cost or because of lack of interest and use. Examples of such indexes are the HAIC index to *Chemical Abstracts,* the continuity index to *Information Science Abstracts,* and the WADEX (word and author index) to *Applied Mechanics Reviews.*

V INDEX EVALUATION AND PROFESSIONALISM

14 Index Evaluation

It should come as no surprise that indexes come in different qualities—just as do diamonds, foods, wearing apparel, and almost every other product and service. Indexers, publishers, and searchers (as well as librarians and other purchasers) are faced with the problem of how to evaluate the quality of indexes. Standards have been developed and can be used in evaluation. Specifications for different indexes can be measured, recorded, and compared in evaluation. The first volume of the *Annual Review of Information Science and Technology* carries an article by Charles P. Bourne entitled "Evaluation of Indexing Systems" (Bourne, 1966). Evaluation is still an important topic, and the literature continues to increase and is occasionally reviewed in the *Annual Review of Information Science and Technology*.

Since the creation of quality indexes has been covered in preceding chapters, it is unnecessary to repeat here the discussion of errors that are to be avoided in indexing. This chapter, therefore, seeks to provide a guide, a set of criteria, to be used by indexers, publishers, and readers in evaluating indexes. The criteria have been selected from the literature and supplemented and organized, so far as possible, into a set of questions that an evaluator might reasonably ask in judging the quality of an index. Measures are suggested for some of these criteria.

In considering procedures for evaluation, we distinguish between "criteria concepts" and "criteria measures" (Evans, Borko, and Ferguson, 1972). Criteria concepts are aspects of the index being evaluated, for example, the size and structure of the index. Criteria measures are the techniques, data, and calculations used to quantify these concepts, for example, using the number of entries in the index as a measure of size; and using the number of entries per book page as a measure of indexing density.

14.1 CRITERIA FOR EVALUATING BOOK INDEXES

The Committee on Ethics, Standards, and Specifications of the American Society of Indexers (ASI) prepared drafts of criteria for the evaluation of indexes, prior to producing a set of accepted guidelines. Although not all of these have been approved by the members of the ASI as yet, the drafts provide a basis for the following list of criteria.

1. *General*
   a. Type:
      What kinds of indexes are provided?
      Is one of the indexes a subject or a concept index?
      Are all indexes combined into one alphabet?
      Are other indexes needed, e.g., molecular-formula, report or patent-number, classified or taxonomic.

   b. Introduction:
      Does the index have an introduction?
      Is the introduction adequate?
      Does it contain examples?

   c. Size:
      What is the size of the index?
      Size may be measured by the number of entries; the number of subject headings; the number of lines; and the number of pages.

   d. Density:
      How many entries are there per page of text?
      What is the ratio of index pages to page of text?

e. Authority:
Are the subject headings those of the author?
Are they those of other indexes?
Are they from a thesaurus?
Is a nomenclature used?

f. Errors:
Are there any errors? Errors may be measured by the number of each kind or as a percentage of the total number of entries.

2. *Entry structure*

a. Modifications:
Do all entries have modifications of subheadings? Do these adequately define the subject indexed?
Use of modifications can be measured by dividing the number of entries by the number of modifications.
Does the index have blocks of undifferentiated references?
Lack of differentiation can be measured by the number of blocks of undifferentiated references; and the percentage of blocks of undifferentiated references based on the total number of references.

b. References:
Are there reference numbers that are in error? Reference errors can be evaluated by calculating the percentage of errors based on the total number of entries. The number of errors can be determined by sampling.

c. Ambiguity of entry:
Are ambiguous headings used?
Are ambiguous abbreviations used? For example, APA can stand for the American Psychiatric Association, the American Psychological Association, and the American Pharmacological Association, among others.
Are names of people given in full, e.g., "Miller, Henry John"? Or are they incomplete, e.g., "Miller, H. J." or just "Miller"?
The number of ambiguities can be counted and their percentage calculated.

d. Entries to nonsubjects:
Are entries restricted to subjects, or are concepts and words indexed as well?

Nonsubject entries in a sample can be counted and reported as the average number of nonsubject entries per page; and the percentage of nonsubject entries based on the total number of entries.

e. Omissions:
Is there indexable material that is not indexed?
The number of omissions in a sample of indexed pages can be counted and recorded as a percentage of the total number of entries on those pages.

f. Specificity:
Are subjects indexed at the maximum level of specificity?
Is there posting-up?
The number of entries lacking specificity in a sample of indexed pages can be counted and recorded as a percentage of the total number of entries in the sample.

g. Scattering:
Are entries on related subjects scattered among headings?
Are modifications of related subjects scattered under the same subject headings?
Scattering can be measured during editing by counting the number of transfers (thrown cards); it can be expressed as a percentage based on the total number of entries.

3. *Syndetic system*

a. Cross-references:
What kinds of cross-references are used? Examples are *see, see also, see under, use, use for, broader term, narrower term, related term.*
How many cross-references are used?
The percentage of cross-references can be calculated on the basis of the total number of entries. Percentages of each kind of cross reference can also be calculated, but this is seldom warranted.

b. Duplicate entry:
Is duplicate entry used in lieu of cross-references?
Duplicate entries can be found by sampling or during editing and reported as a percentage of the total number of entries. This percentage can be compared with the percentage of *see* cross-references.

c. Blind cross-references:
How many blind cross-references (cross-references leading to nonexistent headings) are there?

Blind cross-references can be calculated as a percentage of either the total number of cross-references or the total number of entries.

d. Glosses (parenthetical synonyms, definitions, explanations, "scope notes"):
What percentage of the headings have glosses?
The number of glosses in a sample of headings can be counted and calculated as a percentage of the number of headings in the sample. Glosses can be interfiled with the entries or presented separately in a thesaurus or in some other way.

e. Inversions:
Are inversions used in headings to bring together related entries?
Are inversions used in modifications for the same purpose?
Headings and modifications with inversions can be counted and calculated as a percentage of the total number of headings and modifications, respectively.

4. *Typography*
See Criterion No. 2 in Section 14.3.

14.2 CRITERIA FOR EVALUATING INDEXES TO SERIAL LITERATURE

The evaluation of indexes to the serial literature is, in general, no different from that for indexes to other kinds of literature; however, the type of literature may affect the form of the index.

The following list of criteria for evaluating indexes to the serial literature has been influenced by similar lists in Winchell (1967) and Katz (1969) for determining the value of published indexes to periodicals.

1. *General*

a. Instructions:
Are instructions provided on organization and use?
Are the instructions adequate, and are sample searches included?

b. Scope:
What is the specific subject field covered?
How many periodicals are covered?

Is there, in each issue, a list of the periodicals covered? In each volume?
Are works other than articles covered, e.g., books, reports, patents, etc.?
How many languages are indexed?
Is there serious overlap with other indexes?

c. Abbreviations:
Is there a list of authorized abbreviations?

2. *Duration, Frequency, and Promptness*
   a. Duration:
   For how many years has the series of indexes been in existence?
   What significant changes have occurred in the content and form of the index over the years?

   b. Frequency and promptness:
   How frequently is the index published, e.g., monthly, annually?
   Are there accumulations? What is their period?
   What is the time lag between the appearance of an article and the entries to it in the index?
   Is issue regular?

3. *Completeness of Coverage*
   a. Coverage:
   Are all articles indexed?
   Are items other than articles indexed, e.g., book reviews, obituaries, notes, notices?

   b. Basis for selection:
   Is the basis for selection of materials to be indexed fully explained?

4. *Quality of Indexes* (See also the criteria for evaluating book indexes.)
   a. Type:
   What kinds of indexes are there, e.g., subject, author, title, classified?
   Are all indexes merged into one alphabet?
   Is letter-by-letter or word-by-word alphabetization used? Is this choice explained?

   b. Density:
   What is the average number of index entries used per article or abstract?

c. Authority:
Are the author's terms used in the index?
Is a thesaurus or subject-authority list used?
How frequently is the thesaurus or list updated?

d. Completeness of entry:
Are authors' names given in full or are initials used? Is the form consistent?
How are identical names distinguished from one another?
Are all of the co-authors indexed?
Is the full title used as the modification?
For languages other than English, is the title in the original language, transliterated, and/or translated?
Are titles of periodicals given verbatim; if abbreviations are used, are they intelligible? unambiguous?
Are numbers (volume, issue, date, and inclusive pages) given, and is the form consistent?
Are other data noted (e.g., illustrations, maps, number of references)?
Are there cross references; are they adequate?
Are there errors?

5. *Quality of the Printed Index*
See Section 14.3.

14.3 CRITERA FOR EVALUATING THE PRINTING OF INDEXES

It is desirable to evaluate the quality of printing and paper of the finished index, and to consider the value received for the price paid. These variables make the index easy or difficult to use and to own.

There are user studies of preferences regarding format (Drage, 1969; Lancaster, 1971; Gould, 1974), and these may be of use in designing indexes. Typography has been evaluated by Wicklen (1958) and by Spencer, Reynolds, and Coe (1975). In 1975, an international study institute on the design and evaluation of printed subject indexes was held in Aberystwth, Wales (Keen, 1975). The results of these and other studies are incorporated into the following list of criteria for evaluating the printing of indexes. Choices are effectively made by the publisher, printer, and indexer in matters of quality; the purchaser and user may have no choice, since the index may be the only one available.

1. *Paper* (in the case of separately printed indexes)
   a. Page size and quality:
      Is the page size convenient to handle?
      Is the paper durable (low-acid)?
      Is the paper sufficiently opaque?
      Is there glare from the paper?
      Is the index bound sturdily and attractively?
   b. Columns and margins:
      Is the page divided into more than two columns?
      Are the columns separated by a rule or white space?
2. *Typography*
   a. Type size and style:
      What is the type size?
      Is the typeface pleasing and complementary to that of the text?
      How much lead is there between lines?
      Are different typefaces used effectively?
   b. Layout:
      Are modifications indented or run-on?
      Is there space between alphabetical groups of entries, and are the letters of the alphabet used to label these groups?
      Are the various components of index entries distinguishable one from another?
3. *Price*
   The price of an index may limit its distribution and use.
   Is the price about equivalent to that of comparable indexes?
   Can the subject area be covered by another index or set of indexes?
   Will the value derived from use justify the cost?

14.4 CRITERIA FOR EVALUATING BIBLIOGRAPHIC DATA BASES

Indexes to bibliographic data bases in computer files are evaluated by criteria different from those for printed indexes. Entry structure in the file is of little concern to the user. There are no modifications; subheadings are rarely used. The headings have large blocks of undifferentiated references. Cross-references, rarely included in the index, are generally in a thesaurus external to the index—if there is a thesaurus. Bibliographic data bases are not standard. For data bases to the primary literature, the reference must include the name(s) of author(s); the title of the work; the language; the name of the journal or a report number and code; and numbers for the volume, issue, series, inclusive pagination, and year. Some data bases may have indexer-assigned terms based on author usage or they may have headings selected from a thesaurus or an authorized subject-heading list. BIOSIS includes a taxonomic index. ERIC uses both "descriptors" and "identifiers" as headings. The descriptors are carried in a thesaurus; the identifiers are not. Identifiers are highly specific terms, such as trade names, the name of a school, or the name of a test.

Some data bases include no preassigned headings; retrieval is by matching words in the title with words of the searcher or by search of abstracts and author names.

Multiple-word terms may or may not be allowed in indexing and in search. For example, **Automatic indexing** may be a subject heading in some data bases while others require that **Automatic** be "ANDED" with **Indexing.**

In more sophisticated systems, stems of terms can be used. That is, words can be truncated by the removal of suffixes and sometimes of prefixes as well. For example, the truncated index heading, **Program$** is equivalent, in search, to: **Program**, **Programs**, **Programmer**, **Programmers**, **Programming**, etc. The dollar sign is used to indicate, in the computer program, that truncation is desired.

Rather than suggesting criteria to evaluate the data base itself, emphasis has been placed on determining the effectiveness of the index in retrieving references relevant to the search—effectiveness as judged by the searcher. This kind of evaluation was developed by Cyril Cleverdon in the Cranfield experiments (Cleverdon, 1962, 1967), as was the use of recall and precision as evaluation criteria.

The two ratios, recall and precision, are the most important measures in evaluating retrieval effectiveness. However, a number of other variables, such as cost (Kollin and Harris, 1968) and accuracy (Bourne, 1976) need to be used in the evaluation of computer-based systems as well as of printed indexes. Since data-base systems are primarily for the serial literature, many of the criteria given earlier for evaluating indexes to the serial literature are also appropriate.

The following is a list of criteria for evaluating the index characteristics and index quality of bibliographic retrieval systems.

1. *General*
   a. Type:
      What kinds of indexes (author, subject, title, etc.) are there?

Is the vocabulary controlled by the author or by a thesaurus?
Are subjects, concepts, or words indexed?

b. Size:
How many entries are there?
How many subject headings are there?

c. Vocabulary:
Is the vocabulary hospitable to new terms?
How frequently is it updated?

d. Arrangement:
Is the file direct or inverted?
Is the file accessible on-line or batch mode or both?
Can subject headings be listed on-line?

2. *Search*

a. Correlation:
Must the words of multiple-word terms be correlated?
Can both single words and multiple-word terms be used?
What Boolean operators are available?
What level of nesting is allowable?

b. Truncation:
Can truncated terms be used on search?

c. Vocabulary:
Is a subject-heading authority list or thesaurus used?
Are portions of the vocabulary displayed on request?

d. Accuracy:
What percentage of subject headings are misspelled?
What percentage of references are incorrect?
What percentage of entries guide to concepts and words, rather than to subjects?

e. Symbol-string searching:
Can search be by a free (uncontrolled) vocabulary as well as by preassigned subject headings?
Can text as well as title be searched?

15 Indexer Qualifications and Training

Indexing can be fascinating and challenging. It has certainly been an enjoyable vocation for the authors of this text, one of whom has had 40 years of experience with indexing, indexers, and indexing organizations. Indexing in one's area of specialization is stimulating and rewarding; it is a way of keeping up with the current literature in that area. Reference librarians, next to scientists and scholars, are probably the largest single group of index users. Indexers and librarians are allied, in that both work with the record of knowledge, and both guide searchers to relevant references. The interdependence of librarianship and indexing is recognized by the teaching of indexing in some library schools; it should be taught more extensively.

The basic concepts of indexing and the structure of indexes are applicable to many subject fields. This chapter deals only with the acquisition of indexing skills. It starts with an examination of the traits and characteristics that are desirable in indexers, then reports on the educational and training programs that are available prior to and during employment, and as continuing professional education.

15.1 INDEXER CHARACTERISTICS

Indexing is a complex decision process involving perceptual discrimination, concept formation, and problem solving. Indexers select specific subjects reported by the author; paraphrase the subject *via* words that guide to the broad subject areas; select terms from the paraphrases that best guide to them; translate the selected terms, if necessary, into standard subject headings; coin modifications; note the references; and make cross-references where necessary. To make the correct decisions, the indexer should, preferably, know the subject field, either by education or by experience. Bernier and others have repeatedly stressed the importance of knowledge of the subject being indexed (Bernier, 1974). Some employers recognize the value of specialized education and pay indexers with a doctorate more than are those with a lower degree. The higher salary is cost-effective because the Ph.D. will nearly always accomplish more work with fewer serious errors than will indexers with less formal education.

Motivation is another trait that is almost universally stressed. The productive indexer is seen to be interested in the subject field and in indexing. Dedication (related to motivation) may develop when indexers understand that, by indexing and providing guidance to the literature, they are making a great contribution to their chosen field.

Indexers should have a good command of English, and for some subjects, for example, medicine, they should also be proficient in Latin. Knowledge of foreign languages is essential if English-language abstracts are not exclusively used as the basis for indexing.

An experimental study (Oliver, 1966), funded by the National Science Foundation, sought to investigate the basic processes involved in the manual indexing of scientific documents and the qualifications and traits of good indexers. Data were collected by means of questionnaires completed by 64 indexers and 24 index supervisors in 22 organizations. Each index supervisor was asked to rate the "best" indexer and also one who was regarded as "not so good." Both rating forms were to be completed at the same time in order to identify differences between the good and not-so-good indexers.

More than 30 indexer characteristics were studied. In each case it was hypothesized that there would be statistically significant differences between Type 1 indexers (good ones) and Type 2 indexers (not-so-good ones). It was found that fewer than one-third of the variables differentiated significantly between the two types of indexers. As judged by indexing supervisory personnel, the following traits characterized good indexers:

1. A higher indexing rate
2. A greater flair for indexing
3. A higher reading rate
4. A greater familiarity with search techniques
5. A greater familiarity with user information requests
6. Work preferences more related to documentation
7. Greater age
8. More reading and less scanning while indexing
9. Less difficulty in understanding the material indexed

Some variables that did *not* distinguish the good from the not-so-good indexers were:

1. Interest in indexing: Most indexers of both types were rated as having either high or medium interest in indexing.
2. Motivation: All indexers were judged to be highly motivated.
3. Error rate: Most indexers (80%) were judged to be low or very low in error rate.
4. Absentee rate: Very few indexers (only 6%) were rated medium or high in absentee rate.
5. Familiarity with indexing techniques.
6. Familiarity with subject matter.
7. Industriousness.

These variables distinguish people who become indexers from those who do not; but they do not—in this study—distinguish between good and not-so-good indexers. One possible reason for these results is that all of the indexers were reasonably good. It is unlikely that a really unsatisfactory indexer would continue to be employed in these organizations.

The responses of the indexers differed somewhat from the ratings of the supervisory personnel. The following is a list of indexer qualifications, in no particular order of importance, derived from an analysis of indexer responses.

1. Educational background
2. Breadth of knowledge
3. Depth of knowledge
4. Interest
5. Motivation
6. Judgment
7. Experience in subject field
8. Experience in related fields
9. Indexing experience

10. Thesaurus familiarity
11. Direct user contact
12. Appreciation of user viewpoints
13. Knowledge of user current requests

Employed indexers apparently believe that an indexer needs knowledge, interest, motivation, experience, and an appreciation of the needs of the index user. This belief is consistent with the experience of the authors of this work.

15.2 EDUCATION AND TRAINING

Indexers need a good general education, advanced subject knowledge, and specialized knowledge about indexes and indexing. Whenever possible, these general educational requirements should be completed while at a college or university and before employment. Indexing skills are taught both at the university and in indexing organizations.

15.2.1 Learning at School

Courses in indexing are taught in university library schools. Librarians study subject analysis, cataloging, and classification; indexing is another, more detailed, level of subject analysis and it is a useful library skill. Reference librarians use indexes to guide patrons to the information they seek, and the more the librarian knows about indexes and the publications of the abstracting and indexing services, the better will be the guidance provided. Special librarians should know how to index, for their job frequently requires the preparation of indexes to special materials. Some special librarians work as freelance indexers.

College students in all majors can benefit from courses in indexing, for a knowledge of reference tools improves a student's ability to locate and use the indexes found in libraries, as well as book and journal indexes. Learning about indexes should increase the percentage of recall of relevant material in a collection and also increase the percentage of relevance of the material recalled.

Study of the principles of indexing is necessary to promote better indexing and design of indexes. Proof that students understand the principles is demonstrated by their application. Students must index. In some indexing courses, students are given the option of creating an "external memory," a collection of indexed abstracts for their personal use. In preparing this memory, students learn by abstracting and indexing works of value to them. The abstracts are filed in serial-number order, and the serial number is used as the reference in the indexes, which are made up of 3- × 5-in. cards filed by subject heading. Author-index cards are interfiled with the subject-index cards. It is anticipated that the external memory will be maintained throughout the students' professional careers.

Some courses in indexing require students to index a book, or a significant part thereof, and then to compare their work with that of other students, that of the instructor and the published book index.

Other assignments in indexing courses include

1. Preparation of several kinds of indexes, e.g., subject, KWIC, precorrelative, and postcorrelative for the same work and a comparison of the advantages and disadvantages of each
2. Indexing of articles and reports in library and information science, for the library of the school
3. Indexing student-selected articles and then comparing student entries with those created by a professional indexing service, such as ERIC
4. Indexing a collection for a faculty member

Programmed instructions, with appropriate exercises to provide practice, have been developed to:

1. Identify subjects
2. Select terms leading to the subjects
3. Paraphrase the subjects
4. Translate, where necessary, the selected terms into standard index headings
5. Coin modifications
6. Write cross-references

The importance of practice cannot be overemphasized. Indexing is learned by doing, and it should be required in every indexing course.

15.2.2 Learning at Work

Indexing and abstracting services always provide training for newly hired indexers. Employees of adequate subject background are sought because they index faster and make fewer and less serious errors. Relatively few new employees have a general knowledge of how to index.

15.2.2.1 *Coaching*

All new indexers work with an experienced indexer of the organization, called a coach. The coach checks the work of the novice, makes changes as necessary (the word *error* is avoided), and shows the changes to the trainee as soon after the indexing as possible. The trainee is given every opportunity to discuss all changes as well as the general principles of indexing with the coach. It should be noted that, in a formal educational setting such as a university, the coaching of students is also feasible for small classes; in large classes, the students can be advised to work together in or outside of class, share experiences, and bring unresolved differences to the instructor for resolution. Working together provides opportunity for effective group interaction and feedback, such as is found in working for a publisher.

Coaches may change as many as 75% of a new indexer's first index cards; 50 to 65% is common. To speed finding of the changed cards, they may be indicated with paper clips to identify them clearly in a drawer of cards. The large number of changes will not be discouraging if the coach explains that this is expected and that learning is speeded by the coach explaining all changes to the new indexer. New indexers commonly overindex or underindex. The coach creates the omitted entries, shows them to the trainee, and discusses the reasons for the extra entries. Some entries prepared by the new indexer may lead to concepts, topics, and words, rather than to subjects reported by the author. The coach crosses out these entries and takes the opportunity to explain precisely why this is necessary. At first, the abbreviations and the format are frequently incorrect; these are corrected and shown to the learner, often without comment. It has been found unsatisfactory to give the new indexer a drawer of clipped cards *without* explaining the changes; many changes cannot be understood without explanation.

At the start, modifications are usually not specific enough; the coach adds words to increase the specificity, explains how to estimate the degree of specificity required, and even why, in a given instance, more specificity is needed. Sometimes modifications are redundant or too specific. Again, the coach has the opportunity to show how to eliminate redundancy and superfluous specificity. The words used to begin some modifications may be injudicious; the coach reorders the modifications, shows the new order to the trainee, and gives the reason for the changed order. Discussions are reassuring to the learner and give the coach the opportunity to improve his or her knowledge of the subject matter indexed and skill in indexing and in teaching.

15.2.2.2 *Training Aids*

The training of indexers can be expedited by aids. This volume is an example of such an aid, as are publishers' manuals. In teaching and in the use of aids, the attitude of the coach is important. Mutual exploration (in a kindly, relaxed way) is effective. Treating all changes as tentative suggestions open to discussion also serves the purpose of keeping the beginner relaxed and of focusing on the reasons behind the changes. No change made by the coach should be arbitrary; reasons, where not obvious, should be available, and they should be given where requested.

Since the trainee is required to use the accepted abbreviations in all cases, a list of the standard abbreviations used in the index is an aid that expedites training. Cardboard backing of the list facilitates reading, handling, and filing for ready use.

Card files of decisions made by the trainee with or without the help of the coach have been found to be useful in maintaining consistency. Such a card file is also useful in reviewing earlier decisions upon which both trainee and coach have agreed. Writing the decision on the card (usually 3 × 5 in.) fixes the decision in the memory of the trainee better than does mere discussion and observation of the changed card. Also, making and filing decision cards gives the trainee further experience in indexing; success or failure in finding a decision filed earlier will depend on indexing skill.

A most effective training aid is the indexing of material for an index that is to be published. The prospect of publication and of the usefulness of the published index makes the indexer take the work more seriously because all uncorrected errors will appear in the printed index. Indexers like to participate in real-life situations and not just to train for participation.

If it is the organization's practice for indexing to be dictated, it is important for the trainee to start with a dictating machine so that its use becomes an integral part of the training.

Programmed instructions have been found useful in launching the novice indexer, and a number of such programs are available.

15.2.3 Continuing Education

It is necessary for the indexer to keep up with advances in the field of indexing. As new equipment and techniques become available, the indexer should learn about these. It is, for example, important for indexers to know how computers can be used in the production of concordances and other indexes. Newer techniques and better procedures are being developed to make indexing more efficient. The indexer with a professional interest in indexing needs to become aware of developments. This learning is part of being a professional—of professing to know.

Continuing education in indexing is obtainable through short formal courses offered by universities and by professional societies. The meetings of the Society of Indexers are devoted entirely to discussions of indexing problems and techniques. In addition, the American Society for Information Science, the Medical Library Association, the Special Libraries Association, and other organizations devote part of their annual meeting program to indexing. Indexers are well advised to attend these courses and meetings and to talk shop with other indexers. These encounters are both educational and enjoyable.

16 Indexing as a Profession

Although indexing is an old profession—it may have started millennia ago with the filing of cuneiform clay cones or tablets—the first professional organization of indexers was founded only in 1957. From ancient times to the present, the number of items to be indexed has increased at an exponential rate. Guidance to the accumulating record has become ever more extensive. Indexing procedures have been greatly improved in the last century and been made more uniform. Indexing practices currently considered acceptable have been described in this volume. Further improvements, for example, in computer-aided indexing, should continue to be researched.

Librarians seeking to organize works for efficient storage and for efficient retrieval are guided by the Anglo-American Cataloging Rules, a set of procedures on how to catalog and a standard or criterion by which specific cataloging tasks can be measured. Unquestionably, the acceptance of the Anglo-American Cataloging Rules has furthered the practice of librarianship. For indexing to make similar advances, a formal set of indexing standards may be needed.

16.1 THE RISE OF PROFESSIONAL INDEXER SOCIETIES

G. Norman Knight, who founded the Society of Indexers in Great Britain, stated that the need for such a society first occurred to him when he realized that he was not acquainted with anyone else who worked as an indexer. With the launching in July of 1957 of the Society of Indexers, the publication in 1958 of *The Indexer*, the official journal of the society (Knight, 1958), and the increase in organizational activities, the feelings of isolation among indexers faded.

The constitution of the society gives as its objectives:

a. to improve the standard of indexing and to secure some measure of uniformity in technique;
b. to maintain panels of indexers in all fields from which authors, editors, publishers, and others may be furnished with suitable names on application;
c. to act as an advisory body on the qualification and remuneration of indexers to which authors, editors, publishers, and others may apply for guidance;
d. to publish and communicate from time to time books, papers, and notes on the subject of indexing;
e. to raise the status of indexers and to safeguard their interests.

Stimulated by the success of the Society of Indexers and by the belief that U.S. indexers also could benefit by organization, a group of U.S. indexers and teachers of indexing met in New York City in 1968 to form the American Society of Indexers (ASI). This organization was founded in 1969 and elected Alan R. Greengrass as president pro-tem. The ASI has close liaison with the British society and shares the journal, *The Indexer*. The statement of purpose is similar to that of the Society of Indexers, but the ASI has added:

- To cooperate with other societies in the field of indexing, librarianship, and information science
- To provide for information exchange concerning methods and developments in the field of indexing, and
- To promote higher standards and to encourage education in the field

Both societies provide a structure within which indexers can meet, discuss common problems, and become acquainted. It is interesting to note that the first items of new business discussed at the initial meeting of the ASI were standards, evaluative measures, and the remuneration of indexers (Harris, 1969). These are still topics of concern.

The ASI has regular, institutional, and honorary members. Life membership may also be granted by vote of the regular members at a general meeting. The annual general meeting usually takes place in April. The normal complement of officers—president, president-elect, treasurer, secretary, and corresponding secretary—together with a board of directors, manages the affairs of the society between meetings.

Much of the professional work of the society is carried on by the committees on membership; programs; ethics, standards and specifications; nonprint media; certification of indexers; publisher–indexer relations; getting started as an indexer; chapters; and indexer economics.

16.2 ETHICAL CONSIDERATIONS

Interactions among indexers, index publishers, and searchers have raised questions of ethics. To deal with these issues the ASI established the Committee on Ethics, Standards, and Specifications as well as the Committee on Publisher-Indexer Relations.

16.2.1 Aims and Conduct

Professional indexers index for a livelihood. In order for them to earn a living, the indexes produced must be at or above a certain level of excellence. The fact that many of the qualities of indexes are subtle places a premium on ethical conduct. In practice, maintenance of quality means reducing errors in the index to as close to zero as is possible. To do this, the indexer must be aware of likely errors and know how to prevent and remove them.

Ethical indexers aim to reduce the load on the searcher to a minimum. Lack of knowledge about indexes by searchers is compensated by the skill of the indexer. Poor indexing, as has been pointed out throughout this book but may be usefully repeated here, results in load on the user, especially in the form of:

- Missed guidance to relevant references and possibly being held responsible for the missed references
- Insufficient guidance within the index

- Having to search for incorrect references
- Having to solve unnecessary puzzles
- Finding guidance to concepts, topics, and words rather than to subjects; and
- Having to decipher special nomenclatures

Professional indexers ideally produce the best indexes possible and still seek ways to improve them. They resist degrading index quality through untried innovations while welcoming improvements in printing, automation, and format—after these have been tested and shown clearly to be superior. Indexers keep up in their subject fields—perhaps better than others in the same fields because they read all of the latest material. They also keep up in the developments in indexing, such as the dictation of index entries and the use of computers as indexing aids. Keeping up in one's profession is an ethical responsibility that indexers observe.

Indexers maintain professional relations with publishers and participate in the design, testing, and implementation of improvements in indexing and indexes. They accept useful advice, guidance, and suggestions from users as well as publishers. As the process of building indexes has become clearer and more widely known, it has become more obvious what indexes actually are and how much better they can be made. The conduct and skill of professional indexers can lead to the production of indexes that more and more closely approach the ideal. Of course, not all indexes meet the ideal.

16.2.2 A Code of Ethics

"An index is intended to provide accurate and complete guidance to the type of material specified in the title of the index. Hence, indexers and index publishers have an obligation to provide, within specified limitations, such an index." This statement was authorized to be published by the American Society of Indexers as a result of the work of its Committee on Ethics, Standards, and Specifications (1975). The statement is a good introduction to the subject of ethics in indexing. It has been recommended by the ASI that *how* the "specified limitations" affect the use of the index be described in the introduction, in instructions on the use of the index, and in advertising about the index. This recommendation was necessitated by the fact that unspecified limitations can have a drastic effect on recall percentage as well as on whether or not the index is useful for a given search. It is ethical to be accurate, frank, and honest in matters that affect the purchasers and users of indexes: It is ethical to detail the limitations of indexes that affect their use. It is ethical to be careful not to take advantage of naive users.

Several of the qualities of indexes are subtle and difficult to observe. Omitted entries are generally invisible. Entries not leading to subjects, for example, those leading to concepts, topics, or words, can often be detected only by looking up the entries. Searchers may be puzzled to discover that the references to which they have been guided by the index are unrelated to the subjects studied and reported by the authors. Another subtle characteristic is that of the scattering of related entries among synonyms, antonyms, and terms related in other ways, or among modifications under a heading.

Because of the subtlety of some of the qualities of indexes, it is entirely up to the indexer to protect the user against loss of references on search and against having to expend extra time and effort in using the index. It is an ethical responsibility of the index publisher to support the indexer in this effort. Support of index quality may add to the cost; however, it is the combined responsibility of the indexing and publishing professions to convince libraries and individuals that the quality is worth the price. Users, in general, appreciate quality, so this task is not too difficult. *Caveat emptor* (let the buyer beware) is as shortsighted a policy for indexes as it is for quality jewelry or any quality product.

Ethical responsibilities, specified by the ASI for indexers, index publishers, and index users can be paraphrased as follows:

For Indexers:

- To index only in subject areas in which the indexer is qualified
- To plan, specify, and maintain the quality of the index
- To accomplish the work in a professional manner
- To reduce scattering of like entries in the index
- To have each entry provide guidance to all relevant material in the work that might logically be subsumed in the work under the heading for that entry
- To specify the user's responsibility to compensate for scattering, for example, among synonyms and modifications
- To inform the searcher as to where to find expected material that is not in a logical place
- To supply cross-references and other syndetic devices in or with the index, and to inform the user, in the absence of syndetics,

as to the searcher's responsibilities for compensating for their absence

For Publishers:

- To evaluate the effect of the plan for the index upon the user so that the user can avoid loss of data, money, and time
- To state clearly all of the index's specifications in advertising, catalogs, and documentation of the index
- To specify all precautions necessary for the effective use of the index

For Users:

- To study and to understand the structure and organization of the index so that it will be used as intended
- To report deficiencies to indexers and index publishers as well as to other users via media that report on indexes and indexing

For Both Indexers and Publishers:

- To bring relevant prospective changes in indexing policy to the attention of the user, preferably before implementation
- To entitle indexes accurately, clearly, and succinctly so that, for example, "Title–Word Concordance" is used, rather than "Subject Index," if this is correct, and not to imply that the two kinds of index are equivalent
- To provide errata (a list of errors in the index) and to bring these to the attention of the user through inserts, cumulations, the next edition, or reprints, or in the next index of the series

It is important that professional people have and maintain high ethical standards in order to ensure the integrity of, and confidence in, the work that they do. Ethical considerations are especially important when the quality of the work or product is subtle, as in indexing. Only when all three of the prinicipals involved in the production and use of indexes accept their responsibilities can the quality of indexes approach the desired ideal.

16.3 ECONOMIC CONSIDERATIONS

In addition to promoting higher professional standards and ethical behavior, the American Society of Indexers is concerned with the economic aspects of indexing, including employment, pay scales, and helping new indexers to get started in the profession. On request, the society will help to adjudicate any differences that may arise between publisher and indexer. All of these functions are the proper responsibilities of a professional society.

16.3.1 Employment Opportunities

One of the appealing aspects of indexing is that both full-time and part-time employment opportunities are available. Indexing can be a satisfying full-time profession and an equally satisfying part-time avocation. Librarians are especially advised to become cognizant of opportunities as indexers. Some organizations, such as special libraries, prefer to hire as indexers, librarians who are qualified in a particular subject area as well as being trained librarians. This is sensible, because librarians with MLS or equivalent degrees do have an undergraduate subject background. In addition, graduate education in librarianship ensures competence in cataloging, classification, bibliography, and reference services, much of which involves the use of indexes. Also, employers may find it advisable to hire librarians as indexers because most indexes and bibliographic data bases are sold to, or used by, libraries and their supporting organizations; employers benefit by having on their staffs those who know the problems and needs of libraries.

Indexers are employed by (*a*) publishers, (*b*) abstracting and indexing services, (*c*) special libraries, (*d*) research organizations, and (*e*) information-analysis centers. Indexers may also be self-employed as free-lance entrepreneurs.

16.3.1.1 *Book Publishers*

Publishers of technical, trade, and text books must see to it that their publications are properly indexed. Some publishers employ indexers as full-time members of the staff; often they do so in order to ensure quality as well as compatibility among all indexes to a set of volumes. For example, the *Encyclopaedia Britannica* employed more than two dozen indexers to prepare the *Propaedia*. Since this index is continually being updated, the work is ongoing, not temporary.

Most of the indexing in book-publishing houses is part-time. The author may be required by the contract to provide the index. If the author does not wish to (or cannot) index the book, the publisher will hire an indexer, and the cost may be paid out of the author's royalties. The publisher keeps a card file of indexers, alphabetized by subject and language competence. Some publishers may hire an indexer on a retainer basis, for example, $5000 per year. By this, the publisher guarantees to provide the part-time indexer with a certain minimum of work during the year. In return, the indexer agrees to give retainer work priority and to meet the publisher's deadlines. Obviously, if more than the minimum amount of work is done, the indexer receives additional pay. This arrangement appears to benefit both the publisher and the indexer.

16.3.1.2 *Abstracting and Indexing Services*

Secondary or surrogate publications provide access to the primary literature—mostly that part of the literature contained in journal articles and technical reports. The publishing organizations that undertake this work generally employ full-time indexers and index editors. In some organizations, the same person may function as abstract editor, indexer, and index editor at different stages of the publication process, necessitating subject knowledge as well as editing and indexing skills.

In addition to full-time employees, surrogate publishers may use the services of part-time people, both paid and voluntary. Volunteers are those who have full-time employment, for example in libraries and universities, but who undertake such work because it promotes their profession, is interesting, and provides an opportunity to keep up with the current literature. For specialized subject expertise or language competence, the organization may employ part-time indexers.

16.3.1.3 *Other Employers*

Librarians and subject specialists are often employed to index the collections of special libraries, research organizations, and information analysis centers and prepare bibliographies, abstracts, and technical reports. While librarians do much more than index, an extensive knowledge of indexing is desirable.

16.3.1.4 *Free-Lance Indexing*

Organizations that need indexers only for special projects employ free-lance indexers. Other organizations use free-lance indexers for most or all of their regular indexing. Free-lance indexers are in business for themselves; they sell their indexing skills on the open market. Getting started requires no capital investment beyond the cost of the education and training, plus a typewriter and some stationery. Book publishers, some publishers of abstract journals, research organizations, industrial firms, authors, scholars, and others sometimes need a book, journal, or collection to be indexed; they employ free-lancers.

16.3.2 Pay Scales

Starting salaries for full-time indexers working in publishing houses, libraries, and research organizations are about the same as for the beginning librarian. In highly technical fields, say chemistry, the starting salary may be about that of chemists starting in the laboratory. In addition to salary, the full-time employee qualifies for the usual fringe benefits: vacations, health insurance, and retirement. Some organizations have an educational program and encourage their employees to continue (or complete) their education at local universities or by correspondence, and by attendance at conventions, institutes, seminars, and symposia. The employer pays at least a part of the cost. Employers benefit by not having their employees become obsolescent.

The pay scale for part-time and free-lance work is more difficult to determine. The *Newsletter* of the American Society of Indexers (June 1973) supplied some interesting statistics on charges for book indexes. These are worth quoting in full.

> Based on data from 83 free-lance jobs, it was determined that the average book indexed was 282 pages in length, for which an index of 1045 lines was produced at a price of $304.69. The typical index contained 3.7 lines of index per book page indexed; for such jobs, indexers charged an average of $1.08 per book page, or 29.1¢ per index line. The typical grade level of these jobs is 1st-year college or general trade. About 75% of indexes are submitted as typed manuscripts (rather than on cards), and over 90% are analytical indexes (with subentries). The average deadline for such jobs is 2 weeks, during which time the indexer puts in 50 to 60 hours. Since the labor component of these jobs is about $300 (after deducting a small amount for cash expenses), indexers are presumably earning $5 to $6 per hour.

Additional data from the *Newsletter* are:

- The least price paid for an index was $35; the highest was $500
- The smallest index had 200 lines; the largest had 4300 lines
- The smallest book indexed was 88 pages; the largest was 800 pages
- The lowest educational level was seventh grade; the highest was college postgraduate
- The shortest deadline was 3 days; the longest 9 months

- The fewest number of jobs done annually by an indexer was 2; the most was 25
- The fewest publishers worked for by a single free-lancer during the year was one; the most was nine
- The lowest reported income from indexing was \$775; the highest was \$13,000
- Most free-lancers work by the hour plus expenses; the next most popular basis is a flat rate, set in advance; next is a rate per index line
- The lowest hourly rate at which work was billed was \$4 per hour; the highest was \$7
- The lowest line rate contracted for was 10¢ a line; the highest was 35¢

In summary, for book indexes, the average rate of pay can be stated as any one of the following:

\$5–6	per hour
\$0.25–0.30	per index line
\$1	per book page
\$300	per book

Clearly, these figures are meant only for guidance and are *not* a schedule of indexing rates. The reader should also allow for inflation since 1973.

16.3.3 Getting Started

Finding employment requires ingenuity, initiative, and an aggressive program. Advice is a poor substitute for dedication and determination, but the following are a few helpful ideas:

- Check the want ads, especially in *Publisher's Weekly* and in the large-circulation newspapers
- Place a "job wanted" ad in trade publications read by publishers and writers
- Write letters to publishers, including government agencies. Be specific in stating your qualifications; few people can "index everything." It is usually helpful to follow up on your letter with a personal phone call
- If you know (or can arrange to meet) the author of a book about to be published, convince her or him to let you index it. Also, have the author recommend you to the publisher

- The American Society of Indexers publishes a *Register of Indexers*, which is a list of members who accept free-lance indexing assignments. The Society of Indexers of Great Britain publishes a register of indexers selected for their qualifications by a panel of judges. The ASI also has a Committee on Getting Started as an Indexer

16.3.4 Indexer–Publisher Relations

As can happen in any employer–employee relation, there are occasional disagreements between the indexer and the publisher. It would be folly to try to list all possible areas in which disagreements could arise; however, major areas are (*a*) compensation; (*b*) schedules; (*c*) index size, style, and structure; and (*d*) recognition (inclusion or omission of a by-line). Dee Atkinson (1973) has pointed out that indexer–publisher relations are a two-way street. As happens when automobiles travel on a two-way street, there are occasional crashes and altercations. Some means is needed to adjudicate differences.

In the matter of compensation, publishers are generally willing to pay a fair price for indexing. Disagreements occur because most publishers, as well as most indexers, do not seem to know what indexers should be paid. For example, many people believe that short indexes should cost less than long indexes. However, some short indexes are more difficult and more time consuming to prepare than are some longer indexes. The ASI has collected some data (see Section 16.3.2) on how much indexers are actually paid. The ASI will, if requested, help indexers and publishers to reach a reasonable agreement.

Schedules are a very sensitive subject for both indexers and publishers. More communication between the parties is needed. Production schedules allow little leeway. However, if the printer falls behind in delivering page proofs, the indexer should not be expected to make up for the time lost by the printer. Nor is it right for the publisher to set the indexer's schedule shorter than it need be, nor to require the index to be delivered a few days before it is actually necessary.

Should the publisher have a preferred style for, say, indentation rather than run-on or in the matter of punctuation or of indexing illustrations and footnotes, then the indexer should be informed of these before the work is started. It is difficult and time consuming to make style changes in a partly completed index because many entries are interrelated.

Indexers are creative people; they like to receive recognition, in addition to pay, for the work they do. Indexers as well as authors should get a by-line or other acknowledgment. This recommendation is made in the foreword to the ANSI's *Basic Criteria for Indexes* (1968). Publishers generally send authors copies of reviews of their works. If the reviewer has mentioned the index as being noteworthy, the indexer would certainly also like to receive a copy of the review and would certainly also appreciate the thoughtfulness of the publisher.

Whereas the copyright of books and other media has received extensive coverage, the copyright of indexes is rarely mentioned. G. Norman Knight, founding president of the Society of Indexers of Great Britain, states the case very well. He contends that

> Any agreement between publisher and indexer, whether it be a written contract (as by the interchange of letters) or a vocal contract (as by telephone), applies to that particular publishing alone.
>
> Should the original publisher sell the right to reproduce the whole book to some independent publisher overseas or to a separate paperback publisher in this country who intends (as he probably will) to use the existing index, then I contend that, unless the index copyright has been assigned, the situation is changed; now the compiler is free either to arrange an assignment or else demand a copyright fee from the new publisher [Knight, 1972, 74].

In view of the interest generated on the subject of copyrighting indexes, the council of the society established a copyright subcommittee "to seek and obtain counsel's opinion on the subject [Society of Indexers, 1972, 82]." The conclusion was "that an index is the subject of copyright, independent from that in the appurtenant text (Society of Indexers, 1972, p. 86)." The legal counsel also suggests that questions about ownership of copyright be raised during negotiation of the contract between indexer and publisher. The indexer can, in writing, assign the copyright to the publisher, and may get some additional remuneration for so doing.

No comparable discussion of copyright for indexes in the United States or any other country could be located. Copyright, and many other of the topics of this chapter, are problem areas that a professional society can help to resolve for the benefit of its members and the entire professional community.

References

Aitchison, J., and Gilchrist, A. 1972. *Thesaurus Construction: A Practical Manual*, Aslib, London.

American National Standards Institute (formerly United States of America Standards Institute). 1968. *Basic Criteria for Indexes*, ANSI Z39.4, New York.

American National Standards Institute. 1974. *Guidelines for Thesaurus Structure, Construction, and Use*, ANSI Z39.19, New York.

American Society of Indexers. 1973. "Index finances," *Newsletter*, June 5.

American Society of Indexers. 1974. "Specifications for printed indexes," *The Indexer*, Vol. 9, No. 3, pp. 121–122.

American Society of Indexers, Committee on Ethics, Standards, and Specifications. 1975. *Ethics of Indexing*. Statement authorized for publication.

Angell, R. S. 1968. *Two Papers on Thesaurus Construction*, International Federation for Documentation, Committee on Classification Research, Report No. 8, Danish Center for Documentation, Copenhagen.

Armitage, J. E., and Lynch, M. F. 1968. "Some structural characteristics of articulated subject indexes," *Information Storage and Retrieval*, Vol. 4, No. 2, pp. 101–111.

Artandi, S. S. 1963. *Book Indexing by Computer*, Ph.D. dissertation, Graduate School of Library Service, Rutgers—The State University, New Brunswick, New Jersey.

Atkinson, D. 1973. "Indexer–publisher relations: A two-way street," *The Indexer*, Vol. 8, No. 3, pp. 172–174.

Austin, D. 1974a. *PRECIS: A Manual of Concept Analysis and Subject Indexing* Council of the British National Bibliography, London.

Austin, D. 1974b. "The development of PRECIS: A theoretical and technical history,' *Journal of Documentation*, Vol. 30, No. 1, pp. 47–102.

Austin, D., and Digger, J. A. 1977. "PRECIS: The preserved context index system,' *Library Resources and Technical Services*, Vol. 21, No. 1, pp. 13–30.

Bakewell, K. G. B. 1975. "The PRECIS Indexing System," *The Indexer*, Vol. 9, No. 4, pp. 160–166.

Barlow, H., and Morgenstern, S. 1948. *A Dictionary of Musical Themes*. Crown Publishers, New York.

Bernier, C. L. 1957. "Correlative indexes IV: Correlative chemical-group indexes," *American Documentation*, Vol. 8, No. 4, pp. 306–313.

Bernier, C. L. 1961. "New kinds of indexes." *Journal of Chemical Documentation*, Vol. 1, No. 1, pp. 62–67.

Bernier, C. L. 1964. "Correlative indexes X: Subject index qualities," *Journal of Chemical Documentation*, Vol. 4, No. 2, pp. 104–107.

Bernier, C. L. 1968. "Alphabetic indexes," *Encyclopedia of Library and Information Science*, Vol. 1, pp. 169–201. Marcel Dekker, New York.

Bernier, C. L. 1974. "Index specifications," *The Indexer*, Vol. 9, No. 3, pp. 9–12.

Bernier, C. L. 1976. "Microthesauri," *Encyclopedia of Library and Information Science*, Vol. 18, pp. 114–119. Marcel Dekker, New York.

Bernier, C. L., and Crane, E. J 1962. "Correlative indexes VIII: Subject-indexing *vs.* word-indexing," *Journal of Chemical Documentation*, Vol. 2, No. 2, pp. 117–122.

Bernier, C. L., Gill, W. N., and Hunt, R. G. 1975. "Measures of excellence of engineering and science departments: A chemical engineering example," *Chemical Engineering Education*, Vol. 9, No. 4, pp. 194–197, 204.

Bernier, C. L., and Heumann, K. F. 1957. "Correlative indexes III: Semantic relations among semantemes—the technical thesaurus," *American Documentation*, Vol. 8, No. 3, pp. 211–220.

Bernier, C. L., and Langham, C. C. 1955. "Dictating machines as indexing aids," *American Documentation*, Vol. 6, No. 4, pp. 237–238.

Blagden, J. F. 1968. "Thesaurus compilation methods: A literature review," *Aslib Proceedings*, Vol. 20, No. 8, pp. 345–359.

Borko, H. 1970. "Experiments in book indexing by computer," *Information Storage and Retrieval*, Vol. 6, No. 1, pp. 5–16.

Borko, H. (editor) 1967. *Automated Language Processing*, John Wiley & Sons, New York.

Borko, H., and Bernier, C. L. 1975. *Abstracting Concepts and Methods*, Academic Press, New York.

Bourne, C. P. 1966. "Evaluation of indexing systems," *Annual Review of Information Science and Technology*, Vol. 1, pp. 171–190.

Bourne, C. P. 1976. "Frequency and impact of spelling errors in bibliographic data bases," *Information Processing and Management*, Vol. 13, No. 1, pp. 1–12.

Brandenberg, W. 1963. "Write titles for machine index information retrieval systems," *Automation and Scientific Communication: Short Papers, Part 1* (H. P. Luhn, editor), American Documentation Institute, Washington, D.C., pp. 57–58.

British Standards Institute. 1976. *British Standard on Indexing. BS3700:1976; Preparation of Indexes of Books, Periodicals and Other Publications*. London.

Burt, C. 1959. *A Psychological Study of Typography*, Cambridge University Press, Cambridge.

Busa, R. 1971. "Concordances," *Encyclopedia of Library and Information Science*, Vol. 5, pp. 592–604. Marcel Dekker, New York.

Campbell, D. J. 1963. "Making your own indexing system in science and technology: Classification and keyword system," *Aslib Proceedings*, Vol. 15, No. 10, pp. 282–303.

Chomsky, N. 1956. "Three models for the description of language." *IRE* (Institute of Radio Engineers) *Transactions on Information Theory IT*-2, Vol. 2, No. 1, pp. 113–124.

Chomsky, N. 1957. *Syntactic Structures*, Mouton and Co., The Hague.

Citron, J., Hart, L., and Ohlman, H. 1958. *A Permutation Index to the Preprints of the International Conference on Scientific Information*, SP. 44, System Development Corporation, Santa Monica, California.

Cleverdon, C. W. 1962. *Report on the Testing and Analysis of an Investigation into the Comparative Efficiency of Indexing*. College of Aeronautics, Cranfield, England.

Cleverdon, C. W. 1967. "The Cranfield tests on index language devices, *Aslib Proceedings*, Vol. 19, No. 6, pp. 173–194.

Cohen, S. M., Dayton, D. L., and Salvador, R. 1976. "Experimental algorithmic generation of articulated index entries from natural language phrases at Chemical Abstracts Service," *Journal of Chemical Information and Computer Science*, Vol. 16, No. 2, pp. 93–99.

Drage, J. F. 1969. "User preferences in technical indexes," *The Indexer*, Vol. 6, No. 4, pp. 151–155.

Ellison, J. W. 1957. *Nelson's Complete Concordance of the Revised Standard Version Bible*, Thomas Nelson & Sons, New York.

Engineers Joint Council. 1967. *Thesaurus of Engineering and Scientific Terms*, Engineers Joint Council, New York.

European Atomic Energy Community. 1967. *Thesaurus Part II*, Brussels.

Evans, E., Borko, H., and Ferguson, P. 1972. "Review of criteria used to measure library effectiveness," *Bulletin of the Medical Library Association*, Vol. 60, No. 1, pp. 102–110.

Fischer, M. 1966. "The KWIC index concept: A retrospective view," *American Documentation*, Vol. 17, No. 2, pp. 57–70.

Garfield, E. 1963. "Citation indexes in sociological and historical research," *American Documentation*, Vol. 14, No. 4, pp. 289–291.

Garfield, E. 1970. "Citation indexes for studying science," *Nature*, Vol. 227, pp. 669–671.

Garfield, E. 1972. "Citation analysis as a tool in journal evaluation," *Science*, Vol. 178, pp. 471–479.

Garfield, E. 1973. "Citation frequency as a measure of research activity and performance," *Current Contents*, No. 5, pp. 5–7.

Garfield, E. 1974. "The citation index as a subject index," *Current Contents*, No. 18, pp. 5–7.

Gluck, D. J. 1965. "A chemical structure storage and search system developed at Du Pont," *Journal of Chemical Documentation*, Vol. 5, No. 1, pp. 43–51.

Gould, A. M. 1974. "User preferences in published indexes," *Journal of the American Society for Information Science*, Vol. 25, No. 5, pp. 279–286.

Harris, J. L. 1969. "Annual general meeting of the American Society of Indexers," *The Indexer*, Vol. 6, No. 4, pp. 189–190.

Harris, Z. S. 1962. *String Analysis of Sentence Structure*, Mouton and Co., The Hague.

Heald, J. H. 1966. *DoD Manual for Building a Technical Thesaurus*, prepared by Project LEX, Defense Documentation Center, AD 633 279.

Hines, T. C., and Harris, J. L. 1970. "Computer-aided production of book indexes," *The Indexer,* Vol. 7, No. 1, pp. 49–54.

Katz, W. A. 1969. *Introduction to Reference Works,* Vol. 1: *Basic Information Sources,* McGraw–Hill, New York.

Keen, M. 1975. "Design and evaluation of printed subject indexes," *Final Program of an International Study Institute,* College of Librarianship, Aberystwyth, Wales, July 14–18. (No proceedings were published.)

Kennedy, R. A. 1962. "Library applications of permutation indexing," *Journal of Chemical Documentation,* Vol. 2, No. 3, pp. 181–185.

Kim, C. 1973. "Theoretical foundations of thesaurus-construction and some methodological considerations for thesaurus-updating," *Journal of the American Society for Information Science,* Vol. 24, No. 2, pp. 148–156.

Knight, G. N. 1958. "The society's progress," *The Indexer,* Vol. 1, No. 1, pp. 5–6.

Knight, G. N. 1969. *Training in Indexing,* MIT Press, Cambridge, Massachusetts.

Knight, G. N. 1972. "Copyright in indexes," *The Indexer,* Vol. 8, No. 1, pp. 74–75.

Kollin, R. and Harris, J. L. 1968. "A criterion for evaluation of indexing systems," *American Society for Information Science, Annual Meeting,* Vol. 5: *Information Transfer.* Columbus, Ohio, pp. 79–81.

Lancaster, F. W. 1971. "The evaluation of published indexes and abstracts journals." *Bulletin of the Medical Library Assocaition,* Vol. 59, No. 3, pp. 479–495.

Lancaster, F. W. 1972. *Vocabulary Control for Information Retrieval,* Information Resources Press, Washington. D.C.

Lane, B. B. 1964. "Keywords in-and out of-context," *Special Libraries,* Vol. 55, No. 1, pp. 45–46.

Lewis, R. F. 1964. "KWIC . . . is it quick?" *Bulletin of the Medical Library Association,* Vol. 52, No. 1, pp. 142–147.

Luhn, H. P. 1957. "A statistical approach to mechanized encoding and searching of library information," *IBM Journal of Research and Development,* Vol. 1, No. 4, pp. 309–317.

Luhn, H. P. 1959. *Keyword-in-Context Index for Technical Literature* (*KWIC Index*), RC-127; also in *American Documentation,* Vol. 11, No. 4, pp. 288–295 (1960).

Lynch, M. F. 1971. "Computer-organized display of subject information," *The Indexer,* Vol. 7, No. 3, pp. 94–100.

Lynch, M. F., and Petrie, J. H. 1972. "A program suite for the production of articulated subject indexes," *Computer Journal,* Vol. 16, No. 1, pp. 47–51.

McColvin, L. R. 1958. "The purpose of indexing," *The Indexer,* Vol. 1, No. 2, pp. 31–35.

Machine Indexing: Progress and Problems. 1961. Papers presented at the Third Institute on Information Storage and Retrieval, American University, Washington, D.C. February 13–17.

Margolis, J. 1967. "Citation indexing and evaluation of scientific papers," *Science,* Vol. 155, pp. 1213–1219.

Montgomery, C., and Swanson, D. R. 1962. "Machine-like indexing by people," *American Documentation,* Vol. 13, No. 4, pp. 359–365.

Oliver, L. H. 1966. *An Investigation of the Basic Processes Involved in the Manual Indexing of Scientific Documents,* General Electric Co., Bethesda, Maryland, PB 169 415.

Payne, M. D. 1938. *Melodic Index to the Works of Johann Sebastian Bach,* Schiermer, New York; Second Edition, McAll 1962.

Powers, W. T. 1973. *Behavior: The Control of Perception,* Aldine, Chicago.

Price, D. J. de S. 1963. *Little Science, Big Science,* Columbia University Press, New York.

Rooney, P. 1974. "*Descriptive guide to the TOPIC indexing system*," mimeographed.

Ryan, V. J. and Dearing, V. A. 1974. "Computerized text editing and processing with built-in indexing," *Information Storage and Retrieval*, Vol. 10, No. 5/6 pp. 211–228.

Salton, G. 1975. *Dynamic Information and Library Processing*, Prentice-Hall, Englewood Cliffs, New Jersey.

Salton, G. (editor). 1971. *The SMART Retrieval System: Experiments in Automatic Document Processing*, Prentice-Hall, Englewood Cliffs, New Jersey.

Schultz, L. 1976. "Data processing support to indexing," lecture delivered to the New York chapter of the Special Libraries Association, May.

Selye, H. 1966. "Symbolic shorthand system (for physiology and medicine)," *Rutgers Series on Systems for the Intellectual Organization of Information*, Vol. 6, Susan Artandi (editor), Graduate School of Library Service, Rutgers—The State University, New Brunswick, New Jersey.

Society of Indexers. 1972. "Copyright in indexes," *The Indexer*, Vol. 8, No. 2, pp. 81–87.

Soergel, D. 1974. *Indexing Languages and Thesauri: Construction and Maintenance*, John Wiley & Sons, New York.

Sparck-Jones, K. 1974(a). *Automatic Indexing 1974: A State of the Art Review*, Computer Laboratory, Cambridge University, Cambridge.

Sparck-Jones, K. 1974(b). "Progress in documentation: Automatic indexing," *Journal of Documentation*, Vol. 30, No. 4, pp. 393–432.

Sparck-Jones, K. and Kay, M. 1973. *Linguistics and Information Science*, Academic Press, New York.

Speight, F. Y. 1967. *Guide for Source Indexing and Abstracting of the Engineering Literature*, Engineers Joint Council, New York.

Spencer, C. C. 1967. "Subject searching with *Science Citation Index*: Preparation of a drug bibliography using *Chemical Abstracts, Index Medicus*, and *Science Citation Index*," *American Documentation*, Vol. 18, No. 2, pp. 87–96.

Spencer, H., Reynolds, L., and Coe, B. 1975. "Spatial and topographic coding in printed bibliographical materials," *Journal of Documentation*, Vol. 31, No. 2, pp. 59–70.

Stevens, M. E. 1970. *Automatic Indexing: A State of the Art Report*, Monograph 91, National Bureau of Standards, Washington, D.C. First edition 1965.

Sussenguth, E. H., Jr. 1965. "A graph-theoretic algorithm for matching chemical structures," *Journal of Chemical Documentation*, Vol. 5, No. 1, pp. 43–51.

Tasman, P. 1958. *Indexing the Dead Sea Scrolls by Electronic Literary Data Processing Methods*, IBM World Trade Corp., New York.

Tukey, J. W. 1962. *The Citation Index and the Information Problem: Opportunities and Research in Progress*, annual report, Princeton University.

United Nations Educational, Scientific, and Cultural Organization, 1973. *Guidelines for the Establishment and Development of Monolingual Scientific and Technical Thesauri for Information Retrieval*, SC/MD/20, UNESCO, Paris, July.

United Nations Educational, Scientific, and Cultural Organization. 1975. *UNISIST Indexing Principles*, SC. 75/WS/58, UNESCO, Paris, September.

Veilleux, M. P. 1961. "Permuted title word indexing: Procedures for man/machine system," in *Machine Indexing: Progress and Problems*, American University, Washington, D.C., pp. 77–111.

Weinstock, M. 1971. "Citation indexes," *Encyclopedia of Library and Information Science*, Vol. 5, pp. 16–40. Marcel Dekker, New York.

Wheatley, H. B. 1879. *What Is an Index?* Longmans, Green, and Co., London.

Wicklen, S. I. 1958. "The topography of indexes," *The Indexer*, Vol. 1, No. 2, pp. 36–41.

Winchell, C. H. 1967. *Guide to Reference Books*, 8th ed., American Library Association, Chicago.

Witty, F. J. 1973. "The beginnings of indexing and abstracting: Some notes towards a history of indexing and abstracting in antiquity and the Middle Ages," *The Indexer*, Vol. 8, No. 4, pp. 193–198.

Wolff-Terroine, M. 1975. "Multilingual systems," paper presented at the Second European Congress on Information Systems and Networks, Commission of the European Communities, Luxembourg, May 28–30.

Wooster, H. 1970. "0.46872985 square inches—A naive look at subject analysis," *Digest of 1970 Annual Meeting*, National Federation of Science Abstracting and Indexing Services, Philadelphia, Pennsylvania, pp. 41–48.

Youden, W. W. 1963. "Characteristics of programs for KWIC and other computer-produced indexes," in *Automation and Scientific Communication: Short Papers, Part 2*, (H. P. Luhn, editor), American Documentation Institute, Washington, D.C., pp. 331–332.

Subject Index*

*Index prepared by Charles L. Bernier, Past President of the American Society of Indexers, in accordance with the recommendations of that society.

C

A 8
B 9
C 0
D 1
E 2
F 3
G 4
H 5
I 6
J 7

CONVERSATIONS WITH CUBA

Conversations

The University of Georgia Press *Athens & London*

with CUBA

C. PETER RIPLEY

Published by the University of Georgia Press
Athens, Georgia 30602

Set in 10 on 14 Palatino
Printed and bound by Maple-Vail Book Manufacturing Group

The paper in this book meets the guidelines for permanence and durability of the Committee on Production Guidelines for Book Longevity of the Council on Library Resources.

Printed in the United States of America

03 02 01 00 99 C 5 4 3 2 1

Library of Congress Cataloging-in-Publication Data

Ripley, C. Peter, 1941–
Conversations with Cuba / C. Peter Ripley.
p. cm.
ISBN 0-8203-2163-X (alk. paper)
1. Cuba—Description and travel. 2. Cuba—Politics and government—1959– 3. Cuba—Social Conditions—1959– 4. Cuba—Economic conditions—1959– 5. Tourism—Cuba. 6. Ripley, C. Peter, 1941– —Journeys—Cuba. I. Title.
F1765.3.R56 1999
972.9106'4—dc21 99-16371
CIP

British Library Cataloging-in-Publication Data available

Some things you have to see to believe.

Others, you have to believe to see.

This is for Bob, Hal, and Martha,

three who know some things about fellowship.

CONTENTS

FOREWORD *Bob Shacochis*

"Are books dangerous?" I asked Ricardo Alarcón, the president of the Cuban Parliament. "Do you think that a book can be a weapon?"

Implicit in the question were years of imprisonment suffered by Cuban writers judged subversive by the state, poets made to eat their own poems, novelists whose work would never be published and read in their homeland.

The year was 1995, my second visit to Cuba, this time as a guest of the American Publishers Association, which had organized the first-ever U.S. book fair on the island. Literary intrigues were heating up. The Cubans maneuvered to block the public display of one of the more blatant anti-Castro books the APA had slipped into its luggage. The U.S. Interests Section in Havana hosted a party for the group to introduce us to a collection of writers whose lives had been made difficult by government harassment, censorship, isolation, and, occasionally, incarceration. Dissident writers were barred from a joint meeting between American authors and members of the Cuban Writers Union, whose president at the time, Abel Prieto, was verbally attacked by human rights activists traveling with our entourage.

"Can a book be a weapon?" Alarcón repeated dismissively. "No, I don't think so, unless you hollow out the pages and place a gun or a bomb inside."

It was, any reasonable person would agree, a most disingenuous answer, coming from one of Fidel Castro's inner circle. For Cuban writers, free and independent expression was, and often is, a crime against society, enforced capriciously by the authorities as their mood of siege waxes and wanes.

Mr. Alarcón and the Cuban authorities certainly are aware that books can be dangerous, highly effective weapons in any campaign against ignorance, intolerance, authoritarianism, and repression. Alarcón's duplicity reminds me of a second anecdote, of equally sinister import. When contra rebels, financed by the U.S. government, launched their ugly little war against the Sandinista regime in Nicaragua in the 1980s, the operation inspired an anti-contra demonstration, replete with calls for the end of U.S. involvement in Central America, in downtown Miami. The demonstrators were, for the most part, Anglo activists, and they were set upon by counter-demonstrators, for the most part far-right Cuban Americans, who charged into the crowd, fists swinging in fury. A few days later, a friend of mine spoke with a prominent attorney in Miami's Cuban American community, arguing with her about the violent manner in which her ideological fellow travelers had broken up what was otherwise a peaceful demonstration.

"You and your people don't understand the First Amendment to the Constitution," my friend argued. "People have the right to demonstrate and express themselves freely."

"On the contrary," the lawyer, herself an exile, replied. "We understand it. We just don't agree with it."

To understand freedom and yet to not agree with it is a breathtaking admission, given the magnitude of suffering it engenders, and one that provides valuable insight into the complexity of the ongoing Cuban tragedy and its ever distant resolution. "Necessary rules"—muzzling the opposition, for instance—are, throughout the ideological spectrum of unchecked power, responsible for unnecessary sins: the purges, the violence, the hatred and absolutism that contaminate the righteousness and purity of cause on both sides of the modern Cuban experience.

So goes the story of the twentieth century and its revolutions, especially those decades that encompassed the Cold War. When the left and the right butt heads, common people pay the price with their liberty. When the extreme left and the extreme right butt heads, the common person is devoured. When the bottom rises against the top, the middle is swept away in the flood. When the bottom replaces the top, any genuine movement toward the middle is seized upon as counterrevolutionary. And far too often, the difference between the old masters and the new masters is simply rhetorical, a matter of language, a matter of style.

For a while at least, the Cuban revolution seemed different, seemed to break the mold, seemed to be a victory for the dignity and freedom of the common person—and then it didn't seem that way at all—and on both sides of the Florida Straits, one rule was constant: If you disagree with us, you'd better keep your mouth shut.

C. Peter Ripley's *Conversations with Cuba,* I think, is indeed dangerous, and will be seen as such by the irreconcilables within the Cuban communities, exiled and indigenous, and their die-hard supporters. And on still another level, this account of the author's travels in Cuba and his illuminating dialogue with its citizens poses a threat to the complacency of inside-the-beltway thinking about Cuba. As such, Mr. Ripley's book is a weapon not against people, American or Cuban, but against wrongheaded policies, aging stereotypes, dogmatic clichés, intransigence and arrogance, and the brittle but enduring myths of Cold War politics.

The essential, driving motivation behind *Conversations with Cuba* is the author's struggle to know, to know truly and clearly, beyond the headlines, beyond the policies, beyond the hatred and blind allegiance, beyond the cult of personality, beyond his own naiveté and earnestness, and beyond the strange seductive glamour of the revolution itself. It is a struggle to understand what lies at the heart of a sense of community, the collective energy that gathers itself into a grand cause, a struggle to understand the awfulness of the history between the United States and the island nation of Cuba.

An informed citizen presents a danger to all those who would wield power over the life of their societies, for an informed citizen, first and foremost, measures the use and abuse of power by its impact on the common person, which is to say, by its humanity. Most important, a citizen who has informed himself or herself has earned the right to speak out, a most provocative act, even in a democracy.

The virtue of this book, I believe, is the author's unflinching honesty, which also serves as its greatest point of vulnerability. Ripley, by vocation a historian, steps away from the strictures and orthodoxies—and, one must add, the illusions—of his profession to allow himself the opportunity to bear witness to history in the making. When a writer assumes the role of correspondent or chronicler, immediately certain fundamental decisions must be made, certain conventions and received beliefs reexamined and resolved anew. At the top of this list rests the notion of objectivity, or neutrality, one of the great conceits of journalism. Frankly, our most respected periodicals and news outlets and our most respected reporters are no more models of neutrality than, say, Switzerland, which we now know negotiated a rather duplicitous posture during World War II. While one can acknowledge the honorable intentions of objectivity and its appropriateness for gathering hard evidence, one must also recognize that the ideal leaves room for intellectual dishonesty among its practitioners—or room for an aesthetic that chills me, like T. S. Eliot's insistence on the "impersonality of art."

Identity—who the writer *is*, rather than who the writer *isn't*—is most definitely a part of the story, regardless of the precious detachment coolly manufactured by so-called objective reporters. Objectivity is a matter of degree, and its threshold is rigid; past a quickly reached limit of purpose, the principle itself becomes a guise, a ruse. And even the most "objective" reporting is obliged to serve the higher agenda of the establishment press and its unanimous support of the status quo. In this context, objectivity is a comforting lie, a tacit endorsement of a system. Trust us, it urges. We are disinterested messengers. Well, not even a camera is a disinterested messenger; rather, it is an extension of the personality holding it, and a picture might well be worth a thousand *irrational* words in a society so easily swayed by imagery. "I think some people come to Cuba to find our unhappiness," says Paulo, the young man from Havana who became the author's steadfast companion. I think Paulo is right, and I think the behavior he describes is inevitable and wrong.

At the most basic level, a writer earns credibility by getting the slippery, shifting facts of the moment right, of course, but it's never as simple as that, and beyond accuracy, beyond convention, there's plenty of room for disagreement about the nature of the correspondent's role. Objectivity, for someone trying to understand the most complicated and difficult things about the world—politics and power, the human heart, betrayal, sacrifice—is a false, or at least an inadequate, science. In its stead, fair-mindedness and open-mindedness, expressed in the envelope of the writer's own value system, are the best we can hope for—are what we *should* hope for. A writer shapes what we know as much as any other player invested in a story—policy analyst or historian, spin doctor or diplomat, leader or peasant or exile or anyone else, and to report from a vacuum of self becomes a political, and perhaps ethical, sleight of hand.

To have a direct, unobstructed view of the person writing, to have access to his or her inner thoughts and moral universe, is a vital component of our ability to judge a work clearly, judiciously, responsibly. Correspondents as separated in place and time and sensibility as Mark Twain and Martha Gellhorn knew this instinctively: that they were not some sort of truth machines—not neutral transmitters—that what they saw and heard and, just as significantly, what they felt and believed, mattered. That they had a point of view, and it was as much a part of the story being told and interpreted as anything else. Rather than diminish credibility, point of view places the writer's integrity on the line and diminishes the fiction—the self-righteous bluff—that objectivity invites onto the page.

The bottom line is, when sometimes all the facts in the world don't quite add up to the truth of a people or a nation or a revolution or a war, hot or cold or interminably lukewarm, the writer must step forward.

Read with this understanding, *Conversations with Cuba* is not solely an intimate account of the roller-coaster drama of postrevolutionary Cuba's survival at the end of the millennium, the Soviet Union's last Potemkin village collapsing in decay (yet simultaneously buttressed by an invading horde of joint-venture capitalists and dollar-fat tourists). More than that, the book presents itself as one man's quest to comprehend his vestigial romance with revolution, to come to terms with his yearning for "a society with a grand purpose, where service in a good cause had the strength it once did in America, when part of a generation was inexorably drawn to the Peace Corps, or the civil rights crusade, or the antiwar movement." Many readers might question the author's reverence for the soul of the Cuban revolution, but they would be missing the point. Ultimately, although Mr. Ripley undermined his own myths on his travels to Cuba, he reaffirmed what was good within himself, the universal values that bring light to humanity, and became, to our benefit, a rare visitor—an American without another stale rationale for why things are one way or another, who, in the process of discovery and rediscovery, created a guileless and compassionate book qualitatively different from the available literature delivered by mainstream journalists or self-deluded leftists or imperial daydreamers. In keeping the reader very close to him, to the ambiguities and contradictions, to the inspirations as well as the indignities, to the pain and the charm of the day's experiences, the author has brought us all closer to the Cuban people themselves, and to their abiding spirit.

And that, unlike the revolution he writes so tellingly about, is a triumph, and a dangerous act for those who cling, whether through bitterness or fantasy or inertia, to the past. "Why does the United States hate Cubans so much?" a taxi driver in Havana asked the author. "How can we be that important?" I share the driver's perplexity, as does Mr. Ripley, given that the central reasons for our government's antipathy toward Cuba withered long ago, and the continuing estrangement between the two countries seems more a product of laziness and petulance and political cowardice than anything else, than anything solid and insurmountable.

Here, then, is this book's lasting contribution, and it should not be taken lightly. *Conversations with Cuba* moves us forward along the path toward the day in the future that most Cubans and most Americans believe in, when "the United States and Cuba would get back together, like long-separated lovers with a lingering attraction," a day, perhaps, when Cubans "will decide they liked us most of all for the possibilities we represented, not for who we actually were." It is that faith, created out of the things we hold in common, and that irony, created by our history, that the author explores most poignantly and writes about most eloquently—the grace and sadness of the gestures that underpin the bonds between the people of the United States and the people of Cuba.

ACKNOWLEDGMENTS

I accumulated a lifetime of appreciation during the making of this book.

I don't know how to properly acknowledge the people of Cuba, those friends who welcomed me and those strangers who paused with me for a moment of conversation. No matter how pressing my questions or how difficult the times, they never turned away or turned me away. I hope that Paulo, Víctor, Neddie, and those many others who accepted me at face value will find their trust justified.

Hal Williams and Pam Ball read and reread the manuscript, saving me from mistakes and vanities while improving the work with their suggestions. Those friends and others who encouraged, or lent a hand, or gave a damn about this book and Cuba—Martha, Murph, Phil, Joe, Trish, John, M. A., Tom, Cynthia, Connie May, Mika, Jimmy, Elly, Joe M., D. K., Dan, Catfish, Carol, Nancy, Paul, and B. K. among them—provided the comforting grace of a redemptive community, for which I am most grateful.

Thanks to Joan Didion, W. E. B. Du Bois, Graham Greene, Michael Herr, Tim O'Brien, Frank País, Robbie Robinson, Bob Shacochis, and Bruce Springsteen for the power of their imaginations, which made me want to try, and then try harder.

After more than a quarter century of professional association I am delighted to publish this book with Malcolm Call, my editor at the University of Georgia Press and my good friend.

BATISTA'S VASE

A book about Cuba wasn't part of the plan when I began scheming to travel to Fidel Castro's embargoed island. I set out in 1991 with an ambition common to most travelers, to satisfy a curiosity, in that instance about a place prohibited to Americans for three decades, after Cuba was first damned as Communist and then sequestered as dangerous during the crudest days of the Cold War. My curiosity was elevated by a personal need as well, to settle up with a handful of youthful fantasies that over the years had developed into a romantic attachment to Cuban society.

More than any other piece of foreign geography, Cuba was fixed in my imagination like a set of snapshot photos dating from the mid-1950s. As a fifteen-year-old, I was ready to travel there with a group of Florida lifeguards whose tradition was to end the summer season with a warm rinse of Havana's whiskey and women. I wanted to know what sort of place attracted such dissipated men, Korean War vets mostly, who closed down the bars every night and seldom went home alone. They told stories of narrow, cobbled streets and smoky bars, honey-smooth rum and fat cigars, and live shows that titillated a poor boy's imagination. I longed to know about all of it—to share their experiences—but I never did. Fulgencio Batista's tyranny governed Cuba then, but my parents ruled no less harshly, I thought, reasoning from the limited insight of a 1950s teenager.

We knew something about Batista in my Florida beach town because he had a home among us, a lovely high-walled residence along the river, one of the better addresses of our small community. During one night when my friends and I were driving around and drinking beer, the talk went to bravado; a challenge was made, and accepted, for me to scale Batista's wall and break into his house. This had nothing to do with politics or understanding the cruelty of Batista's rule. It was a simple matter elevated not one notch above teenage boredom and bad judgment, for we all knew with youthful certainty that the home was heavily guarded when Batista was in town and well protected at other times as well. Rumor certain, men with guns had been seen there. Be that as it may, men with guns or not, there was little I could do but take myself to Batista's wall. And just as I was about to leave my older brother's 1954 Chevrolet convertible my friends declared that a certification was needed, a proof of some sort that I had been inside the house.

Given a boost, I grabbed the top of the stuccoed wall, which I scaled, then dropped onto the ground and ran, crouched and stealthlike, through the moonlight, across the close-cropped Bermuda grass to the house. I loosened one of the long, narrow panes of glass in a jalousie door, reached my hand inside, and turned the knob. I was horrified when the door opened, would have been satisfied to scramble back to the car to confess a shameful failure had there been proper locks to prevent my entry. What could Batista have been thinking to leave his home so poorly prepared to meet an unskilled vandal, let alone someone with a more serious purpose? But I was trapped, chose to steal from a dangerous stranger rather than give up the challenge, so I stepped inside the house. I was in and out of there in one fearful moment's time, returning to my friends with a small vase clutched in a hand dripping with blood from cuts made by broken glass embedded in the top of Batista's wall.

Two years later, with the 1950s drawing to a close, Cuba tugged at me again, this time to celebrate the victory of Fidel Castro's revolution. I knew little of the politics of the situation, but I do remember what caused me to try to forge an identification with those distant rebels. It was a spread of pictures I saw in my high school library, in *Life* or a similar magazine, featuring Castro's guerrilla army just as it marched into Havana, ragtag and victorious. The pictures would have been dated January 1959, when the Triumph was brand new and I was seventeen years old. The single photograph I remember like yesterday's memory was of a group of happy young men in fatigues, kids actually, no more than teenagers, but members of Fidel's army, grown up in arms and suddenly in charge. They were posed against the wall of a building with their arms around each other's shoulders, locked in the time-honored stance of brotherhood. Looking at that smiling photograph I thought, "Whatever else they may do with their lives, they will always remember being part of this," and that idea moved me in unfamiliar ways.

That emotional response is clearer to me now, though I still would make no claim to a real understanding. But I think I admired—envied—those young men for what they were a part of, for what they had experienced and what they would bring away in a fair exchange for their commitment: a sense of community, a dramatic moment shared with comrades, and participation in a transcending experience that changed history.

Cuba was never very far away from me after that. The Bay of Pigs invasion and the missile crisis kept Cuba in the news and twisted America with Cold War tensions. But like many others born during World War II and raised in the easy affluence of the 1950s, when I went off to college I was drawn into the student movements of the 1960s. For those of us pretentious enough to claim the label of radical, events involving Cuba and the United States meant something different than they did for the rest of the nation. Where most of America found evil and despair in the "Godless" Communist state just ninety miles from Florida, we found heroes and inspiration—men we could admire and achievements we could only dream of.

The Cuban Revolution was perfect for us. We studied it and quoted it, we fantasized it and romanticized it. It was not our own, but it was of our time. It had unfolded before us, on television and in the newspapers. We read the words and saw the images. And we learned that it was advanced by students, artists, writers, the middle class itself—the sort of people we knew, the sort we were. In the Cuban Revolution, history gave us hope in the form of a powerful lesson: people like us could change a nation.

That idea never left me, and it was forever associated in my imagination with Cuba. So in the spring of 1991 when a writer friend was asked by a magazine to sneak into Cuba and bring back a report on Castro's emerging tourism trade, I begged him to take the assignment, and to let me tag along, so that I might test my romantic attachment against a Cuban reality.

Defendamos

Por la VIDA, NO al Bloqueo

Revolution and Tourism

MAY 1991

Gettin' Inside

The trip went nearly out of control even before we were properly on our way to Havana. The flight crew of the hand-me-down Iluyshin-8 Russian airliner shut down one, then another, and finally all four of the plane's engines, leaving us stranded on the tarmac to swelter in worrisome silence under Mexico's tropical sun. The captain and co-captain left the cockpit to make their way down the aisle, mopping their brows with handkerchiefs, mumbling to upturned faces that everything was fine, the delay would be brief, as they passed through the length of the cabin to the rear exit, leaving behind a sea of turned heads looking at the sweat-stained backs of their uniform shirts. Then they were gone, presumably to wait in air-conditioned comfort for the electrical problem to be solved.

Even before we boarded the threadbare Cubanacan airliner, the list of delays had grown so long that less persistent travelers might have abandoned the idea of getting into Cuba. A near-total U.S. State Department ban on travel to the island—punishable by a $250,000 fine, loss of passport, and ten years in jail—we regarded as an obstacle, but little more than that. Yet not everyone shared our casual indifference to government regulations; countless hours spent on phone calls to travel agents, political contacts, savvy travelers, and the Cuban Interests Section in the Swiss embassy had netted us nothing more than an irritating list of crossed-out phone numbers—no visa, no plane ticket, no ETA for Havana, and no hope of getting there anytime soon.

Finally we abandoned protocol and flew to Cancún, Mexico, where a local travel agent, Pepe, picked us up at the airport in a rusty green VW bug and made happen in one morning what we had failed to accomplish over several weeks. He got us tickets and visas and issued us a caution about reckless behavior and its attendant penalties: "Don't let Cuban immigration stamp your passport; it will cause problems with your government." To certify his caution Pepe invoked rumors then circulating throughout the Caribbean basin about U.S. customs agents harassing Americans who foolishly collected evidence of their travels to Cuba, threatening them with punishment and a fine so large we laughed at the idea the government might ever collect it from us. But our laughter held a nervous edge that acknowledged thirty years of meanness in U.S. policy toward Cuba, which made anything seem possible.

Yet there we sat, bathed in perspiration, honoring the rumors and wondering aloud if we might be plucked off the plane by Elliot Ness look-alikes, and wondering too what mysteries awaited us in Havana, assuming we ever got airborne over the Gulf of Mexico. Being from Florida made us neighbors of Miami's Cuban exile community, whose anti-Castro sentiment swept out of south Florida like a ferocious tropical storm. Those expatriates had fled the Revolution in successive waves for more than three decades, then formed themselves into a self-conscious community of 500,000 that was regarded in the States as the respected authority about life in Cuba, an authority backed up by a power in politics all out of proportion to their numbers.

My traveling companion Bob visited south Florida regularly, where he had collected a surplus of exile wisdom which he shared while we waited for the technicians to repair the plane. His purpose was unclear, leaving me confused as to whether he was trying to prepare us for the worst or was thinning out his own anxiety by spreading some of it around, but his information was unambiguous. "The end is near, *el jefe* is tightening things down, food is scarce, spies are everywhere, people are fearful, repression is rampant, arrests are increasing, racial tensions are rising, Castro doesn't have another year"—and on it went until our concerns about entering Cuba rose as high as the temperature in the plane. His last bit of information, gathered from a phone call to a Cuban exile friend just before we boarded the plane in Miami, had included the warning "Be careful."

Our conversation led us into some fierce anticipations about what we might find on Castro's island—a sullen population living in a country where everyone was hungry and nothing worked; secret police positioned on every street corner; a population of spies ready to denounce neighbors and *yanqui* visitors for the smallest infraction; a country without soap, coffee, or the gasoline we would need for our planned trip across the island; a hellhole of a Communist nation in the final stages of accelerated collapse under the blood-stained hands of the last Communist, America's most enduring enemy, the bearded Prince of Darkness in green fatigues.

While we Americans tormented ourselves—about the U.S. government, the Cuban government, the quality of Russian airplane technology, our chances of survival in the air and on the ground—a trio of extremely merry Mexicans took charge of the situation on the plane. "*No problema,* don't worry," announced the obvious ringleader in a take-charge declaration, "everything is under control," which brought everyone to laughter, including, or perhaps particularly, the flight attendants. The head *muchacho* produced a bottle of tequila and passed it around, assuring passengers and crew that tequila was a drink well regarded in his community for its calming effect, a claim that caused another collective roll of the eyes to pass through the cabin. Then the trio began singing "Don't Worry, Be Happy," making a fine time out of a sweaty, miserable situation.

The electrical failure repaired, the pilots finally returned, cranked the engines, and started down the runway, with the young Mexicans rocking in their seats and chanting "Go, Go, Go," until most of the passengers joined in, wishing and grunting the plane off the ground, heading us toward Cuba. Airborne at last, the air-conditioning returned, and as the chilled air hit the humid cabin icy flakes began to drift down from the vent above my seat, showering me with a misty snow—another absurdity among many, real and imagined, causing me to confide in Bob, "The only fitting end to this day would be for us to be hijacked back to Miami by an unhappy Cuban."

My companions were an experienced writer paired with a photographer on magazine assignment, well-established professionals whose experiences made them cautious, whose work made them skeptical. They were headed for Cuba looking for a story about a revolutionary culture flirting with tourism, a tale about Marxism blowing kisses at capitalism, seeking it out against a backdrop of Cuban exile opinion, American journalistic wisdom, and their own professional skills. There was little else to draw from.

Good judgment demanded that I be attentive to the apprehensive opinions of my friend Bob Shacochis, a contributing editor of *Harper's* magazine, where he regularly published nonfiction, and a National Book

Award winner for *Easy in the Islands*, a collection of short fiction set in the Caribbean, where he had lived for many years. His ungoverned need for exotic travel and his chosen trade had left him rubbing shoulders with martial law more than once. Bob's personality ran straight toward the intense, even obsessive, about nearly everything, small or large—his insistence on Camel Light cigarettes, two-pocket shirts, and Pilot pens, his unchecked curiosities and loyalties, and his need to be right in all arguments, which he usually was, but not always to his advantage. I imagined him in an earlier life as a steel-eyed councilor exercising a fanatical control over a weak-willed monarch, a man admired for his brilliance and feared for the fierceness of his convictions. In this life, he was most intense—make that hyper—about his work, which in the present instance meant Cuba, and he radiated a sense of worry as we headed in country.

At the first impression, photographer Bob Caputo seemed an uncommon modern man at ease with everything that came his way, giving no sign of alarm even when his camera equipment failed to arrive in Cancún when it was scheduled to. And he actually accepted at face value the airline's pledge that his gear would arrive later that evening, on the last possible flight if he was to leave with us for Havana with cameras in hand. Caputo's twenty years in Africa, often in the service of *National Geographic*, had him lugging his aluminum camera cases across so many international borders he had his passport number committed to memory. Perhaps those African years had rendered him too philosophical about the possibilities of life's true miseries to fret about its lesser insults.

These guys had been around, and knew some stuff, that was certain. So I accepted a touch of their concern by the time we arrived in Havana's José Martí Airport. We three Americans, queued up in front of the immigration booths, were easy to spot with our slumped posture and downcast eyes, the international sign of guilt or fear, never mind which. "What will happen to us if they stamp our passports?" asked an earnest young American woman clutching hers, its cover embossed with the U.S.A. spread eagle. Feeling edgy and weary of hearing American anxieties about Cuba, I told her, "You'll probably be arrested as soon as you return to the States and will never see your mother again."

"God, I wish we had never left Belize," she moaned.

My friends and I inched along down the line not knowing what to expect, pushing our bags forward with our feet while looking ahead silently to see what was going on, hoping for some advance notice of what awaited us, until finally we reached an immigration official. A young woman in a military-style uniform stationed behind a glass partition greeted us with a smile—she smiled, she flirted—hardly glanced at our passports before she stamped a separate document to be picked up when we departed the country, leaving us with no official trace of ever having entered Cuba. Then we swept through customs without a single bag being touched or examined, just waved through, as though Americans were welcomed into Cuba every day.

Stepping outside into the moist Cuban afternoon I poked fun at our deflated worries. "These Communists are going to wear me down fast. I don't know if I can endure much more of this Marxist-Leninist oppression." Bob joined in. "How clever of these Communists to lull us like that, to get us to drop our guard with a charade that is sure to end any second." We were approached at the curb by the three Mexicans from the plane, whose leader ambled over to us and with a wagging finger and sly conspiratorial grin announced, "Sooner or later we knew you Americans were going to come."

Yet as we joked away our Cold War arrival anxieties and reassured ourselves that Cuba would soon have us acting as playful as our newfound Mexican friends, I glanced at a large crowd of Cubans gathered behind a chain-link fence. They were craning their necks, standing on tiptoe, hooking their fingers in the wire trying to get a better look as they searched for relatives among the crowd of arriving passengers, exiles most likely, returning home to visit the country that called them *los gusanos*, the worms, yet had just greeted us so warmly. Cuba, the land of irony and contradiction—at last.

We had two weeks to road-trip through Cuba, to walk the streets of Havana and the guerrilla paths of the mountain range, the Sierra Maestra, trusting that Cuba would reveal herself as we covered the time and space that separated the two ends of the island. Ours was a modest ambition, which we began to pursue at Havana's Hotel Comodoro, where we were escorted to sunlit rooms, beautifully appointed with colorful ceramic tile and highly polished teak woodwork, with balconies overlooking the water that caught the comforting sound of surf splashing against the breakwater. The Comodoro lacked only phones in the bathrooms to qualify for a five-star rating, at one-third the cost of most other sand-and-surf resorts in the world. An unlikely front line for continuing Cuba's Revolution.

Castro had decreed that tourism would be Cuba's future, a decision we wanted to evaluate for ourselves, having read numerous newspaper stories about an economy poised on the near side of ruin. The U.S. embargo against Cuba, then in its third decade and respected by most of America's allies, had punished the island economy, choking it for trade, tourists, friends, and finally food and medicine. Then, on the eve of our arrival, the dissolution of the Soviet Union ended nearly all assistance to the only Communist nation in the hemisphere, costing Cuba nearly $8 billion per year and instructing her once again about the unreliable nature of patronage among nations. Going it alone, Castro had decided to blend Marxist purity with joint ventures, in a program that invited companies from Spain, Mexico, Germany, and Canada to bring fat checkbooks and ambitious blueprints for rebuilding Cuba into the for-profit tourist paradise it once had been, under another government.

Everywhere we turned, the telltale signs of Cuba's revised ambitions were revealed in muddy construction sites. Prerevolutionary hotels were being lifted out of 1950s neglect, foundations for new luxury resorts were poured every day, and 50/50 deals were being cut with foreign companies that would test whether the Revolution's virtues could withstand a harsh assault by the international corporate community and the rush of tourists that Cuba hoped would soon follow. A hand-painted billboard, perched high on the steel and concrete skeleton of a hotel under construction, announced: "To defend tourism is to defend the Revolution."

Perhaps so. But we would have to see for ourselves, would need to examine Cuba's gritty mix of tourism and revolution in a society grinding its way toward an uncertain future without benefit of patron, or even neighbors with sufficient passion and power to offer a helping hand in plain view of the United States. Our inquiry began in earnest during a cab ride down the Malecón, the lovely seaside boulevard that stretches along the edge of Havana, from below the Hotel Comodoro to our afternoon's destination in Old Havana.

From the window of our taxi we looked out upon a Cuba spread along the Malecón's seawall. Lovers clutched and leaned into each other; young boys and old men fished, some with rods and some with handlines; teenagers gathered in conspicuous knots, while younger children swam and played with inner tubes, riding the gentle waves of Havana Harbor. The scene was relaxed, informal, and lacking in political or national characteristics, a view we might have seen in any number of warm-climate locations, including the Florida Keys.

We sped past American dream cars from the 1950s and people pedaling one-speed bicycles, contrasting images that served as appropriate symbolism for our inquiry about tourism, a contrast that hinted at the confusion in Cuba's shifting identity. Would she trudge forward with slow-paced revolutionary determination, or would she select a sleeker style, one drawn from a historic past that was big-finned, plump, and glitzy?

For Bob, the skeptical journalist, the answer was obvious. "Fidel has chosen a reckless solution to Cuba's problems. If he invites Americans to overrun the country they will corrupt thirty years of social progress and Cuba's most valuable asset—its revolutionary culture." "Suicide by tourism," he called it, an artful description that was hard to dispute. Castro's choice seemed a desperate decision as we arrived fresh from Cancún, Mexico, where another revolutionary government had constructed a seaside city to attract foreign dollars, where the only things that felt authentic were the handicrafts trucked in from the countryside and sold in brightly lit shopping malls to roving gangs of tourists, ravenous in their pursuit of native bargains.

The cab dropped us at the Plaza de las Armas on the edge of Old Havana, a destination that turned out to be our gateway into Cuba's postrevolutionary society. We followed a web of narrow streets as inviting as any in the Americas, where sidewalks meet the foundations of homes and walls rise straight up like parapets protecting the cobblestone lanes. We passed sites in Old Havana that pointed back into Cuba's history: fortresses that guarded the city from pirates and foreign invaders in tall sailing ships; a limestone cathedral that acknowledged the one-time Jesuit influence; the statue of Carlos Manuel de Céspedes, always honored as the founder of the country; the Plaza de las Armas, a reminder of Spain's colonial occupation; and the nearby Museum of the Revolution, celebrating Cuba's Triumph. This was Hemingway's neighborhood for a time, where his room in the Ambos Mundos Hotel on Obispo Street is preserved as a museum. The nearby bar that he frequented, La Bodeguita, needed no preservation—it had endured by the force of its own presence and served as our destination that day.

We were four when we landed at La Bodeguita, having acquired the companionship of Pedro, a paper-thin, sixtyish plumber neatly dressed in pressed khakis and white shirt. He had approached us on the street to ask for a cigarette. Bob obliged. Then Pedro asked for a light, and then the lighter, which Bob produced like the polite guest he was, only to change his mind fearing he would find no replacement in a depleted Cuba. "Mother of God," Pedro gasped when told we were from the States, so rare were such creatures in Cuba in 1991. Then, a grateful and smiling Pedro volunteered his services as guide, black marketeer, and social critic—"Things are very bad, Castro is unpopular, we never have enough to eat, I can get you cheap cigars, let me exchange your money. . . ." Pedro was our first contact with the streets of Havana, and the possibilities of his real intentions were limited only by our ability to imagine the trouble he could cause. I wondered if his practiced spiel started with "Fuck Castro" and concluded with "You are under arrest for trafficking in black market cigars and crimes against the Revolution." No matter. We pushed on, taking our place in the line of people waiting for La Bodeguita to open at noon on Sunday.

While we waited, children asked for gum—young kids who the next day would exchange their street ways for school uniforms, transforming themselves, much the way Cuba appeared to be doing, daily. Three agreeable young men, spotting us as foreigners, offered to exchange money at eight times the official rate, then lingered for a passing conversation after we declined their generous proposal. Our refusal caused no begging or complaining, and no bad aftertaste. They were polite, unlike their brotherhood in most other countries, causing me to marvel at their good manners and to wonder if their mothers worried about their dangerous trade. At straight-up noon the doors opened, and we moved forward, pressed in line with anticipating Cubans.

Small, cramped, and good humored, La Bodeguita radiated the atmosphere of invitation common to the world's best bars. We stepped inside, well prepared by the bar's reputation to be pleased, and most certainly ready to sample the house specialty, *mojito*, a mix of Cuban rum, lime juice, sugar, soda water, and a mint leaf for delicacy of taste. Harried bartenders made them a dozen at a time throughout the afternoon and were never idle. Dark-paneled walls showed a forgiving attitude toward graffiti, which included names so easy to recognize and so substantial in achievement they immediately reassured strangers in a new country: Hemingway, Allende, Márquez. It was easy to believe that those three men had visited La Bodeguita and stayed awhile, content to lend their endorsements to such a fine establishment.

The place tingled with families out for a Sunday meal, tourists out for the memory, and neighborhood folks out for the day's pleasures, who appeared and reappeared throughout the day to greet us like regulars once we lingered past the time usually allotted for tourists, which we did, by a comfortable margin. Groups of sightseers, pressed together on the narrow sidewalk, stared through the open-air front of La Bodeguita at the bar's indifferent patrons; guides explained in several languages that Hemingway drank inside, then footnoted their history with Ernesto's own words: "My mojito at La Bodeguita, my daiquiri at La Floridita." Two uniformed tourism police spent the day across the street leaning against a wall, loitering with a passive psychological effect, in contrast to their companions, two pained-looking plainclothes cops, whose crossed arms and open disdain cast a suspicious pall over the Sunday gathering. Trendy young women, artists and musicians, baseball fans, off-duty workers, black marketeers, money changers, complainers and loyalists, wobbly drunks, and proper families joined the assortment of Cubans, all churning toward a common euphoria, Cuban style.

Photographer Caputo won over the house in no time. He shot roll after roll of film, climbing on a bar stool for one shot, leaning over the bar for another, waving people out of his line of fire, stopping to sip his *mojito* and to push his slipping glasses back up on his perspiring face, then back at it again until his flash became part of the texture of the place. Everyone took his manic professionalism with a smile that matched his own, delighted to have him among them, cooperating like skilled extras in a finely scripted documentary on Caribbean charm.

Bob found an observation spot leaning against the rear wall, where he sipped his rum, chewed his pen, and scratched pages of notes in his journal, occasionally running his hand over his perspiring forehead and through his curly hair, which was just beginning to show some gray. He added another Pedro to the group, a thirtyish waiter on his day off who announced, "I am taking English lessons, so is my wife. We think tourism will make us a better life if we know English." His appetite for rum matched his enthusiasm for rambling on with Bob in English. Tourism had put the scent of change in the air, even at La Bodeguita, which felt like a solid institution, impervious to the temporary shifts in the authority of politics or ideology, beholden only to its customers, as a great bar should be.

We drank, we talked, we asked questions, we answered questions, we told countless people, "Yes, we are from the States"; we craned our necks and our imaginations, and we tried to fit in but we were too much of an oddity by the fact of our nationality and the power of our uncommon curiosity. After a time, with appetites sharpened by several *mojitos* and the rapacious culture of the La Bodeguita, we joined the line wending its way up the narrow staircase to the second-floor restaurant, to a small table wedged into cramped quarters. The air was as warm and close as you might imagine for a second-story restaurant in the unair-conditioned Caribbean during May. And it radiated comfortable sounds—ice on glass, bar chat floating up from downstairs, the clanking of dishes and the rhythm of mealtime conversations from the tables surrounding us—and the noisy air was scented with garlic, shredded pork, grilled chicken, fried plantains, and black beans and rice, a sensory presence so delightful it pulled us to the edge of our chairs when the waiter arrived with an oversized aluminum tray covered with piled-high plates of food and misty bottles of cold Hatuey beer.

Pedro the plumber paid close attention to his pork dinner, hardly looking up until the food was gone and the plate was polished clean with a chunk of bread. Then he politely turned to the few leftovers on the table, focusing on the process of eating Sunday dinner with a determined manner that answered the question we were too polite to ask: *Are you bone-showing thin because you don't have enough to eat?* We ate and talked and drank beer and flirted with the young woman at the table next to us. She was a brown-eyed teenager who seemed terribly bold for someone sharing a table with her parents and younger brother, catching my eye with an inviting smile and then turning to Bob. She was our first real contact with Cuba's social style between the sexes, an introduction that became more elaborate after we finished eating and returned to our station downstairs.

The two young women sitting beside me at the bar struck up a conversation in a Spanish spoken so rapidly it sounded as though each sentence was one long word—a word that contained no *s*'s at all. "*Más despacio*," I pleaded—slower, slower. They laughed and tried again, then a third time, until I thought I had it. How unusual, I thought, attractive women at a bar were engaged in a universal appeal, asking a man, a foreigner, a rich *yanqui* tourist, to buy them drinks. When I paused and stared at them, taking a few indecisive seconds to consider which idiom to mangle and which barroom response to invoke, one of them pressed folded pesos into my hand. Baffled about what was going on, and starting to feel the full effects of Cuba's ambiguous charm, I looked around for Bob, hoping he might lessen my load of language if not of obligation, but he just looked back with a smile of absolute comprehension that said, *You're on your own, brother*.

So I started over with a proper introduction, with another plea to speak slowly, to tell me, please, "What is going on?" And they did. Jennifer and Liza had not asked me to buy them drinks, just to accept their pesos and pay for the drinks in dollars, in a fair exchange, or close enough to ignore the slight tilt toward the locals. It was 4:00 P.M., they explained, and from then until 7:00 La Bodeguita accepted no pesos, only dollars, which Cubans were forbidden by law to have under any circumstances, the penalty being jail. Finally I got it—this was the foreigners-only revolutionary happy hour. But around the bar, no one missed a beat as drinks, laughter, and conversation continued to fuel the day's merriment. In a country with numerous inconveniences, this one, like most others, was accommodated in good spirits, at least here, where the crowd, pressed three and four deep at the bar most of the day, showed little sign of thinning out its numbers or cranking down its energy.

The exchange of currency with Liza and Jennifer led to an exchange of words that drifted easily into improvisation and communication with a most common intent. I taught the English word "flirt" to Jennifer, a tall, smiling *mulata* whose angular face was set off by dangling brass earrings that she flipped with the back of her hand when she was animated. With a smiling charm she taught me the most common expression in Cuba in 1991, *"No problema,"* after I explained to her that we could not go to the Hotel Comodoro for drinks, for dinner, for whatever might be percolating between us. It was against the rules, I told her—"no Cuban guests in the rooms"—a regulation clearly spelled out in a letterhead statement I had picked up at the front desk at check-in time, but not specifically handed to me for examination, a subtle distinction between policy and behavior that suggested certain complexities in Cuba's changing culture. *"No problema,"* Jennifer assured me again as she looked up from the document, clearly amused by my failure to grasp one of the fundamental characteristics of Cuban society in transition, the imprecise struggle between the expectations of a revolutionary culture and the changes brought into that culture with the arrival of hard times and tourism.

As the afternoon moved toward evening I felt an impulse to seek relief from the *mojitos*, the too-fast Spanish of Jennifer and Liza, and the wicked allure of La Bodeguita. I needed fresh air, to clear my head, to put into proper order the jagged pieces of our introduction to Cuban life, so I drifted out of the bar into Old Havana's strange and marvelous streets for a few moments alone.

But Cubans made it impossible for an American to stand alone for long. Within minutes a young man approached, a slightly built teenager in baggy shorts and an "I Love Miami" T-shirt, offering to trade, straight up, his well-worn state-issued shoes for my Nikes. I declined. He abandoned the negotiations in favor of continuing the conversation, and, when I proved agreeable, he grabbed my arm to pull me along the sidewalk, heading a few doors down the block to his house, where I would meet his mother. She was a sailor, he said. Had been to Canada and other ports. Would love to meet me. I surrendered, let him drag me where he wished in a passive expression of my willingness to be swept along by well-meaning Cubans determined to entertain or inform or simply pass time with a curious visitor.

Down San Ignacio Street we pushed through a narrow bright-orange door and made a right turn through a hallway into a small apartment. Blinking away the sunlight I saw well-worn furniture pushed against the walls, a bare fixture hanging from the ceiling, a yellow, Formica-topped kitchen table commanding the center of the room, chickens pecking at morsels on the floor, and shafts of light slicing through the one window—a room cast from a crumbling texture too unfamiliar for me to connect with, except for the black-and-white TV sitting on a small table. A fortyish woman not dressed for visitors and startled by our presence stood over a two-burner enamel stove stirring a bubbling pot of black beans that scented the apartment with Cuba's national aroma.

After the moment it took her to recover, she offered me coffee and pulled out a chromed chair, as an invitation for me to sit and visit at the yellow-topped table. We talked and drank coffee for a time, working through the awkwardness of strangers. She was a sailor, as the son had promised, a well-traveled citizen among people for whom travel was the odd, rare luxury or the refugee's desperate choice. From a large ceramic pot situated on top of a wooden hutch she produced a set of documents, held together by an elastic band and dark-stained from the familiarity of many hands. The official pages, affixed with an overexposed photo and the ink of government stamps, confirmed her status as a merchant marine named Marie and documented her entry into Canada, Hong Kong, and other foreign ports. As she started to close her papers and put them away, out fell a family photo that she carried for a mother's comfort whenever she left the country, and as she gazed at the photo on the table her face turned sad, then weepy. Apologizing for her tears, she placed the tip of a single finger over the face of her eldest son, who, she explained, was in prison for five years, sent there for the crime of possessing foreign currency. Dollars.

Standing over the table, her crossed hands pressed over her heart, Marie looked down and asked in a whisper, Didn't I know someone in the Cuban government who could help her son? What about the U.S. government? Didn't I have some way to help? Couldn't I do something for her son, who was a good son, who had done nothing more than what many people did every day? Couldn't I do something? *Please?*

I told her I knew no one in power in Cuba, no one at all in Cuba, really; it was only my second day in the country. I was there illegally according to the U.S. government, could not consider going to the embassy. There was nothing I could possibly do, not in Cuba, not in the United States.

Marie stood there looking down at me, saying nothing, just looking at me through her tearful sadness. For that Cuban mother, the power and authority of America and Americans was such that I don't think she believed my protests of impotence; from the expression on her face, I suspect she reasoned my explanation down to a cruel unwillingness to help a mother and son in their misery. I sat there for the longest time, as long as I could anyway, while the silence took hold of the room, and then, unable to stand it any longer, I pushed back my chromed chair and left her alone in that terribly uncomfortable place. I fled the apartment actually, eager for a quick return to La Bodeguita's good times.

As soon as I walked through the doors Liza and Jennifer greeted me as an old friend or a new possibility, the style in Cuba being the same for either, as far as I could tell. They evicted one of their girlfriends from the bar stool that had been mine before I stepped outside. I took the stool without apology or protest, thanked the scowling girlfriend, kissed Liza and Jennifer on the cheek, ordered *mojitos*, and collapsed into the idea that there was no escape from Havana's assault upon my sensibilities. *Give it up*, I thought, *and wait until later to sort out the confusion that arose out of what Cuba had already revealed of herself,* which I tried to do, planning to spend the remainder of the day adrift in the warm sea of Cuba's social swirl.

But Jennifer presented a different program, based, I presumed, on the idea that if we shared a common understanding about life in Cuba we might also share a common destination at the end of the evening, the dining room at the Hotel Comodoro for certain, but perhaps only as a starting point for further adventures and a genuine test of the rules. With a mix of flirtatiousness, entertainment, and youthful authority she assumed the role of tutor, confident she could sharpen my blurry images of Cuba gathered during just a single day. A charmed confusion of potent images shaded with ambiguities and contradictions.

How could she and the three young currency traders we had met on the street be so carefree about dollars while Marie's son, and presumably many others, passed their young years in jail for possessing foreign currency?

Life was hard, Pedro the plumber had assured us and others had hinted as much, so how could it be possible for Sunday at La Bodeguita to give off the feel of a carnival day, a joyous festival, a celebration of food and drink and socializing?

It was commonly accepted that Cubans suffered wholesale oppression; why, then, did so many among them stop me on the street for freewheeling conversations or offers of illegal opportunity?

If food was so terribly scarce, how could everyone look so healthy, positively radiant compared to the extended-belly look of a nation suffering from a real hunger?

The agreeable Jennifer wanted to help me smooth out the bumpy inconsistencies between what official Cuba said and what everyday Cubans did. She pursued her task with a delight that was often more animated than edifying, laying her hand on my arm for emphasis one moment, clasping her hands over her mouth to mask amusement at my woeful ignorance the next, and keeping a careful eye on things, she paused in her lessons to catch the bartender's attention for another round of *mojitos* each time the need became obvious.

What Jennifer asked me to understand, in her rapid-fire Spanish without sufficient *s*'s, was this. The rules were surely the rules, for they were well established and acknowledged by nearly everyone; but their power and authority stopped there, or at least slowed down enough to invite negotiation, a cultural and political subtlety that helped explain a good deal about Cuba in the moment. Castro needed tourism to revive the national economy and save the Revolution, so he invited megabuck international companies to help build hotels, to create a comfortable architectural landscape for lounging and sunning and drinking and socializing. It's an old story: build it right and foreigners will come from Berlin, Paris, Madrid, and Toronto to sit in the sun and spend that foreign currency so prized as the salvation of the Revolution. *Yes, of course,* reasoned many Cubans, *"to defend tourism is to defend the Revolution." We will do what we must.*

But Jennifer and Liza were among many Cubans whose aspirations and expectations included a time at bat in this new game with foreigners, a chance to improve their daily lives in small, personal ways, to offset the shortages and rationing with a nice dinner, a T-shirt, a fair exchange of dollars for pesos at a bar, an offer of black market cigars for sale (at half the state-store rate), despite the certainty of jail time for holding dollars. But try as Jennifer did, it took a good deal more than our barside chat for me to begin understanding a Cuba nervously edging her way from revolutionary society to sun-and-sand tourist attraction.

We departed La Bodeguita late that evening looking like a ragtag, sloppy parade of three Americans, Pedro the waiter, Jennifer, Liza, and the plainclothes cops, who lurked behind as we made our way to the plaza in search of a cab and some temporary relief from the day's hurricane-force activities. We ambled along in a state of disorientation, brought on by the *mojitos*, La Bodeguita's exhilarating society, the strong sample of Cuban culture, and the near total breakdown of language skills—another effect of the *mojitos*.

"There is a problem," said Pedro, casting an anxious glance around the shadowed streets of cobblestone. That worried comment started me, Bob, and Pedro off on a three-party conversation, with Jennifer offering an occasional upbeat *"no problema"* by way of aside. In one instant Pedro's round face tightened into a frantic look, and the next it glistened with sweat—probably from the rum, but who could tell? A rapidly deteriorating Bob switched from Spanish to English and back again with Pedro, but the day was having its effect, and the collective conversation never got much wiser than Pedro's free-floating, eye-twitching worries about "men watching." The cops were gone, and so were Bob's Spanish and Pedro's English. Our arrival anxieties returned in a rush. Jennifer and Liza were having a delightful time, clearly entertained by the ranting of four men unable to make themselves understood, sinking into some form of paranoid dementia while standing under the illumination of a street light in Old Havana. Finally, waiting in the plaza for a cab, I told Jennifer one last time, "No Comodoro," then she lifted her cheek for a brush with mine to bid me goodnight with a good-natured smile that excused her having to tell the thick-headed American once again, "*No problema.*"

Necessary Rules

After a sluggish, post–La Bodeguita wake-up, we Americans grazed our way through a European-flavored breakfast buffet in the bright sunlight of the Comodoro's glass-walled dining room. Fortified with coffee, cold meats, and eggs, Bob and Caputo set off with professional determination to confront Cuba's government bureaucracy, half worried, half certain that securing press credentials and arranging for our cross-island trip would be a day spent in Marxist-paperwork hell. I went off on my own in search of a more traditional introduction to Havana than the previous day's manic experience. I walked and cabbed through the beautiful city, a welcoming place that appeared seized in time by the 1950s.

Automobiles, architecture, and a skyline slung low across the Caribbean horizon dated the success of the Revolution and the start of the U.S. embargo, that point when Batista and the American mob left town and Castro moved in. From that difficult juncture in her history, Cuba's always-thin national economy of tobacco and sugar began financing revolutionary change and national survival rather than new foundations of poured concrete and imported steel. Havana construction slowed, then stopped except for new housing programs, capturing one of the world's most lovely cities in a museum-quality freeze-frame of neglect. Basic maintenance ended, and so did the application of fresh paint. Thirty years after Fidel's troops first marched down the Malecón, Havana's lovely architectural façade remained beautiful but lay peacefully shrouded in a bleached and faded patina. Centuries-old structures flaked, then weakened until their mortared walls cracked and crumbled, transforming Havana into a landscape where cosmetic beauty surrendered to fatalism. Havana accepted her circumstances, wore them proudly, and remained strikingly beautiful. The modern epilogue to Havana's low, aged silhouette is the Hermanos Ameijeiras Hospital, twenty-three stories of glass and steel named for revolutionary heroes; the city's tallest structure serves as a functioning monument to Cuba's national health care program, its form and purpose appropriate for the most conspicuous addition to the revolutionary skyline.

After walking through the city center to the Avenida Malecón, I paused at the seawall to look across the four-lane street at several blocks of two- and three-story apartment houses. The once elegant buildings share an attached façade, offering a dramatic architectural presentation of tall chiseled columns, brightly colored ceramic tile treatments, open balconies with elaborate curved railings, and massive wooden doors hinged and trimmed with ornate metalwork. But that striking presence had long since eroded into indifference. Missing doors and windows left dark, gaping holes in some houses, and all but a few of them possessed only a lingering hint of paint, pale blue and salmon and light green so worn and faded that bone-white stucco showed through in large splotches. An occasional collapsed wall arched down to the ground to touch the rubble lying undisturbed where it had fallen. Havana was no place for the aesthetically fainthearted.

Those buildings looked out over Havana Harbor, making them prime real estate in any culture where the term "ocean view property" has the value of precious metal, but not so in Havana, where they were occupied by people whose claim to them was validated only by the grace of history. "Squatters," I was told by one young man who could not bear to leave me unattended. "Whole families of many people," he said, "live in two or three rooms; many of them used to be servants of the owners," referring to those once wealthy Cubans who had fled to Miami, abandoning country estates and city homes on the Malecón in a desperate flight, forsaking everything except their possessive love for Cuba and the promise of a return.

Like the Malecón, the rest of Havana wore a fragile look of worried decay. But the people were neatly dressed, even fashionable in a manner appropriate for a Caribbean setting. Cubans in clubs and hotels appeared downright trendy, wearing white cotton, starched and pressed; shirts and dresses in lively prints; and shoes well polished if well worn. Theirs was the look of people out for a good time and accustomed to doing it in style. There was no walking around in rags, sleeping in the streets, feeding from garbage pails, or begging handouts from strangers, even though the pinch was on and starting to tighten.

We had arrived just as a new round of rationing was making shortages and economic adjustments Havana's obsessive topics of conversation. *Life is hard,* more than one Cuban told me, even though the signs of neediness weren't as absolute as their language of protest, allowing a touch of skepticism for the visitor familiar with third-world suffering on an apocalyptic scale. One woman explained, "My month's ration of rice is gone in days; chicken and pork are difficult to get, even on the black market." She was a seamstress, not working, and terribly upset about the changes that tourism and rationing had brought into her life. "Everything is for the foreigners," she said. "We can't get perfume or lipstick or anything like that. It all goes for the tourists." And a walk through stores and hotels testified to the fairness of her protest. Clothes, cosmetics, personal items, and foodstuffs were plentiful in foreigners-only shops at hotels, as part of the program to support tourism and raise much-needed foreign currency, but not available to Cubans in everyday stores, not at any price, and Cubans were excluded from the foreigners' shops, barred at the door.

Castro had decreed a series of policies that allowed a regulated flow of people and goods into and out of the country, trying to ease political and consumer tensions in a society that possessed too much of both to keep the Revolution smiling. Disenchanted Cubans over forty years old could reserve a seat on a U.S.-bound airplane, providing they abandoned almost everything they owned and paid a hefty passport fee. Exiles could return to visit, as many did, their identity easily confirmed at José Martí Airport by their many suitcases and duffel bags bulging with soap, toothpaste, razors, clothes, coffee, and other items once commonplace in Cuba but now treasured by waiting relatives. Or they could plop down much-prized U.S. dollars at the foreigners-only store, a loophole in the system that netted Castro's impoverished government huge sums. In 1991 the U.S. government allowed Miami Cubans to send $100 per month per household to relatives back home, while at the same time threatening to jail any American citizen who spent dollars in Cuba, the most damning violation of the U.S. Treasury Department regulations. The Cuban government unofficially tolerated incoming packages mailed from the United States for the good they did in a country with empty shelves and strict rationing. Out with the complainers, in with the Levi's.

The net effect of these revisionist economic policies boosted the Cuban economy $200 to $300 million a year in cash and goods—not a lot, but significant for a nation that in 1991 imported less than $2 billion in goods for lack of foreign exchange, down from a high of over $8 billion in the late 1980s.

Still, it was hardly enough to keep Havana from radiating the feverish look and sounds of a city sliding toward economic emergency and physical collapse, just as Cuba's skeptics in the States had promised. The lovely architecture, surrendering to its destruction, yielded entire blocks to the snapshot look of war-zone rubble; the dependent economy, teetering on the rim of ruin, relied on foreign guests, who brought dollars and ate Cuba's rice, and former Cuban citizens from Miami, who brought toothpaste and fed Cuba's despair. Empty buildings, empty stores, empty purses, empty stomachs marked Havana's appearance and characterized the complaints of many Cubans. Havana's day-long hum of decay and hard times suggested that a low-grade misery was commonplace in the country.

But Cuba's modern identity extended beyond the obvious, shifted from face to face to reveal competing impulses that suggested a caution. *Listen carefully and look closely,* she seemed to say, *and I will tell you tales in which very little is absolute, where almost everything is provisional.*

That day took me along the length of the Malecón and back into Old Havana, where I bumped, literally, into a tall, handsome couple on a narrow sidewalk as Luisa and Pascual emerged from an apartment flushed from a lovers' rendezvous. We apologized, Pascual asked the time, which led to conversation, then to a brandy at the nearest bar, leading to more brandy and more conversation in messy Spanish and English. A lingering good time at the bar produced an invitation to hop a cab for the ride across Havana to the apartment they shared with Luisa's mother, Neddie, and Luisa's grandparents. Neddie, an English teacher, could ease the burden of language, if not of culture and politics, perhaps help us to express sentiments best left unspoken while standing elbow to elbow at a bar in Castro's Havana. I had no way of knowing, but off we went. Without hesitation I grabbed a cab with strangers, to go God knows where, or to what end. After only two days in the country, I was hopelessly seduced by Cuba's friendliness and charm, her good manners and curiosity.

We left the cab in a working-class neighborhood and walked up two narrow flights of stairs to the family apartment, where we were greeted by Abuela, tiny, gray, slightly bent, and more than a bit curious about who the kids had brought home. We settled in as Abuela looked on, rocking in her chair and twisting her hands in her lap while we sat and talked, waiting for Neddie. Luisa, a professional dancer, produced a large scrapbook. Laughing and pointing at memories, she showed me photos and press clippings, the history of a young woman who had been dancing since childhood. Luisa's shy personality and modest demeanor were beguiling counterpoints to pictures of her at work, a mocha beauty with an athlete's physique, dancing in sequined costume at one of Havana's most famous clubs, looking very much the provocative woman. Luisa explained with a schoolgirl's fussy distress that she had no pictures from her recent tour with a national dance troupe because there was no film for her point-and-shoot Kodak, even on the black market. Pascual, angular and loose-jointed, was as quick with a smile as he was with his rapid-fire Spanish. He showed me his hands, palms hard with calluses from hours playing the bongos and congas at a social club. His family was musical, his work a tradition. His uncle was well known throughout the Caribbean for introducing a particular African drum technique to the rhythms of the islands.

Luisa and Pascual possessed an innocent curiosity in their genuine pleasure at meeting an American—I was their first—and they were eager to know about me, and for me to know about them, a Cuban fellowship that in the days ahead I would learn was more commonplace than unique. Their interest was personal, concerned with the three of us and everyday matters. *What is your work? Do you own a car? Where do you live? In a house? Are you married? Why did you come to Cuba? Are you having a good time? How long will you stay? What hotel is yours? Are you here alone?*—and on they went without a touch of interest about the spiteful history shared by Cuba and the United States, or about my opinion of Castro's Cuba either. Abuela listened attentively, silently except to instruct the children in rapid Spanish, with wagging finger and great animation, "Say nothing to him about Castro."

Politics in that household were the exclusive jurisdiction of Neddie, the matriarch of the gathering, who returned home from a day of teaching English to scientists to find a foreigner—an American at that—sitting in her living room, facing her family lined up in a row across the room. She clapped her hands in delight. "Could I practice my English, perhaps ask a question or two?" she asked.

"Anything," I said. "I am grateful to be here."

With Neddie's arrival the three-room apartment appeared to lose proportion, creating the sensation of a space too confined to accommodate everyday Cuban home life—my American's perception, to be sure, because the gathering was the family, plus one outsider. Neddie and I shared a faded blue couch that rested against one wall in the small living room. Luisa, Pascual, and Abuela sat side by side on straight-backed wooden chairs along the opposite wall, which opened onto a balcony behind them. Sunlight filtering through the balcony shutters cast the three of them in thin slivers of light in which afternoon dust particles danced. At one end of the room was the front door, a table with TV and stereo, and a floor lamp; the other end opened onto a kitchen cramped with a small refrigerator, two-burner gas stove, and tiny countertop covered in burn-blackened pots and pans, assorted boxes and bags of food, and bottles and jars of drinks, spices, and sauces that were so close that I could read the labels—rice, black beans, olive oil, hot sauce, coffee, sugar, rum. Beyond the kitchen lay the single bedroom with a bath. The apartment's paint was institutional green, the place was clean and neat, and the whole scene was faded, well worn, like Cuba herself.

A woman of commanding form and presence, Neddie wore a sundress once patterned in bright colors but long since reduced to near white by repeated washing. She leaned forward on the edge of the couch with her hands folded in her lap as she spoke seriously about life becoming "more difficult in the past two years. . . . No, no, Peter, I think 'inconvenient' is a better English word than 'difficult'"—with the food rationing and with such items as soap and coffee so scarce. "This is all true, but our problems will be temporary. Castro will get us through this difficult period, just as he has many times in the past. It is important that we all remember how much Castro has done for Cuba. Sometimes in very difficult circumstances. Dangerous circumstances. I'm certain you know what I mean, don't you? He will do it again. I'm confident of it," she said, nodding her head up and down to accent her conviction.

Neddie spoke faultless English with an old-fashioned attention to pronunciation. She was well informed and thoughtful with her information and history, not a person given to excessive claims or denials to explain Cuba's new circumstances, but possessing enthusiasm for her life, her family, and her country. She smoked Popular cigarettes, the inexpensive national brand. While we sipped Cuban coffee from chipped porcelain cups, I said, "I am embarrassed by what my country has done to yours. The blockade, the assassination attempts against Castro, the Bay of Pigs, the drive to overturn the Revolution."

"No, no!" she responded with one of the explosive exclamations that punctuated her conversations. "The Cuban people understand that it is not the American people who have done these things, but the government. The American people are our friends," a dubious statement I let pass, preferring at the moment the warmth of community among Cubans over the truth about politics in America.

"Everything in Cuba will be clearer if you visit the Museum of the Revolution before you travel to Santiago," said Neddie. "It is very important for you to understand our past before you can understand Cuba today. It was a terrible time before the Revolution. Some people had everything, and people like my family had nothing. We were hungry and despised. We had no place to live for a time. We worked very hard but had nothing. It was a very difficult time," she repeated, without a trace of self-pity.

"Many of the people who complain the most today don't know or remember what Cuba was like in the past," she continued. "They forget. That's very dangerous. Yes, very dangerous. For them. For Cuba too."

I told her that many Americans knew something of what Cuba was like before the Revolution, when Batista ruled, and about the revolutionary struggle.

Neddie, assuming the common characteristic of her profession, cast a doubting look, folded her arms, and started a schoolteacher's tutorial. "Tell me, Peter, what do you think about the attack on the Moncada Army Barracks?" she asked, referring to the first military action of Castro's revolution, and an absolute disaster. "Was it a reckless act?" she began, then walked me through several of the Revolution's historic high points.

"Why do you think Batista exiled Castro rather than executing him?

"Do you think Castro was always a Marxist?

"Have you seen the Sierra Maestra where Castro and his army made the Revolution?" And on it went, with me respectfully answering the questions with as much information as I had until the discussion gradually shifted from quiz back to conversation.

Apparently satisfied that I was not a one-fact wonder, Neddie the teacher softened to Neddie a daughter of the Revolution and the mother of Luisa with another point to make that slipped past pure politics. Staring softly at her mother, Luisa's bent and gray grandmother, she said, "Since the Revolution, we have national health care. The Revolution brought that, and gave my mother two lifesaving operations. *Two*. That would not have been possible before the Revolution. Not at all. Without the Revolution, my mother would be dead by now.

"My daughter has had dance lessons paid for by the state since she first enrolled in school," she said, reaching over to gently rub her daughter's arm for a moment. "The Revolution did that too. Before, only the rich went to school. There was no opportunity for people like us. One of the first things the Revolution did was to end illiteracy. It was a very big campaign. An important effort. Thousands of people went throughout the country to teach people to read and write.

"The education system gave my daughter a profession. A chance in her life. She has a job and respect. She has a future.

"Why do I tell you all this? Because I am a Communist? No. I am not," said Neddie, squeezing her eyes shut and shaking her head from side to side. "Because I am a Cuban proud of our Revolution? Yes. And because I want you to see what the Revolution means to me and the people I love most. What it means to people like us. People who had nothing before the Revolution. Not even hope."

In the silence that followed I could find nothing to say that felt appropriate to Neddie's personal manifesto. I had neither the political values nor the personal inclination to doubt her testimony of loyalty and gratitude to the Revolution; and no stories of my experiences would have advanced that conversation, so I acknowledged Neddie with a sober promise to visit the Museum of Revolution. Delighted with her success, she offered to accompany me as guide.

When the afternoon drew down I invited Luisa and Pascual to come to the Hotel Comodoro with me to meet Bob and Caputo, to have dinner, drinks, and conversation. But my invitation was misdirected in that household. "That will be impossible," said Neddie firmly. "We have rules to keep Cubans out of the tourist hotels; we must have them because some Cubans are taking advantage of foreigners, causing Cuba to look very bad. They want things. They do things. We can't allow people to make trouble with the tourists. Tourism is too important to us, Peter. I hope you understand. These are necessary rules. You are always welcome to come to our home, to share what we have, but Luisa and Pascual cannot go to the hotel."

Not willing to surrender the point, I headed for the technicality. "Don't the rules allow Cubans to be with foreigners in hotel bars and restaurants? Only rooms are off-limits?"

"That's true but changes nothing; my family will not give the appearance of breaking the rules," said Neddie, with a straight-backed tone that closed the discussion.

Already late to meet Bob, I gave up the argument and said good-bye to Neddie, Luisa, Pascual, and Abuela with a pledge to visit again before I left Cuba.

While I was being swept into the embrace of Neddie's family, the always-working Bob had parlayed a stroke of good fortune into a breathtaking bonanza. He had been introduced to Abraham Maciques, the head man at Cubanacan, a state-sanctioned independent tourism agency that was ravenous in its pursuit of dollars to save the Revolution. When Bob asked Maciques if he might help us secure severely rationed gasoline for a trip into the island's hinterlands, Maciques said, "*No problema.*" He would take care of that, and more. Cubanacan would provide car, driver, and translator for such a distinguished writer interested in tourism.

Bob hesitated. Fully vested with the skepticism of his trade, he feared he might lose control of the trip, convinced that Maciques had in mind a state-controlled romp through the glitzier aspects of Cuba's unrefined tourism industry. Bob stalled for time to think, to figure out how to get what he needed without surrendering too much in return. Our need was clear, but the dangers of a bad bargain were manifest.

Maciques, the gentleman executive properly outfitted in dark dress slacks and a white guayabera, kept working the deal until Bob softened on the car and driver, but he remained firm about no guide (*no bilingual, ideological, government-minded imposition who would surely monitor our every move, contest our every decision, and become an unacceptable cramp on our freedom,* imagined Bob). But Maciques soothed and persisted, until finally an anxious but opportunistic Bob accepted Maciques's full package—car, driver, *and* translator-guide. But it would be Bob's show, "Agreed?" "*No problema,*" responded the courtly statesman of tourism.

The deal was cemented the next morning when Eric, an Afro-Cuban in his fifties with a bearlike build, an easy smile that filled his face, and the most reassuring eyes, pulled into the circular drive of the Hotel Comodoro in a new air-conditioned Toyota van. He carried with him Roberto, a man of thirtyish good looks just starting to show signs of thickening flesh, neatly trimmed black hair and mustache, a rakish charm, a knack for languages, and a consuming curiosity about Americans. Bob presented Eric with a five-gallon gasoline container brought from the States as a precaution in the land of rationed fuel, a precaution transformed that morning into a much-appreciated gift.

Without prodding, a smiling and agreeable Eric pronounced Bob the *jefe* of the expedition who would sit up front with him, who would give the orders and directions that Eric promised to follow, which turned out to be true without exception. Bob liked being in charge, and it was, after all, his gig, his trip, and his story to write. Caputo, Roberto, and I shared the van's back seats with our gear and a Cubanacan cooler filled with ice, juices, Coke (imported from the Netherlands), and Hatuey beer (the 12 percent stuff), and beside the cooler sat a case of seven-year-old Cuban rum. Perfect. Outfitted for the trip, we headed for Varadero Beach, where the rules of the road made themselves known before the end of the day.

As soon as we were on the move, the wiring among the five of us began to harden, with hot leads and solid grounds and lots of energy—sometimes too much. Bob, Roberto, and Caputo shared an unrelenting need for nicotine and a tendency toward sardonic humor.

English was the near-universal language in the van, placing Eric a bit out of range much of the time, although over the miles it became clear that he understood far more than he was prepared to comment on, making him the only one of us with the least bit of restraint about saying whatever came to mind. By the nature of our lesser obligations, Eric and I were drawn together, the two who could shut down and just cruise easy when the need or desire hit us. For Bob, Roberto was more a source of information for this story than a traditional guide to Cuba's historical past and modern highways, which was how Roberto saw his role, at least for a time. The affinity of the two namesakes seesawed between competition and friendship, and began almost immediately when Roberto went to work, practicing his skilled English and spreading his charm, smooth. "Give me a chance," he said with dramatic sincerity, referring to Bob's earlier reservations about accepting a guide and translator. "You're my first Americans."

"We're every Cuban's first Americans, as far as I can tell," I said.

"And we may be the last unless Castro gets busy," said Bob. "Do you think Cuba will survive the loss of Russian aid and Castro's decision to court foreign tourists?" he continued, off and running, after that story.

"Who knows," shrugged Roberto. "The future is the future."

"Yes, and just around the corner," said Bob. "There's a lot a capitalist could teach you about running your tourism industry, but you seem to have already learned a good deal about how to turn a profit."

"Ah," said Roberto, quick on the uptake and warming to the game, "you know Karl Marx says, 'Take what you can of your enemy's good points and use them for yourself.'"

"Good luck with that," said a skeptical Bob.

"What?"

"It's a little cynical humor."

"Okay, good. I like the American sense of humor. But listen, we are aware of the dangers of tourism and the need to maintain the principles of the Revolution."

"Time will tell," said Bob, establishing his provenance for getting the last word.

Heading along the pastoral coastal highway leading to Varadero Beach, we made a number of side trips with stops at historic points, not feeling pressed, and actually paying more attention to what was going on inside the van than to the outside landscape, making small shifts and adjustments to meet the demands of random personalities thrown together and cooped up in a van for ten days. Everyone kept to their best behavior as we passed a series of beaches with clusters of modest bungalows and cinder-block hotels that catered to local customers, a place where faithful workers might go to redeem their work bonuses or incentives. The beaches were spiked by the occasional oil well, a rusted, ugly reminder that the Revolution needed whatever resources it could extract from the Varadero Peninsula.

As happened to us repeatedly in Cuba—a land shut off to Americans, not only its landscape, but its essence too—we had given little thought to what we would find. Perhaps a bucolic twelve-mile stretch of sandy beach, a Caribbean paradise of whitewashed cottages with red-tiled roofs, home to longtime residents whose stories of living on the edge of the sea would make us nod wisely, grateful for having read Hemingway.

Whatever we expected, it was not the 218-room, $18 million, four-star Tuxpan Hotel that Eric pulled up in front of with the announcement that we had arrived. With its lavish lobby decorated in exotic woods, piped-in music, color TV, glass-walled views of postcard-perfect water, tiki-lit lounge area, and bare-breasted German sunbathers, the Tuxpan—an extravagant monument to the concept of one-stop resort vacations—was a succulent offering in the competitive marketplace of international tourism. Twenty-four hours earlier, when we had visited Havana's rustic Marina Hemingway, I had remarked ruefully to Bob, "I can see Florida developers poised with blueprints, ready to raze this place and airlift in a ready-built modern facility. You know they could get the job done in a wink, so practiced are Americans at snatching up such an opportunity." At Varadero Beach there appeared the incarnation of our dark capitalist humor in a series of high-rise hotels in various stages of completion, beckoning to rich international travelers to come, spend, bail out the Revolution. Joint ventures with the Spanish, Germans, Mexicans, French, Canadians—anyone and everyone (except Americans, who were forbidden by the U.S. government) with the capital to finance a 50/50 deal with the Castro government—had created a scene that left us dumbfounded.

We were in Cuba for the adventure as well as the story and eager for whatever Cuba might present to us, but we were not ready for the Tuxpan Hotel. It was cheap enough in price, but too costly in concept for travelers like us, too much the turbo-jet, slick-brochure, package-tour accommodation. It was Cuban by the circumstance of geography, not Cuban in culture or personality.

Bob was distressed. In rejecting the offer of a Cubanacan-pride-in-tourism tour, he had made a deal that he would be in charge, no exceptions, no sidetracking. Yet there we were, in the Tuxpan lobby. Then things began to spin out of control when Roberto explained that he and Eric would leave us three Americans at the Tuxpan while they found lesser accommodations for the night. Bob barely held it together.

"What are you talking about?" he asked, his rising voice catching the attention of the lobby staff. "Just stay here. If it's over your budget, we'll make up the difference."

"Bob, it's not that," said Roberto. "We can't stay here. Cubans aren't allowed here. This is a foreigners-only hotel."

The look on Bob's face first surprised me, then told me what was on the way. Bob had not been part of my conversations with Jennifer or Neddie, and while he had some inkling that everything was not as it should be for Cubans in tourist hotels, he had no real understanding that Cubans were excluded as guests. For that matter, neither did I, assuming, without giving it a great deal of thought, that this absolute prohibition was governed by the winking flexibility we had already come to admire in Cuban society.

"That's bullshit! If you guys leave, we go with you," said Bob in a near fit of outrage at the idea of our traveling companions being banished from the place—an unforgivable breach in the democratic rules of road tripping.

Roberto appeared panic stricken. He tried to reason, to explain this was how it had to be, for the sake of the Revolution. It was all right. "You must stay . . . you are expected here . . . it is all arranged . . . special guests of the manager," he pleaded, wiping the nervous perspiration from his brow.

Bob is a personality with the interesting but sometimes problematic quality of feeling everything keenly, intensely, and in that setting he was insulted, even hurt, by the national policy that refused hotel service to his newfound friends. His political reactions are sometimes difficult to predict, but his sense of humanity lies close to the surface, and it bubbled over in that sunlit lobby in the form of a series of uncharitable references, including one to "Cuban apartheid."

Caught in his own dilemma, Bob failed to appreciate Roberto's. Caputo and I tried to make peace. Actually, Caputo tried to make peace by quoting Bob's own article on Mexican tourism in which he concluded that Mexico's seaside resorts were a source of great national pride; given the circumstances, soothed Caputo, couldn't we accept Roberto's need to have us experience one night of Cuba's salvation by four-star tourist attraction? Bob snarled. I chose politics over peacemaking, suggesting that Bob ought to let Roberto decide what sacrifices he was prepared to make for his Revolution. Bob snarled.

Finally Bob accepted an amended program, though he didn't like doing it. The three Americans would stay the night and schmooze with the manager, but from then on we would all travel, eat, drink, and sleep only where Cubans were allowed to do the same. A grim-faced Roberto fled the lobby just as the hotel manager arrived to set a time for us to view the place and chat over coffee. A truly unhappy Bob snarled once again.

Later, we gathered in the café, where Tuxpan manager Eamonn Donnelly introduced us to the workings of tourism on Castro's island. The effusive, sandy-haired Irishman worked for a German management firm that ran the Mexican-built hotel, which was owned jointly by the Cuban government and Spanish investors and serviced and supplied by Cubanacan. Cranked up on coffee laced with sugar and surrounded by an appreciative audience, Donnelly told us how much he loved the place, totally, hopelessly loved it; not the hotel itself exactly, but the country, Cubans, the situation, and not just because an astounding 95 percent occupancy rate during the winter high season guaranteed his success, but because it all worked so well.

"Cuba is a safe destination, free of the racial strife found elsewhere in the Caribbean. It has the best reputation on the European market," he said, straightening the collar of his oatmeal-colored linen shirt.

And he was as proud of the hotel's employee arrangements as he was of the occupancy rate. Each professional staff member—manager, chef, housekeeper, bookkeeper—mostly foreigners, trained a Cuban understudy who someday would inherit the position. The Cuban trainees also attended a tourism school run by Cubanacan. "Cubans are great workers," Donnelly said, "the best employees I have ever had. Brazil was a nightmare, and the Germans overseeing things were so strict. Cubans are educated and eager to do a good job. They really believe in what they are doing. They believe that tourism is the future of the country. This is the real Caribbean socialism, if you ask me. It's all quite lovely, actually," he said with a sigh. "I don't ever want to leave."

This charming man's enthusiasm for Cuba's revolutionary society *cum* tourist paradise had me wondering if Castro might not pull it off after all, mix up the two contrary forces and then patch up the damage to the Revolution when the exchequer said the time was right.

But the conversation took a difficult turn when Donnelly remarked that a group of fifty Young Pioneers, the Communist Party's youth group, would arrive the next day to do volunteer work, spruce up the hotel grounds before a convention of international travel agents met there that weekend. My companions responded with such loaded words as "overseer" and "slave labor." Playing the social coward, I bit back the urge to offer my own comparison. Not forced workers, by any fair-minded judgment, but American Boy Scouts collecting litter along the highway, eager youths in khaki uniforms who dragged bright orange bags filled with the discards of indifferent travelers, young men learning the virtues of public service. I was distressed that my friends saw the situation so differently, put such a harsh twist on Cuba's revolutionary doctrine of *voluntarismo* that Cuban youths traditionally accepted as their own.

Neddie's claims on behalf of the Revolution and the need for necessary rules and personal sacrifices—including hers—found a pressing context at the Tuxpan. What would she contribute to this conversation, I wondered? If tourism and joint-venture hotels on the Tuxpan's scale were Cuba's best hope—perhaps last hope—of surviving in a hostile world, then why not invite the Communist Party's youth brigade to help out? The idea of public service had fallen to the level of quaintness in the United States during the Reagan eighties. But sitting in that conversation I found appealing a society with a grand purpose, where service in a good cause had the strength it once did in America, when part of a generation was inexorably drawn to the Peace Corps, as Bob was, or the civil rights crusade, as I was, or the antiwar movement, as so many of us were. Was it softhearted and wrongheaded to consider Neddie's view of things? To accept the idea that some Cubans were ready to serve the common purpose of a shared struggle, which made teenage Communists willing to spend a weekend pulling weeds, made Roberto and Eric willing to walk out of the Tuxpan to seek lesser accommodations, because it was for the Revolution in crisis? Sacrifices for the cause. An easy enough proposition to understand, however uncomfortable its ground-level application.

Yet for all my romantic high-mindedness on behalf of revolutionary sacrifice, the bone-deep, long-after-the-fact reflective truth of that situation was this: I never asked Roberto and Eric where they stayed the night; never asked, *Did you travel an emotionally difficult distance before finding a place that would take you in?* I never asked in the most pressing, personal way how they really felt about being turned out of the tourist hotels, about "necessary rules." And the even more complete truth is that after sharing coffee with Donnelly I went to my lovely room and then trotted down to the gorgeous, sugar-white, *foreigners-only* Varadero Beach to swim in the beautiful sea, acting like the privileged tourist that I surely was, floating in the last rays of Caribbean sunlight.

Playa Girón

At the front desk the next morning I talked Donnelly into cashing the first U.S.-issued traveler's check since the start of the embargo. "First exceptions," he chimed, "are happening minute by minute these days in Cuba." Roberto and Eric appeared, and we loaded up the van for a long day on the road. A reconstituted Bob shook out the map and told Eric, "I think we should take a sharp turn here, back to reality." The ever-smiling Eric shoved a rock 'n' roll cassette into the tape deck with a flourish and swung the van out of the hotel drive, onto the open highway.

Mile after mile we watched cane fields and farms, the land as flat and monotonous as south Florida, an appropriate comparison, for the farther south we moved into Matanzas Province the closer we got to the Zapata Peninsula, Cuba's own Everglades, a major wildlife preserve for crocodiles and manatees and home to 388 species of birds, many of which are found nowhere else in the Americas.

We stopped at Guamá, the Revolution's first tourism project, an Indian village in the middle of Zapata National Park that includes a crocodile farm. Boats carry visitors down five miles of canals, through water and jungle teeming with fish, reptiles, and birds. We were less interested in the village than in lunch, which we already knew would be accompanied by an installment of Roberto's machismo style, his quixotic flirting with every waitress in every restaurant we visited. While we waited in the beautiful thatched-roof restaurant for our grilled crocodile, a *trova*—a musical poem—played on the radio. Its lyrics were political, revolutionary, and considered passé by some Cubans, advising listeners not to emigrate from the countryside to the city, since there were no beds for so many people. The newer *trovas*, in contrast, were street smart, urban based, rock oriented, and often critical of the Castro regime. One of them had an antitourism theme, but not antitourist, for that would violate Cuba's impeccable good manners; it chided the government for the tourism industry's double standard in its treatment of Cubans.

While the rest of the crew toured the rickety crocodile farm, Eric and I lingered at the café, something we would do occasionally, having discovered a common sensibility along the fringes of the group dynamics, away from the steady obligations held in common by writer, photographer, and guide. Every Cuban I met was curious for details about life in the States, and so was Eric, but his particular interest concerned race relations, what it meant to be black in white America. He knew a good deal about the civil rights struggle, its heroes and martyrs such as Martin Luther King Jr. and Malcolm X, and its flash points, most of them violent and bloody. He and I always drifted back to that subject, normally when he sought clarification for some fact or idea we had previously spoken about. But this conversation took a different form.

"Do blacks in the States know about life in Cuba? Do they think we live like they do?"

"I can't really say for certain. I suspect some blacks, those widely read and fully informed, have an idea, but I don't really know."

"Our life here before the Revolution was a lot like in the States, I think. Maybe worse, I don't know. But I know what the Revolution has meant for people like me. There was prejudice. It was very bad, to be black. To be black and poor. It was very bad. We could do nothing. I wish my English was better so I could explain better.

"Now we can do whatever everyone else can. Be here or there. Hold important jobs. When people in the States talk about Cuba, they never ask people like me what I think, what we think.

"We will never go back to the way things were. We can't. Won't. I think the Revolution was most important for blacks. More than anyone else," said Eric, his thoughts trailing off as our companions returned to gather us up.

Back on the trail of exploration we fell into one of our intermittent language lessons as we ticked away the miles. I entertained the group with repeated failed attempts to properly pronounce the main course of our lunch, *cocodrilo*. Every few minutes a mischievous Eric called out the word, carefully and dramatically articulating each syllable with exaggerated clarity, and I faithfully responded each time, but my mind got locked on stressing the wrong syllable, and the harder I tried the worse it got, and I never did get it exactly right, causing my comrades to fall into fits of laughter and uncharitable attacks on my language skills. Bob gave Eric an English tutorial based on mocking statements about Roberto's social life, which Eric repeated with great delight: "Roberto loves every waitress in Cuba." Then Bob helped Eric with his driving etiquette: "Eat dust and die, dickhead." Bob told Roberto to get out his notebook and write this one down: "Cuba has put all its eggs in one basket," one of Bob's regular attempts to get Roberto into a discussion about tourism. And on it went. Caputo cautioned Roberto and Eric that for each of the many rules in English there are even more exceptions, a statement about language that we all appreciated for its symbolic application to life in Cuba, so much so that when we passed by the Holy Spirit Artificial Insemination Factory we were too preoccupied to even joke about it.

The shift in mood sent Roberto and me into an earnest conversation about medical practices in the United States, particularly in the treatment of HIV and AIDS. Roberto was horrified to hear that in the United States HIV-infected people are allowed to walk the streets free and unchecked, and was absolutely appalled to learn that the U.S. government made no provision for their medical treatment. A truly disbelieving Roberto sought confirmation from Bob in the front seat, then from Caputo, both of whom testified to the truth of it. "That's crazy," he said with a shake of his head, "just crazy.

"In Cuba," he went on, "whole neighborhoods are given blood tests at one time. Infected people are taken to a sanatorium in the countryside where many of the best medical people are. They get the best medicines and healthy food. They don't have to work; everything is provided for them. Only when the doctors think a patient's health is okay and he's learned to act responsibly can he leave and go home. Usually someone from the hospital, a psychologist or someone, goes along to explain to the neighbors and the people at work that everything is okay. The papers say that AIDS patients in Cuba live longer than any place in the world. Cuba is very proud of that."

Roberto, it turned out, was an informed voice on such matters because his wife was a doctor, a Chinese woman, and his third partner in marriage. To that information I remarked, "I'm surprised you've gone through only two wives, given the way you try to seduce every woman you meet."

With a sigh Roberto bummed a cigarette from Bob, lit it, and said, "Yes.

Yes. I know. It's a big problem. It has been since I was a kid. I love women. Cuban women, Canadian women, German women. I just love them. I know I make them feel good. I was expelled from the Young Pioneers because of that. They didn't approve that I went with so many women. I was young, but that didn't make any difference. They threw me out for what you would call 'womanizing.' All it really meant was I can't join the Communist Party, and that's not really important to me anyway. My life is fine."

About the time I was explaining to Roberto the principles of civil liberties in the United States to help him understand why we didn't—couldn't—make sweeps to round up citizens other than criminals, we slipped off the main route and dipped toward the south coast for a side trip to Playa Girón, a beautiful stretch of beach, preserved as a tourist resort, that is remembered in the United States, but not in Cuba, as the Bay of Pigs. As we approached, simple, solemn concrete monuments rose intermittently, and then with greater frequency, out of the mangrove swamp and thick palmetto scrub, honoring Castro's warriors—161 killed in action during three days of battle, April 17–19, 1961. We planned to mark the historic site, visit the museum, and be on the road again soon. A quick stop to nod at history, urged Bob. As we piled out of the van, we couldn't help but comment on the irony of such a gorgeous place being the locale of such an ugly business, Americans sending 1,500 Cuban exiles, armed and trained by the CIA, into hopeless battle against fellow Cubans and the Revolution. After the fighting, Castro had more than 1,000 prisoners and the start of what became the 1962 missile crisis.

Being in that place sharpened the memory of what our government had done there, causing Bob and me to shake our heads in wonder over one of America's most outrageous Cold War blunders, an act so arrogant, so incompetent, that it stands on its own, even after all these years, as a crimson-stained affidavit to American hubris.

Roberto and Caputo headed for the museum while Bob and I lingered at the van to discuss the invasion. Eric, standing nearby and listening to us, casually remarked, "I was with them."

Failing to catch Eric's exact meaning, Bob asked, "What are you saying?"

Eric, in his understated style, explained, "I was a student, just nineteen years old, when I came on the second day of the fighting with the brigade that Fidel brought from Havana. I stayed until the fighting ended. After that I guarded the prisoners and helped take them back to Havana. "Yes," he laughed softly at our look of discovery, "I became a major in the air force. But don't worry, I'm retired now." He fished out his wallet to show us a military identity card, with a younger Eric, smiling, dressed in an officer's uniform.

His revelation sobered us further. History changed into a face we knew. A man we found so easy to like for his soft charm and humor, who had been so welcoming to us, had suddenly presented himself into one of our sensitive historical memories by the act of defending his country against the shameless intentions of our own. Bob and I looked at each other. Neither of us knew how to process the information Eric had offered so casually, a report made without malice or regret, so we simply told Eric what was clutching at our emotions: we were honored to visit the Bay of Pigs with one of its veterans. Eric smiled affectionately at me, we embraced, pulled back, smiled again as if we had shared a secret, which I suppose we had, and embraced once again, a commonplace act to confirm a most curious bond. Eric stayed with the van listening to music while Bob and I headed for the museum, lost in our separate thoughts as we passed beneath a billboard that proclaimed the Bay of Pigs as the site of the "First Rout of Imperialism in Latin America."

Outside the museum sat a prop-driven plane, a camouflage sentinel guarding the artifacts of an embattled nation's Revolution. Was this one of the planes that downed the CIA aircraft, then sank the invader's supply boats, leaving the 1,500 civilians in fatigues abandoned on the beach, while the U.S. Navy watched offshore and President Kennedy, cutting his losses, decided not to send in air support? No one appeared to know.

Arriving just weeks after the thirtieth anniversary of the invasion, we were presented with commemorative pins and a pamphlet complete with several maps that described the invasion by the *mercenarios*. The maps were detailed, the text accurate in fact and revolutionary in language.

Our tour guide shared the national characteristics of a pleasant countenance and an enthusiasm for Americans, although Caputo was instructed, "No photographs, please," for reasons never made clear. She walked us through the museum, a re-creation of the invasion with maps, charts, photographs, and displays of weapons and military paraphernalia under glass, mostly World War II surplus arms and materiel—

30-caliber M-1 carbines, khaki rucksacks stamped "U.S.," military-issue field glasses—a collection of national treasures protected from even the camera's flash. The invasion story was told with war's universal imagery. Grainy black-and-white photographs of smiling Cuban militiamen gathered around a tank, hands raised high in the V-for-victory sign, jubilant over the "first defeat of imperialism in Latin America," were positioned beside pictures of captured *mercenarios*, exhausted after seventy-two hours of combat, faces grim with apprehension, eyes fixed with the thousand-yard stare so common to fighting men who had seen too much. Except for the pictures and a few captured documents, the displays resembled an army-navy surplus store in the States, a reminder of how current this major event in Cuban-U.S. relations truly was, but giving no hint of its enduring importance.

A Texan who had shared our plane from Cancún offered his opinion, his drawl coming from under a straw cowboy hat. Tall and lean like someone sent from central casting, he had "agricultural interests in Mexico" and visited Cuba regularly. "I can tell you why the United States is so wrongheaded about Cuba," he said. "The United States is so wrongheaded about Cuba because at the Bay of Pigs our government got egg on its face, and every time it tried to wipe it off, all it did was smear it around even more." Not a bad take on U.S. policy toward Cuba since the Revolution.

The Bay of Pigs invasion, or something like it, was inevitable given the long-standing relationship between Washington and Havana, a sticky union that gave the United States enormous influence in the island's affairs for decades before the Revolution. For years, a flow of culture, aspirations, investments, vice, tourists, gangsters, shoppers, adventurers, commerce, and industry had locked the two countries in a relationship that left Cuba dependent on the United States for its good fortune as one of Latin America's most prosperous countries, explains historian Louis A. Pérez Jr. There was a time following World War II when Pan Am ran several flights daily between Havana and Miami; ten thousand Cubans visited Florida during the peak season. Cuba was a hungry market for companies with postwar money to invest, F. W. Woolworth, Coca-Cola, Pepsi Cola, Armour, Swift, Singer Sewing Machine, Texaco, Shell, Standard Oil among them, and hungry for American books and films, for radios and TVs and automobiles, for sun-seeking tourists—and sin-seeking tourists as well. And many Cubans liked what they saw, finding in American culture and society an aspiration for themselves and their country: the good life.

The United States held the key to Cuba's treasury. In 1958, Americans controlled a staggering proportion of Cuba's economy: 90 percent of telephone and electric services, 80 percent of public railroads, 70 percent of petroleum imports and distribution, and on and on. Seventy-five percent of Cuba's imports came from U.S. companies, from machines, motors, automobiles, refrigerators, televisions, and radios down to the very nuts and bolts that held Cuba's factories together. And the United States bought more Cuban sugar each year than any other country in the world.

Enter Fidel Castro and his 26th of July Movement, the most powerful and best organized of several groups trying to oust the shaky Batista government during the 1950s. The time was right, the conditions near-perfect, made so by official corruption, colonial economics, organized crime, girlish prostitution, and a boom-or-bust economy, too bound up with the United States, too long on its down side. Underscoring these problems was the Platt Amendment, America's turn-of-the-century license-by-fiat to intervene in Cuba's internal affairs. The culture and commerce of American dependency made many Cubans resentful, eager for a change in national style—or in government, if that's what it took. In early 1958, Castro's movement, flush with wide support across the island and active in every province, initiated a plan to destroy property, particularly foreign-owned property, particularly American-owned property.

A bad economy got worse. As it approached collapse, it drew labor, peasants, students, and the middle class into the struggle. Washington grew unhappy with Havana. Political disorder threatened American lives and businesses, disrupted commerce, and destroyed millions of dollars in property. With Cuba on the edge of catastrophe, the United States stepped into its traditional role as arbitrator. Washington withdrew support from Batista, first by way of an arms embargo and finally by sending an emissary—a New York banker with interests in Cuba, a perfect choice given the situation—to convince Batista to step down before the country was lost to Castro's rebel army. Batista said, "No," in the petulant language of tyrants.

The Washington-Havana axis ruptured on January 1, 1959, when the rebels took control of the country through force of arms. The United

States was on the outs with Cuba for the first time in half a century, discredited by its partnership with a corrupt and brutal past, by its economic hold on the country, by its imperious attitude toward Cuba. It took two more years for things to sour completely between Washington and Havana, in a contest that had many phases, none more important than ridding Cuba of American privileges.

The Revolution's earliest decrees had dual objectives: to improve life for Cubans and to lessen American control over the island. By May 1959 Castro had issued decrees affecting wages, rents, costs of services, land ownership, health, and education, often at the expense of foreign owners. In cutting utility and telephone rates and raising wages, Castro let American business interests know that their reign in Cuba was at an end. In nationalizing over 2.5 million acres of land with the Agrarian Reform Law, he restructured the relationship between Washington and Havana by reducing the power of American sugar and cattle interests, some of which lost nine-tenths of their holdings. Power follows money, and Castro clearly intended to break America's authority over both in Cuba.

Events tumbled quickly from there. In early 1960, Cuba and the Soviet Union signed a trade and economic aid agreement, swapping sugar for crude oil and netting Cuba $100 million in low-interest loans.

June—Castro nationalized Shell, Texaco, and Standard Oil refineries after they refused to process the Russian crude, a corporate decision reached under threat of retaliation by the U.S. Treasury Department.
July—Washington cut Cuban sugar imports to zero.
August—Castro nationalized North American–owned utilities, sugar mills, and banks.
October—The United States established a partial economic embargo.
October—Castro nationalized all remaining American property in Cuba—166 holdings, from hotels to export firms—ending U.S. investments on the island.
January 1961—The United States broke diplomatic relations with Cuba.

The Revolution was then just two years old; plans for an invasion at the Bay of Pigs were nine months old, having been authorized by Eisenhower in April 1960.

With diplomatic relations ended, Washington's drive to control Cuba had shifted from Havana to Miami, passing through the powerful Cuban exile community in south Florida, thus making the Washington-Miami axis the keeper of the ambitions from the Bay of Pigs—topple Castro, overturn the Revolution. This was a natural transfer. By 1960 Miami was home to more than 125,000 refugees from the new revolutionary government, men and women of wealth and property who had long looked to the United States to keep Cuba solvent and peaceful, safe from dramatic change or ruin. Cubans fled the Revolution, unable to gather themselves into a reasonable opposition to Castro. Having fallen into political atrophy under the comfortable assurance that the United States would always protect their shared interests, the exiles arrived in Miami certain that their stay would be temporary, confident that Washington would not tolerate a Communist government just ninety miles off the Florida Keys—near enough to travel by auto ferry, which many exiles did, their cars carrying hidden packets of money and jewelry, treasures small enough to slip past an emigration official but large enough to help them make a fresh start in Miami.

These *exilios* found the United States a welcoming place. History and ideology worked on their behalf—the Cold War and the Statue of Liberty were warm friends to white, well-educated refugees with middle-class enthusiasms and fierce anti-Communist sentiments. The State of Florida and the federal government set up assistance programs unseen since the post–World War II GI Bill, programs that included loans and outright grants for resettlement, education, businesses, language lessons, retraining, and state jobs for Cuban professionals unable to pass license examinations.

Unrepentant *Batistianos* arrived in that first wave, some fleeing revolutionary courts, or firing squads, or grim prison cells where in the past they had sent, guarded, tortured, or otherwise helped brutalize—whether through the exercise of their authority or the wickedness of their silence—those just come to power. They were greeted by a generous nation's embrace and a CIA plan for their return to Cuba—Washington's gift to the Miami-Havana axis.

The CIA and the *exilios* constructed a gossamer network of anti-Castro adventurism. Honest-to-God spies, saboteurs, and assassins used weapon caches, safe houses, and training camps to envelop south Florida in a web of Cosmoline intrigue. With Miami at the hub and the eastern edge anchored along the beaches of the Atlantic Ocean, fragile runners extended north, to guerrilla camps in the Everglades swampland, and south, to jumping-off points in the Florida Keys, all with ambitions toward Havana. Within the web operated the largest gathering of CIA employees outside Langley, Virginia, writes Joan Didion in *Miami,* her breathtaking discussion of the relationship between Miami, Washington, and Havana. Some three to four hundred case officers each ran a handful of contract men, who in turn each ran agents, thousands of them all told, mostly exiles, all with ambitions toward Havana. The CIA station in Miami controlled a flotilla of small boats and mother ships, its own airline, hundreds of pieces of real estate, front companies, stores and businesses, and millions of dollars in cash, all with ambitions toward Havana.

The mischief they did was well recorded by the U.S. House of Representatives Select Committee on Assassinations during its investigation into the U.S. government's role—particularly CIA involvement—in plots to kill foreign leaders. From the summer of 1960, the same summer Castro nationalized millions of dollars' worth of U.S. property, the CIA started tracking two objectives, to eliminate Castro and to overthrow the Revolution, by murder and invasion if one or both became necessary. The CIA plotted assassinations (Castro's certainly and other Cuban leaders' as well), offering cash money and sweet deals to the Mafia, to former revolutionaries, to damn near anyone promising to rid them of Castro. Shadowy figures were promised riches, public figures were promised power, *exilios* were promised repatriation. The CIA dispatched saboteurs in small boats laden with the tools of covert operation, offloading them from larger ships into Cuba's silky waters with instructions to blow up refineries, to ruin the sugar harvest, to do anything to discredit Castro and the Revolution. As many as 20,000 such acts were committed, according to one former CIA official. Seagoing saboteurs were so common that the Piracy Museum housed in historic Morro Castle at Santiago de Cuba devotes a separate room to them, displaying rubber boats, weapons, and pictures of failed adventurers—"imperialist pirates," by any other name. No plan was too bold, no expense too costly for an operation that spent millions before it lost momentum.

This was serious business. In late 1961, some six months after the Bay of Pigs fiasco, President John F. Kennedy approved Operation Mongoose, an umbrella code name that included the Miami-based network and spelled out a carefully layered, six-part plan to overthrow Castro from within. The final phase, should all others fail, would be another armed invasion, this one to include U.S. forces and scheduled for October 1962—the month of the missile crisis. By the time the United States and the Soviet Union stepped back from the brink, Kennedy had made a secret promise to Premier Khrushchev: there would be no further invasions of Cuba, no United States Marines wading ashore on the Revolution's sugar-white beaches.

In Cuba, Playa Girón is a place. In the United States, the Bay of Pigs is a lingering idea, a touchstone for promises made to the Miami-Havana axis but never kept—and never forgotten. Thousands of *exilios* trained in weapons, explosives, sabotage, and assassination by the U.S. government were all pumped up with no place to go after Kennedy swore off plans to bring down Castro by invasion. But the *exilios* had made no such pledge and felt no loyalty to it, or to Kennedy, the man who had courted them and then abandoned them, more than once, leaving them stranded first on a Cuban beachhead and then again in Miami. Committed to ousting Castro, they were better trained in paramilitary actions than in the clumsy workings of democratic institutions, so, writes Didion, they stayed with what they knew best.

Men and organizations from Miami's glory days, when south Florida pulsed with energy spun off from the Bay of Pigs invasion and Operation Mongoose, continued their work, occasionally making the news. Former CIA *exilios* stood convicted at the Watergate trials, having been led to the locked doors of the Democratic National Headquarters by E. Howard Hunt, their old CIA contact from the Bay of Pigs, the man who had promised them air support. *Exilios* appeared on court dockets from Miami to New York to Caracas for an eccentric list of violent acts—for shooting a bazooka at the United Nations, for assassinating politicians and citizens sympathetic to Castro, for blowing up a Cuban DC-8 out of Barbados and killing seventy-three people, for bombing the Cuban consulate in Miami. They turned up in the 1978 House Select Committee on Assassinations report, which stated that twenty exile groups had the resources and motivation to take part in the assassination of John F. Kennedy. During the Reagan years, the Miami-Havana axis joined forces with the Contras—Reagan's "freedom fighters"—against Nicaragua's Marxist government. Still hopeful after thirty years, the Miami-Havana axis labored under the slogan "*¡Nicaragua Hoy, Cuba Mañana!*" In 1991 the updated slogan, seen on bumper stickers in Miami, read, "Christmas in Havana."

Casa Grande Hotel

Back on the road, stuffed with history, we headed along the secondary highways that hug Cuba's rugged south coast bound for Trinidad, one of the most lovingly preserved colonial sites in the New World. Founded in 1514 and home to sixteenth- and seventeenth-century adventurers and conquistadors, it later prospered with profits in sugar, tobacco, and slave trading. The houses of its historical ruling class are now museums devoted to natural history, archeology, decorative arts and architecture, and the "Struggle against Bandits," bandits being the last remnants of the old regime, whose members fled to that part of the island in a last effort to resist Castro.

Trinidad's beautifully preserved pastel buildings—with twelve-foot-high ceilings, massive wooden doors, ornate wrought-iron grillwork, and gorgeous ceramic tile—and her charming citizens turned the normally subdued Caputo into a wild man, fully devoted to the love affair between Cuba and his camera. We lost him, and joked that in his hyper condition we might discover him either in jail or in church getting married, but he turned up in the town square near the butcher shop operating in a professional frenzy, surrounded, it appeared, by nearly every Trinidad resident, smiling, waiting, joking with each other and delighted with the possibility of having their picture taken.

I wandered into the crowd and opened my haversack to distribute balloons to the kids, making a name for myself, according to Bob's recollection, as the American who started the Great Trinidadian Balloon Riot of 1991. Bob and Roberto and I eventually left Caputo to his euphoria and found a place to listen to troubadours sing traditional ballads, one of which, insisted Bob, would soon be written about the Balloon Riot. We sipped cups of a local drink made of raw rum, lime juice, and honey, a drink favored by the Mambis, the Cuban liberation fighters in the war against Spain.

Although Bob waited patiently for Caputo to finish his work, strain was beginning to show from days of close quarters, long hours, and short nights. Both men were accustomed to working alone and being in charge, Caputo mostly shooting film in Africa, which explained his wardrobe of heavy khaki shorts and quick-dry Supplex shirts in six colors, and a frayed and faded shoulder bag filled with camera bodies, lenses, and film that he was never without. Small tensions had developed between them, mostly concerning the time and travel needed to get the shots Caputo wanted, once causing us to backtrack three hours so he could reshoot a scene in better light. Although Caputo was glad to be in Cuba, to see the place, he complained how badly he was being paid for someone of his professional accomplishments. More than once Bob shot Caputo unacknowledged sideways glances when Caputo ordered expense-account meals from the pricey side of the menu.

But exhaustion trumped everything else that day, ambition, impatience, and curiosity included. As soon as we sat down for an afternoon coffee, we were ready to call it quits. The steadfast Eric shepherded us back into the van, and an hour later, after a twelve-hour day of zigzag travel, we collapsed in a hotel in the hills of Sancti Spíritus, barely a third of the way across the island to Santiago de Cuba, our final destination.

The next morning we headed out through the flat provinces of central Cuba, a landscape unbroken except for cane plantations, pineapple farms, banana groves, and citrus orchards. By midafternoon we were in Camagüey, a city to which Canadians can fly directly from Toronto, and from there they are bused to Playa Santa Lucía, a twelve-mile-long stretch of isolated beach and part of a system of hundreds of miles of keys, most of them deserted and many of them unexplored. The underwater network of virgin reefs off Cuba's north-coast archipelago are grander than Florida's in every way and, we were told, second in size only to Australia's Great Barrier Reef. The smallest possibility of snorkeling in translucent waters over genuinely unspoiled reefs had caused Bob and me to pack diving mask and fins.

The idea of planeloads of Canadians jetting nonstop into Camagüey, in central Cuba, or into Varadero Beach, on the Havana end of the island, started us fretting again over the effects of tourism on the revolutionary society. I asked Roberto, "Aren't you worried just a little bit? The hotel and beaches are closed to Cubans. Girls will swap out a night of fun for gifts from the foreigners-only store. Guys will risk going to jail for selling black market cigars, for just having a dollar bill. What do you think Che would say if someone told him, 'No Cubans allowed at Varadero Beach'?"

"Peter, this is not my decision," pleaded an exasperated Roberto. "I am not in charge. Most of us believe that Fidel knows what he is doing. We may worry. We may wonder. You know some Cubans tell you, '*Fidel es loco*.' But I believe that Castro will find a way, will make everything work out. What choice do we have? We must do something to survive. For me, tourism has provided a good job. Do I say, 'I don't want the tourists?' I don't think so.

"I think you and Bob worry too much. That's what I think. We always talk about tourism and a dreadful future. What about the things Fidel has done for Cuba? The schools? The hospitals? Everyone has a chance now. Not like before. You and Bob need to lighten up. Come on. It's Cuba!" said Roberto, raising his hands above his head in an exaggerated flamenco gesture.

The debate over tourism and revolution dogged us across the island and back, much as it dogged Cuba, from the point of inception into an ambiguous future. We never did quite get the Cuban take on things, no matter how many times we pressed Roberto and other Cubans for help in understanding. Roberto usually offered up little more for our consideration than confident statements—*Castro will find a way; The future is the future*—that seemed terribly incomplete or, worse yet, unforgivably indifferent to the double-knit doomsday we envisioned for his country.

Roberto fled that conversation in relief when we pulled up in front of the Villa Coral Hotel, right on the beach. After a tour of the facility, we ate at the buffet and had drinks in the disco, where the entertainment consisted of watching the master of ceremonies persuade a houseful of German tourists to dance in a conga line. While Bob and Roberto hit the dance floor, Eric and I huddled in one of our private conversations and watched. But mostly Bob and I waited for morning, so we could get into the water.

When the time came we were placed under the protective care of Osvaldo from the International Scuba Diving Center in Santa Lucía, who would ride out to the key and dive with us. Roberto declared early in the day that the water was too cold for him, and Caputo had no interest in an undersea exploration, but both were on the job, so they came along for the ride. Eric was eager for his first view of the mysteries beneath the surface. We set off down a sandy road in a hotel van, past salt marshes smothered in hundreds of flamingos, past a fishing village with everyone out to sea, and through a checkpoint manned only by an authoritative billboard: "No Access Except to Foreign Tourists." At a dock in the shipping channel more people joined the expedition, a director from the national theater in Havana and a writer from *Bohemia*, Cuba's most distinguished magazine. We were becoming a party, with lots of joking, wisecracking, and the relaxed behavior that fine beaches and blue waters produce wherever they are found.

We anchored the skiff at Sabinal, a small, sandy island where a guy waited beneath a thatched *ramada* ready to mix everyone *Cuba libres*. A grateful Caputo accepted. Osvaldo, Eric, Bob, and I passed on drinks, too eager to get into our snorkeling gear and onto the reef, about a forty-five-minute swim offshore. Only a few minutes into the water Eric had to turn back, unable to get accustomed to the borrowed mask, a disappointment that he referred to several times over the next few days. The three of us went ahead with the long, easy swim over a sand and rock bottom, then turned to face the current as the bottom became coral fields. The reefs were beautiful and bountiful, gorgeous undersea worlds unlike any I had seen in Florida, and populated with game fish—oversized groupers and red snappers, fat jacks, and a monster moray eel the size of my leg that Bob frantically waved me over to see. We swam, we dove, we resurfaced, over and over, time and again; after an hour, Osvaldo asked if we were ready to go back. "Are you joking?" we answered. He asked again at the two-hour mark. After a third hour, a speed boat came looking for us, dispatched from the Villa Coral; Eric, it turned out, had been rowing around for the past ninety minutes, unable to spot us in the blue expanse of rolling waves. Back on shore, Bob and I were unfit for landed company, so exhilarated by the experience we could only look at each other with wide-eyed grins and shake our heads in delight, and disbelief, at the marvels of the day.

We had missed a prepared lunch that sat waiting for us back at the hotel, and Bob decided we were running behind schedule, although behind *what* schedule was never clear, other than his determination to make Santiago de Cuba, some 250 miles away on the southeast coast, by nightfall. On the road again it became evident that the pace of driving, looking, walking, talking, drinking, swimming, and absorbing the Cuban experience was beginning to wear on us all. Just five days into our trip, and both Bob and Caputo had fallen into a cranky state of job-related numbness, so tired that they ignored each other's irritations and looked past everything and everyone, but too professional not to worry that they might be missing something noteworthy. Roberto, whose ability to communicate in either English or Spanish had momentarily forsaken him, would not even rise to the bait of a discussion with Bob over a point of revolutionary history, a direct challenge to Roberto's status as our guide. Eric was red-eyed from driving, much of it on attention-devouring secondary roads, and from the nightly chore of finding gasoline, which had him working an hour of two after the *gringos* were in the bar rehashing the day's events over Spanish brandy. I lay exhausted across the back seat of the van, whimpering in my sleep as though I was begging for mercy, reported an uncharitable Bob.

It was after nightfall when we passed through the Sierra Maestra to make our way into Santiago, going directly to the Versailles Hotel, where the tap water ran irregularly, where the extensive menu was reduced to three stewy dishes, where you could get Miller beer in a can, where we collapsed, desperate for some rest before we tackled Santiago, a task we approached with an apprehension we had not felt since our arrival in country.

A Cuban exile had issued us a warning just minutes before we departed Miami for Cancún and Havana: "Be careful in Santiago!" He had explained that Santiago was a "colored" city, while Havana was more "white," therefore safer and better run, more hospitable for Americans. Santiago, he cautioned, was in turmoil from racial tension, from shortages, from government inefficiency so bad that the city had no water for hours at a time, a claim that turned out to be true.

Traveling across the length of the island we had visited museums, hung out in bars, honored revolutionary shrines, and visited with citizens, becoming friends with two of the finest in Eric and Roberto. But in those accelerated days and busy nights, there was a great deal we did not see that had been promised, or threatened—painful economic suffering, skulking neighborhood spies, the melancholy faces of a tyrannized people, a repressive military. Paris's Orly Airport had more armed military presence than we saw in all of Cuba. So by the time we reached Santiago, after days of total immersion, we had begun to conclude that, whatever might be wrong in Cuba, she was not as bad off as some in the

States wanted us to think, not nearly what the exiles saw in their thirty-five-year-old vengeful vision.

Yet the specter of racial antagonism in a major city can make the fear rise up hard in an American bosom. In Havana I had accompanied a black marketeer down a side street, turned up an alley, and ducked into a dimly lit building to buy cigars, without the sense of urban menace I would have felt at home. But as we approached Santiago, our apprehension was emotional and personal, reflecting a worrisome concern that our growing love affair with Cuba would be ended in a mean way, in a city that did not work, by a people at each other's throats, with a proper demonstration that everything the exiles had warned us about would come true in the shadow of the Sierra Maestra, in the geography where the Revolution had been fought and won by Fidel's rebels.

The next day we drove to the city center intent on inquiry, and Santiago swallowed us up. It was a festival weekend, an annual celebration of Caribbean music that overflowed the streets with a slow-moving press of joyous people dressed in bright cotton and tight-fitting spandex, who swayed and danced and laughed and inched along good-naturedly. They came in every shade of white, brown, yellow, and black, and everything in between; matched up as friends, families, and lovers, with an indifferent attitude to race or color, as if to say, *Our city is so mixed by race and blood, any distinctions based on color would be difficult to make and useless even if you could do it.* For us three pale *gringos,* this city felt free of racial tensions.

We walked with the crowd, swayed with the music, chatted with the revelers, and looked on in wonder as a laughing Santiago pulsed with a passionate Caribbean rhythm. I was pulled out of the mob by a young desk clerk from a nearby hotel and his girlfriend, who hooked their arms into mine, steered me to a sidewalk vendor, and bought us beers while they bombarded me with questions about the States and about what I thought of Cuba. They finally released me with an invitation to look him up at work so they could show me Santiago in the local style. "You will like us here," they assured me. "I already do," I told them.

"*What* is going on?" I asked Bob when I caught up with him after leaving the young couple. "How could so many people back home be so wrong about this country? How can they get away with such stupidity, such willful lies? This insistence on damning the people and the place because they don't like Castro. You know we won't be able to go back home and talk reasonably about what we've seen without being dismissed as naïve fools. It's crap. No, it's evil. I didn't expect a Marxist hellhole, not in the Caribbean. Not from this revolution. But this? All of what we've seen?"

"It's just another clever Communist ploy to trick us; this is all staged for our benefit," said Bob, offering an answer as improbable as the day's events and fitting for such a test of his professional skepticism and his unrelenting enthusiasm for new places and people.

While we talked and inched along in the close-fitting mob, someone picked my pocket, getting a backup $100 bill, a photo ID, and a useless credit card, but even that didn't take the heady edge off the day.

We eventually moved away from the crowd, down thinning streets into José Martí Square, where we stopped to sit on a bench, to once again let our Cuban observations overtake our American expectations. But we just slipped further into overload. Mothers in housedresses leaned against strollers and chatted while their children played around them. Several young men stood jostling and pushing and punching each other in the arm in the international style of friendship among teens. Gray-haired men wearing short-sleeved white shirts and dress pants sat near us discussing baseball with an enthusiasm that made their unanimous agreement sound like a ruthless argument. They spoke with reverence of the heroes of their youth, even those who had chewed gum and demanded too much money, behavior that did not meet their approval. Across the street a long line of people waited patiently before a sidewalk vendor selling blood sausage; an even longer line waited for pizza. A group of hip-looking, smartly dressed young men and women passed through the square, with one of the women so tall and beautiful, in a city filled with beautiful people—she was Santiago beautiful—that all conversation in the park hushed when she walked past, and when she reached the street she looked back across the square at the staring Americans with a smile that seemed to say, *It happens all the time, but thank you for the compliment anyway.* We caught quick glimpses of her twice again during our three-day stay in Santiago, a Latin beauty appearing and then reappearing as if to instruct us on a most useful lesson—pay close attention or you'll miss the fine points of Cuba and return home with only those images you brought with you.

That day she slipped between a row of big American cars from the 1950s that the owners were washing and polishing, cars that could be hired as illegal taxis if you had the fare, despite the state monopoly on cabs. The stories about American automobiles from the 1950s still looking good and running fine were true. Vintage Fords and Chevrolets were everywhere, with an occasional Pontiac and Buick thrown in for variety, and almost every other brand represented, all well cared for by attentive owners. In one ninety-minute walk through central Havana I counted seventeen 1953 and 1954 Chevrolets pass under the huge mosaic portrait of Che on the face of a multistory government building that looks across the long, rolling Plaza de la Revolución toward the Communist Party headquarters.

From that park bench in José Martí Square, cars appeared as metaphor in Cuba. As metaphor, they set the time when Cuba and the United States were best friends and trading partners, and established the date when it all went bad, soured over politics and ideology. As metaphor, they honored the enduring affection Cubans had for Americans and things American, not solely as objects, but as solid, trustworthy, dependable links to their onetime neighbor in the full meaning that the term *neighbor* once had. As metaphor, these '55 Fords and '56 Chevys, the dream cars of my generation in the States, were tributes to the resiliency of Cuba's revolutionary spirit every day when they cranked up to hit the road, patched and repaired with makeshift foreign parts to keep them going despite shortages, much like the country itself, running on threadbare parts and ancient machinery, but running, and looking good, too. As one car owner told me, *Every Cuban is a mechanic who can keep American cars running with Russian tractor parts*—another sort of metaphor, one that described Cuba.

Despite her troubles of the moment—the "necessary rules," the corrosive mixing of tourism and Revolution, the shortages and the rationing, the politics of the post-Revolution era—Cuba, like those 1950s cars, was also still moving forward, if needing repairs and showing a bit of body rust. She had gone a long way toward creating a society that made many of her citizens proud and resilient, and others downright defiant. The accomplishments of the revolutionary government were well known, and had been repeated by Roberto, Eric, Neddie, and strangers on the street, regularly and often, during our journey. *Cuba is literate, has national health care, has food and housing for her people, has an infant mortality rate lower than most industrial countries and a life expectancy for HIV patients unrivaled in the world.* Judgments about politics aside, Cuba *tried* to care for her citizens equally and fairly, and did a remarkable job of it until the economy crumbled after the loss of Russian aid in 1989. As I reflected on those accomplishments, I reflected on a bit of history. I was in a city where slaves had been brought from Africa and worked by force, a city where emancipated blacks had been dispossessed and despised, until came the Revolution, which forged a racial harmony known to only a few of the world's countries, a social transformation worthy of being acknowledged as a revolutionary triumph.

Those thoughts tagged along as we left the square and drifted back to the crowded center of the celebration, working our way to the balcony restaurant of the Casa Grande Hotel, where we hoped to find something to eat. Once a fine place, as the name promised, the hotel had fallen into neglect, like so much of Cuba. The man at the door checking identification had long since given up trying to enforce the foreigners-only rule; the place throbbed with a crowded mix of intellectuals and artists, TV crews, print reporters, dancers, musicians, hangers-on, and gawkers speaking an indeterminable number of languages. We ordered *whatever you've got* for dinner, having learned days back that asking for a menu in most Cuban restaurants only marked you as either a new arrival or a hopeful fool.

Nowhere in Cuba did we remain strangers for long, least of all on the Casa Grande balcony during festival week. Over the din of loud festival music, a well-known Cuban poet talked earnestly with Bob, curious about the reputation of several Latin American and Caribbean poets, pleased that Bob knew his friends' work, more pleased to know they were respected in the United States. Could Bob send him books? "Of course," he said, making a note in his journal. A baseball player appeared and was introduced to us as someone who had turned down a big offer to join the show to the north, saying he just could not imagine living anyplace but Santiago. We attracted the attention of a wispy trumpet player who bummed a cigarette from Bob, and as he broke off the filter he scoffed at the idea of defecting in favor of the big money in New York City, where he had connections. "Why would I want to leave this?" he asked, sweeping open his arms before him. "Cuba is my home." Then came a twenty-four-year-old woman, a university student and part-time dancer who asked her passionate questions with a hard-edged tone. "Where is the sugar for Cuba? Where is the rice for Cuba? Where is the coffee for Cuba? Most people want Fidel. My feelings are not political, but how can we grow this food and not have it to eat? My answer is, I don't know."

There it was, a set of competing images rising high above the crowd to offer a moment of celestial clarity. Cuba's ambiguities and contradictions, her hope and her unhappiness, were gathered together on the balcony of the Casa Grande Hotel. "Where is the rice for Cuba?," an innocent cry by a latte-colored beauty, challenged by "Why would I want to leave all this?," the rhetorical question asked by a full-hearted musician who felt blessed to live in Cuba.

Which led me to a question of my own: *Where is the single voice of Cuba's despair that had been promised to us in the States?* Promised to us in Miami by Jorge Mas Canosa and his cynically named Cuban American National Foundation and in Washington by Foggy Bottom liberals whose ongoing analysis of Cuba was as stale and false as the rationale for Kennedy's Bay of Pigs invasion. "Trust us," said the CIA agents, dressed in three-piece suits. "Trust us," said the exiles, dressed in camouflage fatigues; "the Cuban people hate Castro and will rise up as one." Whatever Cuba was or was not, whatever she might become, she was not an island where a single opinion prevailed, however much some might claim or hope.

These conversations solidified various free-floating notions about Cuba that had been gathering during the past few days. There was no denying it, Cuba needed tourism—or something—to fend off bankruptcy and ruin, to fill the stomachs of the faithful before they lost heart, to jump-start a country low on fuel of every type, rice and gasoline and caffeine and all the rest. Jesus, *Where is the sugar of Cuba?* How could the complexities of a nation's modern life be reduced to a more fundamental question?

Yet after the first glance, after the first layer of conversation with Cuba, I realized that it wasn't that simple, not that fundamentally obvious what people thought or felt. After walking through Havana and driving across the island to stand on that balcony, I thought I could see a Cuba running hard and strong on an alternative form of energy, something most outsiders could not identify, let alone tap into and harness. What was it? Patriotism would be a good start, were it not a discredited concept. Pride would do, for lack of a word that conveys a grander meaning. *Patria* might work, if it had an emotional equivalent in English. A nationalistic ethos of some sort lay just below the surface, not worn like a badge on every tunic or spoken of in everyday conversation, but infusing that society with an easy confidence, a belief that a country with the force and staying power to transform itself in extraordinary ways—to yank itself out of illiteracy, poverty, and exploitation despite enormous obstacles—could find its way through these troubled times too. When Roberto shrugged off our worries about tourism with the comment "The future is the future," perhaps what kept us from understanding his viewpoint was our inability to share a Cuban trust in the Revolution, to accept tourists, shortages, and closed doors as sacrifices worth making, as tolerable costs for carrying on the Revolution.

We were Americans, accustomed to having choices and finding solutions in the face of problems and crises. We wanted—damn near demanded, at times—policy answers to Cuba's troubles, and we grew frustrated with Cuba's facile confidence and her reliance on revolutionary bromides: *Castro will find a way; The future is the future; To defend tourism is to defend the Revolution.* Many Cubans tried to help us, and if there was a failure of understanding, the responsibility was surely ours, a failure on our part to appreciate the Cuban Revolution and history. For Cubans, their Revolution was not an abstract idea or a flash in time, not something relegated to memory or fixed in history. Most Cubans placed great trust in the Revolution, believing in it as a process as well as an event, an evolution as well as an apocalyptic clash of arms. The Revolution did more than separate 1958 from 1959, or Batista from Castro; it separated the period before the Triumph from today, tomorrow, the day after. The Revolution was regarded as something real, spoken of in the present tense, even in the future: *¡Venceremos!* We shall overcome!

Many Cubans we spoke with, drank rum or coffee with, or just bumped into on the street, were ordinary folks—not politicians or party leaders but dancers, musicians, black marketeers, teachers, waiters, money changers, writers, merchant marines, and kids who covet Nikes and T-shirts. Some of them anticipated help in some small form or another from foreign visitors. But many of them sought something grander. Loyal Cubans wanted outsiders, particularly us Americans, to acknowledge the Revolution, to understand the changes since the day Fidel's boyish army drove Batista's gangsters out of the country. Those still-hopeful Cubans saw the triumphs of the Revolution shimmering gloriously above the gray patina of Havana's buildings and the weary national infrastructure, and they wanted us to lift our eyes away from the obvious, to see Cuba's successes, her possibilities, too, and to give them proper weight in the scale of things.

For an optimistic moment this all seemed very clear as I stood on the balcony of the Casa Grande Hotel overlooking Céspedes Plaza, where the center of the celebration spilled into the streets and beyond, filling every open space as far as I could see with people cheering their past, their culture, themselves. It was a hell of a sight, and an oddly reassuring one. Being in the midst of all that Caribbean revelry and experiencing that fine country with my companions moved me to a comfort of place unknown to me for many years.

I returned to the table and, over the blast of the music, pulled Bob to the balcony, waved my arm over the railing to demand, "Show me the face of oppression in that crowd! Show me the look of tyranny among these people, among any of the people we've met in Cuba!" Bob got out his notebook as I raved on. "Oppressed people don't act this way. Cubans are proud of what they have achieved, proud of their country, proud of the Revolution. Yes, yes, I know. There isn't enough food and some of the services are going to hell, fast. Cuba has problems—big problems—but a lot of them are out of her control. The fuckin' colossus of the north has its heel on Cuba's throat. How easily that gets lost in the discussion!

"And look, whatever the problems, whatever the politics of this place, no one, *no one,* refused to talk with us, about anything. Who is going to believe *that* back home? Christ, almost the first thing we heard on the streets of Havana was 'Fuck Castro.' Remember Pedro the plumber?

"Whatever's wrong here, there's a lot that's right, and Cubans know it, and won't surrender it. Many chose to leave, but most chose to stay. You gotta admit it, Bob, this is an amazing country, an amazing people."

Caputo came over to join us, and we both whipsawed Bob with our feelings about Cuba and Cubans, as though some sort of Gestalt floodgate had broken open, ruptured from too much accumulated pressure. From the day we hit Old Havana an intensity had been working us over, building from one day to the next, not letting us catch a complete emotional breath, keeping us hyped on some untested traveler's mega-crank. It was unrelenting, like a narcotic found pure and uncut in Santiago de Cuba.

When Roberto and Eric arrived back at the table from their nightly search for gasoline, Roberto invoked a running joke by asking Bob what sort of CIA secrets he was working on so seriously in his journal. Roberto then noticed how solemn we appeared, and his face opened, as if to wonder, *what have I blundered into?* No one spoke. We didn't know what to say, didn't know how to translate an epiphany into appropriate language. Bob just handed his notebook to Roberto, who read the latest entry, then looked up, around the table, into the eyes of each of us, and with a constricted throat and trembling lip said, "You damned Americans are going to make me cry."

Roberto's reaction pushed us even deeper into our exposed emotions. Bob scraped back his chair, mumbling something about needing to find the bathroom. I escaped back to the railing, where I stood taking deep breaths, looking out on the crowd, feeling pleased to be on the Casa Grande balcony, pleased for that moment, in that place. And I made this note to myself: To find the best in a country, look into the faces of the people when they are gathered together.

Physically exhausted and emotionally depleted, we returned to our hotel for an easy evening, but Cuba never once offered us such a thing, not to us, not once. Bob and I couldn't let go of the experience, didn't want to relinquish the rawness of appreciation that had come to us in Cuba, so we sat and drank dark rum and talked and argued, sitting in the bar of the Versailles Hotel, in Santiago de Cuba, which in its own right caused us to pause occasionally to consider our good fortune.

Benedictions

The next morning we piled into the van to head out of Santiago under a sky so threatening that Roberto urged us to reconsider our plans for the day. One of the things Bob and I most wanted to do in Cuba was climb in the tropical green of the Sierra Maestra and walk the path of Castro's guerrilla army. Numbering less than two dozen when they arrived here in 1956, they claimed the mountains as a home and as a base of guerrilla operations until they took control of the country two years later.

Bob brushed aside Roberto's worry about wind and rain and insisted we drive to the mountain, hopeful that the weather would clear by the time we arrived. He did so despite the fact that Roberto had failed in the one chore Bob had asked of him during the entire trip, to get us ham and cheese sandwiches and bottled water, our breakfast and liquid for the day's effort. Roberto kept predicting that the weather would keep us off the mountain. Then he tried to cover himself by saying, "Don't worry, we'll find something to eat on the road," to which Caputo responded, "Not unless we hit it."

We drove along the coast, where the muscular, thickly wooded mountains seemed to spring up sheer and forceful from the side of the road and reach into the blackened clouds. The road worked its way alongside bucolic bays and harbors, each with rustic fishing villages. Periodically, from a distance, it appeared as though the road ended abruptly up ahead, appeared as though the mountains rose out of the sea so radically that there was no place for a car to pass without disappearing into the landscape.

Along the route Roberto had Eric stop here and there—to get ice for the cooler, to ask about food. He returned to the van once to announce that a professional guide was required for the climb we had planned, but mostly he just delayed, hoping for some redemptive rain to keep us off the mountain, until Bob, tight-lipped and out of patience, insisted we get moving. "Quit stalling," he told Roberto. "We've already wasted two hours, and won't have any food all day if we don't get going; by the time we get back to Santiago it will be too late to find something to eat."

We were sixty miles from Santiago, where store-bought supplies were as scarce as Americans in 1991, so we began the climb on empty stomachs, with no prospects for lunch, and carried with us only one can of Coke and two cans of juice to see us through the daylong trek to Pico Turquino, at 6,476 feet Cuba's highest peak and the site of a national shrine. Eric begged off with a smile, a wise man who masked his insight about how difficult the day might be with a playful comment about duty, which, he said, required him to remain with the van. Roberto, who held on to his good humor even during the trip's most difficult moments, insisted with an exaggerated bravado a microsecond removed from chest pounding, "I'm Cuban. I'm your guide. It's my duty to go with you. I have to see you to the top if the government is going to award you guys the title of 'Heroes of Tourism,'" citing the accolade he had bestowed on us as praise and complaint for our manic insistence on seeing and doing everything possible. "Let's get going," he said. Which we did, for a few hundred yards, before Roberto turned back, though not without uttering the self-congratulatory declaration, "During the Revolution I would have been an urban guerrilla, not a mountain fighter." Caputo turned back next, a victim of his forty pounds of camera equipment. I pushed on with Bob, who quick-stepped ahead in irritation just as the sun broke through the overcast sky.

We trudged up the low, gradual base of the mountain, past an occasional small farm with fields cut out of the forest. Horses ambled across the trail and goat bells chimed in the distance. For a time the forest was so thin we could glance up from the path to see the series of rising peaks and intervening valleys that lay ahead for the day's effort, a four-mile roller coaster hike to the top. After an hour the trail grew narrower and steeper, the sun grew warmer, the trees and vegetation grew thicker and soon covered the trail in a tropical canopy that held us in a wrap of heat and moisture. We grew less talkative, concentrating on the climb, the beauty of the mountains, and the historic significance of the place.

We wanted to make the top despite Roberto's claim that "you can't climb El Turquino in the rainy season." Years prior to Castro's arrival in the Sierra Maestra, a freedom-minded father and daughter consecrated the highest point by placing there a bust of José Martí, the father of Cuban independence and the one historic figure all Cubans view with nationalistic pride. Over the years, true believers trusted the idea that José Martí's figure looking out over Cuba from El Turquino would inspire patriots to another revolution. Bob and I wanted to see the statue. We had paid proper respect at other revolutionary monuments and historic places, but we wanted very badly to pause before that sanctuary because, I suspect, to do so required more than the normal effort expected from casual tourists, required us Americans to make the extra effort.

We climbed for two hours before the liquids were gone. After three hours the rain started, gentle at first, then harder, filling the narrow trail with moving water, transforming the path into a mountain stream that rushed against our boots and started to dilute our determination. The rain turned the trail into a mass of thick red clay that sucked at our feet with every step; rocks and small boulders caused us to slip and stumble, claiming our energy just to keep our balance, and more than once the slick, jagged trail dropped us in painful falls. After five hours we were covered with mud, bruises, and scrapes, and we sat our exhausted selves down to rest rubbery legs, indifferent to the cold rain and body-shaking chill that crept into us each time we stopped moving. We sucked rain off leaves to slake our thirst, and nursed our battered bodies.

As I sat there with my fatigue I flashed on another country lush with tropical greenery, thick moist air, and rugged terrain: Vietnam, a country unknown to me personally, but not to tens of thousands of my generation. I put my face in my hands for a sorrowful moment trying to imagine what the days might have been like there, trying to capture the feeling of a year's tour of duty filled with exhaustion, heat, humidity, rain, danger—and death and dying. But I could not. The similarities in landscape and climate common to Vietnam and Cuba, particularly the indescribable green of the forest, were evocative, causing me to feel for that instant that I could make other connections as well, but that was a false impulse. The look and feel of a shared topography could not bridge the distance between the experience of American friends who went to Vietnam and my own experience that day in Cuba, or any other day, for that matter. That distance was too great for the imagination to travel.

I shook free of that thought to consider the idea that Cuba and Vietnam represented competing touchstones for my generation. Then I raised my head from my hands to look down the mountain, over the thickness of the trees to the base of the mountain and past the base to the point where the land meets the clean, fresh sea, just across the road from where the mountain starts its steep rise toward Cuba's highest point. Then I turned to look up to El Turquino peeking through the forest, shrouded in fog that protected the bust of José Martí.

But there was no protective shroud for our adventure that day. We turned back at 4,000 feet. The two-hour descent down the muddy trail was more solemn than it should have been, more solemn than it would have been in other circumstances. Bob and I were quiet with our disappointment. We weren't disappointed that we had failed to finish the climb, exactly, or that our physical abilities were not equal to our ambition, although that certainly did not please us. It felt more as though we had failed to meet an obligation, one too imprecise to render clearly but one that we felt keenly nonetheless.

Two days later, as we headed out of Santiago toward and then home, Bob and I and Caputo let our intoxication with Cuba spin out of control. Driving over the flat agricultural landscape of the island's central plains, past yet more sugarcane fields, pineapple farms, and banana groves, and through small towns, nearly all of which had dusty baseball diamonds, we Americans struggled with the pure excitement of discovery brought on by Cuba. We had walked through Havana, drunk *mojitos* at La Bodeguita, watched dancers at Cuban night spots, snorkeled an untouched coral reef, hiked in the Sierra Maestra, seen sobering bullet holes at revolutionary shrines, repented for America at Playa Girón, gotten swept away during the music festival at Santiago de Cuba, and crisscrossed the island. We were overcome by all of it, pushed into overload by the breakneck pace, the beauty of the country, the charm of the people, the grace of the culture, the vigor of the society. All of it. Everything. It was not just the physical demands and wonderful pleasures of those days that put us on the edge, sent us into double alert. It was something more, something we could not put into words at the time because it was too close to bring into sharp focus, to define, to even describe. We were just in it.

More than anything else, the humanity of the trip held us in a tight grip, like our experience on the balcony of the Casa Grande Hotel, only with less pressure, which made the close feeling tolerable, if still terribly intense. Roberto and Eric had played their role, as had the many

Cubans, like Neddie, who welcomed us without rancor or suspicion, had asked nothing more of us than that we try to see Cuba through their eyes, to put politics and personality aside and judge their country fairly and evenly. Cubans liked us, and we liked them. Strangers one minute, sharing a coffee or rum the next. No one denied us. It was all quite extraordinary.

Roberto and Eric had become more than guide and driver along the island's highways. They had directed us through the culture and the society, never refused us an opportunity or an answer to the most pressing question about Cuba, or about themselves. Traveling in the van, the five of us—with luggage, camera equipment, the cooler of beer and soft drinks, and the case of Cuban rum—created a fellowship that continued through the day's meals and into the late night's last drink. We traded ideas and even a few confidences, the first tentative steps toward friendship taken in the most traditional fashion during an uncommon journey. Consider Eric's memories of being a young man at the Bay of Pigs, where he went with Fidel, where he collected American arms and Cuban prisoners but no bitter memories.

There were jokes and good humor and language lessons and promises to stay in touch, but late that afternoon, as the lowering sun cast the sky and the land in a bright illumination, we lost control. It started with yet another lesson in *yanqui* idioms, which Roberto, the faithful student of English, particularly its slang, scribbled in his notebook.

"Fuckin' A," I began, following it with examples of the expression's subtle and exact usage.

"Dickhead," contributed Caputo.

"Wiseass," offered Bob.

"Attention, please, Kmart shoppers"—and on it went, with Roberto using each term in a few sentences until we were satisfied he had the true feel of it. Before long we were giddy and laughing like fools.

It was I who sent everything off on a wrong course, without meaning to or ever suspecting it at the time, and it began when I asked Roberto, "Who is the Minister of Culture? We must speak to him as soon as we arrive in Havana. I have the answer to Cuba's future. A theme park!"

"Right," said Caputo, catching on. "If you want American tourists back in Cuba, you've got to be ready to give them what they want."

"Exactly," I said, "and what they're going to want is a Revolutionary Theme Park situated at the base of the Sierra Maestra. That is the natural place, the place you Cubans refer to as the 'Cradle of the Revolution.' We can get the Disney people to come in on this; it's a natural for them. Just look at what they did for Florida."

"They can make up life-size robots of Che, Fidel, all the Heroes of the Revolution," said Bob, joining in the tasteless letting-off of pressure.

"That's right," I continued. "They can make up a really wicked Batista, and every afternoon they can put him on trial for his crimes against Cuba. Then they can shoot the motherfucker at sunset, just as the park closes. Jesus, it's perfect. Perfect!"

"Ride the Guerrilla Mountain Water Slide."

"Visit the AK-47 Shooting Gallery."

"Don't miss the Revolutionary Dance Revue—topless, of course."

"If Cuba really wants tourism, then we can help you do it right. We're Americans. We understand these things. It'll make millions, Roberto, hundreds of millions. Trust us on this. We'll make you famous for this idea."

We were laughing like madmen, holding our aching sides, tears rolling down our cheeks, each hoping the others would say no more so it would come to a painless end, until finally it did, and we slumped into quiet exhaustion, like three hysterical people after a body-racking fit of crying.

Only later, when we were alone, did Bob describe the hurt he saw in Roberto's eyes, and only then did Bob confess that Eric had wanted him to translate so he could understand what we found so funny, which Bob could not, would not, do.

We had gone too far, and I had no idea. What I had done, without understanding its purpose or offense, was to act out my concern for Cuba in a merciless skit of dark, capitalist humor. Being an American, and having fallen in love with the country, hopelessly, pitifully in love, I grieved over a future too tied to tourism, grieved from knowing that each time I returned to Cuba, as I knew I surely must, I would find a loss of the qualities in that country I had come to respect and admire so much.

You don't have to measure the worth of a society by the most wicked acts of its government, unless that is your choice. You don't have to judge politics and political personalities to care about a people and a culture, revolutionary or reactionary, unless that is your choice. I found in that revolutionary place, among those welcoming people, a national purpose that had succeeded after centuries of suffering at the hands of tyrants, homegrown and foreign, Spanish and Cuban, Russian and American, by both proxy and clear purpose. I wanted the suffering—whatever its origin—to end, to stop. Then. At that very instant. In my admiration and affection, I wanted to preserve Cuba before things got even worse, and I would have done it had I the power and authority. Would, in a miracle of imagination, have lifted the American embargo and loosened the close-fitting politics at home for my new friends, our old neighbors. But I couldn't. And I recognized there was no stopping the progressive ruin that would follow the chosen remedy of the day.

Tourism, I feared, would eventually bring hordes of Americans descending on Cuba, and American tourists would surely bleed the revolutionary culture with a series of small cuts and slashes that would likely go unattended until Cuba was pale and anemic from her losses. Why not, then, build a Revolutionary Theme Park at the start, mock the Revolution and market its heroes, its purpose, its meaning, its accomplishments? It was bound to come, I was warning in my crude way, so why not just be done with it?

That afternoon, in the illumination of failing Caribbean sunlight, in exhaustion and exhilaration, in a fondness for Cuba, and in a fear for her future, we created Fidel Land as a caution and as a benediction.

If Roberto and Eric were offended by our excess, they gave no outward sign of it, but it was difficult to know because we were all quiet and subdued during the rest of the drive to Havana. Only Eric, who alone among us seemed not to be searching for something on this trip, remained alert as he drove on into the late afternoon and evening. When he finally pulled into the curved drive of the Comodoro, back where we had begun ten days earlier, we startled awake and piled out of the van like whipped dogs.

Before we parted for the night, Roberto and Eric insisted on driving us to the airport the next day, although we assured them there was no need. I don't know then if they persisted out of duty or friendship, but persist they did, and I was glad for it; I did not want to leave them without a proper good-bye. When the time came we all stood in the middle of José Martí Airport like awkward young lovers at the end of a summer romance, not ready for it to end, but realizing it must. Surrounded by knots of loud tourists, pushcart bars with overpriced *mojitos*, and lounging immigration officials waiting for the flight to arrive that would take us back to Cancún, we three Americans said good-bye to our Cuban friends with a teary embrace. "You damn Americans," said Roberto as he turned to leave, "you're going to make me cry again."

Bob and I made no attempt to sit together during the flight home. Such a hard reentry was best done alone. The wacky last day's drive from Santiago to Havana, the emotional farewell at José Martí, followed by a postmodern rush through the brightly lit Cancún airport to make our connection to the States, seemed an unusually harsh combination of sensations.

On the Miami-bound airplane, a kindly gray-haired woman, apparently determined not to let me sulk, leaned across the aisle and asked if it was true that I had just come from Cuba.

"Yes, that's correct," I told her.

"What did you think?" she asked.

"It was my best experience since Richard Nixon resigned," I answered.

Ignoring my remark, she explained that she had traveled to Havana as a teenager with her mother and two cousins, in the 1950s, before the Revolution, and remembered the trip fondly, but after so many years carried but a single image in her memory, that of young children in rags rummaging though garbage pails for food.

Too absorbed with my Cuban experiences to comment, I turned my head to the window and thought, "Oh, I wish you could see it now."

The Special Period

JULY 1992

Resolviendo

By the summer of 1992 I had cracked the code of legal travel to Cuba. A phone call to Marazul Tours in New York brought a set of paperwork, which, when completed and returned, produced a visa, plane ticket, and hotel reservations, all without delay or difficulty, because I could squeeze into the exemptions in the Treasury Department's near-total embargo on travel to the island. The U.S. government tolerated three charter flights per week from Miami to Havana to accommodate the U.S. Constitution—those with First Amendment claims for open travel and free inquiry, including reporters and academics—and to accommodate Cuban exiles who demanded the right to be shuttled across the Florida Straits to visit relatives on the island, while at the same time insisting that few Americans be allowed to make the same trip.

I queued up at 6:00 for a 10:00 A.M. flight, the conspicuous Anglo in a long line of dressy south Florida Cubans wrestling bulging suitcases and duffel bags filled with clothes, medicine, cosmetics, and household goods, all of it destined for relatives on the island, and all of it levied a dollar-per-pound overweight fee. The Miami airport was a tedious place, where nothing happened when it was scheduled and everything was driven by a clear indifference to efficiency and courtesy. In the slow-moving snake of a line a bored fellow passenger told me that Castro had more than seventy homes and slept in a different one each night. The Air Haiti charter left Miami three hours late, and after reaching Havana's José Martí Airport we suffered through another painful line while Cuban customs agents leisurely conducted meticulous inspections of each piece of baggage brought before them by the exiles, only to wave me through untouched.

I arrived at Havana's Hotel Inglaterra in the late afternoon of a very long day that had started with a 5:00 A.M. wake-up call in a Miami hotel—too long a day for ninety miles of air travel over the Gulf of Mexico. Out of energy and out of patience, I was irritated with airports, with the U.S. Treasury Department, with Cuban customs agents, with U.S.-Cuban antagonisms, and particularly with the absolute and repeated stupidity of the U.S. embargo—with everyone and everything associated with getting into Cuba from the States. I vowed never again to travel with proper U.S. government authority if it required undertaking the cumbersome process of passage from Miami to Havana.

The next morning, cranked up on double espressos, I approached the line of cabs stationed outside the hotel, an orderly row of four-door Mercedes Benzes, Nissan sedans, and LADAs, an international assortment of brightly polished, state-owned taxis. Trying to play the savvy traveler, I approached the driver of a sparkling black LADA with a bargaining proposition, only to be told, "We are not permitted to bargain taxi fares, señor. The rate everywhere in Havana is what the meter reads at the end of the ride." So into the backseat of his cab I climbed to start a day of friendship and obligation.

My driver was Eduardo, a gentleman in his late twenties with neatly trimmed dark hair, fashionable clothes, and a certain seriousness of purpose. We set off first for the *diplotienda*, a series of well-stocked stores that catered to the diplomatic community and foreigners but was strictly off-limits to Cubans. The plan called for me to go there with an engorged shopping list a friend had thrust upon me, asking me to buy food and household goods for relatives, and then deliver the goods to Havana street addresses so incomplete that Eduardo tossed his head from side to side in disbelief as he read them.

As we left the Hotel Inglaterra, on the edge of Old Havana, and moved through the city center toward the northern suburb of Miramar and the *diplotienda,* things did not look quite right. The farther we traveled, the more it seemed as though automobiles had fled the streets, had executed a daring escape from the island; there were perhaps 70 percent fewer cars than in the previous year.

"What's going on?" I asked Eduardo. "Where are all the cars and trucks? Everything looks different from a year ago. What's happened?"

"There isn't any gasoline," he said. "It's as simple as that. The fuel ration has been cut to three liters a month. Three liters! Most people just leave their cars parked and sell their gasoline ration on the black market. What can you do with three liters? Nothing, I tell you," said Eduardo, who had not driven his big-finned 1957 Plymouth Fury for months. "I used to take my wife and daughters to the Varadero Beach almost every Sunday. Now there isn't any gasoline. But what's the difference? The beach isn't for us anyway."

Oil imports had dropped by more than 50 percent since 1989 when nearly all Russian aid ended, down from thirteen million tons to six, leaving Cubans stranded at home and often in the dark, according to Eduardo.

"If you haven't been here for a year, a lot is different. We don't even have enough oil to make electricity. Parts of Havana are blacked out at night. We never know what part it's going to be, or when it's going to happen. All of a sudden, the streets are black. The house is dark. We don't even think about it any more, just light candles and wait. What else can we do?" he asked with a glance in the rearview mirror to judge his audience.

Electricity had grown so scarce that television and movie programming had been cut back, robbing Cubans of their beloved television, a modern amenity so commonplace in Havana it was an accepted staple in nearly every home, so much so that one woman complained because Radio Martí, the U.S. government–sponsored, anti-Castro network, used its jamming capability to interrupt her favorite soap opera. With a mocking tone, the woman mimicked the broadcasts: *People of Cuba, be patient. We have not forgotten you. We will liberate you.* "I don't want those people liberating me," she said, referring to Cuban exiles in the States. "I want my TV shows."

In the center of the city, in the busiest part of the day, the streets had the look of a video game with a prehistoric theme. Just a few months before, cars, trucks, and buses had jostled for space and jockeyed for position, had clogged intersections and rotaries, had filled the city's air with diesel and gasoline fumes to give Havana the look and feel of big-city rush-hour traffic. Now, everything seemed out of proportion. In nearly empty streets, the few cars and buses were surrounded by swarms of bicycles, looking like fragile, slow-moving primeval creatures engaged in battle with mammoth steel beasts.

One million of the swarming, stick-figured creatures, Flying Pigeon bicycles imported from China, with 500,000 in Havana alone, said Eduardo with a shake of his head, and for good reason. The bike riders challenged the outnumbered vehicles in a blood-red contest for control of the streets, sometimes to the death. Weekly casualty rates ranged as high as a dozen; yet the bike-riding survivors conceded nothing to the buses and trucks, riding down the middle of the lane and moving over slowly, grudgingly, if at all, each time Eduardo honked his horn. Before we finished that cross-city drive I had concluded that nearly all of Havana's bike riders were deaf or suffered from an uncontrollable arrogance or an unseemly death wish, either of which could end the game with the same result on a Flying Pigeon. Cyclists and motorists moved through the streets of a Cuban society in transition, trying to work out a new accommodation to the changed order of things, which found both of them sharing the open road with a growing number of oxcarts.

Outside the city center everything thinned out even more, creating an abandoned look, eerie and out of sync with modern urban life. Buses ran regularly, though not in sufficient numbers (I was told nearly one-third of Havana's buses were out of service for want of parts) and not regularly enough to keep them from being pressure-packed beyond the point of good judgment. Every passing bus had riders pressed desperately together on the steps, hanging onto handrails, onto each other, onto anything to keep their precarious balance as the vehicle sped recklessly down the open streets, weaving around bicycles, belching huge streams of noxious diesel exhaust. Hitchhikers were seen everywhere in outlying neighborhoods and on the open road, where upraised thumbs outnumbered cars, where Cuban courtesy tried to compensate for rationed gasoline. Here and there cars stopped along the side of the road near groups of hitchhikers, the drivers leaning out of their windows to inquire about shared destinations. Drivers of official vehicles were encouraged in that practice, but empty taxis were forbidden to help out. Many did nonetheless. Hard times had not robbed Havana of her neighborliness.

We passed by a large crowd formed into an orderly line under the direction of a man dressed in yellow shirt and pants and clearly in charge, but, "in charge of what?," I asked.

"He's *el amarillo*, the yellow one," said Eduardo. "He's a state official. You'll see a lot of them. His job is to stop all cars with red license plates, the official cars, and match them up with hitchhikers going the same place. It's the only way to travel long distances these days," he explained. "It doesn't look good for government cars to ride half empty while we sit at home or hitchhike because there isn't any gas." Ah, I thought, how clever of Fidel, and how good for Cuba, struggling with hard times and traveling on three liters of gasoline a month was not quite finished so long as it sought to compensate for the people's losses with make-do solutions rather than tyranny.

We arrived at our first stop, an elegant address in Miramar, a district once reserved for wealthy Cubans and now the center of the diplomatic community, with fine, pre-Revolution homes two and three stories high and free of the neglect so common in other parts of Havana. While Eduardo waited with the car, my passport got me inside the *diplotienda*. No mere "shop," this stucco-walled compound, with manned entrances and fresh paint, housed an entire city block devoted to commerce. A department store, a grocery, a pharmacy, and a restaurant offered the best assortment of goods found in all of Cuba. I prowled well-stocked grocery aisles, piling carts with canned meats and vegetables, cartons of powdered milk, giant boxes of Tide laundry soap, family packs of bath soap, disposable razors, toothpaste, and sanitary napkins—an assortment of food and personal necessities that were the mirror image of Cuba's shortages. I cleaned the meat locker out of scrawny chickens, got every one and still didn't get as many as I had been asked to. The store was crowded with customers. Only the employees had the look of workaday Cubans, and they seemed unfazed by the extravagance of my purchases or the fold of hundred-dollar bills I used to pay the tally.

Eduardo helped me load the many bags into the backseat and trunk of the LADA without a word or a sign, except for the solemn look of his face, then off we went to search out the elusive families. Eduardo grew quiet after the arrival of the bags, and I could only assume that his needs were no less compelling than those of the fortunate Havanans with the generous relative in Miami. What had started with my willingness to help some hungry Cubans was rapidly sliding into something quite different. In a culture of shortages, even acts of kindness were not without consequences. And I didn't like it, so I tried to reengage our conversation, but Eduardo held his concentration to finding the first address on our list. After driving to the proper section of Havana, he drove in a systematic grid pattern through the cramped and crowded streets, asking questions of one, then another, then a countless number of people, every one of whom listened closely and tried to help, until, his determination finally rewarded, Eduardo found the place, a dull-colored building without numbers located on a street without a sign.

I lugged several bags up the broad, curving staircase to a third-floor apartment in a building fallen into decay but still within reach of redemption. A ballroom-sized entranceway, elaborate plaster relief-work crowning the twelve-foot-high walls, a heavy iron handrail, and white marble steps, so well used each tread had two indentations worn deep by the years, suggested a once grand residence. Standing in the dark third-floor hallway, grocery bags surrounding my legs, I explained my purpose to the elderly woman who opened the apartment door. Her first look registered disbelief, at me, at the bags at my feet, then her face softened and dissolved into emotions. She covered her tears with wrinkled and spotted hands, dropped them down to her thighs with a slapping sound, then back up to cover her face again, repeating the movements several times until a younger woman came to the door. I explained myself once again, in Spanish made sloppy by my alarm over the older woman's dramatic condition, until she righted herself and took over the explanation.

I was eager to leave the bags, along with written instructions from the stateside relative that specified who should get which of the items I had delivered. But the women looked worried, did not want to let me go, tugged at me to step inside, and would not so much as touch the bags. They asked me to stack them side by side in a row on the living room floor and to explain to them once again what should be done with everything. The older woman clutched at my sleeve as a plea for me to remain until the other relatives were gathered from a nearby building for a division of the unexpected bounty. The younger woman explained that she and her mother did not want the others, who were on their way, to have cause to accuse them of misrepresenting how everything should be divided among the several members of the family. I did as she requested, and left saturated with everyone's thanks.

Back in the car, as Eduardo and I drove for another couple of late-afternoon hours to complete the deliveries, I described what had gone on in the apartment, why it had taken me so long to return. Without acknowledging the suspicious family, Eduardo explained the need that had settled over Cuba. "Meat of all kinds is impossible to get. If someone had told me that someday pork or chicken or fish could not be found in Cuba, I would not have believed them. No one would have. But it's true today. Very hard to get. Things like soap, oil, rum, aren't any better." The monthly state ration, cut and cut again since 1989, now stood at five pounds of rice, one pound of beans, four pounds of sugar, sixteen eggs, twelve ounces of chicken, four ounces of coffee, and small portions of oil, garlic, and soy and was gone in days, explained Eduardo, frustrated.

"Tourists get all the food," he said as a flat declaration. "The tourist hotels have all the things we don't. It's worse than it has ever been. Worse than we ever imagined it would be. I see people who are hungry and angry. The government tells us all the time how wonderful everything is, how fortunate we are to have our health care system, our hospitals. But what good are hospitals without medicine?

"It's an impossible life now," continued Eduardo. "I told you earlier that the government turns out the lights each night to save energy. Now let me tell you something else. Bad things happen in those parts of the city when it's dark. Be careful where you go at night. During the day, okay," he said, swinging his head around to look at me in the backseat for emphasis. "But not at night. No lights makes things dangerous; let me leave it at that," he said, and drove on. A few silent minutes later, at a stop sign, Eduardo rubbed his face with his hands, then stared at me to say softly, "There is not enough milk for my babies," words he spoke not in complaint, or as an invitation for me to help, but as a father's woeful lament.

As our day together ended, Eduardo used the most dramatic language I heard during that trip to Cuba when he predicted with rueful confidence, "The future holds blood." Back at the Hotel Inglaterra we shook hands, and as we parted, Eduardo, a proud Cuban, apologized for the look of Havana, for the buildings that needed paint and the roads that needed repair, and, with that, reminded me once again why I found Cuba such a compelling destination.

After my fourteen months away from Cuba, the changes in Havana were so transforming they seemed too dramatic to accept. Yet Eduardo had testified to Havana's look of a city nearly abandoned, by cars and perhaps by happiness, as though it was unraveling, from hunger, from shortages, from a neediness that was wholesale on the streets, if Eduardo could be believed.

Christ, I wondered, what had happened to the nitro-powered Caribbean culture and revolutionary society I had fallen so loopy in love with during my last trip? Cuba stranded, dark, hungry, and subdued, maybe even dangerous—how could that be? Had the last trip been an aberration, created by the particular circumstances of that journey across the island with Bob, Caputo, Roberto, and Eric? Was it possible that we three Americans had played the fool, surrendering our good judgment to Cuban charm, confusing a clever seduction with the virtues of a revolutionary society? The thought left me embarrassed about the dewy-eyed stories about Cuba I had told to friends after the trip. I retreated to the hotel bar, where I drank Hatuey beer and brooded away the rest of the evening.

The Hotel Inglaterra was a good place, for its threadbare restoration and for its location. Havana's oldest hotel, semi-successfully refurbished from its colonial-era construction, it sits across a broad street from Central Park. There, every day, musicians entertained visitors and regulars, mothers played with their children, and older men in white shirts and hats argued sports with such passion, with such loud voices, with such wild gestures, I always expected a fight to break out. Beyond the park starts Old Havana, with its narrow streets and houses built at the very edge of the sidewalk, where architecture offers beautiful evidence of European influence and Spanish rule, a reminder of how much history Havana possesses. In the opposite direction, behind the hotel, San Rafael Street leads through a series of neighborhoods into the more complex society of downtown Havana.

That was my destination the next morning. I planned a walk down San Rafael Street to the city center to examine the changes in the most touristy part of the city. The moment I left the hotel a young man fell into step beside me on the sidewalk. Tall and dressed in T-shirt, shorts, and mismatched running shoes, he was like Cuban society, neat within the limits of possibility. At first Fernando asked only to practice his English as we walked along. "Yes, why not," I said, "if I can practice my Spanish," an agreement he wanted to negotiate, which should have told me more than it did about his personality, if not his intentions. We walked and talked a competitive mix of languages as Fernando drove the conversation with a series of rapid-fire questions: *Where are you from? Are you married? What is your work? How long will you stay? Are you here alone? Why did you come? Can I have your T-shirts when you leave?*

After several blocks of making contact, Fernando elevated his ambitions to a grander plane that included a mix of sightseeing, illegal commerce, and social activity, the standard offering of Havana's street hustlers. Under his guidance we could exchange money at ten times the going rate, find black market cigars for half the state-store price, and discover a source for anything else that might please me during my stay in Havana. "My friend, let me be your friend while you are in Havana. Everything is possible."

"I am certain it is," I said, "but I need nothing, want nothing."

"My friend, don't be that way. We can have a nice time during your visit. Let me help with that," persisted Fernando, and on he went.

When I failed to respond to his proposals with appropriate enthusiasm, Fernando grew more intense. He talked faster, searched for something to say, anything to keep the contact solid. He questioned me, hung on to me, did not want to leave me, did not want to lose me. "I am a proud Cuban," he said, a claim he stated loudly and repeated often to make it passably believable, because his behavior suggested otherwise, until finally it started to feel awkward to be around him.

As we walked along the busy blocks of San Rafael Street, he crowded next to me and waved his arms as though he could keep the conversation alive by the force of his body's energy. When I grew exasperated, he grew worried that he was losing me, so he pressed me to set a time for us to meet the next day, and when I hesitated, then refused, he insisted, placing himself in front of me and walking backward down the sidewalk, and moving his face closer to mine, until finally I sent him away—but not for the last time.

Over the next couple of days, nearly every time I left the Inglaterra Fernando fell into step beside me, in a performance so smooth his appearance at my shoulder seemed magical. I imagined him waiting quietly for hours across the street in Central Park, his focus unblinkingly on the hotel entrance, waiting for me to come outside so he might have a second, then a third, and yet one more opportunity to sell me cigars, or cheap pesos, or perhaps to introduce an altogether new opportunity that he had been holding back as the clincher, too good for me to pass up.

In desperate irritation I finally banished Fernando. My inability to deal with him was making me act like a fool, causing me to hesitate each time I started to leave the hotel lobby, to look up and down the sidewalk and then across the street into the crowded and busy park, wondering if Fernando was lurking somewhere close by, wondering if it was possible for me to avoid him. The answer was no: it was not possible. He was far more practiced at the game than I. So I sent Fernando away, told him, "You have nothing I want or need. Leave me alone," as he walked beside me down the street protesting in bilingual excitement, with me setting a fast-stepped pace, afraid that if I slowed down I would lose an imagined edge in our contest.

I brushed off Fernando with a stroke of rudeness far bolder than I ever thought I would need in Cuba, and did not like doing that. It troubled me because I had previously found in Cuba a culture where such behavior was unnecessary. One of the things I appreciated most about the country was its good manners and gracious style, even toward the foreigner. I liked the fact that strangers approached me on the street with a smile and curiosity, liked the fact that I never had to walk alone, unless it was my choice. Thereafter when I saw Fernando—and I did see him several times here and there on the street—he refused to acknowledge me in any way. I was certain I had hurt his feelings and wondered if I had misjudged him as well. Perhaps, but I don't think so.

After my encounter with Fernando, when I was a tourist alone walking down San Rafael Street into the city, no less than six other young men offered me cheap cigars or a generous exchange rate, and even more tried to start an icebreaker conversation—anything to make contact, to create the possibility. Young men were on the make in greater numbers and displayed a more aggressive style than the year before, which I saw as a disturbing index of the decline of life in Cuba. As an American, I was still an oddity and a special attraction, just cause for the street kids to redouble their efforts, to hang tight to what they hoped would be a deliverance, which might be as small an offering as a T-shirt or as large as the dream of a new life in Miami. When I walked past an open-front café, one particularly persistent young man made his pitch as rock lyrics poured out from inside—"Is this the real thing, or just a fantasy?"—and I wondered the same thing myself. Was this the real Cuba, the new postrevolutionary Cuba created by shortages and tourists?

Face to face with Fernando and his brotherhood at every block, I tried to laugh away their annoying presence by labeling them *molestarios*, a word I made up and then congratulated myself for its cleverness because it defined so accurately the situation on the streets and the mood the *molestarios* created. But they already had a name—*jineteros*, jockeys—given to them by disapproving Cubans, an appellation taken from the image of the jockey hunched over the horse's neck, reins in hand and elbows pumping up and down, riding hard in pursuit, going around and around the track, chasing tourists. It's a good image. But like so many shorthand understandings, this one had its limitations that failed to acknowledge the subtle and complex forces pushing and pulling Cuba in new and often competing directions.

My walks down San Rafael Street always concluded at the Habana Libre, a gritty, urban touchstone appropriate for Cuba in transition. The Habana Libre was the biggest and most active hotel in that part of Havana. It was originally built as the Havana Hilton before both its name and its national ownership changed with the Revolution. It was not Havana's nicest hotel in 1992, not the newest or the best appointed, but it still carried the weight of political and historical character, and it was well located for foreign travelers, not exactly inexpensive, but not pricey like the elegantly restored National, whose rooms went for $200 per night.

With restaurants, foreigners-only shops, guests of a half-dozen nationalities, a long line of available taxis, and Cubans milling about, the Habana Libre was also a social playground where the term *jinetero* expanded to include everyone who hustled tourists, including young women. Easy to spot near the grander tourist hotels like the Libre, women dressed in spandex and body-hugging minidresses wandered in and out of the lobby, leaned against the railing at the guest drop-off point, looked wistfully at displays in shop windows, sipped coffee in the open café, sometimes with friends, other times with new companions for the evening. Day and night they were always there, hopeful, waiting, chatting, laughing, impossible to miss, impossible to ignore, stationed like pacing sentinels signaling a pathway into the titillating corner of Cuba's "special period" of rationing, shortages, and growing need since the loss of Soviet aid.

Loitering in the Libre's lobby, I watched like a voyeur getting off on a preview of Cuba's revolving peep show, a preview that revealed the shifting rules that governed sex, tourism, and shortages—the street trade of downtown Havana's social life. Sitting at a glass table in the Libre's open lobby, I had plenty of conversations and the possibility of almost anything else the imagination might consider. The *jineteros* stopped approaching after a time, once word spread through their community that I was "not a foreigner who wanted to do business," as one *jinetero* later described me. Women passing by tried to make eye contact, hoping for an invitation to sit, to talk, perhaps to eat and drink, or, better yet, to spend an evening together, which might expand the possibilities in a world filled with scarcities.

It took only a hint of encouragement on my part for three young women to pull out chairs to sit and share the table. They smiled at one another with experienced nods when I told them my purpose included nothing more than sharing conversation with them over a sandwich and a beer, a declaration of intent they did not believe for a minute but accepted with a shrug. "*¿Por qué no?*" they agreed among themselves as they picked up menus.

Their features ran from Spanish white to mocha to black, and as we sat and drank our beer they acted like best girlfriends used to sharing laughs and whispering confidences. Marta, a woman with tight black ringlets surrounding a face distinguished by high, chiseled cheekbones, was the acknowledged ringleader who did most of the talking, and even though we spoke in Spanish, Marta would repeat snippets of the conversation to the others in Spanish, occasionally inserting an addendum spoken so rapidly it was clearly intended for their understanding alone, which usually produced laughter and giggles.

Once convinced that the limits of our engagement did not extend beyond food, drink, and the lobby, Marta accepted my curiosity with a Cuban tolerance. She and her friends went out almost every night, she explained, often with a stop at the Libre to see what was going on there, to visit with friends, or to just hang out in hopes of meeting someone.

"Meeting someone?" I asked.

"Yes, a foreign man. We want to go to a restaurant and eat. It's best if we can get them to take us to a disco. We love to dance and have a good time. We aren't allowed in by ourselves. Cubans can't go alone. We have to be with a foreigner. Plus, if we get to know them, or if they are really friendly, maybe they will take us to the hotel shop."

"What do you want at the shops?"

"Anything," Marta said, as all three laughed. "María got that skirt," said Marta, and María stood up to show off an inexpensive-looking piece of Dacron and cotton cloth with badly puckered seams. "We like clothes, perfume, things like that. Anything."

"Do the men expect you to have sex with them?"

"Yes, of course, most of them do. Sometimes I don't go with them. It depends. I don't want to go with a man I don't like at all. I won't do that."

"Do other girls?"

"Yes, all the girls are different. Some just want dollars. They have sex for so many dollars, won't go anyplace with a man unless they know what dollars they will get in return. That's common. We do that sometimes, make that arrangement. But it's usually not like that for us. We want to have a good time, and maybe get a gift, or some dollars. It depends," said Marta with a toss of her hands as if to indicate there was nothing more she could tell me about that.

"What about the tourist police?"

"They're a problem. A big problem. We have to be very careful. If they catch us in the room, they take us to jail. If you get caught a lot, it's a real problem."

"How do you avoid being caught?"

"We give dollars to a baggage person or someone at the desk. It depends who is working and where we are, what hotel we're at. If the police come, they call the room and warn us. Sometimes it's very scary. But funny after," she added with a smile. "You have to grab your clothes and try to get them on and leave before the police get there."

"What about protection, from pregnancy and disease?"

"That's difficult, a real problem. Many men have condoms. That's what we hope for; we don't have any. They are hard for us to get and cost too much. What can we do?

"A lot of the country girls are taken advantage of. They don't know about foreign men. They don't get dollars. Don't get anything. Some get pregnant. Mexican men are bad in that way. They like Cuban women, but a lot of them take advantage. Particularly of the country girls."

Marta and her girlfriends extended the meaning of social life as sexual play or sexual business beyond the essential act of sex for dollars, which in most cases, like nearly everything else in Cuba in 1992, looped back to Cuba's immediate problems and her chosen remedy, back to the "special period" and squeezing dollars out of tourists. Havana's social-sexual scene involved a messy mix of elements conspicuous in Cuba's drift into a dreary-looking, postrevolutionary culture, part old, part new, part Cuban, part import—an idle and bored younger generation, a government courting tourists, a society confronted with rationing, the Caribbean tradition of gift-giving, an active urban social culture, and the pure, don't-give-a-fuck universal attitude of *I'm young and I want to have a good time!*

Marta and her friends, like so many of Havana's young people, were bored and wanted something to do, something to fill their days and excite their nights. Whatever their intent, whatever they wanted or needed in the moment, they spent their time just hanging out, in the streets, in hotel lobbies, in parks, in doorways, waiting for opportunity, waiting for the future, waiting perhaps for something not yet even considered. They were neatly dressed and obviously took good care of themselves—Marta wore a black cotton shift, bare legs, and worn open sandals, and carried the fresh scent of soap. The young women all looked like truant students, which many of them certainly were. Not one of them ever struck me as a cause for alarm, ever ranked higher than irritation on the urban-alert scale. But that's not the point. It just didn't feel right to see so many idle young people hanging around the Habana Libre, and nearly everywhere else you looked, even if only a fraction of them were *jineteros*. The rest just waited. "There is nothing for us to do," said Marta, as did many others, time and again. Jobs were scarce, and the coveted ones—in the tourist trade—were hard to come by without a second language and probably some inside pull from a friend or family member.

In their idleness and boredom, at night they staked out the Malecón as their own exclusive domain. Every night, young people crowded into the area down the hill from the Habana Libre toward the harbor, where they spread out in both directions along the sea wall. A university student named Paulo introduced me to Havana's late-night culture along the Malecón. He heard me asking directions in English and approached me to inquire, with a politeness that was uncommon by any modern standard, *Can I practice my English?* A bit dubious after my experience with Fernando, I wondered if every young person with a few English phrases used them as an ice-breaker with tourists, then began the hustle.

Hollywood agents would market Paulo as a Cuban Tom Cruise. Wholesome looking with neatly trimmed short hair, he radiated the sort of handsome confidence that would make the father of a young girl wince when he opened the front door on a date night. Paulo possessed an absolute fascination with English, and he desired nothing more sinister than an opportunity to practice his language skills and show off his city to a visitor from the United States. When I asked him about missing classes to spend time with me, he assured me it was okay. "*No problema.*"

"The instructors tell us that spending time speaking a foreign language with a native is better than going to class. A very proper substitute, Peter. Really, it's okay," he repeated as I shot him a skeptical glance. He was interested and enthusiastic, almost old fashioned in his good manners, an eager companion tolerant of my curiosities and accommodating of any suggestion to go here or see that. As we shared time together walking, Paulo's initial politeness proved to be bedrock personal, not provisional.

With Paulo—with nearly everyone during that visit—the talk quickly drifted to Cuba's hard times, but in this case it was I who brought it up, not Paulo. His was not a personality given to complaining.

"Yes," he said, "food is very scarce; it is difficult." Paulo and his family—mother, father, and sister—ate one meal every day at 3:00 P.M. and then had a snack at 8:00. "We can't get food at any price. Even on the black market. The rations just aren't enough for us. It all goes for the foreign tourist," he said without rancor.

"A year ago we thought the shortages were temporary. Everyone thought so. That's what we were told. We accepted rationing as necessary. But since then the lack of food has changed everything," said Paulo.

"'Changed everything' how?" I asked.

"Just everything. I don't know. It's hard. There isn't enough food. No clothes. I made this watch band out of a belt I found in the trash. It's a good job, I think, but why am I doing that sort of thing? I don't know. Making things out of scraps. I would not have been doing something like that before. No way."

"Will things improve?" I asked.

"I think so. I don't know. How can I tell?" he said, obviously a bit uncomfortable.

"Are you losing faith in Cuba?"

"No."

"Will there be a big change?"

"Perhaps," he said.

"What does that mean?"

Paulo wouldn't speculate.

"Will it mean an end to the revolutionary government?"

"No," he replied emphatically.

"A change in leadership?"

"Perhaps."

"Has Castro betrayed the Revolution and Cuba?" I asked him.

"No."

"Has Castro made mistakes?"

"Yes. But he will do something," said Paulo, holding fast to a national confidence that was repeated over and over.

Paulo was mindful of the crisis that shaped his every day and sent him to bed hungry each night. But he was equally forward-looking and accepting, given more to considering a hopeful future than to dwelling on the pressing difficulties at hand. Having accepted the idea that tourism would redeem Cuba, Paulo was ready to move ahead without apparent regard for what might be left behind. He joked that one day he would show me Cuba in a high style, when he ran Cubanacan, the tourism agency. He loved studying English, and his ability was substantial after only one year at the University of Havana. Paulo understood, as did most Cubans, that English, like tourism, would be part of their country's tomorrow, and Paulo would be ready, not out of opportunism but out of optimism. If Fernando symbolized Cuba's hard times and her people's edgy response, then Paulo was the best hope for the post-revolutionary period, which Cuba was drifting into in 1992. Paulo represented Cuba's future, if it arrived in time.

With the day getting late I suggested we continue talking over dinner, an invitation no Cuban ever refused during the "special period." But even at one meal a day, Paulo resisted the opportunity to order a proper meal, insisting that the menu was too expensive, that he should go home to eat then return if I wanted to go to the Malecón to meet some of his friends. I parried his objections until he cautiously ordered—exactly what I did, and no more. But when the meal came and Paulo started to eat, the possessiveness of his hunger became obvious.

Paulo paused for a moment when I asked about the possibility of an organized anti-Castro underground movement. "Peter, I suppose you are correct that our difficulties might make something like that, I don't know, appealing to some people. But I can tell you that it would be impossible for people to get together because Castro is so much in control. I don't know how he does it, but he does," concluded Paulo with an uncharacteristic certainty, but with clear respect for Castro's magical hold on Cuban society, whatever its source.

It was full-summer evening when we left the restaurant and set off for the Malecón at Paulo's understated urging. "I think you might be surprised when we get there," he said. We walked from the Morro Castle end of the seawall, a straight shot up the sidewalk with the sea on our right and Havana's skyline to the left. From a distance, through the darkness of a moonlit night, it looked as though the four-lane road had lost all its distinguishing features. But that was a trick of the night; the street was there, it had simply surrendered to the enveloping presence of thousands of young people. When we got closer I could see them, pressed against the seawall, spilling over the four lanes from sidewalk to sidewalk, then stretching into the darkness, a snaking ribbon of the nation's future. The street was theirs. The cars were gone, victims of shortages and rationing, much like the young men and women who took their place.

Paulo and I wedged ourselves into the crowd, twisting and turning, trying to weave our way through the solid mass of people who had gathered in groups, talking and laughing, passing bottles of rum, bobbing their heads and swaying their bodies to rock music from loudspeakers positioned on the roof of an amusement center. Paulo knew many of them and stopped to shake hands or embrace, to pass a comment, to flirt, to take a sip of rum, and each time Paulo paused to be social, everyone's eyes clicked back and forth from Paulo to the stranger. But Paulo played it cool. He never acknowledged their curiosity, just left them looking after us as we moved away, deeper into the crowd.

We got a bottle of rum and found an open space on the seawall to lean against. Behind us, the waves of Havana Harbor splashed on rocks in the radiance of the Caribbean night; across the street, the skyline was pockmarked by the lights of Havana's buildings. It felt good there, sipping rum with Paulo, being part of the wonder of the place, pressed among those sounds and sights, forgetting for an instance how difficult life had become for Cuba. It was a comforting place, offering me not a moment's concern over being the flush foreigner in a land of youthful need.

I asked Paulo why, with half of Havana's young people surrounding us, many of whom were presumably *jineteros*, no one was approaching me to buy cigars, sex, or pesos, as so often happened when I walked the streets.

"Peter, no one will bother you when you are with me. They know you're a foreigner. They would like to ask you. But I'm Cuban, so they will stay away. It's just not done," said Paulo.

"Is that street hustler etiquette?" I asked.

"I guess so. It's just not done. No one would come up to you while you're with another Cuban. They wouldn't know what's going on. You might be a relative from the States, a good friend. It would be embarrassing for them to try to do business with you, and an insult to me. It's okay, relax. Everything's cool," he said—his way of letting me know we had talked to the end of the subject.

A group of Paulo's friends wandered over, seven or eight young men and women, hopeful and eager, who accepted my offer of rum as an invitation to join us. In a quick display of authority, Paulo established himself by making the introductions, explaining who I was and telling me his relationship with each of the new arrivals, a mix of university and street friends, with Paulo at the hub of all the connections. Over the next couple of hours people came and went; some drifted away and then drifted back again, others left only to be replaced by new inquiring faces. We drank rum and joked and talked about nearly everything I could think of, leaving nothing unsaid or unasked.

I adopted the habit of asking every new arrival their opinion of Castro as soon as they moved into the circle, hoping to catch someone cold, with their guard dropped low, who might let slip an unprotected comment, a reserved bit of truth not fit for public ears; but it turned out I was being naive, maybe even silly, not provocative or clever. Nobody cared.

Nobody shirked away; everyone made it clear that they held no opinions that required discretion. They didn't give a damn about my question, or what they said about Castro. A few dismissed the question with an indifferent toss of their hands or a shrug of their shoulders; several said he was *loco*; a number thought Castro was all right but had governed too long, had grown old and stale in power, was, as one of them put it, "a man of the past, not the future."

No one that night broke into revolutionary worship of the maximum leader, no one recited the textbook praise for the Triumph of the Revolution, learned in school and touted on billboards. And no one—not even those who offered the most unforgiving judgments that drew startled looks from friends—cast a worried glance over their shoulder, or adopted a conspiratorial tone, or betrayed the slightest apprehension as they spoke critically of Castro, the Revolution, and Cuba's past or her future, which they all saw shrouded in doubt. Everyone agreed on a single fact: change was needed.

The conversation became more animated when I asked about the black market, something they knew about, cared about, at the bedrock level of eating one meal a day. "It is *the* Cuban economy," stated one woman. Another described it as lively but casual, not a systematic organization of thieves and criminals—no gangsters, American style—but a make-do system involving the whole society, anyone who might have a shirt, a radio, a pair of shoes to sell so they could get money to buy food. "Anything is good for the black market because everything is so scarce," she explained, to everyone's agreement. "You never work in your own neighborhood. You go somewhere else and knock on doors to sell. It's safer that way."

But in Havana during the "special period" even everyday items were so hard to come by, came a comment from the crowd, that "sometimes there's nothing to buy on the black market. There just isn't anything, even if you have some money." "Everything goes to the tourists," someone else offered, repeating Cuba's mantra for the "special period." "The government takes what it needs for the hotels and tells us, *Be patient*."

A young man named Gregorio stepped forward, whose trendy clothes and chunks of gold jewelry—rings, bracelets, neck chains—established a presence that set him apart from the other patrons of the late-night Malecón. Later Paulo told me what was obvious, that he was a professional black marketeer, someone different from the people who traded and sold now and then as opportunity or need presented itself.

"The state has everything," said Gregorio, "controls everything. If we want to do business we have to get things to sell. So there is the *bolsa*," he said, the exchange. The crowd smiled at this exposure of Cuba's worst-kept secret.

"The *bolsa* is very illegal, very dangerous. More illegal than the black market because it involves stealing directly from the state—from stores, from trucks, from warehouses. Very serious," he said, "very serious. If you get caught, you go to jail for sure. For a long time. For a long time," he repeated with exaggerated emphasis.

The hustling of tourists, skimming from the state, and black marketeering, the tendency for men and women to become *jineteros* and *jineteras*, the whole process of getting by along the edges of a society that was pitching and rolling, had become so commonplace, so much a part of day-to-day life during the "special period" that it had aptly earned the name *resolviendo,* resolving things. A near-perfect Cuban term, for it suggested a solution evolving out of hard times, with a touch of optimism and no whining.

Yet as the days went on and the more I talked to Cubans, the more I came to appreciate that *resolviendo* was more tolerated than approved of, was worn by a needy society like a sackcloth woven from the scratchy fabric of failure. In groups, young people joked about it, dismissed it, and accepted it as part of their lives, as something that offered the occasional treat or opportunity. But not every Cuban was so cavalier. For many, particularly the older generation, the life of *resolviendo* was a worry, a reason for concern. Older Cubans fretted like everyone else and complained about the indignities of the special period—not enough food or gasoline, or enough of anything, really, a Cuba on the steady downturn, a hungry life. Yet in their view, *resolviendo* extended the problem, even as it offered a patched-up solution. Cubans were distressed at having to steal, to buy stolen goods, to sneak around, to act like criminals. "It's just not Cuban to do those things," said a fortyish teacher as she struggled to explain *resolviendo*'s place, and its rub, in Cuban society. Everyone accepted why it was commonplace—out of necessity, the need to survive, to get from today into tomorrow. The reason was simple, actually, as primitive as the hunger that had created it, but a lot of people disliked *resolviendo,* even as they engaged in the process.

Cuba's new culture of small rations, of standing in line, working the streets, breaking the law, and bartering whatever you had—including pride and honor—for what you needed, affected Havana's mood, reshaped the way Cubans felt about some things, including themselves. *Resolviendo* added an edgy layer to a society that was changing too fast to track, an anxious society that often appeared to be on the verge of tears—like Eduardo when he told me, "There is not enough milk for my babies."

For the first time, a foreigner could feel the cool stare of the Cuban people, particularly from those standing in line waiting to buy whatever might be left over for them. The weary look on pinched faces came from need rather than resentment or anger, I thought, from the universally accepted understanding that foreigners "get everything"—all the things that Cubans could get only through *resolviendo,* if at all.

One afternoon, as I stood looking at the José Martí Theater, a once-beautiful building now gone to neglect, boarded up and unused, a kid perhaps twelve years old rode by on his bicycle, stared at me, shouted "Fuck you" in English, shot me the bird, and then broke into a full-faced smile. I think the kid knew what he was talking about—Cuba's mood was still good-natured but growing frustrated and getting angry. Trust and faith were growing as scarce as bath soap in lovely Havana.

26th of July

I was in Havana on the 26th of July as part of a romantic plan to celebrate one of Cuba's most honored days. Castro's revolutionary group took its name, The 26th of July Movement, from the date of its first military operation, a reckless and doomed assault on Batista's Moncada Army Barracks in 1953. The attack failed horribly, leaving sixty-eight rebels dead from army gunfire, torture, and execution and sending Castro to prison and then into exile in Mexico. But history is forgiving of blunders by the winners, so in Cuba the attack has long symbolized the start of the guerrilla war, and the date is rivaled as a national holiday only by January 1, the day the rebels claimed power.

During better times, when the Revolution cared for the people in a prideful fashion, before the Russians withdrew their aid and the United States tightened its embargo, before the shortages took hold to threaten Cuba's national well-being, the government celebrated the 26th of July by halting work for the day and distributing presents of food, good rum, and other treats appropriate to the day's historical importance. And out of respect for history—and the Revolution—tens of thousands of Cubans gathered to cheer Fidel Castro's traditional speech, an address to the nation and the world that news film crews loved because it offered images of a tireless Fidel going on and on for hours, his language as animated as his waving arms and revolutionary declarations. It was a moment I had hoped to experience, to stand pressed among proud and grateful Cubans in the Plaza de la Revolución listening to Fidel Castro.

But in post–Cold War Cuba, even the 26th of July was short on rations and low on energy, reducing Havana's holiday to a condition as faded as the revolutionary flags that flew from the city's open balconies. Castro was away from the country, tin-cup begging from Spanish cousins, leaving behind a city with no real thirst for a party. I hooked up with Paulo, eager for the opportunity to spend time with him around the idea of the Revolution.

We returned to the Malecón, one of several locales for the day's festivities of music and dancing and fireworks promised for later that summer evening. People covered the seawall, the sidewalk, and the roadway. We pushed our way through the crowds, looking for nothing in particular, just walking and soaking up the scene. Upon the seawall sat an endless row of young faces, black and white teens dressed mostly in T-shirts and shorts, dangling bare legs against gray chunks of rough sandstone placed there to protect Havana from high tides, harsh seas, and Lord knows what else. One group looked on attentively as we approached, and when we got directly opposite them they sat up straight, smiled, and threw their arms around the shoulder of the person on either side of them, posing, as an invitation for the man with the camera. I went over to them and asked with great seriousness, "*¿Permítame, por favor?*"—may I, please?—to which they all smiled their permission. I took a series of shots, thanked them, and started to leave when a young woman wearing a dress of bright-colored circles that looked like a roll of old-fashioned Life Savers asked with great hesitation, *Don't you need our names?* Feigning an irresponsible forgetfulness and expressing gratitude for her reminder, I assured her I did need them, certainly I did, and as I wrote them in my journal—Luisa, Elena, Rafael, Ramón, and Luz—I considered the value of small courtesies in a land where so many things that contribute to a good life had been reduced to a ration list.

The mass of young people leaned against bicycles in long, sweeping rows, chatted quietly, moved about very little, and acted a bit pensive, even subdued. Mothers and fathers held the hands of small children and carried baskets and bags of food, drink, and games for the day's picnic. Everywhere I turned my camera, people smiled and posed, eager to please. I paused to catch the stare of a young girl, perhaps five years old, who was standing on the seat of a park bench, leaning against its wrought-iron back; she wore a bright red jumper with blue and yellow flowers along the edge, brightly polished black shoes, and white-white socks, and her face was an olive-skinned oval with deep, dark eyes and perfect chubby cheeks surrounded by black-black hair, a healthy, well-tended child who finally could contain herself no longer and broke into a charming smile, one look of Cuba.

Paulo and I worked our way over to join a knot of people who stood watching a man chanting, dancing, and making music, a tall, lean black man with smooth, ageless skin. He was certainly at least sixty years old, and could have been eighty, maybe even older. He was carefully dressed, wearing a shirt with a white-red-and-blue pattern, neatly pressed white trousers, and spotless white tennis shoes with blue laces. He carried a blue-and-white conga drum on a matching leather strap around his neck, and in one hand he held a tin-can rattle painted the same blue color and filled with pebbles; in the other hand he clutched a white handkerchief trimmed with red piping. His left ear was pierced with six stainless-steel hoops of ascending sizes, his front teeth were an alternating mix of gold and steel, both his wrists were ringed with bracelets, some made of metal and others of shells, and around his neck hung no fewer than a dozen necklaces of beads and shells in an assortment of Santería colors, representations from the religion that African slaves developed in the New World. The longest necklaces, made of black and white beads, reached nearly to his waist, and the others worked their way up in size to the shortest, a red-and-white choker at his neck that held a silver-framed picture of a young child. His shaved head, his face, his arms, and the portion of his chest exposed by his open shirt—every visible part of his body including the bridge of his nose, his chin, and his cheeks—were covered with tattoos, bold, intricate, artfully detailed patterns, some of recognizable words and figures, others of elaborate symbols of unknown origin or meaning. He chanted, shook the tin-can rattle, and occasionally made a single, dramatic strike on the conga. His chants were about Oriente Province, the sugar and slavery part of the island; pieces of history and stories elevated into mythology and legend about Africa, about slavery's suffering and heroes, about Spanish cruelty and stupidity—stories that dissolved into silence midway through, when he would pause for a moment then slap his forehead and run his hand over his smooth-shaved skull down to the back of his neck. His liquid eyes and elastic face shifted from hard concentration to full-face delight to deep sorrow, perhaps despair. Another look of Cuba.

The surrounding crowd was attentive and respectful. But nowhere on the Malecón that day did people demonstrate a genuine commitment to a good time. Except for the very young, the innocent children who played among themselves with no knowledge of embargoes or "special periods," the people, young and old alike, appeared to have arrived there without vitality or passion. There was something terribly wrong that so many people generated so little energy or laughter or anger, any emotion that might indicate a capacity to move the emotional meter off empty. It didn't feel right or good for a festival day, or any day for that matter. Even a fistfight or a loud lovers' quarrel would have been welcome as a sign that Havana still had some juice.

Black-and-red Movimiento-26 flags half the size of a bedsheet hung from windows and balconies; 26th of July banners flew on street corners and lampposts, stirred occasionally by a breeze off Havana Harbor, a sight that struck me as particularly poignant. Seen against Havana's low skyline and mixed with the bright sunlight of a clear tropical sky, the flag-draped setting had a dreamlike quality, a sparkling backdrop emotionally unsuited to the gray mood of the people. I flashed back to Santiago de Cuba, to the music festival the year before, where national pride and a festive time had given me and my companions an appreciation for the spirit of the Cuban people and a slice of hope for their country's well-being. The contrast in mood and style was so striking, it caused me to think that if something spontaneous happened in Cuba, a trouble more ambitious than an everyday worry, it would start at the Malecón, where on a moonless night a minor incident could set everything off, maybe something as commonplace as a cranky policeman asking too many kids for the IDs they had forgotten to tuck into their pockets that morning.

I lacked any real idea what that would mean, what it would look like, what the result would be, but the setting seemed perfect—large numbers of idle teens with little faith in the past and too much anxiety about the future. It was not that I considered Havana's young people to be on the verge of rebellion, nor did Havana feel like a national capital ready to change governments. It was just that so much of Cuban life seemed out of proportion, felt not quite right in a manner that defied a reasonable description. The glue that had been mixed during the revolutionary struggle, that had held Cuban society together for three decades, was growing brittle and unreliable, allowing people and emotions and attitudes to shift out of their proper place, out of their proper relationship in an orderly society. Even the optimistic Paulo had little interest in the past. For him and many of his youthful generation, the Revolution and the Movimiento-26 were reduced to mere history, and not particularly compelling history at that, even on the 26th of July, when they were excused from school or work and encouraged to celebrate, to party.

Paulo had gradually assumed the role of my unofficial guide and translator, partly out of his curiosity, partly because he thought I needed someone to keep me out of trouble, although I could not imagine what that might mean in Havana, certainly not danger. He wanted me to see every interesting corner of his city, not in a showy braggart's way, but in a prideful, helpful way, as an act of friendship and exploration, and he was enthusiastic about everything I mentioned or we stumbled across, except the Museo de la Revolución. Thinking that the 26th of July was the appropriate occasion to bring it up, and remembering Neddie's command from my last trip—"You must go to the Museum of Revolution to understand what Cuba was like before the Revolution"—I raised the idea with Paulo. He stammered his hesitation, as he always did at a mention of the Revolution, or any showplace associated with it; he would have gone to the Museum with me out of courtesy and friendship, but his comment that it takes two and a half hours to complete the tour told me what his good manners would not allow.

Curious about Paulo's skittishness concerning the Revolution, I pressed him. "Didn't you study the Revolution in school?"

"Of course, all through school, until it was boring," he said, making a teenager's face.

"Can you name the original Heroes of the Revolution?"

"No, not all of them. It happened a long time ago."

"How many can you name?"

"Not that many, really."

"Come on, give it a try. If you had to memorize them in school so many times, you must be able to name a few," I continued with my good-natured torment.

But Paulo refused to play the History of the Revolution game with me. It bored him.

Many of the revolutionary generation still judged the present against the worst memories of the Batista years, but Paulo and his friends grew up with the Revolution an established fact, with its benefits taken for granted as the minimum level of their expectations. Housing, food, education, medical care was what they knew. It was the Revolution's promise to them, a commitment made long ago and kept until only recently.

The young ones judged their lives against the Revolution's best years, and they wanted to know what had happened, and what was next.

Some of them were starting to ask, *Who is to blame?* No one had a good answer. In return, young Cubans cared little about the history of the Revolution, cared only about its successes and benefits, put into place and preserved for their good fortune, now going bad. Everything else was folklore, done with and gone from their vision, with no relationship to their lives. "What's the big deal?" asked one of Paulo's friends.

If Paulo lacked enthusiasm for revolutionary history, he returned to his attentive self when our conversation drifted into serious political rumors about revolutionary leaders. Banners and flags and posters with pictures of fallen martyrs and revolutionary slogans were everywhere that festival day, including portraits of the Heroes of the Revolution, Cuba's national figures who rival America's own founding fathers. When Paulo noticed a series of images in the distance he grabbed my shoulders to turn my back to them, and with great dramatic effect he recited the names of the Heroes, the ones he had not been able to remember earlier.

I asked Paulo about the theory, much loved by Cuba's harshest critics, that many of the Heroes of the Revolution who rivaled Fidel in popularity had disappeared in one way or another over the years—Che off to Bolivia to die at the hands of the CIA and the local army, Camilo Cienfuegos lost in the crash of a small airplane with no wreckage found, and General Arnaldo Ochoa executed by a Cuban firing squad under Castro's direct authority.

The Ochoa incident was the only one contemporary for Paulo, who was quick to tell me that the general, Cuba's most respected military man and Castro's compatriot from the Revolution, should never have been executed for reputed drug dealing, and he believed that most of his friends thought the same.

"Was Ochoa guilty?" I asked.

"I don't know," shrugged Paulo.

But from our conversation I took it that he believed not, although the more important fact was this: it did not matter. Innocence or guilt counted for little in this case because either way, Ochoa was Ochoa, the last *fighting* Hero of the Revolution from his service leading Cuban troops in Angola, including many of Paulo's friends, said Paulo with a prideful tone of voice, which reflected a greater respect for Cuba's revolutionary tradition than he had granted to himself.

Paulo looked a bit puzzled when I asked about Camilo Cienfuegos, whose story had never been able to go to rest, a story that after many years of fitful discussion in Cuba and Miami had been elevated to mythology and allegory, even in Havana under the flying banners of the 26th of July. A revolutionary leader from the first days of the movement, Camilo was enormously popular, considered second only to Fidel by many Cubans during those dazzling months just after the Triumph. In those parts of central Cuba where Camilo was raised and led a rebel army, I saw his picture—not Che's, not Fidel's, but Camilo's—hanging in the homes of the revolutionary generation. When Camilo's small plane disappeared, Castro personally supervised the search that found no wreckage. Skeptics in the United States speculated that Castro sabotaged the plane to rid himself of yet another potential rival for power. When I told Paulo that story he said, "The rumor in Cuba is that Camilo is wealthy and living in Miami." In death, Camilo Cienfuegos, Hero of the Revolution, served everyone's most suspicious intentions.

My plans called for me to spend the evening of the 26th of July with Neddie and her family, but before I went on my way Paulo said he wanted to take me someplace, to show me something, so off we went. We walked along the Malecón into Old Havana, down its narrow streets into one of the saddest moments of the trip. Paulo took me to a small café near the Plaza de las Armas to buy us a flan. Not a striking establishment, the café was a small, weary place with four or five tiny tables, a café like many others, but a place Paulo knew as one of the very few in Havana that welcomed Cubans with their pesos, and after several days of me paying in dollars Paulo, being a well-mannered young man who appreciated the subtle responsibilities of friendship, wanted to take his turn. We ate our desserts and talked at the outdoor table for the longest time, savoring the moment and the setting Paulo had created.

When we finished and rose to leave, the proprietor refused Paulo's pesos, insisting that the foreigner pay in dollars, and when an embarrassed Paulo could not reason with her no matter how long or hard he tried, trying too long and too hard, I paid without him having to explain, but it was awkward and painful, and Paulo was nearly in tears from disappointment. I put my arm through his in an exaggerated act of fellowship as we turned to walk away from that uncomfortable place, trying to make small talk as though nothing of consequence had gone on, but we both knew better. We never spoke about it. Paulo did not want to; I did not know how to. We just carried it around with us.

My worry over Cuba's choking problems of the "special period" had grown powerful throughout the trip, and I struggled hard to see it clearly, to get it right, to make sense of Cuba's new tone and style, the loss of passion and self-confidence among so many people. Yet all those concerns—about politics and economics, about embargoes and food, about unhappy kids and uncertain futures—were reduced in size for an instant by the insult Paulo suffered on that 26th of July, when he tried to show me something about Cuban friendship.

I left Paulo, even though I did not want to abandon him with his disappointment, but I was expected at Neddie's, was already so late I took a cab to the working-class section where she lived. But I found no relief in the small apartment Neddie shared with her parents and her daughter, Luisa, who was expecting a child.

A changed Neddie started in almost the moment I passed through the door, as if she had been holding herself in check with a discipline that faded the instant I arrived. "I would like to see a happy end to this film. A happy end is the one I want," she said as we sat in her living room sipping Cuban coffee I had brought from the States out of respect for the rumor that there was none to buy in Havana.

I had first showed up at the apartment, unannounced, just after I arrived in Havana, to be greeted by Abuela at the door with open arms, saying, "Pedro, Pedro, Pedro," in an exclamation of hopefulness. Neddie and I made a trip to the *diplotienda* for groceries, then she insisted on cooking a nice meal for all of us, which she did, a traditional Cuban meal of stewed chicken, black beans and rice, and fried plantains, that was the best I ate in Havana. Neddie had invited me to return on the 26th, and I had promised I would. During the days in between I had visited the family more than once, and they had always made me feel welcome, but food shortages made their lives difficult, made their need so complete that it was always there, formed into a separate presence and crowded into a space too confined for its emotional fierceness.

When I arrived that evening after leaving Paulo, I asked Neddie about her family's traditions for the 26th. "Peter, it is unusual for us to have such a complete meal and a bottle of rum this nice. This is a special event because you are here to visit. I feel no cause for celebrating except for that reason. You are here," said Neddie.

"I must say this. I am disgusted with the government and its false claims for the holiday," she went on, making her contempt clear as she went down the list of goods that had been promised as part of the celebration.

"Rum;
soda with rum, a small bottle;
hard candy;
soft candy, like fudge;
a can of Chinese sauce for fried rice;
Chinese noodles;
a package of chocolate cookies, not arrived;
salt crackers, not arrived;
4 ounces of coffee, not arrived;
carrots, not arrived,"

she said with an arched eyebrow and a sarcastic tone. The portions were for a family, regardless of size, and had to be picked up at a distribution point where long lines made the wait intolerable. Everything was not available at one time, so the lines formed whenever a new something arrived, then re-formed for the next item, until Neddie finally quit going, stopped making the effort out of disgust at government promises unfulfilled.

But Neddie's miseries were more substantial than an irritation at the government's inability to deliver crackers and cookies. And the more we talked, the more animated and agitated, emotional and distressed, she became, until her unhappiness and disappointments spilled out.

"I feel betrayed," Neddie said. "I have lost my job. For the first time in my life I have no work, no job. What am I to do, Peter? I must care for Luisa and her unborn child—my first grandchild—now that Pascual has left. And you know my parents live here, too. They are old.

"I worked very hard all my life and have nothing. No shoes. No underwear. Nothing. We eat so little each day. I and my parents . . . we usually have only small portions of noodles so we can save food for Luisa. We must do that to have a healthy baby.

"The government never thanks me for what I have done, only asks me to do more," she said. When the Triumph came, Neddie went to school, an impossible goal before the Revolution, she acknowledged. Then she spent eighteen months building roads in Iraq, returned to Cuba to finish university, and then back to Iraq as a translator, again proud of the possibilities the Revolution gave her but just as proud of the contributions she made on its behalf.

She had many years of service as a "respected teacher of English at a very respected school," a position and a circumstance that had made her life "very happy, very fine, until the 'special period' made everything come apart.

"I knew there would be suffering," she said. "But I got sick, and even though I worked at the school for so long, my contract was not renewed. Peter, I have no job. I don't know how they can do that to me after so long. I worked so hard," she said, nearly in tears. "How can I feel after twenty-three years of hard work? Can I feel fine? After so many sacrifices, in the most difficult time I had, they did nothing for me. Nothing.

"When the Triumph came, I was seven years old. I am now forty.

"What do I have? A black and white TV.

"What do we have?

"What are we?

"What am I? Just a beggar asking for this or that.

"I am in despair.

"The Revolution had many possibilities, but now there are so many problems, it is difficult to see the possibilities any longer.

"I want a better life. I am sorry," she said, not with sarcasm, but with a genuine regret for having to speak the words, for having to tell me that the Revolution had failed her and she had abandoned it.

Abuela sat in her chair in front of the shutters that opened onto the balcony, listening to her daughter, occasionally running a hand over her white hair, cut short and brushed back flat on her head. She always returned her hands to her lap, to fold and wrap them in her dress, as if the faded fabric offered comfort to knuckles and joints swollen by arthritis. During unhappy discussions Abuela paid close attention but remained silent, never offering a comment except for the occasional dramatic moment when she would shake her head from side to side and wave her hand in front of her face, as if she was shooing away flies, not miseries.

But even in Neddie's despair, the Revolution defined the terms of her conversation, her expectations, her disappointments, much as it did the nation. It was her frame of reference—Cuba's frame of reference—

good or bad. Neddie's distress was greatest when she talked about the "special privileges" that had seeped into Cuban society, that had arrived hand in hand with the tourists, the shortages, and the difficulties of the past year.

"I thought that when the 'special period' came we would all live the same, but that is not so. The powerful political people do what they want. The managers of the tourist corporations go here, eat there, watch expensive shows. The people who work in the hotels can get foreigners to buy them things in the stores. Shoes. Food. Even perfume and clothes. It happens all the time. They get advantages, and we see nothing. Nothing.

"I am not being selfish. I do not want more than others. But things aren't right. It's an easy way for them to live," she concluded with a touch of poetic language.

During my previous visit, when I toured the island with Bob and Caputo, our conversation returned again and again to the fear that tourism would strike a ruinous blow to the revolutionary culture that was Cuba's distinct and sustaining characteristic. We had speculated that the imprecise quality—the soul—that held everything together, that made most Cubans proud of what their nation had achieved, was in danger. Just one year later our worst fears seemed to appear before me—the hustling on the streets, the *jineteros*, the catering to foreigners, the lack of food, *resolviendo*, the black market, the broken heart of Neddie, the needy society that more and more looked like it was snatched back from the 1950s.

Neddie's Revolution was in a fast-track race to see whether it could arrive at the treasury with sufficient revenues from tourism before the Cuban people arrived at the palace gates, hungry, weary of shortages, and ready for action.

"When the rationing began in 1989, we all believed what the government said. 'Be patient. The problems will be temporary.' We believed that Fidel would get us through this. We know that Fidel has done wonderful things. We know that. But this has gone on so long. So long. When will it end? Will it ever end? I ask Fidel that. When will it end?"

Historical ironies worked against Cuba, too. For many years the Revolution provided for the people with great success. But with the loss of Russian aid and the tightened U.S. embargo, the difficult times were intensified by their reflection in the recent past. The Revolution had set a standard it could no longer meet. I heard more than once the comments, "We work, work, work and there is nothing to enjoy," a sentiment as keenly felt as the expectations from which it sprang. Many Cubans had become accustomed to a good life, as defined by the standards of the Caribbean or most countries in Latin America, and that bountiful yesterday made a lean today, tomorrow, and probably the day after even more disappointing to the Cuban people.

Neddie's Cuban society was being pulled apart by a struggle between revolutionary behavior and the need to find a place in the post–Cold War world—a struggle between a revolutionary past that was losing its authority and a future that was terribly uncertain, yet wonderfully appealing for those Cubans who benefited from tourism. The irony, and Cuba's problem, was that two sets of rules were working against each other. People like Neddie were expected to be faithful in their sacrifices to the Revolution, expected to go without for the benefit of the tourist trade, expected to accept sacrifices and shortages as the Revolution's last hope; and many Cubans did that willingly. But they were less willing to do so while tourism workers gained advantages in a society reduced to a single meal a day.

Foreigners, including me, engaged as willing partners in furthering the Cuban friction. I never hesitated to offer Neddie a trip to the *diplotienda* to get food for her family, was glad to do it without reservation, and she accepted the offer under the same terms, ignoring the irony of her complaint about others who did the same. And one day in the lobby of the Habana Libre Hotel I took an angry, disaffected, half-mad artist into the hotel shop to buy shoes for his two children—he asked nothing for himself. My list could go on, but it only leads to a common point: it did not take long for the watchful tourist to wonder if his every meal came from the table of a suffering Cuban family.

But in offering help, we also made false promises. "Only you Americans help me," Neddie said, referring to me and to others I had asked to look in on her during the past year. "Peter, you don't know how happy it makes us every time someone comes to say they are your friend from America, then gives us the dollars you send. It means so much to us. So much. We always try to make your friends feel welcome in return." As I talked with Neddie I understood that those small acts of kindness had caused her to believe that Americans were Cuba's friends, and from that she concluded that the United States was a country she could rely upon.

Neddie's leap from personal experience to political principle was a common mistake in Cuba, an alchemist's blend, falsely manufactured by mixing sympathetic American visitors with a belief that an end to the embargo would guarantee Cuba the bountiful blessings of the United States, all at no cost. In some portion or another—from modest to full measure—many Cubans shared Neddie's and Paulo's faith that the United States and Cuba would get back together, like long-separated lovers with a lingering attraction, destined for a renewal of fidelity and trust.

On a visit to Morro Castle at Havana Harbor, Paulo asked me, "Don't you think that the United States will lift the embargo? Will become our friend again? Isn't that possible? I can't understand why they don't do that."

"Why would the U.S. want to save the world's last Communist?" I replied, as we stood looking at the harbor, a calm setting nearly empty of ships, thanks to the embargo. "Cuba has no constituency in the United States. The U.S. hates Castro. He embarrassed us at the Bay of Pigs and has annoyed us at every opportunity since then, not the least of which have been the successes of Cuba's revolutionary society."

Even on the 26th of July, that holiday celebrating the Revolution, Paulo and Neddie cast hopeful eyes toward the United States, seeing Cuba's choices narrowing, tightening down to either absolute ruin or an accommodation with her archenemy of thirty years. Among workaday Cubans there was little appreciation for the concessions the United States would extract before ending the embargo and embracing Cuba once again as friend, or even family, the term some Cubans considered most appropriate to describe the two nations' proper relationship.

Neddie was more willing than Paulo to forsake the Revolution in order to court the United States openly—an unexpected twist, given Paulo's professed indifference to Cuba's revolutionary past and Neddie's earlier insistence that I appreciate it as she did. But when it came down to it, Paulo's youthful optimism encompassed not only his own future, but his country as well. During a thoughtful discussion, as we took shelter from a summer shower under the eaves of the Museum of Education, I asked him if he had ever thought of going to Miami. He said he had, to visit relatives, but when he realized the true intent of my question, he said, "No, I would never leave here. I love my country."

Neddie, in contrast, was worn out, like so much of Cuba, even on the 26th on July. Tired and disappointed, fatigued by shortages, scraping by on not enough food for too long, Neddie wanted rest and comfort, and nothing seemed too great to sacrifice in return. Late into the evening on Cuba's once-proud holiday this once-proud revolutionary woman talked about finding an American husband of convenience for her or Luisa and of accepting the United States on any terms, so long as it brought relief.

"Fidel and brother Raúl out of power?" I asked.

"Cuban Americans back in Havana?" I asked.

"The return of confiscated property?" I asked.

"The rise of political parties?" I asked.

"Yes, yes, yes, and yes," Neddie answered, to all my questions.

"The only happiness is when you help. Please don't forget us, Peter," was Neddie's final comment.

I left Neddie and her family that night sluggish with Cuban food, rum, and Neddie's terrible unhappiness. Just a year ago Neddie had been a woman proud of Cuba's successes, with her mother healthy and her daughter dancing as a professional thanks to the Revolution. Sitting in the living room with her family, she had told me: "That's what the Revolution means to me and the people I love most."

And Neddie's powerful, testifying words—spoken with such conviction and confidence, and appreciation—were the ones I remembered best and quoted most from that first trip to Cuba, the words I had used to smack around the American skeptics, the people who doubted Cuba and her revolutionary culture because their vision could not see past Castro and Communism, those critics who had never been to Cuba, who knew little of the place or the people, those Cold Warriors and their fellow travelers who knew proof certain that what I had reported from there was mistaken, that I was either a patsy for clever Cubans or a fool, misguided by my own politics. Fuck 'em, I finally decided. I knew where I had been, and I knew I was going back.

And I had, and there I was, a few days after saying good-bye to Neddie, sitting in the plane ready to leave Havana. And once again Neddie's parting words had expressed in the simplest of language my own feelings about Cuba, which this time was desperate worry. It felt as though Cuba's confidence and purpose, her revolutionary ethos and passions, her triumphs and successes were leaking away, diminished by want and the loss of a grand ideal. Having fallen into a fit of worry over Cuba, I turned on Castro, for trusting the Russians, for confusing poets with saboteurs, for confusing hostile ideas with attacks on the Revolution, for confusing his critics with Cuba's enemies, for confusing his personal will with Cuba's best interests, for confusing his vain place in history with a national ambition. I cursed Castro for his hubris and for recklessly threatening Cuba's revolutionary society and the visions and hopes it had inspired, including my own.

Food and Dollars

DECEMBER 1994

Dollars

Neddie's heart-piercing final comment—"Please don't forget us, Peter"—kept pulling my thoughts back to Havana. But it was mostly bad news and refugees that came out of Fidel's island during the two years it took me to get back there. Rumors circulated in Miami about a spectacular increase in the number of rafters, about idle children of the Revolution smashing windows in Havana's tourist hotels, about power blackouts lasting as long as twelve hours a day, about a malnourished citizenry eating cats, about Castro facing his final hours. Such pessimistic stories and dismal predictions left me anxious about Cuba and the fate of my friends there. Cuba never let me feel indifferent.

Finally in December 1994 I flew to Nassau and caught an uneventful shuttle to Havana. Hailing a cab at José Martí Airport for the ride across Havana to the Hotel Inglaterra, I braced myself for the worst, certain I was about to enter a desperate and desolate place. But as was so often the case, Cuba was not what she was supposed to be. *Los amarillos* were disappearing from the roads along with the crowds of hitchhikers, many of whom were riding buses donated by sympathetic cities in Canada and Europe, including one yellow school bus with large black lettering that identified a previous owner as the Huron County School Board. My taxi shared the open road with private cars and official vehicles and government trucks filled with produce and construction materials. I checked into the hotel and immediately hit the streets, walking the now-familiar route down San Rafael Street from the hotel to the city center, along streets I knew as well as many in my own city.

The long walk took me through neighborhoods of two- and three-story apartments and handsome homes with arched doors and windows, ornate iron grillwork, and peeling paint. The streets were lined with cars and motorcycles; people sat on doorsteps and chatted, kids played on the sidewalks, family laughter came from open windows, laundry dried on the ubiquitous balconies, and the sticky-sweet, opulent smell of overripe fruit scented the air. I passed stores and shops in buildings time-dated by their architecture of big picture windows set in aluminum frames and double-entry doors made of oiled wood and glass, doors with brass plates on them where customers could place a hand to push their way inside. I had walked past those stores more times than I could count from memory and had never seen the doors swing open for a single customer, had only seen the stores boarded up and empty, like hollow, dusty reminders of Cuba's neediness. But now they were open for business. I wandered in and out of several of them, where milling customers chatted among themselves, held up merchandise for inspection and approval, and pulled companions to investigate discoveries in the next aisle. Satisfied-looking customers once again browsed and handled the stock, which was mostly small household items and uninspired clothing. Convenience-style stores selling soft drinks, beer, candy, cigarettes, and food had popped up here and there, crowded with Cubans clutching pesos and dollars, eager to spend, eager to buy, happy to be back in the game. The energy of commerce had returned to Havana.

Out on the sidewalks and plazas, hyperbusy men shined shoes, women at card tables glued on false fingernails, and people repaired bicycles and anything else that was broken but salvageable in a country where little was considered beyond reclamation, even disposable cigarette lighters. Long lines of patient customers waited for products and services; the longest was stationed beside a shooting gallery constructed from a sheet-metal backdrop, where kids shot pellet guns at crudely fashioned ducks.

I stopped to talk with a barber as he worked on a customer who was seated in an old-fashioned barber's chair of cracked brown leather and white enamel. "I live just over there," he said, looking up from his work to point down the street. "Every morning my son helps me carry the chair from the apartment to the sidewalk. This is where I do business," he said, glancing up and down the sidewalk. "My father was a barber. This was his chair. He had it in his own shop with several other barbers. When the shop was closed down, my father kept the chair. He put it in the apartment, where it has been for more than twenty-five years. He cut the hair for family and neighbors. I did the same thing. We had to be careful doing that; now I am doing the same thing on the sidewalk," he said with a Cuban shake of his head. When I asked him why his father had shut his shop, the talkative young barber ignored my foolish question.

After walking nearly to the city center, I grabbed a cab and headed for another piece of familiar ground—the Plaza de la Catedral and the Plaza de las Armas, situated only blocks from each other in La Habana Vieja—eager for the understanding that comes from measuring change against what's familiar. During the previous visits I had spent many hours in these spots, but the lack of energy and action, the subdued presence and promise, had made them seem like emotionally depressed pieces of urban geography compared to what they should have been, what they must have been in earlier decades, so I quit making the trip after a few times. But when the cab dropped me off, I walked the narrow cobbled streets into a reconstituted Havana.

I went into a *paladar*, without a clear idea of what it was—a two-table restaurant set up in the small living room of an apartment, where the family served homemade meals of black beans and rice, a piece of fish or beef, potatoes, beer, and dessert for $2.50. The husband, who acted as host, waiter, janitor, and social critic, told me that during the several months they had been open business had been good, but several recently opened *paladares* had caused him to start worrying about falling profits. I congratulated him on good fortune and his rapid conversion to businesslike anxieties. They had placed no signs on the building; his only advertising consisted of walking the surrounding streets of Old Havana handing out professional-looking business cards to foreigners and leaving the front door of the house open as an invitation, as a sign of their readiness to do business.

Artists and craftsmen had commandeered strategic spots along the sidewalks, in the parks, and in the plazas. Painters in all media and styles—oils, acrylics, and charcoal, from folk art to abstract—displayed their work against the black wrought-iron fences surrounding the plazas and under the protective eaves of the buildings, particularly the Museum of Education with its broad, wide overhang. The open space of the plaza was filled with tables manned by booksellers, crafters of black coral jewelry, skilled carvers of beautifully polished wooden canes and masks, and vendors of revolutionary artifacts, particularly Che's portrait on postcards, pins, posters, and T-shirts. I walked around, gawking and marveling at the new look of the place, crowded, busy, hustling, seductive, like it should be, like it always should have been, like hip locations in other cities, such as Saint-Germain-des-Prés in Paris and Jackson Square in New Orleans, but unlike anything I had ever seen in Havana.

Like street artists everywhere, Havana's eagerly sought customers, but failing the sale they settled for a conversation to pass time. I was drawn to a set of brightly colored folk-art paintings and drifted into conversation with the artist, Francisco, an extra-tall, extra-gaunt Afro-Cuban who bent his head down every time he spoke. He and his friend, Raúl, traveled across Havana every day by bus—a two-hour ride that involved several transfers—from a neighborhood on the road to Varadero Beach. Crowded buses with erratic schedules made it difficult for them to arrive early enough to secure a good spot, preferably under the protective care of the museum, away from the threat of sun and rain.

When I told Francisco how struck I was by the changes in the area, he said, "There are other places where people sell things for dollars outdoors. We come here because it's the closest one to our home." He wrote out directions to other locations where the underground economy was merging with the official one, creating something new that was feeling its way, still pretty awkward and sometimes messy.

Arts and crafts attracted tourists, who attracted *jineteros* and black marketeers, who staked out turf and worked to establish their reputations. Pointing to a discrete young man with a fixed smile, Raúl said, "He's Old Havana's most reliable source of Cuban cigars. Very honest. Never sells fakes. Has fair prices. He's the man you should see if you want cigars. He has good contacts inside the factory"—the ultimate certification of a black marketeer's credibility. Raúl pointed out another man known for providing "companionship" and a third for operating an unofficial taxi service: "He uses his father's car and is very good. Knows the streets of Havana and is cheap and a safe driver, not at all dangerous."

In his whispering style, Francisco said serious problems developed when it first became legal for the artists and vendors to set up for business. It took some time for the artists and the illegals to work out a streetwise etiquette concerning the tourists, upon whom everyone so depended. "Some of the *jineteros* would come up and start talking to tourists while they were looking at my paintings, trying to take them away. It was really bad," he said. "Some of those guys were really rude. Now it doesn't happen very often." The new protocol called for black marketeers to stay clear of the tourists while they browsed among the artists and craftsmen, but once outside selling range they became a fair target.

I stood a long time talking with Francisco and Raúl, surrounded by their art under the wide overhang in front of the Museum of Education. The friends shared a knowing laugh when I asked for details about the black market. "There is no black market; it's the Cuban business. It's all the same now. Everything is dollars," they explained. "Everything."

What previously had been underground and dangerous had in recent months become open and hopeful. A series of decrees issued during the summer and fall of 1993, and another in the fall of 1994, made it legal for Cubans to possess dollars and to open shops offering goods and services. Everyone who wanted to do business, from artists to manicurists—some fifty thousand Cubans by early 1994—paid 45 pesos to the Comité de Finanzas to acquire a state license of operation; the licenses were easy to get, with the single important qualifying question being *Where did you get the tools and materials?* The only reasonable answer, which was never given, was *Stolen from the state*. Everyone ignored the obvious, and dollars had pumped the juice back into Havana's streets, dropping the black market exchange rate from 120 pesos to the dollar to 50, causing many Cubans for a short time to believe that it was smarter to hold pesos over dollars.

The switch to dollars changed the lives of Cubans. Francisco and Raúl and their companions along the plaza could openly sell their art for profit and make a living from their hard work and talent. "This is the first time we can make money," explained Francisco. "Before, if an artist had an exhibition, even in Mexico or some place like that, the money went to the state. The government gave us some of it, but who knows? No one ever thought it was enough. Not for what was sold." With the single decree that legalized dollars, artists emerged from the shadows of Cuban society into the open space of the plazas, selling their own art and pocketing the cash directly. In a society where a physician earned 500 to 600 pesos per month, $25 per painting gave Francisco an economic edge; even at 50 pesos to the dollar, the math made selling art on the street quite appealing compared to a state job.

Francisco's paintings were dramatically colored and folk-primitive in style, hinting of Haitian influence. Set outdoors amid the vivid greenery of a Caribbean landscape, several pieces told tales of Santería ceremonies, in which dancers and drummers made offerings to the *orishas*, the Santería gods, offerings of chickens, pigeons, eggs, pastries, and candles, as the religious tradition demands. The scenes were festive and joyous; the figures were all black. One two-painting set depicted the story of a man on horseback luring away a resting man's wife, and of the husband trying to reclaim his mate, all the while the *orishas* looked on, laughing, mocking, sequestered among the trees in a shroud of pale orange that contrasted against the green of the trees and the blue of the sky. The conflict expressed in the two paintings was left unresolved. I asked Francisco, "Is the struggle in those paintings supposed to represent life in contemporary Cuba? You know, conflicting loyalties?"

"I am not that clever," he said with a laugh. "My paintings would be well-known stories to any Cuban of color. Most of them come from tales we all heard from our grandparents, in our childhood. Stories that are as familiar to us as our lives."

Hanging out and talking with Francisco and Raúl gave me the impression that Cuba was healing herself in small ways. But the streets always kept my enthusiasm in check. During my first visit to Cuba, in 1991, Caputo the photographer had remarked that savvy Africa watchers considered the black market exchange rate a good indication of a nation's stability, or instability, as the case may be. In Cuba, I had come to think that it might be more accurate, or at least more interesting, to judge the fitness of the society by watching the *jineteros*, those people on the fringes of society who hustled foreigners.

Whatever the utility of that theory, for the first time I felt flashes of uneasiness on the streets, brought on by the growing number and determined manner of the men who tried to make contact, to start the conversation they hoped would lead to a deal of some sort. Impossible to ignore and difficult to send away, they seemed more aggressive than I remembered. One *jinetero* told me that he was a prizefighter, as he shadowboxed beside me down the sidewalk near the Habana Libre Hotel; another boasted he was a karate expert; and a third claimed he was a Tae Kwon Do instructor as he fell in step with me outside the Hotel Inglaterra. Finally it came to me—this was tough-guy street hustling Cuban style, not with knives or guns, not even with threats or intimidation, but with information so vague, so implicit, that it took me time to realize they were suggesting danger without actually threatening anyone. Very Cuban. However harmless and quaint these episodes seemed upon reflection, there was no denying that persistence had displaced politeness, that subtlety and charm were disappearing along with an equal portion of the lightheartedness that had made Havana such an appealing destination.

Late one night I left the Plaza de la Catedral with a man who offered taxi service to my hotel. As we walked across the square to his car he introduced himself as a doctor and presented his card with the promise to treat me for free if I needed medical services. The taxi turned out to be a private car doubling as a nighttime cab, a practice that had grown common in Havana from the time Cubans could have dollars. With a man driving and a women sitting in the passenger seat, my doctor friend began his pitch as soon as the cramped, faded sedan started moving.

I politely responded to all his offers, one after another. *Yes, the woman in the front is very beautiful, but I do not wish her as a companion for the evening. Yes, I am certain you can get me drugs and your PCG will keep me as hard as a man could imagine for the longest time, but I do not want any, even if it will lower my cholesterol as well.* And on it went, with offers of cigars, bicycles, and a handsome exchange rate.

We headed off in the general direction of the hotel, but not by a route that could be considered direct, even in the most flexible definition of the term. The price of the ride was preset, so why would they be stretching out the drive? In hopes of creating a possibility? Perhaps. But a possibility for what? I wondered. Illegal business, without a doubt, but maybe with larceny as an alternative? Brand new at being small-time hustlers, they didn't seem to be able to get it right. What the fuck, I thought, was I going to get mugged in Havana by a doctor, a hooker, and their driver? It didn't seem likely, but with everything in Havana changing, anything seemed possible. I pushed the situation off center by suggesting that I might need to hire a car the next day, which picked up everyone's mood—and the driver's sense of direction. Upon our arrival at the hotel, the doctor got terribly agitated when I refused to give him my name and room number, no matter how hard he insisted—and insist he did, until I thought he might stamp his foot in frustration like a petulant child. Nothing was going as he had planned, so he gave up, returned to the car in a huff, and slammed the door. The vehicle sped off as I turned toward the sanctuary of the hotel lobby, walking past a watchful audience of curious Cubans who had gathered on the sidewalk to see how the show would end.

Polite Cubans preferred to ignore this side of their evolving society. But polite they were, so when pressed they conceded that some Havana streets were no longer absolutely safe for a tourist at night, as they always had been in the past. Violence was still rare, but some of the young men with little but idleness to occupy their days and nights had taken to demanding money or snatching purses and cameras from tourists. I felt a bit disloyal each time I approached one of the helpful cab drivers stationed outside the hotel to inquire whether it was safe to walk here or there. More than once I was told, *In the daylight, yes, but not at night.*

It struck me that Havana was losing its innocence, but it may have been that I had lost some of my illusions about Havana. Either way I was put on alert. During a walk down the Paseo de Martí, a wide, busy boulevard that runs through a well-worn neighborhood near Havana Harbor, a group of four or five young black men fell in behind me. Dressed for hip fashion in baggy jeans and floppy shirts and all wearing shades, they were very attentive—too attentive, I felt. They slowed and watched each time I stopped to take a photograph, then followed again as I hurried on with camera in hand and shoulder bag flapping behind me. When they approached with a purpose, I tensed. The largest among them—quite large for a Cuban, and sporting a shaved head—asked me something I did not quite understand. I just stared at him. He repeated his request, and only then did their purpose become clear. They wanted me to take their picture, which I did, and then they drifted away after each of them thanked me, leaving me standing there alone, reminded of the differences between cultures and countries and embarrassed by my assumptions.

I was not alone in these matters. Three Canadian men I met in the Hotel Inglaterra lobby, making a one-day stop in the city after a stay at Varadero Beach, confessed that Havana made them "anxious," which struck me as a rather timid reaction from an athletic-looking trio of their size and youth, guys in their twenties whose very presence would have stopped any danger I could have imagined in Havana. Try as I might, I could think of few cities where these guys would have felt relaxed if Havana scared them.

My smug judgments of the uneasy Canadians aside, they spoke to a trend in the tourist trade that could offer little comfort for Havana or Santiago de Cuba, the island's main cities. Tourists, particularly Europeans, loved Cuba's vacation beach hotels for their luxury, convenience, good food, green sea, and white sand, loved those resorts for the same reasons their Florida-bound counterparts loved Disney World—they were self-contained, one-stop, and safe. Tourists arrived, ate, swam, got tanned, and went home, without making much contact with the rest of Cuba or with Cubans aside from the hotel staff. If they saw Havana, the trip was arranged by the hotel, which bused them into the city in the company of a guide who took them for a sightseeing tour through Havana's history. Apparently the word was out—if you traveled to the city unattended you would be inconvenienced by *jineteros* and have an "anxious" time.

But then again, there were plenty of tourists who cared nothing for the tranquil, safe, and sunny beach resorts. They sought out Cuba for the same reasons that other visitors avoided the city—the social interplay, the night life, the good times, the thinly masked promise of sex, despite official rules prohibiting sexual contact between Cuban women and foreign men. Cuban law still excluded locals from foreigners' hotel rooms, and tourist police patrolled the plazas and leaned against the entrances of major hotels, conspicuous in their gray-and-blue uniforms, leather belts, and peaked caps, ready to enforce the rules, to nudge Cubans along with their nightsticks, if necessity required it, but clearly not meeting their duty at every opportunity.

The laws were the laws, and the police were the police, but the rules of engagement remained Cuban—vague and not always easy for an outsider to grasp. At many hotels, Cubans came and went, in and out of the lobby with ease; the women, at least, seemed to have earned that right, or possibly they'd paid for it. Doormen passed some Cuban women into the lobbies, where they sat, sometimes for hours, chatting among themselves and trying to make contact with a guest. Other women were kept out. It all depended on their understanding with the man at the door. Women in the company of foreigners were welcomed into the hotel bars and restaurants, but not the rooms, unless money changed hands with someone at the hotel. The women knew how to make that happen.

Kevin, an American, had heard about Havana's social life, so he made the trip to investigate for himself. I reluctantly spent time with him after he chased me down and demanded that we talk. "It's very important," he told me with a pleading look. I had met almost no Americans in my trips to Cuba, and too many of those I had met were puffed up with unreflective Uncle Sam judgments about Fidel and the Revolution, so I had to reason that Kevin would be no different.

He looked like an American poster boy for Caribbean tourism, tall, blond, handsome, well tanned, with gold chains at the neck, a Rolex on the wrist, and a heavy cotton shirt, the sleeves cut off at the shoulder to show well-developed arms. Kevin defined himself and his problem with a small handful of repeated facts, as if his consciousness was a cheap memory chip set on an eternal loop. He began as soon as we sat down.

"I live in West Palm. I own my own company. I'm very successful." With every statement he ran a hand through his stylishly long hair, then shook his head from side to side, partly in vanity, partly in nervousness. "I've got money. A nice car. A great condo. You should see my condo. But American women. I don't know. I don't know how to get along with them. I don't know what they want."

He told me he had read a newspaper article about how Cuban women treat American men like kings. "I mean, everyone wants that, don't they? Everybody does."

Then the loop started over again, with the hand running through the hair, the eyes betraying utterly no comprehension of his own audacity, not caring whether or not I wanted to hear his shit. Only when the salient facts were out on the table for the third time did I manage to sneak in a question. "What do you want from me?" I asked. It seemed someone at the hotel had told Kevin that I was an American who knew about Cuba, and he wanted my advice about something important. I told him I doubted I could help him no matter what his problem was, but that didn't stop him.

"I met a girl, and we're in love, but it's impossible. Every time I sneak her into my hotel room we worry about the tourist police. I always bribe the desk person. I know about that. But twice they called. I got her out of the room just in time. But it's tough, you know. It's hard to have sex with that on your mind. I keep thinking that the tourist police are about to break into the room and take her off to jail. What can I do?" he asked me. "I love her. I plan to come back every other weekend to see her. I've got to do something."

I just looked at him, at a loss for anything to say. In this wonderful, beguiling country, my most bizarre conversation up to that moment was taking place with a horny, dysfunctional, anxious young American. But in a flash it came to me what to tell him. "If you love her and really plan to come back every other weekend, you should buy an apartment."

"Well, yes, but I'm American and can't buy property here, can I?"

"No, you can't. You can't have it in your name, but you can get a place and put it in her name. They're not that expensive. You love her, and if you come back as often as you say you will, it will save you money in hotels over the long haul."

That was the best I could do on the spur of the moment, could only hope that Kevin went to his girlfriend and said, "*Chica*, I've got a great idea," then bought the apartment, and she changed the locks as soon as he left town.

Next to an invasion fleet of U.S. Marines, Kevin was my worst American nightmare for Cuba. Kevin was the net of a Cuban resurrection based on tourism and an accommodation with the United States. He irritated me for what he was, for his own sake, and he worried me for what he represented, a Cuban future tied up with American tourists. Kevin took the satire out of Fidel Land.

But Kevin hadn't invented the game, he'd only carried himself to Cuba so he could play it. It was Cuba's game, Havana's, it was everywhere, and I watched it for the first time in the Hotel Inglaterra. Seated in a circle of white wicker chairs in the small lobby, three young women looked over each foreign male who passed, trying to make eye contact that might lead to conversation, that might lead to a night of possibility. The women were beautiful shades of mulatto, dressed very nicely and not too provocatively, ready for an evening of socializing that they hoped would include dinner and drinks at a club or restaurant, before leading to whatever else the late night might hold.

One woman left the hotel with a very blond, very self-satisfied-looking young man dressed in a blue blazer and khaki pants. One of the remaining two approached me and settled in a neighboring chair to talk. Her name was Damaisys. She had the facial features of Lisa Bonet and the hard-working persistence to devote two hours trying to convince me that I should spend time and money with her. "I am only sixteen, but I will be wonderful lover for you. I have experience. I am young but know things that none of the others know," she told me as we ate shredded pork and drank Hatuey beer in the hotel bar. We sat talking, eating, and drinking as if we were on a date, but we were fooling no one who knew anything about Havana, except possibly Damaisys, who kept bringing the conversation back to the proposition that $40 for a night in my room was a fair price for a memorable evening. But even as she sought to sell herself, Damaisys kept tugging at her modestly short skirt, never touched me in a provocative manner or painted graphic word pictures of the pleasures she offered, never resorted to the gaudy trappings of her nighttime trade.

Damaisys confused my rejection of her invitation with the idea that I was worried about the rules, apparently unconvinced that I simply did not want to accept her temptation for a promising night together. So she presented an alternate plan while she sipped her beer and nibbled at her plate of food in a graceful manner.

"Leave the hotel and come with me. I have an apartment. You can stay with me. We can eat there and be together." I would share her bed for $45 a day—much less than my room rate—with meals and nightly companionship as part of the package.

"How is it you have an apartment?" I asked.

"I don't live alone," she said. "It's my aunt's apartment."

"What does your aunt think about you bringing men home?"

"She's no problem. She's crazy. It's okay. She's head of the CDR," said Damaisys, referring to the revolutionary neighborhood watch, the group charged with preserving revolutionary culture, universally regarded as Castro's neighborhood spies. "Because of her no one ever says anything to me about what I do," she said with a flash of smile to celebrate her enviable situation.

As the evening moved forward and it grew apparent that my plans for the remainder of the night, and the nights to follow, did not include her, Damaisys's charm was displaced by a growing irritation, then anger. She became upset over my unreasonableness, raised her voice in protest, pushed back her chair with a force that nearly sent it tumbling, and, standing up, grabbed my notebook off the table and wrote "*hipócrita*" in bold letters that filled a full page, rebuking me for my willingness to talk but my final refusal to accept the arrangement she offered.

But Damaisys's anger was not so thoroughgoing that it prohibited her from returning the next morning to wait patiently in the lobby for me to come down. Poised and ready with a smile and scented with fresh shampoo, she reopened negotiations as we walked along the sidewalk. "Take this," she said, pressing into my hand a piece of paper with her name, address, and phone number. "I know you will change your mind. Promise me you will think about it," she pleaded, with a tone revealing more anxiety than conviction.

I tried to ignore her as we walked down the street, tried to pretend that we weren't attached by some neocolonial thread, until she got into a shouting match with a young Cuban man who, moving along beside us, began waving his arms and stamping his feet on the sidewalk as he cursed her for consorting with a tourist. She shouted back for him to mind his own business, to leave her alone, to get away from us or I would have him arrested. But nothing deterred Damaisys—not my rejection, not even public criticism, nothing—until I stood within hearing distance of a tourist policeman and told her that I had business to attend to, so she must be on her way.

That incident left me feeling manipulative, as if cast from some sort of risk-free Lord Jim adventure on the sunlit, friendly streets of Havana. I had let her go on and on with her hopeful persistence, her barely disguised despair, because I wanted to learn what she had to say, wanted to know about her life. But my intentions had the rancid scent of a titillating curiosity, unchecked by honesty because I never considered going with her, not for a night in my room, not to her apartment. I had used her time and exploited her life in exchange for shredded pork and beer when her rock-bottom price was $40 a night. There I was, acting like an imperialist bargain hunter, fleecing the locals for time and information and, worse yet, manipulating their neediness.

And I felt a further uneasiness because Damaisys left me without any rationalized doubt that the sexual games that had once struck me as a charming part of Havana's flirtatious social style had become more businesslike and determined, more a matter of commerce and less of culture. The soft glow of Havana's boulevards, even in their toughest places and roughest moments, was still a long distance from the hard streets of New York or Washington, D.C. Havana kept a lingering grip on some of its warmth and coyness, but the end game was moving toward a common destination.

I do not mean to give the impression that Castro had "turned Cuba's mothers and daughters into whores," as one friend described it, because that was not true, not at all. Most women went about their lives as ever before, making their way through the "special period" with hard work and the will to resist the temptations that arrived with tourists from countries of plenty. Yet from what I saw, from what I think I learned from

Damaisys and her sisterhood, there was a new sadness and a harsher resolve among the *jineteras*. Shortages and difficult times and boredom caused many young women to work the tourists, to negotiate time spent for a pretty piece of clothing, for food, for cosmetics, for a night on the town, for whatever. It was an old story. But others, like Damaisys, bartered straight up, sex for money, without pretense or apology. More and more women were doing it, and more and more it was done out in the open, no longer masquerading as anything other than what it was—a quest for dollars in a hungry culture.

Paulo and Neddie

One fresh morning Paulo took me to a small marina at the bay of the Almendares River in Havana's Miramar section, where he docked a crude, two-man boat that he and a fishing buddy had patched together out of scraps of wood and tin and other discards of a society where little was thrown away and nothing was wasted. The boat was dry and floated high in the water, but it was so small it looked like a cartoon creation, with fragile lines, uneven proportions, and only the slightest hint of actually being seaworthy. Still, Paulo and his friend took it out of the bay into the ocean for several hours at a time to catch fish that they sold for dollars. They earned only modest amounts with their rickety boat, but Paulo loved to fish, and he wanted to stay busy at something that might pay off in a currency other than cash, to demonstrate, perhaps just to himself, that he was a hard worker prepared to meet his aspirations halfway.

Paulo had been at the marina in the summer of 1994 during a brief period when Castro permitted Cubans to take their chances crossing the dangerous Florida Straits in search of Miami. During the first hours, when the water churned with boats of every description—many of them makeshift crafts unworthy of ever being called a boat—so many they had filled the mouth of the river, heading for the Atlantic. Paulo had looked on in disbelief.

"People jumped into that filthy water just to try and pull themselves onto anything they could," he said. "But the people in the boats kicked and punched everyone trying to do it," anyone trying to find a dry space and relief from the "special period." Paulo had simply watched. "I never considered even for a second joining in. It was dangerous and foolish," he said. But an estimated 32,000 Cubans made the try and ended up in American refugee camps.

Once the policy reverted to closed ports and Cuban jails for anyone attempting to leave, the price of boats dropped at the marina. Paulo and I walked along the weather-stained dock next to boats of various sizes and shapes, only a few of which looked well maintained. He pointed to several that were for sale, "very cheap, but foreigners buy them, not Cubans, and they keep the price from going any lower." Cubans still made rafts, in the off-chance that Castro might offer another opportunity for them to sail freely out of Cuba without penalty or punishment.

"One of my friends has a raft made out of inner tubes, wood, and Styrofoam hidden inside his apartment," said Paulo. "I don't know what he will do with it. Maybe go. Maybe not. He's just waiting."

Four out of five rafters who braved the trip to Miami were born since the Revolution, were Paulo's age or a decade older, so he and his friends all knew somebody who had tried it, who had stolen or paid several months' wages for three or four truck inner tubes, had sewn scraps of cloth into a sail, had crafted homemade paddles, had filled plastic containers with water in preparation to challenge the tight Cuban security and the dangerous Florida Straits, with its furious water flow equal to a thousand Mississippi Rivers.

Some of the more reckless left in ignorance, without information about prevailing currents or weather conditions, without enough water or food, without thoughtful preparation, and most likely their names are on the unwritten list of the doomed, lost to dehydration or starvation, to the high seas and sharks, or to the erratic currents that carried so many of them south of the Florida Keys into the open expanse of the Gulf of Mexico, known to rescuers in Miami as "the Gulf of Death."

Most rafters probably didn't live more than five days, and best estimates are that fewer than 50 percent made it. Some say one in seven.

Others did better. They went to the library to study ocean currents and nautical charts; stockpiled honey, sugar, potassium, and sodium to fend off dehydration; made up a first aid kit; and bought, stole, or bartered for anything else that might swing the chances to their favor, might help beat the odds. There is no guessing where their reckless courage came from.

Not one of Paulo's friends spoke in disapproving tones about the *balseros*. Unlike the first wave of Cubans who fled just after the Revolution for political reasons, those who left later, in the 1980s and '90s, with economics in mind were not judged harshly.

"They can do what they want, is what I say," said one young man at an informal gathering of Paulo's friends. "We talk some about trying it, my brother and I, and sometimes with a friend." But when I asked him point blank, *Will you try to make it to Miami by boat?* he shrugged his shoulders in Cuba's universal expression of indecision, so commonly seen during those unpredictable times. Younger Cubans like him debated and discussed and plotted on a regular basis, whenever a trusted group got together. But their steady talk about leaving Cuba by sea was more an expression of unhappiness with their day-to-day world than a plan of action for the future.

And they were unhappy, sometimes miserable, from not enough food and from a heartfelt belief that they had no future they could rely upon. Food filled their conversations, with friends, with family, even with strangers on the street, despite claims I frequently heard that it was safe to "be open only with good friends." I could not have escaped hearing about food if I had wished, if I had tried, which, after several days in Havana, I now and then did.

"We really want to know when things are going to get better," said a young woman as she held tightly to her girlfriend's arm. "We worry that things will stay like this, or maybe get worse." Fearful that the Revolution would offer less to them than it had to their parents, they talked about problems, blamed Castro for shrinking their possibilities, accepted the idea of a bleak future, and speculated about the rewards of getting out. But curiously absent from their conversations was any imagination or understanding about what could be done, any inspiration about how they might elevate their lives, their world, how they might make it all better. At times they reminded me of Stateside university students of the Reagan '80s who whined that previous generations had soaked up all of the good jobs and possibilities for a comfortable life.

"What would you want your future to look like?" I asked one of the group. He stared at me for a second and said, "I don't even want to think about that." They saw their choices as limited to suffering or leaving, or possibly reaching out to the United States, but nothing in between. When I asked Paulo what he and his girlfriend, Virginia, did in their spare time, he said, "We sleep a lot."

Over a family dinner, Paulo's mother talked about her son and her Revolution. Speaking as if Paulo weren't seated at the table between us, María said, "We are very worried about Paulo. He doesn't care about school anymore. Won't even talk to us about what he will do when he graduates. He is different," she said in a voice filled with worried resignation. The shortages troubled her, and she possessed a mother's worry about Paulo, but she nonetheless insisted that she did not want to turn back the clock or give up on the revolutionary state. "Paulo will have to find a way to make himself happy in Cuba," she concluded.

"I want to work," said an uncharacteristically solemn Paulo. "I want to be able to live like everyone else, to have a home and family. Can you tell me that will happen for me?" he asked, looking to his mother, then to me. "I don't think so."

His mother sighed a mother's sigh and said that she and her husband, Víctor, had given up discussing the Revolution with Paulo because he refused to pay attention. "It bothers Víctor very much that Paulo has no respect for Fidel, the Revolution. Víctor's very patient about it, but it bothers him. He's still so loyal," she said.

With a mix of boyish humor and adult exasperation, Paulo ended the discussion with the comment, "I'm glad Víctor's away because otherwise everyone would be after me all night about this stuff."

On another occasion Paulo refused my request that he and his girlfriend pose for a snapshot beside a statue of José Martí that stood in the courtyard of a particularly lovely schoolhouse. Never camera shy and always up for the game at hand, Paulo finally confessed that he hesitated because we were in his neighborhood, where he did not want people thinking he was "a Communist or a patriot," which to him was the same as looking silly and acting the fool.

For the first time Paulo asked serious questions about the United States, specific questions—*What kind of job do you think I could get? Could we buy a house? What about a small boat for fishing, would that be possible?*—questions asked with a seriousness of purpose that reached beyond curiosity and conversation.

That was a difficult discussion, I told Paulo. Then I explained how much I thought circumstances in Cuba had improved since I last visited—the renewed vitality, the new shops, the open markets, the general feeling that small things were on the move—but he was skeptical, and I felt the need to be honest, so I was. *In the United States the chances are good that if you work hard, and use your charm and energy, everything will pay off in a comfortable life. You will probably get what you want.* I also told him other things, about competition and crime, about a nation, a land of plenty, that was often indifferent to suffering; I felt the obligation to tell him that he would be entering a culture that lacked the warmth and community he so loved in his own. But Paulo only heard that which matched his ambition—a comfortable life, a job, a home, and a family. During my last trip I had sensed that Paulo was Cuba's future, if it arrived in time; but that afternoon, talking to Paulo and his girlfriend, I believed it would not. It looked as though the Revolution was moving too slowly to capture Paulo's dreams, reasonable though they seemed.

We spent one morning going over a public opinion survey conducted in Cuba by a Costa Rican firm and published in the *Miami Herald* just weeks before. The survey was the work of a firm associated with the Roper Agency and had been permitted by the Cuban government with the sole proviso that no question be asked about personalities—*keep Castro out of it.*

This first systematic survey in thirty years, the first since the Revolution, surprised—even shocked—many people, in and out of Cuba, and none more than Paulo and Virginia. Paulo struggled to grasp the concept of asking people direct questions and expecting candid answers in return, and from the start he distrusted the idea. The process was just too unknown to him, and the majority of responses were too often far removed from a reality he accepted, particularly answers concerning confidence in the government and its ability to manage the nation in crisis. Paulo and I went over the questions and responses in English, then he translated them into Spanish for Virginia, whose facial expressions of shock, surprise, and sheer disbelief told their own tale. Paulo was certain that the pollsters "talked only to older people and no one my age if they got those answers," and he grew downright scornful—uncharacteristically so—when I told him that the poll was conducted in people's homes. "The people would not feel they could be honest talking in their homes," he said. "On the streets, maybe, but not in their houses. Never."

I asked Paulo to consider an alternative explanation. Perhaps a significant portion of Cubans held views of society and Castro's rule that were different from those of his own urban generation, and because he didn't spend time around those people, he found it easy to dismiss their views. Paulo just looked at me without saying a word, the only time that happened in the many hours we spent together, in all the conversations we had.

The *Herald* poll showed that there was general respect for the Revolution, for the advances made by women and blacks, and for the opportunities spread so evenly among the island's people, which was why the inequities brought by tourism and legal dollars rankled so much. I asked Paulo's mother about this persistent, enduring respect among some Cubans. She said, "Most Cubans still try to make a difference between what the Revolution has accomplished and the problems about food. We don't like what is happening today, but I ask you, is that reason to do away with everything? I think not." The crisis and shortages and inequities had shaken many Cubans, left them angry about policies and doubtful about Castro's leadership, yet most still thought of Cuba as a revolutionary society in transition, not in defeat. Paulo's mother and father had no impulse to abandon everything, to discard thirty years of purposeful change and return to the old days, to trade in the revolutionary society for another society, perhaps one designed and managed by long-absent exiles.

Dollars and food filled huge spaces in Cuban life in 1994. They were regarded as a problem and a remedy, a source of concern and a possible salvation that no one was allowed to forget for very long because there just wasn't enough of either to allow Cuba to relax and get comfortable. The one-meal-a-day regimen ruled Cuban life, even though food was more available than it had been in the immediate past, at least for Cubans with dollars or extra pesos to spend. Then, a year after the decree that allowed Cubans to have dollars, came the *mercados agropecuarios*, the farmers' markets, where country people sold produce they grew on their land. There, finally, in October 1994, came the most hoped for reform, the one that people believed would ease their hunger. And they were correct, up to a point.

I asked Paulo to show me one of the twenty or so farmers' markets, located in various sections of Havana, and so off we went to the Vedado district. "I think you will like this, Peter," he said. "It's very interesting to see. When the markets first opened there was so much food, prices dropped. Food was cheaper at the farmers' markets than in the regular stores. There was no more black market food. There wasn't any need for it, everything was so cheap. Everyone with money spent it on food, everything they had saved."

The streets approaching the market were a scramble of bicycles and cars parked every which way, with men and women walking the crowded sidewalks carrying plastic shopping bags filled with fresh food. The market was postcard perfect, a scene found in nearly every Latin country except Cuba, until recently. I walked up and down the narrow aisles between makeshift stalls built from wood scraps, with tin roofs keeping the food and sellers sheltered from the long day's sun.

"Where does all the food come from?" I asked a sun-baked man in threadbare work clothes selling fresh-killed pigs. He told me that collective farmers were required to sell 80 percent of their crops to the state, but the remainder they could take to market, for profit. "Some of us grow food and have animals on our land. The government has nothing to do with it, nothing," he said with a satisfied scoff. He became even prouder when I asked him how his business was. "Very well," he said in English, standing a bit straighter. And it was easy to see why.

People squeezed past each other shoulder to shoulder, looking, feeling and pinching the goods, and negotiating for the day's meal. Onions, tomatoes, roots, and green plantains covered tables; plucked and headless chickens dangled by their feet from tall poles; large burlap bags and crudely fashioned wooden bins spilled over with rice and beans; and dried herbs and spices gathered into bunches with coarse twine filled the air with appetizing smells. Sellers shouted out, advertising their produce and the price, sometimes getting into a call-and-response contest with another vendor as they competed for dollars.

One man selling onions grown on his father's farm told me that he drove into the city every day before daylight to work the market, and while he waited for customers he bottled a paste made of onions and tomatoes used for cooking, a special recipe of his mother's. As I started to drift away he insisted I take a bottle and try it, and I accepted, having found it impossible to refuse Cuba's generosity.

In all the time I had spent in Cuba, I had never before seen in one place the full bounty of her sumptuous agricultural lands, her possibilities for a full stomach and a good life. That market, that bounty, put into sharp relief the unhappiness Cubans felt about not having enough to eat, of knowing that the food they needed—the beans, the rice, the onions, tomatoes, plantains; the chicken, pork, beef, goats, and so much else—a tasty plate in any culture—was raised and grown and harvested in Cuba, by Cubans, and then diverted to tourist hotels.

I spent a full day looking, talking, and soaking the scene in, and I left more hopeful about Cuba, about the prospects of her yanking herself out of the "special period" and getting on the right track again. At the end of the afternoon, as the heat of the day's sun was fading into the cool of the evening, as the vendors were packing up what they hadn't sold, the farmer I had spoken to earlier offered to sell me a dressed and skinned pig for $20, which seemed fair to me, but Paulo killed the deal with a slight shake of his head.

The markets became legal none too soon, at a point when conditions were the "worst they had ever been," a stern-faced Cuban outside the market told me as he stood smoking a cigarette, waiting for his wife. Food was so scarce, I learned from others, that lean rations were endangering the nation's health. It wasn't said straight out by him or anyone else, but Cubans left me with the lasting impression that the farmers' markets had opened just in time, a few hungry moments in history before food riots or something else equally potent.

But the shift to dollars and markets had not brought relief to everyone, not even close, and certainly not to Neddie. I found her living at the same place with her mother and her daughter, Luisa, who had divorced Pascual after the birth of their child, Barbara Anella. Abuela pulled me aside to confide, "When Pascual drank too much, he hit Luisa. Luisa did the right thing. But it has been very difficult for her. She is a poor child, a poor child. She is very young for her age. Still a child. I worry about her so."

Luisa was back at work, dancing with a well-known traveling troupe that had just returned from a four-month tour in Spain and was about to leave for a review sponsored by a swank Mexican hotel chain. Luisa earned $25 a day after expenses in Spain, money she used to help the family by buying new mattresses, pots and pans, a bigger television, and a stereo, all shipped from Spain along with cash for food and other necessities. "I can do the same from Mexico," she told me proudly.

But Neddie was upset and angry, inconsolable despite the small comforts that had come into her life, bitter over the advantages that foreigners received in Cuba. "They can get whatever they want because they have dollars. They are buying cars, houses, everything. We can buy nothing." She had considered selling her apartment only to learn that she would have to sell it to the state for "almost nothing," then the state would sell it to a foreigner for $4,000 or more, by her estimate. "We need a bigger place to live. A nicer place." For the first time she had to pay for electricity and water, a 5-pesos-per-month expense that she saw as one more insult from the state, one more expression of disregard for her long national service. She kept referring to Castro as Tito Gómez, because, she explained, "Tito Gómez is a famous singer in Havana whose best known song goes like this: 'It's still the same old story.' Just like Castro," she said, "the same old story.

"Peter, things have changed so much, have gotten very bad. I don't see how they can continue like this. Everyone is trying to make dollars," she said, quoting a term used in Cuban society the way "make magic" might be used in another. "What am I supposed to do?" she asked. "I have friends in this building who are buying new furniture. Have new clothes. Are able to do things. I can do nothing. I have nothing. I owe $25 to a friend for some fabric so I could recover the couch and the chair. Do you think you could help me with that?" she asked. "All anyone talks about is dollars."

Neddie, like other people in want and need, told stories about neighbors engaged in extravagant behavior, stories that described conditions in Havana as improving, but improving unevenly and erratically, for some but not others, creating inequalities and more than a bit of resentment. Dollars, like magic, changed lives; new possibilities were eagerly sought and keenly felt. But Neddie felt left out, saw no way to make magic *or* dollars.

"Peter, you know about the dollars from Miami, don't you? About how they send dollars to Cuba?" Neddie referred to an old story that was never a secret, even when dollars were illegal. A steady traffic from Miami to Havana had eased the burden of those fortunate enough to have charitable relatives who had fled the island to make good in a new land. After Cuba legalized dollars, the flow increased. "There are families who do nothing, but live very well. Very nicely, thank you!" said Neddie with a dramatic toss of her head. And speculation had it that the exile community had sent millions of dollars' worth of goods and cash in 1994, which helped offset the $8 billion loss when the Russians pulled out.

Neddie insisted that I celebrate New Year's Eve with her family, which expanded for the evening to included Neddie's brother, Boyo, and Luisa's boyfriend, Paul, "a musician with one of Cuba's most famous bands that travels extensively outside the country," said Neddie, scoring status points for herself by the fact of their association. Paul, a large, smiling black man, eclipsed the small apartment when he spent time playing with Barbara Anella and joking with Abuela, displaying obvious affection for both. Neddie confided that Paul helped them out—"I don't think we could make it without him"—and I could see she was correct, because his presence in their lives was noticeable for the good cheer he brought to their small apartment as well as for the food he arrived with.

Boyo worked for the government, doing "something in communications." "He travels a lot, but never brings us anything or helps in any way," said Neddie with a disapproving look. She cautioned me to say nothing important in Spanish in Boyo's presence because she distrusted him, to the point of not wanting him to suspect her unhappiness with the Revolution and Castro. "We have to be careful with him. I know I can trust you though, Peter," she said in a conspiratorial manner, leaning into me so no one else could hear.

We assembled in the small living room to eat dinner, balancing filled plates on our knees, passing conversation back and forth with a forced caution, except for Paul, who alone seemed at ease, impervious or indifferent to the tension that Neddie generated. She insisted on redirecting every conversation back to a place where she held the center of attention, would tolerate no contradiction to anything she said, and interrupted anyone who tried to make more than a brief comment. In the few instances when Neddie grew quiet, everyone sat in silence watching the baby play, as if that were our purpose for gathering together that evening. When the food was eaten and the dishes taken away, Neddie brought out the rum and stood in the center of the living room, where for the rest of the evening she commanded the space and the gathering, controlling the conversation and the mood, moving only to pour more rum. "I like my rum, Peter, and you must drink with me," she said. And she did indeed like rum, so much so that I became concerned that rum was this once proud teacher's single surviving comfort. She had put on a lot of weight since our last visit, and she had had all her teeth taken out. Toothless, dressed in a shapeless shift, and swaying on her bare feet ever more as the evening advanced, Neddie explained that she could find no work until the government provided her with new teeth because her pronunciation was not good enough to be a translator or a teacher. Whatever the fairness of that claim, Neddie was embarrassed by her appearance.

Luisa and Paul looked on with sympathy, nodding their understanding as Neddie described her predicament. Abuela had a terribly sad look about her as she shook her head and waved her hand and, I think, brushed tears from her cheek. Boyo looked exasperated, and I, like him, was a bit skeptical, knowing that a mastery of English—the language of commerce, of Cuba's future—was considered a trustworthy introduction to a job in the tourist trade.

Two of Neddie's neighbors arrived, well-dressed women who stopped in for a New Year's drink of rum and for an introduction to "the American friend." Neddie's style grew more dramatic, almost theatrical, as she made the introductions with a flourish of exaggerated language and bold gestures, animated by the rum and the need to establish her importance. Neddie made a big show of asking, *Would it be possible for you to mail a letter in the States to this woman's relative who lives in New York?*, which I agreed to do. Then Neddie asked, *Would it be possible for you to call the woman's aunt before you mail the letter, to guarantee the address and to report that the family in Cuba is fine?* Neddie spoke to me in English and translated to the room in Spanish, clapping her hands together in delight and tossing her head in exclamation as she reported my willingness to do what she requested, acting out that this was a grand accomplishment made possible only by the loyalty of her "American friend." It could have been the rum, or a peevishness brought on by Neddie's performance, but whatever the reason, I became aggravated at her manipulation and told the women in Spanish that what she asked was a small thing for me to do and I was glad to do it without thanks or gratitude.

Midnight came and went without so much as a passing reference to the fact that New Year's marked the day in history when Fidel's rebel army took control of the country, thereafter making January 1st a day of revolutionary celebration rivaled only by the 26th of July.

The night ended badly, with Neddie insisting that I do this or that for her, for Abuela, for Boyo, and then insisting that I eat every evening meal with her family. The rum and her emotional neediness turned Neddie deaf to everything I said, to the reasons I could not, would not, travel across Havana each night to join them at dinner. The room had gone silent, but Neddie continued, not understanding that she had gone too far, had pushed too hard to establish herself in everyone's eyes as the person with the "American friend." Neddie was lost, could not accept, could not understand or manipulate, the new rules governing her life, governing Cuban society. Legal dollars and a generous exile community had created another layer in her Cuban society, just as tourism had, and that new layer was precariously balanced in a society whose essential promise was equality in everything, including opportunity and suffering.

Even those who shared the rewards gained from legal dollars and open markets and small shops appeared uneasy with what had taken place, as though not fully trusting the transformation that was under way—and perhaps for good reason. Activities once damned as counterrevolutionary and branded illegal—activities that had put more than one mother's son in jail—now received official approval as pathways to a national deliverance. But seed-corn capitalism and the day-to-day obsession with dollars—the twin peaks of Yankee oppression and imperialism—did not mix evenly with Cuba's revolutionary culture, even after government decrees converted those longtime evils into newfound salvations.

Neddie was not alone in her confusion about what all that would mean over time, where these changes would take the revolutionary society of which most Cubans remained fiercely proud despite their frustration with the "special period." Once before, in the 1980s, Castro had opened farmers' markets, only to shut them down, calling them abrasive to state socialism, which they certainly were; now many farmers, doing well and making good money, feared that Castro would change his mind once again. At the same time, there existed a wholesale, free-floating anxiety about the future—about shops and independent stores taking over the culture, about large numbers of people abandoning their state jobs to take a chance on "making dollars," about Cubans living on exile dollars forming a new elite with strong ties to the Revolution's oldest enemies, about the dollar economy weakening government control until the society fell apart, undoing thirty years of extraordinary revolutionary accomplishments.

Castro apparently understood that "supply and demand" and "socialism or death" were unnatural companions. He spoke knowingly about the need to move cautiously into joint ventures, farmers' markets, legal dollars, and mom-and-pop stores, since each step created new contradictions within the revolutionary society. This was messy socialism, made necessary to dodge economic ruin and the fall of the revolutionary government that would surely follow. But even brother Raúl, normally considered the reddest Communist in the government, understood the need for change when he told a reporter, "We must be clear about one thing: if there is food for the people, the risks don't matter."

Whatever the political contradictions, social anxieties, or economic tensions, change had slowed Cuba's slide into collapse. And I was reminded of Roberto's faithful catechism from 1991—"Castro will find a way."

The ironies and contradictions were dramatic. Capitalist ventures and American dollars helped save the world's last Marxist economy; Miami exile dollars boosted the very society that the *exilios* hoped to bring to ruin; Cuban have-nots criticized changes that benefited others while begging to be pulled along themselves; U.S. politicians chortled over Cuba's bronze-age capitalism even as they plotted to tighten the economic embargo; and Cubans on the rise made unhappy noises because the changes were too small and too difficult to harness as an energy that would take them into a life that looked like their Miami cousins'. The new bumper sticker in Miami's Little Havana read, "No $ for Cuba." No one was satisfied, yet Cuba struggled on, without enough food or dollars to make a real go of it, but with just enough to ease the worst pressures of the day.

Forms and Traditions

SEPTEMBER 1995

Fathers and Sons

Paulo's mother, María, sat me down at the table with a plate of chicken and rice as soon as I walked in the door, acting as though I were a regular visitor, not someone who had been gone for nine months. She told me that Paulo's father was in town and eager to talk with me. I already knew Paulo was glad that I was back in Cuba. But from the time he had grabbed my bags and walked me out of the airport he had been a bit enigmatic with his enthusiasm, saying only, "I am much happier than last time, Peter. Things are better for me. Havana is better too. I will show you." As Paulo and I headed for his family's apartment he promised to tell me all his news the next day, teasing my curiosity about his changed attitude. This was a different Paulo from the anxious guy so worried about his future that he had considered forsaking Cuba for Miami.

Paulo had done all I had asked of him during a scratchy phone conversation before I left the States. He'd found me a garage apartment attached to a lovely home with stucco siding, gold paint, and red tile roof, all recently refurbished in the Spanish style common to the tony Miramar section. Situated close enough to Paulo's apartment and just across the street from the ocean, it rented for half the price of a midlevel tourist hotel room. And he had arranged for me to rent his grandfather's Russian LADA. Paulo would be ready as driver for whatever exploration I wanted to do in Havana, and then we would take the LADA on a cross-island journey. "I told you not to worry, that I would take care of everything," he said. "Remember, I'm 'the fixer,'" a term he repeated often after I started using it during my last trip as a praise and a thank-you for his help. "Whatever you want to do, boss," he said proudly, with appropriate mockery attached to "boss." "Let's get to work."

My first job was to satisfy my curiosity about Paulo. Like Cuba itself, Paulo appeared in a new incarnation each time I arrived. In July 1992 he was a young college student eager to practice his English and to show off his city while avoiding any contact with the history of the Revolution. When I returned in December 1994, he was despondent and depressed, asking worrisome questions about life in Miami, convinced that Cuba held no future that would meet his aspirations. Now, less than a year later, he confided, "I have changed my thinking about many things, Peter. I understand things I didn't before." Then came his surprising declaration: "I even care about the Revolution."

But I wasn't altogether certain what was up with Paulo, found him harder to read than in the past, despite his testimony about what was going on with him. For the first time I felt a touch of skepticism, wondered whether Paulo's transformation was the genuine article, a true epiphany, or just a temporary change that corresponded with my arrival in the city. I didn't like that idea, it embarrassed me, but I hadn't invited it and couldn't make it go away. That would be Paulo's responsibility.

When I finished my meal at the family apartment, Paulo and I climbed into the LADA to drive around the city so I could get a sense of the place, look for what was new and what was not. And I found Havana looking good, a scramble of cars, bicycles, buses, pedestrians, and commerce, legal and otherwise. Gas rationing was gone, replaced by twenty-four-hour service stations, new to Havana's city landscape, with bright green and red signs advertising all the gas you could afford to buy, any time, day or night. A Fiat dealership was ready for a grand opening, its long expanse of plate glass windows looking across the Malecón. And just down from the dealership was a block-square flea market, a sea of umbrellas that shaded small tables where vendors sold arts and crafts, wood carvings, black coral jewelry, papier-mâché figures, nativity settings, crocheted hats and vests, leather belts and shoes—everything from original art to the tackiest Caribbean tourist artifact, much like the Plaza de la Catedral, which had grown so busy on the weekends there was no room for more sellers.

Havana radiated a feel of energy and enthusiasm, spinning off a renewed hope that Cuba was moving ahead. Paulo had promised as much. "Havana is better," he told me first off. And I liked that, liked leaving behind the O. J. Simpson trial, the Ruby Ridge hearings, the Susan Smith case, the planned retrial of the Menendez brothers, and the social fault lines they represented in American society. It was not as though Cuba lacked problems—it had lots of them, like not enough to eat. But Cuba's struggle now, it seemed to me, was to redefine her proper place as a distinctive society and her place as a nation, a struggle of renewal and affirmation, involving more than just holding the line against decay and decline.

Paulo talked as he drove no place in particular. But distance wasn't what he wanted to cover that evening. What Paulo needed to do was tell his tale, which turned out to be a story of renewal and restoration inspired by family and culture and self-examination, the most bedrock traditional sources in a most unconventional set of circumstances.

He told it as we drove through Havana's lovely streets. Paulo's real father, Frank, lived in Miami, where he had been since Paulo was seven years old, his age when they had last seen each other. After many years of little or no contact, for the past year father and son had talked on the telephone many times. Eventually the discussion turned on the inevitable point, the idea of Paulo moving to the States. Frank had reassured Paulo that he was welcome, would have the sort of future Paulo dreamed of, guaranteed by his personality, his skill with languages, and his willingness to work hard to meet his ambitions.

Paulo had been enormously curious and seriously tempted, had talked of visiting Miami to find out for himself what life would be like in the States under the protective care of a father who had made it big in the import-export business. But whatever his temptation, Paulo held back on making any commitment to move for good, remained unwilling to forsake Cuba and his family there without first sampling the States. He wanted a proper test.

Paulo's indecision and foot-dragging started to irritate his father, who grew exasperated and at one point announced, "I have a successful business, a big house, and a $70,000 car, and you tell me you might reject all that. What is wrong with you?" Paulo's friends asked the same question, said he was crazy not to go, insane to resist the golden dream of so many unhappy young Cubans—a new life in Miami with a flush start.

"My stepfather, Víctor, talked to me a long time nearly every day," said Paulo. "I really respect him a lot. But it was hard. I didn't believe what he did about the Revolution and Fidel. We had many hard times. A lot of arguments. It made my mother very unhappy. Víctor is a smart man and is really crazy about Fidel. Really believes in him. We argued a lot, but he never told me what to do. He just wanted me to understand what the Revolution had done for Cuba. He wanted me to think about the idea that a difficult life in Cuba is better than a life of having everything in the United States. But it made no sense to me at the time. Just words."

Relations between Paulo and Frank continued to bump along, good one call, not so good the next, but never getting any better once Paulo spoke of his reservations about moving to the States, a hesitation that could be understood only with suspicion in Miami's exile community. At one point Paulo was invited by a teacher to spend a month in England, and he dearly wanted to get on a plane and travel to another country, to see a slice of the outside world—a nearly sacred quest among younger Cubans. But he needed $1,000 to do it. Paulo sold everything he had and worked hard trying to raise the funds, but he fell short, so he asked Frank for the loan of half the money. Frank agreed.

Then Frank began to manipulate that promise to leverage a commitment out of Paulo about moving to Miami. An anxious Paulo held fast. No matter how much he wanted to travel, he bit back the temptation, the fierce temptation, to strike the bargain—a trip to England for a move to Miami.

Finally, in anger and annoyance, Paulo's father withdrew his pledge, telling Paulo, "I don't care about your trip to England," and when Paulo tried to recover the situation, to calm his father, to restore the peace by talking about other subjects, Frank grew even angrier and finally lost his temper, shouting at Paulo across the crackling, undersea telephone cable between Miami and Havana: "It's not my problem if you don't have enough to eat."

"I still can't imagine anyone saying that to another person. Not a father to his son," said Paulo, hurt and confused, and telling his story behind hushed tones and sad eyes. "'I don't care if you have enough to eat.' How could that be? Does life in the United States do that to people? Make them selfish even to their own family? Is that right, Peter, makes them *frío*?

"Before all of this I did not agree with the Cuban government, but I loved my friends and family, and I loved the Cuban people, the way they are. This is now more important to me than a house or car. That's why I worried that going to Miami might be a mistake. Now I see I would have been unhappy the rest of my life if I had gone.

"We may not have total equality in Cuba, but we don't have the very rich and the very poor, and we try to take care of each other. Not just family and friends, but neighbors too. Everybody. That makes me very proud to be Cuban," said Paulo with a determination that left me feeling bad for having doubted him and proud to have him as my friend.

Víctor's many discussions about the Revolution had begun to take on a different meaning for Paulo, who found definition in the reflection of his own experiences. "Now I see why the results of the Revolution are important." Paulo carefully explained to me that the benefits of government health care, food, and housing created a better society, making possible a life free from the tension of accumulation that hardens and chills people, diminishes them as individuals and robs them of their best human qualities. Cuba's revolutionary culture assumed an enormous appeal for Paulo, making him proud of the Cuban Revolution as he never had been before, causing him to appreciate Cuban life for what it offered, not for what it lacked, for what it had given the people, not for what it could no longer provide.

"I knew about the Revolution before this, but none of it was real. You know what I mean, Peter? Young people in Cuba study it in school, learn the facts, memorize the history, know that Fidel led the Revolution, but it doesn't have real meaning. We just know it; that's all," said Paulo.

"Now I *feel* it. It means something to me. I have been waiting for you to come back so I could tell you all of this. I can't tell my friends. They would laugh, think I was crazy. But I knew you would understand.

"This is all even stranger than you might think, Peter," he said, referring to the fact that he could more easily confess his political transformation to an American than to his Cuban friends, who were mostly hip kids in Havana, often indifferent if not cynical about the Revolution. He said that he had been unclear about my views on the Revolution until my last visit when I ate dinner at his house, the night his mother, María, and I worked him over a bit for his lack of revolutionary spirit.

Then Paulo told a story that took place just after we first met in July 1992. A friend of his who had seen the two of us on the street asked Paulo what he was doing hanging out with me.

"He was really excited, really curious and worried," said Paulo, smiling at the memory. "I told him you were an American I was showing around Havana, a way to practice my English. But he thought that was a risky thing to do, told me, 'Be careful,' and I couldn't help but wonder about you after that, but not a lot. We were having a good time and you seemed like a nice guy."

"Why would he think that?" I asked, rising to Paulo's bait.

"Well, it seems my friend had seen you before, when you were here the first time with your two American friends. He saw you guys in a government building talking to officials, all big Communist Party members," he said.

"'Watch out,' my friend told me, all worried; 'I think that American is a Communist.'"

Paulo laughed as he told that story, which he had never mentioned before, had kept tucked away until he started to see the Revolution in a new light that allowed him to acknowledge the wonderful irony of two children of Cuba's Marxist Revolution fretting over whether or not the visiting American might be a Communist.

Paulo wanted me to meet Víctor, the stepfather he so liked and respected despite their long-standing differences over life in Cuba and Castro's government, differences that had been replaced by a renewed bond that pleased both of them enormously. During my previous visits Víctor had either been traveling outside Havana or doing volunteer labor, something many Cuban true-believers continued to do as part of the revolutionary tradition established by Che, making the extra effort, usually by doing agricultural labor in the countryside. Víctor and I finally met in the family apartment, ready to talk into the night as he broke out a bottle of rum.

As it turned out, Víctor had been raised in Miami, the son of a Cuban mechanic who served as an agent for Fidel's 26th of July Movement. For a time, Víctor's father worked at an airfield near Fort Lauderdale that serviced Batista's B-26 airplanes, a job that provided him a good wage and the opportunity to commit small acts of sabotage on behalf of the Revolution. He also distributed *Revolución,* the Movement's newspaper, picking up copies at the airport early in the morning, taking them home for Víctor and his sister to roll, and then distributing them in Miami.

After the Triumph, Víctor's father stayed in Miami with his family to continue serving as an agent for the Movement, now transformed by force of arms into Cuba's legitimate government. But Miami was a changed place. With legitimacy in Cuba came greater danger in the United States; he now found himself a target for unrepentant exiles newly arrived in Miami and for the FBI, which considered him a "dangerous Communist agent," as Víctor remembered it. In June 1960 his car was bombed, and then their house was shot at, so he went underground and sent Víctor and his mother back to Cuba. In her luggage his mother carried a roll of film taken by Víctor's father, pictures of men in fatigues in swampland camps training for what turned out to be the Bay of Pigs invasion. When Víctor, then twelve years old, arrived at Havana's airport, his mother was picked up by a government car that carried her and the film to the seat of power. His father, a target for assassination and hunted by the FBI, stayed with his dangerous trade until the Cuban consulate in Miami was shut down; he then sneaked out of the United States by masquerading as a member of the consulate staff.

"He was awarded a medal and a pension from the government for his service to the Revolution," said the proud son Víctor through the smoke of an unfiltered Popular cigarette.

"After I got to Cuba and until this day I never had a doubt about the Revolution," he continued. "Even during the 1960s when I wore long hair and funny clothes and the police cracked down on us, I never blamed the Revolution. Cops are cops," he concluded, an insight that we both shared, and a clear sign of how much both our lives had been defined by the 1960s, his in socialist Cuba and mine in capitalist United States. *Yes, yes, cops are cops*, we agreed.

Víctor sparked another historical contact when he said he admired the 1960s student movements in the United States, admired the way they mixed culture and politics to challenge the government and the rest of the country over Vietnam when it was such an unpopular cause. "I hold those movements very dear," he said.

Falling into the mood, I told Víctor how important the Cuban Revolution had been to those of us who were sufficiently arrogant to claim the label of "radical" during those powerful days of trying to end segregation and the war in Vietnam.

"Cuba gave us ideas and heroes like no other revolution. We celebrated Castro for what he was doing at home and the way he refused to bow down to the U.S., stood his ground. And Che. God, we loved him. His poster was everywhere. We admired him so much. He was living out our fantasies, we thought. Many of us wept when he died, the same way we did when Martin Luther King Jr. was killed and when Bobby Kennedy was gunned down.

"We studied Marx and Lenin and other revolutions, but Cuba's was the important one for us. It inspired us. Made us think anything was possible. I suppose Cuba influenced our ideology and political ideas. But it was really important because it captured our hearts. Gave us optimism. Gave us hope of finding a new way. We didn't like the Soviet bureaucracy any more than we liked democratic capitalism. But we admired the way Cuba was dedicated to caring for the people who had so little before the Revolution. It was," I told an attentive Víctor, "a hope and a promise for a better world that the Cuban Revolution gave me and my comrades."

And then I asked him how the Revolution had gotten itself into such trouble.

"I am a Marxist," he said in response. "I believe it's the solution for the third world. But I am also a humanist, and our Revolution's great contribution was that it gave the individual man a dignity, a liberty, a freedom. If you know our past, you understand that. You know how bad things were before the Revolution and how much the Revolution changed Cuba. Our Cuban viewpoint was very different from those of China and Russia. We had an original way, a Cuban way. Because our culture was very different, so was our Revolution.

"Our big mistake? I'll tell you. To compromise with the Soviets. We took their model of government and society and lost our own way. The Soviet ideology in which the state has to control everything, even education and the media, and looks over the lives of everybody should never have been adopted in Cuba. Never.

"But that's what we had to do to survive against American guns. Fidel's wisdom is that he saved the core of the Revolution, even until today. Fidel did it the only way possible. Without Fidel there would be nothing. *Nada*."

Víctor was a bright, thoughtful man given to reflection and crisp analysis, but his comment about following the Soviet model was as far as he would extend his criticism of Cuba beyond his loyalties, as specific as he could let himself be about how the Revolution got off track. He spoke vaguely of talented Catholics whose work and contributions to the country had been ignored because they were religious, and he drifted through the conversation with a number of wordy euphemisms when terms such as "political prisoners" and "human rights" might have been more appropriate. He passively acknowledged that people had gone to jail for speaking against the Revolution, for criticizing Fidel and government policies. But Víctor could not bring himself to say anything more direct than that in following the Soviets Cuba had lost its revolutionary emphasis, the quality that had set the Cuban Revolution apart from all others and made it so appealing to so many people around the world. When I pressed him for more information, for greater clarity, for deeper insight about what had happened to the Revolution, his voice lowered and his face looked so pained I let it go.

Víctor thought that the farmers' markets were important for the obvious good they did by opening up the economy and making available more food, but also because they were "an important step away from the Soviet model," an important step in Cuba finding her own way for the future, a future that he felt must somehow be tied to the United States.

"The end of the embargo would bring some good things and some bad things, but that is the only way for us to live in a normal way." Not that he wanted intimate relations with the old colossus of the north—"I don't want that trademark back, 'Made in the U.S.A.,' not at all"—but ending the embargo would be important so the rest of the world could have normal relations with Cuba.

"If the embargo was ended, a Mexican businessman would not have to think two or three times about investing in Cuba out of concern for what the United States might do. The United States controls the world, and no one wants to feel her anger," reasoned Víctor. "That's why we need an end to the embargo.

"I criticize the Revolution for one thing—let people leave Cuba if they wish. Most people think that what we have here is natural, is found everywhere. The education, the doctors, the hospitals. Most people who have lived in this system for thirty-five years can't imagine that it's not the same for nine-tenths of Latin America. They just don't know. I have been to other countries, have seen the reality. One night I heard gunshots all night long. So I come back to Cuba because I think it is the best place. The very best place. Those who have not seen do not know the value of social peace, friendship, love, solidarity, a humanistic government, and the society it creates. Here in Cuba we have the will to help others. How can you evaluate that? So I say, 'Let people go,' let them travel. They will come home with a better appreciation for Cuba."

"What about Angola?" I asked. "Was it a mistake to spend Cuba's limited resources in Africa when so much needed to be done at home?"

"No," he said, "it was not a mistake. It was the right thing to do, a very important accomplishment. Two countries are free because we were in Africa—Angola and South Africa. It was important for a small country such as Cuba to help others through the power of our intelligence. It was important for blacks in South Africa to know that South Africa's white army could be challenged by Cubans and Angolans. That example helped to free South Africa. No, Angola was not a mistake. Fidel did the right thing."

But not without fear of U.S. reprisal. Víctor held the rank of captain in the militia, a local military force that was constantly on alert during the Reagan years, on alert to the extent that the smaller arms in the national armories were removed and distributed to local neighborhoods, hidden in small caches here and there so they would be more difficult to capture in the event of an invasion, which many people feared, partly because of Cuba's efforts in Africa.

Víctor said the word went out, which he repeated to me with a grin. "If you see a U.S. Marine in your neighborhood, get your gun and start fighting, even if there is no official announcement. The Marines would not be here by invitation."

Víctor spoke for the most resolute, optimistic, and philosophical Cubans, whose faith and future remained bound with Castro and, above all else, bound with the Revolution, trusting it as an organic reality with a life and destiny. He gave voice to the ideals of the majority, expressed in his father's revolutionary past and in his own experiences, ideals that, however keenly felt, most Cubans could express only in smaller sentiments. I wished Paulo had been there to hear it all and wondered why he wasn't, though I assumed it was his choice.

I asked Víctor how he held on to such strong conviction and clear understanding about the Revolution given the difficulties since the start of the "special period" in 1989.

"Even at our worst, this society is so fond of human progress it can't fail. It would be such a setback, a catastrophe for humanity, if it does. All other socialist experiments in the past have failed because of a lack of human solidarity. Because we have that, Cuba won't fail.

"Let me tell you why I know this with such passion, why I believe as I do. You are right to ask that question. I have even asked myself that many times."

Then Víctor began to tell his personal story. Not a story about politics or ideology, not about what men believe in or trust, but about what they feel in their hearts after they have been touched by the magical hand of history. When Víctor landed in Cuba in early 1960 as a twelve-year-old, he arrived fresh from Miami, fresh from a life in the United States with his bicycle, TV, rock and roll, school dances, the wide slice of American pop culture of the 1950s.

Víctor knew very little about Cuba, knew more English than Spanish. But those were exciting times. The revolutionary government was full of energy, full of ideals and ideas, full of plans to free the people from the past, particularly to liberate them from the ignorance forced on them by an indifferent nation—one in three in Oriente Province was illiterate, with an average of 25 percent nationwide. Under the slogan "If you don't know, learn; if you know, teach," 104,000 young Cubans, mostly urban youths and nearly one-third of them women, moved to the countryside to teach reading and writing to the 1.4 million Cubans who could do neither.

Víctor had barely landed in Havana with his mother, with his father still in Miami in harm's way, when he picked up and went to the Sierra Maestra to teach peasants to read and write. He left in a flush of revolutionary enthusiasm, without telling his mother.

"I was afraid she would keep me from going if I told her what I wanted to do. I could not have endured that. It was as if I *had* to join the literacy campaign. I wanted so much to be part of it. I needed it.

"It was very romantic and very important for me. I was away from my mother. Away from my house and family for the first time. Away from the life in Miami with everything we had. I was twelve years old when I passed through Havana and went to the mountains of Oriente Province, to the Sierra Maestra. Remember, I was just from Miami. It was shocking to see how the peasants lived, without power, without enough food, without sanitation, without anything but their ignorance, it appeared to me as a child. I was shocked. So shocked.

"We felt we were bringing the Revolution to them. They were so eager to learn. So eager. I was a twelve-year-old teaching people in their forties how to read and write. Can you imagine how important that was to me? I will tell you. It set my feelings for life about Cuba and the Revolution.

"We had to teach at night after the peasants finished their work. They worked so hard every day. We had only the nights. There was no electricity where most of us went, so the government bought one hundred thousand Chinese lanterns, like a Coleman with the silk wick that you pump the fuel vapors into. Each of us took one with us. I was living in a *yaque* house made of palm fronds.

"I'll never forget lighting the lantern the first time to start the lessons. I pumped the fuel into the lantern and lit it with a wooden match. I watched the faces of the peasants as they saw the light starting slowly, then growing brighter and brighter as I pumped more fuel into it, making it become brilliant. It was like filling the hut with sunshine, but something even more brilliant than sunlight.

"The look on the faces of those peasants filled my heart to overflowing. It filled my heart like the light filled the hut. To this day—this very night—I still have in my heart the faces of those people. When they saw that light they knew the Revolution was for them, too. And I was a part of it. A twelve-year-old. I was there.

"You ask, what does the Revolution mean to me? I tell you, everything," said Víctor, the whisper of his emotions pulling him to the edge of his chair. "It means everything to me."

Things Held in Common

Next to a vacant parcel of oceanfront land in Miramar, the city's nicest neighborhood, sat three eight-story buildings that showed all the signs of a construction project abandoned for so long it could never be redeemed from neglect and decay. Those buildings, made of precast concrete and never possessing the possibility of being attractive, were in ruin, with broken windows and doors off their hinges and long, rust-colored tear stains on the concrete from iron fastenings that long ago surrendered their dignity to the salty sea air.

These buildings housed Russian workers until they went back home, housed Russians in the ugliest architecture in the city, maybe in the entire country. The Cubans never liked the Russians, found them cold, badly dressed, lacking in generosity, and incapable of having fun—which may be the harshest criticism of all in a Caribbean culture. No one was sorry to see them go, at least no one who would later admit to it.

Cubans liked the Mexicans better because they knew how to have a good time, but some Mexicans tended to be too loud and appeared indifferent to good manners, which Cubans considered an unattractive quality in guests. And in more recent times Mexican men, the younger ones fit and trim and well dressed, the older ones often sporting heavy chunks of gold jewelry, arrived in Cuba in search of her young women. Although some of the older men returned home with youthful Cuban wives, most Mexican men returned home alone, with a few nighttime memories, while the Cuban women remained behind, with a few pesos or some new clothes.

Everyone loved Americans, but I never felt I had a good fix on the reasons why. No Cuban ever made me feel uncomfortable as a scorned outsider, never made me feel anything but welcome. Maybe they liked Americans because so few of us made the effort to travel there, not like the Mexicans or Germans or English or Spanish who visited in large numbers. Or maybe because the few Americans who made the journey arrived with an open curiosity and a tendency to be sympathetic, if not a bit too repentant for America's sinful history with Cuba. Not much, I suspect, like the average U.S. tourist who will flood the country once the embargo is lifted. Over the long haul, once Americans have their choice of three or four shuttle flights a day between Havana and Miami, Cubans will probably decide they didn't like us that much after all, but always did like our culture, our films, our rock and roll, our Levi's, our Nikes, our TV shows, our cars. And I think they will decide they liked us most of all for the possibilities we represented, not for who we actually were.

In the years just after the Revolution the Cubans who fled to the United States were given the impolite label of *los gusanos,* the worms. More recently, those exiles who returned to Cuba to visit family, who returned with offerings of dollars and suitcases full of necessities from Kmart, have been called *las mariposas,* the butterflies. Such is the power of the bounty the United States brings to the Cuban imagination, the possibility of a transformation as magnificent as butterfly from worm.

Of all her neighbors, the United States alone matched Cuba's proud sense of what she aspired to, of what she hoped to be after the transformation; not for our politics or our rough-edged capitalism—in spite of those qualities, actually—but for her culture of middle-class sensibilities and style. That's what Cubans liked about America and Americans.

And as Cuba struggled out of the most difficult time of 1992–1993, as legal dollars and farmers' markets and living-room *paladares* and small shops began to renew the life of the nation, Cubans started to renew their aspirations in their daily lives. Every park in Cuba that I visited, from Havana to Santiago de Cuba and back again—and there were a lot of them, lovely green spaces, showcases of civic pride in the center of even the smallest towns—told part of that identifying tale of how Cuba thought of herself. The parks were neat and clean and safe, free of litter and neglect and danger, and they were carefully tended with trees and flower beds of newly turned soil. Without fail, in every park could be found a bench of gray-haired gentlemen neatly dressed and pressed, usually in light green or beige shirts and pants, sitting and talking about themselves with courtly ease. Mothers in skirts and blouses watched children whose hair and clothes, manners and playful behavior, and ready smiles showed sure signs of being well loved and well tended.

One end of every park belonged to the young people, animated, joking, curious, sometimes looking for the hustle, but always fashionable in a style that revealed the close attention to American TV, especially MTV. Just as surely, some visitors in every park wore the downcast look of hunger and despair, but the image of want and need did not dominate Cuba's green spaces or linger in the memory, at least not for long. Revolutionary Cuba even at its lowest point, at its most discouraged, at its worst hour of too little food and hope, never fell into a ragged, hangdog culture of neglect and indifference about how people took care of themselves, how people presented themselves to friends and neighbors, to say nothing of strangers and visitors.

A Sunday drive through Havana's better neighborhoods showed small but unmistakable signs of a revived attention to the details that characterized a strong attraction to home and community. People were tending their yards, cutting grass with machetes; they were planting flowers and shrubs, repairing concrete steps and broken windows, building fences and rehanging doors, and painting everything they could after years of forced neglect. They were making repairs and fixing up, doing the Sunday chores of people creating their future, not waiting anxiously for a dramatic end to the present.

Even Neddie's inconsolable unhappiness could be located in Cuba's attachment to home and work and family, in the need for an orderly and productive life, which Neddie felt was lost to her. With new teeth and a new hairstyle, Neddie had gone job hunting, but without success. Finally, over time, she had lost all hope that her bad fortune would ever change. She was certain that a joint-venture cruise line had turned her down for a job because she was black. "I want to work. I want a job. But they don't care how well I speak English; they are looking for blond, blue eyes, and slender," she said. "I am well prepared, but they say there are no openings. I am very sad. I know I am not the same. I am losing my English. I was so good, Peter; you remember how good I was. It's true. You know it's true."

Neddie lived in a constant state of agitation over the lack of possibilities in her life, over feeling she had neither control nor understanding of what was going on. "Everything is turned upside down. Things are never together as they should be," she said. "When there's coffee, there's no sugar; when there's beans, we have no rice; when there's fuel, we have no car." And on she went. For Neddie, life had lost its proper rhythm of events and circumstances, and lost with it was her ability to understand what was happening in Cuba's changing society, a loss that left her anxious and afraid. Life as she understood it was out of control. In Neddie's world there was no place for bad fortune, no place for failure, no place for life not working out properly with home, job, and family, not after so many years of hard work on her part—the quintessential expectations in a society based on the concept of proper rewards for services rendered, of a decent life in exchange for hard work.

In the many conversations I had in Cuba, no one better explained how Cubans felt about themselves and their place in the community of world societies than Neddie. She said that Cuba was "at the back of the pack, behind all nations." In that observation Neddie did not rank Cuba with other countries in Latin America or the Caribbean. When I raised that point, asked her if she meant Cuba was behind her island neighbors, she looked a bit puzzled and said, "No, of course not, not behind Jamaica or Haiti, but you know what I mean. We are behind Spain, Canada, and even Mexico. Behind the United States for certain."

What Neddie meant by "all nations" was those blessed with a standard of living commensurate with Cuba's before the "special period," before the rationing and shortages, and what she meant was that her own expectations were very much like those in the United States, the proper point of comparison for so many Cubans when they spoke of jobs and homes and the good life.

In matters of hope for the future Neddie thought that Cuba and the United States were respectable points of comparison to set her expectations; just as in affairs of fashion and manners and social style, Cubans and Americans were very much alike; just as in the world of well-trimmed lawns and Sunday choirs, Cuba and the United States were very much like close neighbors. And that was why Cubans favored Americans who came to visit, liked us more than history should have permitted, if history were governed by good sense, which of course it is not.

Just down the street from the abandoned buildings that once housed Russian workers there sat a wall, probably twenty-five feet long, painted light blue and embellished with the slogan *"¡Por la VIDA, no Bloqueo!"* This declaration against the American blockade, all in oversize black and red letters, the colors of the 26th of July Movement, was a pledge of loyalty to Cuba. The rest of the wall was spotted with graffiti, earnest sentiments written mostly by foreign visitors, including one American. The sentiments supported Fidel, Cuba, and the Revolution and criticized the United States, Jesse Helms, and *"los yanquis cabrones"*—the yankee motherfuckers. There was even one neatly lettered, epic-size poem. And there was the matter of another sign, the one at Playa Girón, which reads, "First Rout of Imperialism in Latin America"—Cuba's reminder of how much and how little America was willing to risk to topple Castro and reestablish a political reality on the island that suited American tastes, to bring Cuban politics back in line with shared social and cultural sensibilities.

Yet Cuba's attachment to the United States was unmistakably firm, in spite of the armed invasion at the Bay of Pigs and the economic abuse of the blockade. Even as the U.S. Congress debated a tightened embargo with the Helms-Burton Law while I was in Cuba—a truly brutal and punishing blockade for Cuba and anyone who violated it, friend of the United States or not—Cubans spoke with hope for closer relations and an end to the embargo. This was partly a topic of economics, even national survival, but nonetheless what came through in those discussions was a belief in the ultimate goodwill of the United States, a belief among Cubans that what our countries shared in the world of culture and society must inevitably be more compelling than what separated us in the world of politics and ideology—a belief created out of the things we held in common.

Rumors of big deals between the Cuban government and America's powerful businesses went hand in hand with discussions about the embargo, as if the embargo lacked the authority to do exactly what it was intended to do. A Cubana Airlines official told me, "Two U.S. hotel companies have purchased large tracts of land in Cuba. Millions' worth. They will build soon, I am certain." His confidence in these words seemed as misguided as I suspected his facts were. Another Cuban, who was a bit of a mystery because of frequent travel to the United States and other foreign countries, a mystery compounded by his unwillingness to explain how or why he traveled so much, swore to me that he had "seen the paperwork on a $300 million deal with a U.S. firm."

"Which one?" I inquired.

"Sorry, I can't tell you that. You must understand it's a secret arrangement," he said.

"Yes, of course. It must be all of that and more. How foolish of me to ask," I said with an open skepticism that escaped him.

He went on to tell me that within eighteen months the embargo would be lifted and relations would be normalized. "Many ports in the U.S. are preparing for that time. It will come soon. You'll see. Soon," he concluded with a Cuban certainty. Yet for all my skepticism, I knew that the director of the Jacksonville, Florida, Port Authority had just recently been in Cuba courting customers for that inevitable day when Cuban ships would find their way to Florida once again—a day that may not be as far away as I and the U.S. Congress think.

The United States embassy building in Havana served as parable for the enduring yet enigmatic attraction shared by Cuba and the United States. In the recent past that building, like Cuba, had been quiet and subdued, needing paint and purpose to give it the appearance of possessing goals and ambitions. Now the building, which dominated much of a small block along the Malecón, was experiencing a massive renovation—again like Cuba herself, painting and repairing for a busier day.

Suddenly it was an active place, a curious circumstance for an embassy that lacked formal relations with the host country. New guidelines agreed to by the two governments in the summer of 1995 ended America's welcome to fleeing Cubans who arrived in Florida uninvited, without proper papers; there would be no more makeshift rafts or stolen boats, proper visas and formal arrivals only, much to the outrage of Miami's exile community.

High scaffolding surrounded the embassy building; an authoritative iron fence surrounded the embassy compound, and the most serious-minded police in Havana stood watch outside the iron fence. The day I went there a snaking line of hopeful Cubans filled the compound, spilled out onto the sidewalk, and filled the sidewalk along one edge of the property and beyond it into the next block—one day's presentation of Cubans for twenty thousand visas per year. No one was allowed near the compound without legitimate business, not even to walk down the sidewalk on that side of the street, not Cubans, not Americans, no one without legitimate business. As I stood in the street taking pictures, a Cuban policeman waved me back, away from the embassy. I kept shooting and waved my U.S. passport at him, too far away for him to see clearly what nationality it was but hoping to buy a couple more minutes to get what I wanted. He blew his whistle and started toward me, returning to his post only when I went back to mine, which was across the street, away from the embassy.

Curious about the police style there, I asked a few questions of one of them who went about his duties with a formal and forbidding manner, uncharacteristically so even for his profession. Only when I admired the Che button on his uniform shirt and commented that I didn't see as many of them being worn in Havana as I once had did he warm a bit, telling me that I would be seeing more of them in the future. But his standoffish style, which he shared with his comrades around the compound but not with most policemen in Havana, told me why Paulo was unusually nervous when we arrived at the embassy, and why he moved a safe distance away from me as soon as we got out of the car—a safe distance being around the corner and out of sight. "They may think I am doing something wrong if they see us together," he said. Which of course he was: he was driving a foreigner around for money. But "making business" had never bothered Paulo before, nor did it ever again; only that one time did it become a real topic of conversation, let alone concern.

The fact and circumstance of business and friendship between the two of us took on an exaggerated importance near the U.S. embassy building in Havana. In that setting, though, everything seemed to take on an exaggerated and a metaphorical importance, for that was a setting where, in reality and in the popular imagination, the things Americans and Cubans held in common were regarded with such a seriousness that they required the guardianship of high iron fences and serious-minded police.

Seeking Santiago

Havana is Cuba's most sophisticated city. She has always thought of herself as the island's central place, causing her to be a bit self-consciously vain and properly so, for more than one good reason. Havana is the seat of political power and an exciting destination with handsome buildings and stunning architecture, but Havana is not Cuba. So I felt the pull to travel again, to see the countryside and Santiago, as I had in 1991 but not since.

Paulo and I would make the drive across the island to Santiago de Cuba in his grandfather's LADA, Soviet Russia's attempt to provide her people with what the Volkswagen beetle had been for Germans, but with a body style much like that of an old Fiat. Not my first choice of transportation, but Paulo had made the deal, and he was the fixer, a role I had gratefully assigned to him and felt bound to respect.

Paulo had resurrected the car from the indifferent hands of his grandfather, had taken it on as his project of repair and restoration—as much as he could in a country chronically short on spare parts. He had it looking good and running fine; the daily rental rate was right, and the money went to the grandfather, a chance for him to "make dollars," enough to make a difference. Paulo was crazy about that car, loved it, pampered it, protected it, and worried about it. He was proud of having brought it back from neglect—replacing parts, repairing the upholstery, getting it painted, keeping it running and clean and looking better than its years should have allowed. In return, it had changed his life. He could get around as he never had been able to on his bicycle, see more of the city, go fishing in distant places, lead a richer social life, and "make dollars" now and then by driving tourists. He was a young man with his first car.

Heading east from Havana the road was mostly four lanes for the first 200 or so miles, in good repair with the grass along the shoulders, running up to the fence lines of farms and orchards, freshly cut and free of litter. Groups of workers were planting flowers and shrubs in the median that separated the oncoming lanes of traffic. Roadside billboards and signs hanging from overpasses showed clear evidence of fresh paint and revolutionary eagerness: "The most beautiful word is *patria*"; "Reason and heart lead us together"; "You must be vigilant in the struggle."

The countryside was flat and green, with standing fields of sugarcane and low flat trees and scrub bushes with the occasional palm, an open territory interspersed every few miles with small farms. This was an area given over to low, wet fields for rice growing. At several spots along the highway, long stretches of the inside lane were covered with rice that had been cut the previous day and spread to dry on the less-used part of the road. We stopped to talk with a group of resting workers, sun-darkened men who worked the fields in the old way and then laid their rice out on the sunbaked highway. As they explained the process to us, a modern tourist bus blew by at a high speed, whipping the rice against our legs as it sped on, carrying Cuba's future forward with little apparent regard for her traditions.

Near Santa Clara, cowboys worked the fields along the side of the road. Sometimes there were so many cowboys, men mounted on horses, wearing boots and chaps and wide-brimmed hats, that they outnumbered the cars on the highway, making us feel like interlopers in a less complicated time and place. On the roadside there appeared the occasional open-sided *ramada* made of bamboo and palm fronds where vendors sold juice, cane, and cheese or pork sandwiches, another addition to the culture since dollars became legal. Even more people sold food and agricultural goods from roadside tables. Others stood patiently on the side of the highway offering strings of garlic or balls of cheese, holding their products high in the air for inspection as each car approached. The people were back to work in the countryside, returned to their traditional jobs of farming and planting and growing, as well as getting into the new business of making dollars and supplying the farmers' markets. People were getting busy because the peso was so strong it was worth more than it had been for several years.

At one roadside stand operated by the government, an employee made a fifteen-to-one exchange for us, rather than the going rate of thirty pesos to the dollar; then he fed us in pesos at such a low cost it meant we ate lunch for half price, while he made two dollars on the exchange at the expense of the government—"making dollars." He warned us that the peso was so strong in Santiago it was difficult to find anyone who would give a decent rate for dollars. He recommended that we get what pesos we might need before arriving in the city. All this translated into something quite extraordinary, even as rumor: it was better to hold pesos over dollars if you knew where to eat or where to shop in Santiago. This was a remarkable development in Cuba, where for a time many people had simply stopped going to work because the peso was so devalued it bought practically nothing; then, suddenly, the word went out that Santiago's black market was a peso market. Pesos over dollars, quite an idea, and one that turned out to be partly true, yet the very existence of the rumor as an expression of hope and as a definition of changing times surprised even Paulo, who had predicted we would find more suffering as we moved farther from Havana.

East of Santa Clara the highway narrowed into two lanes and took on the character of a well-maintained secondary road in rural, central Florida, except we were in a Latin country, provincial and agricultural, where the harvesting of bananas, rice, and sugarcane meant sharing the road with carts and wagons pulled by horses, oxen, mules, and tractors, and farm implements of various shapes and nationalities that were slow moving and filled our car with a black mist of diesel fumes as we passed them. Casual driving on the open road had not returned to Cuba, although gas, at approximately $2.50 per gallon for regular, was still cheaper than in Europe. There were fewer private cars than buses, government trucks, and rental cars, a fact that Paulo shrugged off with the comment that "people in the countryside must not be able to steal gasoline the way they do in Havana."

Cuba possessed the sharp instinct required of a society dependent on the ability to quickly make-do under pressure, and she had set a high standard, too, as she went about her business of surviving. The rural areas of smaller towns and cities had developed new ways of getting around, in addition to hitchhiking, which held its place as a respectable if time-consuming alternative to car ownership. Private buses in a variety of shapes and forms materialized to meet the people's needs once new laws allowing small businesses created the opportunity. The sharpest-looking vehicles on the road were Ford and Chevrolet six-wheel dump trucks dating from the 1950s, recently refurbished to carry people; most of them had fresh, bright coats of paint and beds outfitted with frames for passengers to hold on to; the deluxe models had sail-white canvas tops to shelter passengers from the Caribbean rain and sun. Bicycles as well as riders crowded into truck beds; other bike riders held onto truck bumpers and tailgates as they sped down the road, a small but frequently seen demonstration of why so many Cubans died on the highway after gas became so expensive and Flying Pigeons so plentiful. In the towns, people paid modest fares to ride in horse-drawn carriages, many of which displayed an unmistakable pride in ownership. High, curved metal fenders covered wooden spoke wheels that gleamed with varnish and polish; handgrips and seats had been fashioned out of ornate ironwork, and skillful flourishes of pin striping and fancy swirls of contrasting colors accented the natural lines of the wagon, all showing Spanish influences from another century. This was countryside Cuba, getting by with solutions that fused artful improvisation with necessity.

Those were strong and vivid images from the first day's driving across Cuba, but not nearly as strong and vivid as Paulo with his LADA. Paulo had been driving for four or five months and had developed admirable skills for whizzing around Havana. He had perfected the urban driving style, down to a professional-styled finesse in his mix of clutch and brake and gas and horn play—particularly horn play—as he worked his way through busy streets filled with indifferent pedestrians and oblivious cyclists, cyclists so careless that six or seven of them died each week in Havana. I was relieved during the few days we spent in Havana that Paulo did nothing to add to those statistics, although not to the credit of the bike riders.

But Paulo was a close-quarters driver, not trained by habit or opportunity for the open road. He had not yet developed a clear sense of spatial relationships on the highway, always worried that he was too close to everything on his blind side—the ditch, the car he was passing, the parked trucks and buses on the side of the road, anything, everything. And every time he needed to pass he fell into a minor crisis of white-knuckle anxiety. He would pull out, start to accelerate, linger in the passing lane unsure what to do, and then often fall back when he could have gone ahead—clearly the lesser sin, but the longer passage to Santiago. Finally in impatient desperation I offered to spell him at the wheel, and he was glad of it, I thought, relieved to be rid of the constant worry of not knowing if there was enough road in tight spots, enough open lane to pass.

I took the wheel, the busy American, feeling the compulsive need to chase after lost time, as if I needed to be somewhere, slingshot passing trucks, buses, farm equipment, anything in the way, so long as it was going under 60 mph, the upper limit for the LADA, which started to quiver at any greater speed. Paulo reclined his seat back as if to sleep, but maybe he sought relief from my driving, not relief from road weariness. Whatever he was avoiding or seeking, he kept his head down for most of the next five hours while I drove on to Camagüey, arriving with frayed nerves and red eyed from fatigue, diesel fumes, and the summer's hot air. I wondered what I had been in such a hurry about, aside from the plain bad habit of it, picked up as part of a cultural tradition that had no place in Cuba.

We checked into Camagüey's finest hotel, with rooms going for $35 a night, a most reasonable rate that included cable TV with HBO, CNN, and a couple of music channels. We could catch up on the news with Bernard Shaw, watch Dusty Rhodes on World Championship Wrestling, or be entertained with a subtitled version of *Free Willy*. Paulo went off to explore, returning a short time later, breathless with the news that there were three peso restaurants within two blocks of each other downtown. Not fledgling eateries set up in someone's living room, but "real restaurants with music, tables where they seat you, give you a glass of water, and a menu printed on paper. Peter, you won't believe it! There is nothing like this in Havana."

It became clear that Paulo had never been served a meal in a real Cuban restaurant, in a peso restaurant with Cubans, rather than a dollar restaurant with tourists, where he was rendered a lesser customer by the status of his currency if not the fact of his nationality. For that matter, neither had I. One of the things that I always found maddening during earlier visits was the near absence of places to eat aside from tourist spots, usually found in tourist hotels whose menus catered to foreign visitors, not local tastes. There had been no sidewalk vendors, no local grills, no neighborhood bars or restaurants where Cubans met with friends and family and paid in pesos, few places to even get genuine Cuban food, which was why the meals at Neddie's and Paulo's were always such a treat.

So off we went, and Paulo was right. For less than fifty cents each we were served a small piece of beef, a portion of beans and rice, and an avocado salad. But the sweetest aftertaste of the evening came from being with Paulo and from his excitement at having his first sit-down dinner in a Cuban restaurant, where he could come and go without a sideways glance from someone in authority, where he could pay in pesos, which he did, with an air of uncommon satisfaction.

For the rest of the trip to Santiago and back we ate in *paladares* when in the cities, with Paulo usually making a serious job out of finding the best meal at the best price, arguing with owners who insisted on dollars because I was a foreigner, and often deciding that we should try another place if he could not get an arrangement that met his standards. The fixer at work. A couple of hungry and tired nights, as we trudged through the late-summer humidity to a second and then a third *paladar*, I almost regretted ever giving him the title and the responsibility.

The main street of every town and village we passed through was dotted with food vendors lined up side by side along the dusty edge of the sidewalk. Men and women sat at rickety tables under faded umbrellas that offered relief from the September sun, selling small pizzas, hand-squeezed juices, fresh breads, and sandwiches. Without failure, each row, in every town, had one table with the head of a small roasted pig staring out at passing cars, with the rest of the body covered by a white towel as protection from flies. For twenty cents, the cook would fold back the towel and slice off pieces of fresh-cooked pork to make a sandwich, sometimes with meat and bread still warm from the cooking. At another table a cup of fresh pineapple juice chilled by an oversize block of ice could be had for two or three cents. If Havana was "making dollars," the countryside was "making pesos," and we did our best to contribute, eating local food at every meal and making the trip across the island without once eating among tourists—another Cuban first for me.

We left Camagüey the next morning, the lush green vegetation still covered with dew and the sun beginning to burn off the mist that gave the day a translucent start. We were slow getting out of town because of struggles with bicycle riders. They had numbers on their side, there being so many of them and so few cars that they refused to respect our size and the natural laws of the road. Cyclists moved three abreast down the single lane, ignoring horn, car, and driver's impatience, acting as if the majority ruled on the highway, as if one gain of the Revolution was their right to slow us down and piss us off. I finally gave up, surrendering to their attitude of superiority.

Cuba's prideful ways were evident throughout the culture, in the dress, in the hard work, in the ambition for a good life, in the generous nature, and in the good manners—except while riding a bicycle. Or perhaps in riding a bicycle those prideful ways were most evident. Bike riding irritated Cubans, many of whom had been accustomed to driving their own cars until the hard times arrived and gasoline rationing put the cars up on blocks. Bicycles fell beneath their expectations of a proper form of transportation, did not fit their self-image or their vision of how others should perceive them. If many Cubans felt a small loss of dignity each time they had to sit on a hard bike seat, they in a sense made up for it when they refused to concede anything to anyone driving a car during the "special period."

Although our departure out of Camagüey was slow going, we had less than a day's drive ahead of us to make Santiago. The land began to dip and roll as we turned south off the Central Highway at Las Tunas onto a secondary road heading for Bayamo and Santiago. The Sierra Maestra started to take shape off to the right. At first glance it was difficult to be certain the mountains were even there; their distant, misty peaks blended so well into the clouds that I was forced to look hard before deciding whether I was being fooled by nature. As we drove on, the mountains became more obvious, a series of green valleys and peaks, the tallest over 6,000 feet, peaks so high they couldn't be denied once you got close enough and knew where to look, just as the history held in those elevations could not be denied, once you understood what to look for.

Those mountains were the base of military operations for Fidel's guerrilla army for two rugged years, the place where peasants from the countryside and students and workers from towns and cities went to join the struggle, where they hid from the troops and planes sent by Batista in his repeated efforts to rid his rule of the troublesome rebels. The Revolution had been fought and won on the Santiago side of the island, a place of spilled blood and sacrifices like no other in Cuba. Havana had sent money and fighters and support and good wishes and embraced Fidel and the 26th of July Movement, but the heart of the Revolution had pulsed in the Sierra Maestra, drawing from nearby Santiago money and guns, passion and determination, and men and women—those who did not stay at home to fight and possibly die for *la lucha,* the struggle, in the violent streets of that city, as so many did.

Those mountains divided Cuba, separating the Cradle of the Revolution from the rest of the country in more substantial ways than simple geography, in ways that sharpened regional and political viewpoints from the time Fidel landed there, throughout the revolutionary period, and continuing into the future. Havana reassured herself with the belief that she was Cuba's central place, as she may have been in commerce and culture. But of all the places in Cuba, Santiago alone held the title "Hero City," a singular honor earned and awarded for her role in the revolutionary struggle. As we passed through the mountains and approached Santiago we entered a piece of geography with its own history, a place steeped in Revolution, self-confident, self-aware, and understated, where the armed past made conceit unnecessary and false pride unseemly.

Known in Santiago

The first place I went in Santiago was Céspedes Park to see the Casa Grande Hotel and revisit the central scene of the music festival from the 1991 trip, where Bob and I gave emotional expression to our affection for Cuba and our appreciation for the journey across the island made with Roberto and Eric. I wondered what I would find this time, remembering the contrast between the faded look of the hotel and the passion of the people as they celebrated their culture that festival day. But once again my American expectations were no match for Cuba. The Casa Grande was being redone from scratch, scenting Santiago's humid September air with the smell of new paint and fresh-cut lumber.

A striped awning shaded the second-floor balcony where Bob and I had stood looking out at the park, more than four years past. The hotel was busy with the look of reclamation and the sound of saws and hammers as skilled workers fashioned a new stucco façade; women cleaned construction dust from twelve-foot-high glass doors; men laid a luscious marble floor; laborers carefully unwrapped a beautiful mahogany bar and prepared to install it along the rear wall of the balcony, the centerpiece for a series of fine couches and chairs where guests could lounge with rum, coffee, and conversation. At the side of the hotel an old man picked through the pile of construction rubble, carefully wrapping scraps of marble and a single worn-out rubber sandal in an aged plastic bag, bent low at his task and obviously thankful for what he could scavenge. The Casa Grande was like the country, fixed up and ready for a new start.

Every view from the balcony had the look of renewal. The cathedral to the left, built in 1522 and housing newly opened tourist shops on the ground floor, was freshly painted a subtle yellow with white trim, its alabaster steeple reaching into the Santiago sky where its Angel of the Annunciation watched over the park. The municipal building to the right had been redone in sea blue with white accent, looking very Caribbean and inviting. To the front, Céspedes Park was filled with fresh plantings, cared for by men who used machetes to cut open tin-can containers of new plants that they carefully set in hand-dug holes.

I took a seat in the park, soaking up the look and feel of the place, trying to bring back the texture and emotions of that first visit, nearly squinting in my attempt to bring the memories into sharper focus. There, as in most of Cuba, it was difficult for a stranger to remain alone for long, to sit free of invitation or interruption by the curious or the friendly or the ambitious. Gracus, a tall man in his late twenties who walked with a loose-jointed confidence, took an uninvited seat next to me. We talked for a good while, and I saw him several times over the next few days in what developed into an ongoing and increasingly weird saga. He turned out to be a local character, whose first comments consisted of passionate declarations about how much he hated Santiago, hated Cuba, hated Castro, which I listened to patiently. Claiming achievements as an actor and sculptor, he nervously fingered one then another of the several rings he wore. As our conversation continued, he invited me to see a children's theatrical presentation he was producing the next day, which I promised to attend but missed because he gave me the wrong curtain time, off by two hours.

After sitting on the bench for a time, Gracus directed us to a small shop just off the park, where he bought us shot glasses filled with delicious amber honey which we ate with delicate silver spoons. He slipped into our conversation a casual invitation for me to consider staying with his aunt during my visit to Santiago, a "beautiful woman with a nice house," he said, with an intent that was clear but not so specific as to make it distasteful had my sensibilities inclined me to be offended by such a proposition. We walked the area for several blocks around the park, in and out of busy and crowded shops where he introduced me to clerks and customers in an offhand manner while showing me this and that item, taken from the store shelves for inspection. I was never certain of his purpose, except perhaps to demonstrate that he was a person who knew his way around.

We returned to the park, where Gracus returned the conversation to the idea of life in Cuba being a misery, of how pressed down the people felt, living in unhappiness and despair without hope or promise. Gracus asked me to "look in the faces of the people" as an illustration of his passionate opinions, which startled me, for that was the exact language I had used to Bob in 1991 with such a different meaning, to convince him that the people in that very park were not suffering as we had been led to believe they would be.

I did as Gracus asked and looked around the park, where the faces didn't tell stories of a consuming misery or anguish that day, any more than they had four years earlier. Maybe I could never see Cuba as Gracus did, as many Cubans did in their unhappiness, and that idea worried me, made me feel the need to look harder, with more skill and insight, to make certain that my vision was as fine as I could make it, so that my romance with Cuba did not cast what I saw there into a dishonest image. That afternoon I did see people sitting quietly with somber expressions, discouraged people who possessed more time to wait in the park than trust that a better day could be theirs; their defeated spirits were clearly mapped on their faces, like faces I had seen elsewhere in Cuba, a country and people with real pain and suffering.

But I saw more than that too, as I inevitably did wherever I turned in Cuba, saw what I suspected some people wanted me to see in their willingness to visit with a stranger, in their willingness to talk with me about their lives, often in sorrow, but just as often in the steady sentiments of everyday life. In that Santiago park I also spoke with a young black woman who was studying to be an engineer, who loved American poetry, particularly Walt Whitman, who looked forward to graduating from college and getting on with building her life. A retired college professor joined our conversation, a philosopher who looked a bit threadbare and asked if I had a pen to spare, but he had no complaints, at least none he wanted to share with me and the young woman who would be an engineer. Mothers tended children, teenagers joked and high-fived, two young lovers smiled and touched tenderly with obvious affection as they posed for my camera, and a group of girls wearing brightly colored baseball caps turned backward whispered among themselves and flirted shamelessly, and innocently.

After a time I found Gracus exhausting to talk to in Spanish, not so much for the problem of language but for the way he thought, which seemed to lack a certain linear precision, so I drifted away for a rest. When I ran into him again I invited him and his girlfriend to join Paulo and me for dinner at a *paladar*. So off we went to collect Paulo and the LADA for an evening out.

Gracus claimed to know just the place for us to eat, a perfect destination, he reassured Paulo, as he directed us across Santiago into the countryside. He commanded Paulo to stop the car at a series of locations he considered historic spots, where he explained the importance of each, and then steered us to one, then another, then a third small house along rural roads until it became clear that Gracus was riding us around in an indiscriminate sightseeing tour while trying to find a local family to feed us. After more than two hours of driving and stopping—accompanied by Gracus's nonstop chatter—I began to grow irritated at his behavior and impatient with our lack of destination; finally, with dusk turning to dark, I told him to get us back to the city, now, fast, which he did, but by a roundabout route past yet more scenic sites, as if my irritation meant nothing to him, which was clearly the case. By then I was hungry, tired, and genuinely annoyed and making no attempt to hide it. Gracus finally got the meaning and became eager for us to part company, which we did as soon as we arrived back in the city.

Later that evening, while Paulo and I sat before a *paladar* dinner, he lectured me about the cross-cultural collision of the evening. "Peter, Gracus does not seem exactly right to me. You know, not right. His Spanish makes no sense even to me sometimes. No wonder you're confused. But he really didn't do anything wrong, did he? I think he just wanted to show us Santiago. Wanted to help us, show us around. That's all, I think."

The following day I ran into Gracus at an outdoor coffee shop located around the corner from Céspedes Park. Gracus approached my table with a worried look and a rueful tone, apologizing for the evening by telling me that "life in Cuba makes people crazy" and describing himself as "too close to the moon" and liking rum too much, a cultural and personal explanation of his behavior that I took at face value. He was sorry—and not because he had missed an opportunity for food or favors. I had already concluded that Paulo was correct, that Gracus had simply been delighted to do something different, something interesting, something useful in a small way. In a life filled with uneventful days—days of sitting in parks, sipping rum, feeling idle and bored and weighed down with despair—showing off his city to an American must have passed as a major event, a welcome break in the routine. I invited him to sit and have a coffee, tried to assure him that everything was okay, that there were no hard feelings, that the night had been a problem about cultural differences over how time gets used and how time gets spent, about Gracus needing to pass time while I felt the need to make use of it. I wanted Gracus to accept that explanation as a fair interpretation of what had passed between us, but he would not be reassured however much I tried, and he left without comfort and without so much as touching his coffee.

The coffee shop became part of my Santiago routine, a hangout for actors, writers, and a variety of people who drifted in and out, many of whom were trying to "make business." Good, strong coffee was all they sold there, for one peso, about four cents. But there was a lot going on at the café aside from good coffee. At a back table, Paulo and I tested the roadside rumor that in Santiago's black market it would be difficult to exchange dollars for pesos, which turned out to be a hopeful exaggeration. We could buy pesos there, and did, for our nightly visits to local *paladares*, but it was a seller's market just as we had been told it would be, causing Paulo to haggle hard to get as many as 25 pesos for the dollar, where 30 pesos was commonplace in Havana. The café was an interesting place where whispered conversations between people bent low across small tables was a common sight. Women held hands and talked earnestly; men gathered at tables to comment among themselves about males who passed by on the sidewalk.

After a couple of days of popping in and out of the coffee shop I began to recognize faces, including Hazel's. She sat at the café because "sometimes there are many businesses here." The day we met she needed to "make business" because her monthly food ration was gone and her payday was not until the end of the week. So she sat and waited patiently, hoping for good fortune and opportunity, but so far that day her only success had been a cup of coffee offered by an old friend. She was a university student with a good job as a teacher, but the money she made was "just not enough to live on, so we have to do something else to get by. Sell rum to tourists. People go to hotels with foreigners. Something. Anything.

"Today is trouble," she said, because if something did not come along she and her sister would go hungry. Her life was better than it had been a couple of years before, but progress was too slow for her tastes and needs and her energetic style.

"We are bored," she said. "The government must make life better and more exciting for young people. There is nothing to do on weekends or on vacations. If you try to go to the beach there is only one bus every day, even on Sunday, and it's impossible. There is no time to enjoy ourselves because life is so hard we have to make business," she said, repeating Cuba's mournful litany, that life was always balanced on the edge of need and disaster, creating a day-to-day existence filled with stress and anxiety, creating an uncertainty about tomorrow that prohibited feeling secure in the routines of daily life. "In the big picture, life is better, yes, but every day it is very difficult. Every day is too hard," she said, capturing the emotional heart and the practical reality of Cuba's fundamental insecurity with a firmness that did not invite negotiation, a determination that seemed uncommon for a young woman in her early twenties who was no larger than five foot two and one hundred pounds.

Bored and anxious and determined to do better for herself, the previous year she had decided to forsake Cuba by going to the United States Naval Base at Guantánamo Bay. "My friends and I made a plan. I was the youngest and the only woman. One of my friends traded his old Chevrolet for a ten-foot boat. We all worked hard to collect food and water. We got juices and seasick pills."

Their plan was to make the short sea voyage from Santiago's Morro Castle to the sanctuary of the base, less than 60 miles skirting the shoreline of Cuba's eastern tip. They planned and plotted and gathered what they needed during the period when emigration from Cuba was open, so they had no worries about Cuban patrol boats or police.

"But when bad weather started," said Hazel, "the boat owner grew nervous. We tried everything to get him into action, but he refused. Finally the time of open emigration expired, and there we were, still in Santiago."

Hazel was without bravado or dramatics as she told her story, but it was clear that she was still angry at the captain's lack of resolve to see the plan through.

I asked her why she wanted to go to Guantánamo, where all the Cuban refugees lived in tents, suspended between two lives while the two governments negotiated. She looked up at me and said simply, "I wanted to change my life," a quiet statement of honest ambition that left me without comment.

She had no confidence in Fidel, the Revolution, or *el futuro*, which she was certain would be worse than it was that day, even with no food at home. "Fidel goes on the TV and says, 'Next month things are going to change,' but next month comes and everything is still the same, so the people don't believe him or the Revolution anymore."

She thought that Fidel would have to leave and there would have to be a change in government. When I asked about Raúl, she just looked at me with a sideways glance, as if to say, "That's a very stupid question," which of course it was. Critics of the government distrusted Raúl more than Fidel; he lacked Fidel's charisma and warmth, and had a reputation for being even more strident and ideological than *el jefe*.

Hazel was rich with street stories and nicknames for Fidel, most of them a mix of humor, satire, disrespect, and wit. Her clear favorite was a riff on the government's current slogan, "We must resist," and involved graffiti that pictured Lasso, a large black man who served as mayor of Santiago, standing behind Fidel such that they looked to be in the act of lovemaking; above them was the slogan, "Fidel, you must resist."

We sat for a couple of hours sipping coffee and talking while Hazel kept a watchful eye on what was going on around us, wanting to miss no opportunity to "make business." She was pleasant and cheerful, quick with humor and charm, and animated in her conversation, as funny with her stories as she was unforgiving in her criticism of Cuba. And like most Cubans I met, she told her story without complaint or self-pity, without seeking sympathy or compensation. Hazel's unhappiness was nothing like Gracus's, with his despair and defeat, his daily comfort found in rum, and his surrender to the idea that he was "too close to the moon" in a life without choices. Gracus was lost to Cuba, regardless of her future. Hazel was energetic and lively, determined to "make business" when necessary, to make chancy and even risky decisions when the opportunity seemed right, and to hold tight control of her life regardless of what Fidel or Cuba did or did not do.

Hazel would make the best of things just as Paulo would make the best of what Cuba's tomorrow had to offer. Somewhere between Paulo and Hazel, somewhere between her mix of dissatisfaction and determination and his newfound respect for Cuban life and society, lay Cuba's mood. In those conversations with Paulo and Gracus and Hazel and other Cubans, the mood was one of uncertainty. Yet I found that sentiment of ambivalence comforting after the terrible sadness of 1992. It possessed a forward-looking, even optimistic, quality, under the guardianship of the likes of Hazel's adventurous spirit and Paulo's willingness to see Cuba in a positive light as she struggled to redefine herself after the worst times of the "special period."

As Hazel and I said good-bye I promised to meet her at the café the next day so she could give me a letter to her aunt in Miami. I also asked her if she had a preference for what name I might give her when I wrote about our meeting. She asked why I would not use her real name, and I told her that I wanted to avoid even the possibility of causing her problems. She looked at me with another sideways glance, flicked the air with the back of her hand, took my notebook, and wrote her name, saying, "Please, use it," a request I honored.

At the café, "making business" with foreigners was part of an imaginary chalkboard menu, like in the park—in all of Cuba's parks—where working the foreigners was a respectable if illegal trade. Yet even in those circumstances, Cuba's polite behavior prevailed, governed by a set of social rules that covered nearly all situations, even in the fast-changing society. Gracus, for all my irritation with him, never asked for anything, aside from a bit of understanding. Neither did Hazel, as she sat waiting to "make business" so she would not end the day hungry, yet unwilling to forsake her pride in exchange for a beggar's handout from a stranger. When Paulo was with me, other Cubans kept a respectful distance, even the *jineteros,* who sometimes made the occasional offer to him on my behalf but never directly to me, which would have been rude, bad manners even on the street. But sitting alone in the café or in the park, I was considered approachable for the casual introduction and for whatever else might follow. There was always a group of *jineteros* around the park, and usually a couple of them would make their way over to me, although they would also go away at my first casual refusal, displaying rather timid behavior considering their chosen profession, particularly in comparison to their fellowship in Havana. That was just another sign of an easiness that characterized Santiago, a more relaxed approach to nearly everything than in Havana.

The park regulars had been curious when I arrived a second and a third day, moving in and out of the park and the surrounding area, taking pictures and talking to people. It was low season, so there were few tourists, and those foreigners who did pass through looked the part, in guided tour groups like wandering gangs, wearing Bermuda shorts and sandals and fanny packs cinched tight. It didn't take long for the regulars to acknowledge my presence with a nod and a hello. After a few visits I lost my status as a special attraction, although I remained a subject of curiosity. When Paulo came to the park to meet me one day—he had been out chasing down LADAs trying to buy parts from the drivers—more than one person approached him to ask if he was looking for the American journalist, an assumption they had made based on my camera and notebook. As he sat waiting for me, Paulo was provided details of my day's activities: where I had gone and with whom, when I was last seen, and in what direction I had headed. The *jineteros* filled him in with the help of a group of kids no more than seven to ten years old, who the previous day had hounded us for money, for a pen, for something, for anything, refusing to be denied and refusing to leave us be, making their demands in the most dramatic fashion, hoping that loud and pathetic pleas would move us to charity, which they did not. But all was forgiven and forgotten when they came over to chat with Paulo, sharing information and asking questions about him and the American. Among the *jineteros* and the kids, as with Hazel, whom Paulo bumped into later while he was looking for me, this was small-town gossip among newfound friends trying to be helpful. Paulo told me the story of his wait in the park with delight, a bit amused at what he considered Santiago's country mannerisms, yet more than a bit surprised that the park regulars were familiar with our comings and goings, that anyone had paid us that much attention. "Peter," he said, "we are known in Santiago."

Indeed we were. We met people on the streets who often stopped to chat in the custom of neighbors, sometimes in parts of Santiago removed from the park area. Hazel and her sister, "too-close-to-the-moon" Gracus, the flirtatious young backward-baseball-capped girls, the waitress from the coffee shop, an actor we met at the café (and then ran into again back in Havana), a young woman who asked me to take a letter to the States for her, and people we hadn't actually met but who acknowledged us with small gestures of recognition. Havana may think of itself as Cuba's central place, but Santiago was a good and friendly city, and I liked it there, liked the people and their easy style. So it pleased me to think that Paulo was correct when he said, "We are known in Santiago."

Following Fidel

Standing in the courtyard of the Hotel de Santiago, waiting for the Dream Away Disco to open so she could buy a ticket for the night's entertainment, María said, "I am a revolutionary," words spoken with an easy confidence that placed María's political sensibilities far in advance of her young years. She was part of a crowd of young people who could be found there, day and night, milling around outside the sharp angles of glass and steel that was the city's finest, newest hotel, some of them waiting for entertainment, others just waiting for an opportunity. María was quick to clarify that she was not a *jinetera,* although that statement was unnecessary because she possessed neither the appearance nor the style of a young woman on the make, in fact had a reserve that could be described as proper, perhaps even a bit old fashioned; and when a fellow student from the university approached to urge María to get me to do her a favor, María sent her away with the frosty comment, "That is not my business here."

María was a medical student planning a night away from her studies, not someone on the hustle for favors offered or favors asked. She spoke patiently and listened attentively, as curious about my purpose in Santiago as I was about her attachment to Fidel and the Revolution, which was considerable.

"The days are very difficult sometimes, but they are getting better and will soon be even better," she assured me. She explained that by building the hotels that brought in the tourists and the dollars, Fidel had created the opportunity for her to attend medical school at no cost, a bounty and a benefit that would not be available to her in any other country. "Without Fidel and the Revolution my life would not be possible," she said in an understated tone. She disliked being excluded from the hotels and not always having enough food, but, she said, "The hotels must be stocked, and that is the cost of the Revolution just now."

María spoke of the relationship between tourism and the continuing Revolution with appreciation and gratitude, with an understanding that reached well beyond what many Cubans were prepared to accept. Her declaration that she was a revolutionary, spoken aloud among a group of young people without embarrassment or awkwardness, something that would have been a rare occurrence on the streets of Havana, was not so unusual in Santiago, the "Hero City" of the Revolution.

An enduring commitment to the Revolution was a serious ideal in María's life, a way for her to measure people and behavior as well as political values and national policy. María's mother, a teacher, and her father, who repaired sewing machines, she also described as revolutionaries. Among her friends, she said, "some are, some aren't, but my close friends are. Some students talk bad about the Revolution and others talk about what's good from it. I keep away from those who are critical because I do not want to get into trouble, which could happen from being around people who talk against the Revolution. Perhaps go to jail for it," she said in an offhand manner, and then added, "The police are very strict here."

As in Havana, as in most of Cuba, some people in Santiago "made business" to get by, but here, more than in other parts of the country, the police kept a close watch on those who might commit crimes against tourists—a very rare occurrence—or who sold black market cigars—a very common one. María insisted that it would be unlikely for the Santiago police to accept a bribe to overlook even the smallest offense, as was the practice in Havana—dollars for the blind eye of the law. Paulo agreed. "It is very hard here," he said with a shake of his head, after having spent several days talking with groups of *jineteros*, clearly not wanting to test his Havana street skills against Santiago's country police.

But even in Santiago's strict environment the "special period" brought exceptions to the rule of what was proper to say and do. The crimes and offenses that attracted police attention, those that could send a Cuban to jail, María disapproved of, and presumably so did her close friends. But there were lesser offenses, acts that fell within the more forgiving domain of *resolviendo*—buying, selling, and trading whatever you had for whatever you needed, legal or not. María accepted this fringe world of *resolviendo* as being altogether different from the world of out-and-out petty crime. *Resolviendo* made María anxious because it violated the rules, the Revolution, yet her attitude softened when she spoke of people needing "to do something when there is no food in the neighborhood and no money to buy any." A forgiving Cuban grace slipped into her voice as she described the problem of "no food in the neighborhood," reflecting a concern that went beyond herself and her family to the neighborhood, the community—the essential quality that marked Cuba as a society where the word "neighbor" still meant something. She spoke wistfully about better times before the "special period," when the black market and *resolviendo* were unnecessary, when "food was everywhere," when life in Cuba seemed less ambiguous to her.

María had reached an uneasy place in our discussion, a place made uncomfortable by the conflict between political loyalties and the day-to-day demands of the "special period." María braced herself, much like the strictest teacher you ever had, as she announced, "*El Comandante* says, 'We must resist,'" quoting Fidel's latest slogan, saying it so loud and clear that people around us heard her unmistakably—billboard language uttered in everyday conversation. María was not the only loyal Cuban I talked with, not the only person whose passions for the Revolution and its leaders remained in full force; but she was among the few whose revolutionary ethos was held so strongly and comfortably that she would repeat the Revolution's articles of faith in public to a stranger. And in that setting, with the late afternoon sun reflecting off the steel and glass structure built for tourists, I found in María a person most willing, perhaps most needing, to invoke Fidel's name. His words of encouragement steadied her in the face of what she considered to be her own backsliding from the pure faith, but which in truth was the much lesser offense of extending grace to friends and neighbors who had sinned against the Revolution. María possessed the hard head of a revolutionary and the soft heart of a good neighbor, distinctive qualities of a society that had been forced into a future so vague that few people would speculate about what it might bring.

María was confident that a majority of the people in Santiago still supported the Revolution, and she stood with a look of disbelief when I told her that a majority of the young people with whom I had spoken in Havana were quick to criticize Fidel and the Revolution, that they appeared to have no respect for either the man or the movement which they would declare. I doubt that she accepted what I had to say about Havana's infidelities, so far removed were they from the commonly held sentiments in her part of Cuba. María's response, a statement of skepticism made without challenge or rebuke, was as simple and well stated as nearly everything else she said that afternoon, so wise it was difficult to believe she was so young—"All Cuban people feel something for this country."

María's revolutionary commitment was a fact of family tradition as much as a circumstance of Santiago geography. The politics of María's family dated from the early days of the struggle. Her grandfather, a fisherman with ties to one of the revolutionary groups, was killed by Batista's police, murdered with such brutality that his casket was closed at the funeral. Her eighty-year-old grandmother talked often about those days, when guns and men passed through her Santiago house bound for the Revolution. Her grandmother became known for her ability to hang the Movement's flag in conspicuous places throughout the city without being discovered, a seemingly playful act of defiance for which she would have gone to jail, as the lesser punishment. When victory came and the revolutionaries moved down from the Sierra Maestra to claim Santiago and victory, a band of bearded men in fatigues collected María's grandmother at her house so she could ride with them in an open jeep through the city, giving her a proper place in the ragtag parade as a testimonial to her service in *la lucha*. On occasion, María's grandmother showed visitors her medal awarded by the government, a reminder of deeds that had made Santiago and her people conspicuous in Cuba's past.

Paulo didn't quite know what to make of María, of what she said and what she represented, a revolutionary loyalty at which Paulo had scoffed until recently and which his friends in Havana would have surely mocked. He was suspicious of her, doubted her convictions and even doubted that she was a medical student as he waited for her to make a pitch for help of some sort, but his skepticism softened when we three were eating dinner at a *paladar* and he saw her discreetly fold a piece of chicken into a napkin, presumably to take home for her family or to satisfy a later hunger.

But Paulo was on a trail of his own, following Fidel's revolutionary path in search of deeper meaning for his newly discovered respect for the Revolution, a meaning rendered more compelling in Santiago than it could have been in Havana or any other part of the country. Paulo and I picked up Fidel's trail seven miles outside of Santiago at the Siboney farmhouse, where in 1953 Fidel, Raúl, and a small band of rebels from points all over Cuba gathered; armed with only a pitiful assortment of guns and Fidel's grand ambition, they attacked the thousand-man-strong Moncada Army Barracks, Batista's largest outpost. This was to be the first armed act of the Revolution.

The little farmhouse, now preserved as a museum, is a record of what happened that day when the *Fidelistas* began their revolution with an absolute disaster that had been prophesied by one revolutionary group that traveled from Havana to Oriente Province not knowing what Fidel had planned; as they rode they sang these words: *Iré a Santiago en coche de aguas negras*—I'm off to Santiago in a coach decked with mourning tears. Today, the road leading to the farmhouse is lined with stone memorials to the rebels who died that day—not small, polished headstones, but massive, larger than life–sized, rough-edged pieces of rock rising up from the ground—appropriate representations of the revolutionaries and their mission. The stones' form and size command the attention of all but the most indifferent traveler along that road. Each is embedded with a brass plate inscribed with a name and occupation, honoring with careful simplicity the Revolution's first martyrs, who earned their place in history on the 26th of July, 1953.

Paulo and I set out for Siboney on a beautiful Cuban day, driving on a nearly empty road that gave the heavy stone memorials a greater presence than they might otherwise have possessed. Several times they seemed to pull us onto the side of the road, where we got out of the car for a closer inspection, each stop more somber and respectful than the last. We arrived at the white farmhouse, which looked much too small to accommodate the large gathering of revolutionaries, enough men and women to fill twenty-six cars when they left in the predawn dark to start the Cuban Revolution.

Inside the house, displays told the story of that day and of the sad, painful days that followed. There was a mixed assortment of shotguns and small-caliber rifles and pistols, a pathetic collection of weapons with which to attack the armed might of Batista's largest army barracks. Glass cases housed the Cuban army uniforms the rebels wore to try to fool the guards, Fidel's being the largest they had yet still so that one picture of him showed bare wrists and ankles. Also on display were the two-tone shoes of one rebel, a newly purchased fashion statement he could not resist wearing into battle, and the newspaper stories with bold front-page headlines that described the aborted attack and the death of sixty-eight rebels, though without mentioning that many of them had died of torture as their companions listened to their screams.

Batista ordered that ten rebels die for every soldier killed. While the prison guards went about the business at which they were so practiced, one woman prisoner, sitting in her cell, was shown the eye of her brother, removed with a spoon by a guard known as *Ojos Bellos*—Beautiful Eyes—a nickname that witnessed to his practiced trade as a man of torture.

The brittle uniforms and guns and personal effects of the rebels looked terribly dated—wearing two-toned brown-and-white shoes into battle, for God's sake—and the newspapers were over forty years old, the pictures of dead and captured rebels possessing a grainy, inferior quality. I wondered what imprint such things from the past could make on Paulo, who had once described the history of the Revolution as "boring" when he all but refused to visit Havana's Museum of the Revolution.

But now he moved carefully through the small house, reading the news stories with particular attentiveness, scrutinizing the photos of Fidel and the others under arrest and heading for a dangerous fate. As we walked outside a rather pensive Paulo said, "Víctor will be surprised to know that I was here. It is strange how this history never meant anything to me before, but now it does. Castro attacked the largest army barracks, didn't he? He must have been very brave to do what he did." I was struck by Paulo's intense but inarticulate response to what he had seen there, by the fact that he was beginning to see Cuba in a different way. Just as he had found a new understanding of the present by looking across the Florida Straits to his father in Miami, Paulo followed Fidel as a guide into Cuba's past. Understanding what happened on that one day in history, the 26th of July, caused Paulo to reconsider his image of Castro. What Castro did that day had redefined his image for Cubans of the revolutionary generation, transformed him into a heroic leader, set him apart from several rebel leaders as a man of courage and action. Always before, Paulo and his friends had considered Castro without respect or honor, had seen him as the bloated, red-faced head of state—*jamón con ojos,* ham with eyes, Paulo had once called him. On this day, though, a walk through the Siboney farmhouse changed everything.

Captured after the Moncada attack, tried, and convicted, Fidel was sent into exile in Mexico in 1955, where he set about planning the next phase of the struggle. Meanwhile, the daring barracks assault, disastrous though it was, had gained for Castro an elevated place among the leaders of several rebel groups in Cuba. Among those who journeyed to Mexico to take Castro's measure was Frank País, the youthful leader of the well-developed underground movement in Santiago and Oriente Province. Fidel was twenty-nine years old at the time, the charismatic veteran of Moncada, prison, and now, exile. País was twenty-one, a thoughtful, handsome man, the son of a preacher, with organizational abilities as keen as Fidel's were undeveloped. They struck a deal in 1955, and País's network became the in-Cuba wing of the 26th of July Movement.

Castro told País to plan a massive uprising in Santiago as a diversionary action to cover Fidel's return to Cuba with a rebel army—one that hardly existed when that order was issued. November 30, 1956, was the day Fidel set to arrive from Mexico aboard the yacht *Granma* with his small band of 82 poorly equipped men. But things went badly, and the Cuba-bound rebels were still two days from land when, as promised and planned, País directed some 240 men of the Santiago underground in attacks against the National Police and the Maritime Police Headquarters. They captured weapons and left the police headquarters in charred ruins, but they also left 3 of their own men dead and the planned uprising in a shambles. For the first time, the black-and-red armbands of the 26th of July Movement had gone into battle, with Castro still at sea and Batista's army now on the alert that Fidel was on his way home.

On December 2 the *Granma* either landed or wrecked in the mud of Cuba's south coast, depending upon whether you wish to rely on Fidel, a man with an eye to his own place in history, or Che, a man with an ironic view of life. Grateful to be alive, the men built a makeshift cross for the Virgin of Charity, the patron saint of Cuba, as they knelt on the beach at Purgatory Point, a mile off target and too late to be greeted by the rebels who had waited until driven away by the roving presence of Batista's military. Exhausting marches and attacks by army units filled the days that followed, leaving Che wounded and others killed, until Fidel and some 18 men finally made their way to the Sierra Maestra; from there they would wage war for the next twenty-five months, protected by the grace of the mountain terrain and the courage of the peasants of Oriente Province, who offered the rebels support without reservation or limits.

Frank País held the impressive title of National Chief of Action of the 26th of July Movement; commensurate with his title and skills he had built a substantial rebel organization that extended throughout Oriente Province, while Fidel probably had fewer than fifty men in the mountains. Through the spring and summer of 1957 Frank País intensified the war in the cities, causing him and his men to live in the dreadful threat of Batista's police. In June, Frank's brother Josué was murdered by the police. The next month Frank was chased down an alley by an assassin known as *Mano Negro*—Black Hand—and killed, shot in the back. But Santiago did not grow quiet, nor did she forget. After the Triumph, the National Police Headquarters, attacked and burned by Frank País's rebels in 1956, was converted into a museum to celebrate Santiago's role in the revolutionary history, with greatest honors reserved for Frank País.

Paulo and I had a difficult time locating the museum, which my guidebook called the "Museum of the Underground Struggle in Santiago," an awkward title that lacked a graceful translation into Spanish for the several people on the street of whom we asked directions. We finally found a striking two-story building positioned on Santiago's high ground, well suited for looking down upon the city below—a fitting citadel of arms for a despotic leader.

Paulo and I toured the museum with a guide, who paid close professional attention to the foreigner while Paulo drifted about on his own, absorbed by how much history there was in such a confinement of two rooms. Paulo stopped to read a set of documents and a series of newspaper stories, to inspect the handmade M-26 armbands that the rebels wore into battle; and there were guns, a printing press, parts for time bombs, and gallon gas cans with "ESSO" printed on them—American oil company containers used to carry gasoline to a bomb factory in the city center. But it was the pictures that did Paulo in.

The sorrowful faces of Santiago's revolutionary struggle put the look of humanity on Cuba's history. Young rebels, young Cuban men and women, lying in the street in pools of blood, their arms and legs twisted in the unnatural shape of violent death. Josué País, dead on the street with men standing over him, government men posing for the camera at parade rest with shotguns in their hands as cold as their deed just completed. And the huge funeral procession of thousands for Frank País, as though the entire city had turned out to mourn the loss, a long line following behind the hearse, stretching far beyond what the camera lens could see, far beyond what Batista's secret police could see that funeral day, which is still memorialized every year by Santiago. Another procession, this one reserved for women, all of them dressed in black, the sad-faced mothers of Santiago gathered to march in protest with signs asking the government to stop assassinating their children, in the streets, in the jails, in the homes late at night and in broad daylight, anywhere, anytime.

Paulo moved from one picture to another, slowly, carefully, standing alone, looking at the faces, the people, the losses. The dead revolutionaries, and those who survived—the young, unlined faces of Fidel, Raúl, Che, Frank País, and the others, redeemed from a forgotten place, as men of history, as men in charge, as men long dead, as men studied and transformed into heroic figures that day.

The images held Paulo for the longest time until finally he called me over to ask with a solemn face, whispered words, and trembling lips, "How did they know so much? How did they know what they had to do? They were so young. *They were so young, Peter.* Frank País was my age. Look what he did. I had no idea. No idea. I never knew. No wonder Santiago is so proud of the Revolution."

Paulo had come to realize that people like him, of his age, with parents like his, from families like his, from the university and from the workshop, from places he knew and understood, had made the Revolution, many of them barely grown adults in their teens and twenties, and he was struck by what they had accomplished.

For the rest of our time in Santiago and on the trip back to Havana, Paulo returned again and again to what he had experienced in that city, the "Hero City." He switched back and forth between the Havana Paulo and the Santiago Paulo, angling his own way through Cuba's history and society much the same way Cuba was making her way in the world, without agreement over the past or the future. First he was the hip street kid from Havana, the one who hung out and joked with the *jineteros*, who knew where to get dollars changed at the best rate, who found the right *paladar*, who tried to keep me from making a fool of myself. Then he was the young Cuban with newfound respect for his own history and its heroes, and for the nation they made, which, for all its problems, Paulo had decided he loved and would not abandon.

In his swing back and forth, in his changing moods and attitudes, in his transformation from historical skeptic to revolutionary patron, Paulo reflected Cuba's ambivalence of 1995, holding onto the past one minute yet fearful that Cuba's Revolution and the society it had created held too little promise for the future. I joked with him, saying that I knew his friends back in Havana would be pleased to hear about his new enthusiasm for Fidel and the Revolution.

A bit sadly Paulo said, "I will tell Víctor—who will be so proud, you just don't know—and I will probably tell my girlfriend, but I don't think I'll tell my other friends. Peter, they'll think I'm crazy to tell them what I feel now about the Revolution. They just don't think about this the way I do now. I can't tell them. I probably never will," said Paulo, setting the limits on how far he could follow Fidel.

In Search of Saints

The next day we left Santiago for Havana with one planned stop, to look into Cuba's most important religious tradition—a tradition more important than I could have imagined, as it turned out. The church of El Cobre stands high in the foothills of the Sierra Maestra overlooking the town, a town as needy as any in Cuba, a town surrounded by a landscape ruined and depleted by open-pit copper mining, a town so poor that local children tried to sell us pebble-sized pieces of copper.

In 1608, at a time when the town prospered, two Indian brothers collecting salt at the Bay of Nipe spotted something floating in the sea. They pulled into their boat a foot-tall wooden statue of Mary carrying the Christ Child on one arm and a gold cross on the other. The image was supported in the water by a plank that bore the inscription *Yo soy la Virgen de la Caridad*: I am the Virgin of Charity.

Legend holds that the statue, brought back to Cobre and placed in a thatched hut away from the main church, was so dissatisfied with her lesser position that she disappeared three nights in a row only to be found in the morning at the top of the hill. The people were so convinced of her miraculous power that early in the next century the people built a second church and showed their proper respect by placing her high on the main altar. Over the years she was credited with all manner of miracles, including siding with the local slaves in their rebellion of 1731, which gained them freedom. In 1916, at the request of the veterans of the Cuban War of Independence, the Pope declared her the patron saint of Cuba. In 1926 she was moved into a new church, a beige and red basilica that backs up to the mountains and looks down upon the destitute community and the ruined land.

As Paulo and I walked into the church, our eyes were drawn immediately to the back, to the top of the rear wall where, sequestered in an air-conditioned alcove, stood the diminutive figure of the Virgin dressed in a satin gown with a gold cape and a golden crown, her dark-skinned face watching quietly. Paulo and I paused when we saw her, out of respect for the tradition. In the dignified setting of that beautiful church, surrounded by a landscape that had endured such suffering, and newly arrived from our tour of Santiago's revolutionary shrines, we both felt quiet and thoughtful. All we could do was stop and look at her. Paulo asked me if I "believed," and I told him, "Not so much," a more tentative response than I might have given at another time, in a different setting, but a response that considered my respect for the place, with its religious mythology and its ability to turn a skeptic solemn, if not religious, for one ethereal moment.

Part of the tradition of El Cobre was the belief that anyone might make an offering to the Virgin, leave flowers or something personal—a picture, a piece of fabric, something insignificant or something important—and she would grant the right to make a wish, to ask something of her in return. In that setting of religious distinction, and seeing a part of Cuba in such anguish, and feeling so grateful for all that Cuba had given me, I left an offering and made the only wish to that dark-skinned saint that seemed reasonable to me: "Good fortune for Cuba, please, good fortune for Cuba."

With the spiritual air around us filled with my benediction for a better Cuba, Paulo said, "Most people in Cuba believe in the story of her rising out of the water. Almost everyone believes in her." This declaration set my curiosity working. If Paulo was correct, if all of Cuba believed in *la Virgen de la Caridad*, then she might be the only thing in the country, fact or fancy, truth or legend, real or imagined, that everyone honored with faith and trust. Cuba's ambiguities and complexities, her unresolved history and enduring struggles, her competing ambitions and unfulfilled aspirations, made it difficult for me to interpret her with any reasonable certainty. If all of Cuba believed in the Virgin of Charity, I wanted to understand that marvel. I also wanted a representation of her to take with me that might outlast the visit and keep her importance well defined in my memory; I wanted a representation, a token for the selfish fact that if she loved Cuba, and Cuba loved her, I wanted her close to me, too, for comfort in an unsure world.

The search began in Old Havana as soon as we got back. Almost immediately—as soon as we stepped out of the car, as though our quest were guided by a spiritual hand—we passed the open door of an apartment and spotted a likeness of the Virgin on a small table. Without hesitation or self-consciousness, Paulo knocked on the door to inquire. A gray-haired woman graciously invited us in and offered cool water to sip while she explained that she had owned the small brass figure for thirty years, that it was the centerpiece of her living room as a statement of its importance in her life. She said she would consider parting with it, but her voice was filled with a reluctance that embarrassed me, and in my mind my quest for the Virgin of Charity turned into a selfish drive for an old woman's treasure.

She softened the situation by directing the conversation to a conspicuous, three-foot-tall statue of Santa Barbara standing in the corner, complete with the traditional sword in one hand, to open life's passages, and a light in the other hand, to illuminate the way. That Catholic figure, like the Virgin of Charity, had a long history with the woman, and it also carried a tale of religion and politics, of faith and retribution.

Just after the success of the Revolution in 1959, a friend asked this woman if she would like to have a statue of Santa Barbara. Being a religious person, she said, "Yes, of course," but was surprised when the friend arrived at her tiny apartment with the huge likeness, and a story of her own. The statue needed a new home because the woman's son, a Communist puffed up with the victory of the Revolution, wanted all religion removed from the family home. The woman did as he insisted, though with great reluctance, and left the saint with a sorrowful goodbye. The story ended like a morality play. A month after the statue changed hands the son died without clear cause or explanation and the mother became paralyzed on one side of her body. Our host concluded her story, and our visit, with the comment that when she died, Santa Barbara would be passed on to her favorite grandson, leaving no doubt that it was a family treasure, not a subject for sale or barter. I left more grateful for her Cuban story than I would have been for anything else she might have offered.

Now that the saints were a party to my journey, they started making their presence known. As Paulo and I walked along the street we passed two young women, one of whom made reference to "El Cobre" with a flirtatious backward glance at Paulo. It took Paulo time to make me understand that the term was used as a salutation with many meanings, including respect and admiration and approval, but always offered as a compliment—another sure sign of the widespread acceptance of the Virgin of Charity, not only in the religious tradition but in the popular culture as well. I caught her likeness where I would never have noticed it before, on bracelets and charms and pendants hanging from gold chains. Seeing the Virgin of Charity's conspicuous presence among Cubans, I refused to accept Paulo's statement that I was not likely to find even one traditional Catholic medal of her for sale in all Havana. It didn't seem the least bit reasonable that among Cuba's commodities, no matter how scarce, there would not be a religious medal of the nation's patron saint.

At the Malecón flea market a vendor sold beaded bracelets and necklaces in color patterns that represented Catholic saints or Santería *orishas*, whichever you wished, or both if you had no preference. When the Spanish conquerors of the New World sought to force Catholicism on the African slaves brought to work the Caribbean land, the slaves accommodated their masters by accepting the likenesses from the Catholic church but resisted by investing those likenesses with African names and spiritual qualities, hence the rise of Santería. When the Yorubas saw Santa Barbara, the patron saint of thunder and lighting, clothed in red, the color of fire, they immediately recognized Changó, a great warrior who controlled that element, and from then on both Catholic saint and Santería *orisha* shared the colors red and white. So I bought a bracelet in those colors, to honor the woman's statue of Santa Barbara, and another in blue and white for the *orisha* Yemayá, which I put on for its protective value for travelers, thinking ahead to when I would pass through U.S. customs without the paperwork necessary to make me a legal traveler to Cuba.

We left the market no closer to finding a token of the Virgin of Charity, but luck—or fate—caught up with us once again on the streets when a religious painting of the Virgin of Charity herself looked out at Paulo and me from the open door of a small art shop, set up in the living room of a private home. The place was crowded with artists and their friends and a group of Spanish tourists who were excited in their examination of oil paintings of flamenco dancers and beautiful women draped in gossamer gowns, vividly accented against black backgrounds. Hopeful at seeing paintings of several religious figures—Catholic or Santería, I was not clear which—I inquired about a religious medal, and one of the local artists said, "There have not been such things for many, many years, more than thirty years. Do you understand why?" Which, finally, I did. There had been no religious medals since the Revolution, and the existing supply had long ago been exhausted by Cubans who had held their beliefs, so I accepted as fact that what I sought was simply not for sale in Cuba at any price.

I looked at paintings of the Virgin of Charity and Santa Barbara and other religious figures, asking questions and receiving appreciative answers; and Paulo and I then joined the group of artists for part of the afternoon in a lesson in religion and art. At one point one of the artists quietly approached to say that if I planned to stay at the shop for a time he had a medal of the Virgin at his home that he would like to give me. He left and returned with a collection: an Indian head penny, an FBI pin, a Cuban Revolution pin, and a coin from a Caribbean country dated a decade before the United States was a nation; he also had a medal of the Virgin of Charity, which he insisted I accept as a gift despite my embarrassed reluctance.

I left the shop with paintings of saints and *orishas*, vivid in color, primitive in style, and rich in stories of the synchronicity between Catholicism and Santería. Like myths from a time when the Old World and the New World met in the Caribbean, the stories told about the ways oppressed people adapt and make do, and they were as fine and true as any found in history. As I prepared to leave that fellowship of artists, one of the company asked if I kept the art I bought in Cuba or sold it for profit. I told him that I selected pieces with friends in mind and ended up giving most of it away, but I always had a hard time doing that because the act of selecting a painting was so absorbing it made the parting difficult. In this case, I would keep the painting of the Virgin of Charity but would likely give away the two others; the one of Yemayá, I told the group, would go to my friend Bob with whom I had made the first trip to Cuba. Bob deeply needed Yemayá's promised protection of calm seas and safe trips, I explained, because twice in the recent past his work had taken him too close to death, once in the Himalayan Mountains and another time in Haiti. I told them I was now confident that Yemayá would bring Bob home safely in the future, without harm or close calls. As we walked out the door Paulo looked at me a bit quizzically and said, "Peter, that was a very Cuban thing to say."

Perhaps that was so, although it would be hard for me to judge. But I knew that Cuba had moved me around in certain ways, and as it turned out she wasn't done with me yet, even though I was about to leave for the States. I still needed to say my good-byes to Paulo's family, whom I had not seen since returning from Santiago. As we drove across Havana, Paulo told me that the night we had returned from our cross-island road trip he and Víctor had talked into the early morning. The conversation had been animated by Paulo's stories of his visits to revolutionary shrines—the Moncada Barracks, the Museum of the Underground Struggle in Santiago, and the Siboney Farmhouse. Paulo's newfound admiration for Cuba's revolutionary past and for the smooth-faced men and women who had made it delighted Víctor. For the first time Víctor found it the proper setting to tell Paulo of his grandfather's role in the Revolution and Víctor's own revolutionary trek into the Sierra Maestra during the literacy campaign.

In Paulo's telling of this story, it was clear how important the evening had been for stepfather and son, a coming together that neither of them had ever thought possible, so estranged had Paulo been from the revolutionary society that held Víctor's heart with such fierceness. The struggle of words and ideas between them over Cuba's past and future had been an enormous source of tension within the family and a matter of terrible worry for María, Paulo's mother; but that tension and worry were now gone, disappeared into the long night of conversation about Paulo's experiences in Santiago and Víctor's reminiscences. And even though Paulo mentioned that Víctor was really looking forward to seeing me again, I failed to make any connection between our planned reunion and the renewal that had already been completed between father and son.

As soon as Paulo and I arrived at the apartment it was clear that Víctor had something pressing he wanted to talk to me about. He struck me as anxious to pull free from the family and find a private moment in the small space of the apartment. When we were alone, Víctor immediately revisited our last conversation, our talk about Fidel, the Revolution, about life in Cuba, about his crazy love for the Revolution and his modest criticism of it—about revolutions made and revolutions lost. He told me he had been thinking about what he had said, about what impressions he might have left me with. I suspected he wanted to revise his observations, to smooth and polish them a bit, or, worse yet, ask me not to write about any of it. I began to worry.

"No one is happy in Cuba," he said. "Between Cubans we might agree that Fidel is crazy, but that's when we are upset and angry, because it's very hard and difficult right now. It's not an easy road we have chosen. Cuba is standing alone. It's not an easy trail. Now after more than thirty years we have a time on the trail when we pause and say, 'I am tired.' That is how I feel now. Tired.

"But when you were here and we began to talk, I said to myself, *This person is a friend of my country and a friend to Paulo, so I must answer his questions,* and your questions made me think. When I tried to be fair in my answers, your questions brought back to me all the reasons the Revolution is important and must not fail. That is what your questions did for me. Reminded me during this difficult time why I am for the Revolution still. Yes, still for it.

"I know that Paulo told you how he feels about the Revolution now, told you that he and I talked all night when he returned from Santiago. I am very happy about that, so happy. His mother and I were very worried for him before, I can't tell you how worried. I never asked Paulo to believe everything that I do. But I wanted him to love this country, this Cuba. Sometimes we thought he might try to get to Miami by boat or something like that. But now we are relaxed. We have Paulo back.

"And there is something I want you to have, something to show you my appreciation," he said, extending a small, rigid cardboard folder as my worries vanished.

Inside was a black-and-white photograph of Che, the familiar image seen on every poster and postcard and billboard and revolutionary artifact that honors the fallen hero, the one in which Che looks off to his right, wearing a black beret with a star, a leather tunic, and that expression of defiance and saintliness, of resolve and humanity—the image that Che carried into a youthful grave, and into an adoring place in history. The picture was exactly the one seen so often, only Víctor's print was of professional quality, a beautiful, high-resolution, black-and-white photograph that set it apart from the ordinary.

Then I noticed something else. There was a signature at the bottom.

I looked at the picture, then glanced up at Víctor in confusion and with a creeping apprehension as Víctor began to speak. In 1960, a photographer friend of his had taken the original picture at a rally in Havana, and it had caught hold of the Cuban imagination for the same reason any photo finds an enduring place in a society—the ability to capture an essence as well as a likeness, to capture a spiritual substance as well as a physical image. The people loved the photo because in the face of their hero they found an emotional expression of their own mood and that of revolutionary Cuba—a defiance filled with purpose.

At a subsequent meeting between photographer and subject, Che autographed twenty copies, including the one Víctor handed to me that Havana evening.

In an act of uncommon generosity, Víctor presented to me that object of such personal importance and national symbolism, asked me to accept it so we might honor what Paulo had come to value about Cuba, to honor what Víctor loved about his Revolution, and to honor our new friendship, bound with its shared ideals.

That gift stunned me. I was unsure what to say or do. I stood there at a loss for words, with tearing eyes, nearly swept away by the memory of Víctor telling me that the Revolution meant "everything" to him, that Che had been *his* inspiration for joining the literacy program as a twelve-year-old child, that Che had been *his* inspiration for lifelong volunteer service to the Revolution. And there was Víctor giving me with outreached hand the most dramatic image of that Revolution preserved in its most intimate form.

I did not see how I could accept such an offering, yet I could find no way to say no to Víctor's gesture of friendship and gratitude, and in truth, I did not want to. I was stunned by the gift, the treasure of that picture, but I was absolutely overcome by that moment of fellowship, the true treasure of that Cuban evening. So I accepted the picture with words of thanks that were as true as the moments Víctor sought to honor. I did not know what else to do.

But I did know that Cuba and Cubans had taught me some things, had shown me a great deal for which I was grateful, including the pure, true fact that a people possessing a grand purpose can preserve admirable forms and traditions even as they look with worried eyes at a national crisis and an uncertain future. In that society, among that mix of people who had been pushed and pulled in so many ways since the start of the "special period," Cuba had preserved a faith and trust in the Virgin of Charity, her black patron saint; a faith and trust in Santa

Barbara, a Catholic saint, and in Changó, her Santería counterpart; a faith and trust in Che, the hero of a "godless" Revolution; and a faith and trust in her own generous spirit, even when there was so little to spare. And that is the true test of a society—the ability to hold fast to its best values when they have grown scarce.

So I accepted the picture of Che—as I had accepted the medal of the Virgin of Charity, as I had accepted the many gifts that Cuba had offered me—with gratitude and appreciation, with a hope that Cuba's generosity would not be misplaced and that the future would be as kind to her as she had been to me.

Gold and Scandals

MAY 1997

Havana Gold

Things are good, Peter. Better than ever," a dramatic Paulo reported as he grabbed one of my bags and directed us out of the airport. "Really good, for me. I'm making business, buying and selling gold—coins, watches, bracelets, rings. I am not making a lot of dollars, not getting rich, but I make enough to have a nice life. To buy rum, to pay for dates, have a good time, and take care of my car. I do okay. Not everyone is pleased. Those who have no job, no way to make dollars or something like that, they are unhappy. They don't know what is happening, I think. Don't know the changes that have come to Cuba. But my life is good. Really. Come on, let's get going, I'll show you." And off we went, first to the Miramar garage apartment I had stayed in during the previous trip and then for a drive around Havana.

"It's all really interesting. As soon as people began to make dollars with businesses, other things started to happen too. People had money to spend. All of a sudden expensive things came into big demand."

Particularly gold jewelry, left hidden under Cuba's mattress for more than thirty years. Hidden away for lack of a political sensibility that tolerated buying or selling much of anything, including gold, especially gold. And hidden away because a cultural embargo had tainted the flashy conceit of an earlier life, an embargo imposed by a society that cheered green army fatigues and untrimmed beards as symbols appropriate for a country poised at a new beginning, a fresh start made by a force of arms. In revolutionary Cuba, gold jewelry fell to a secondary place, an unseemly token to be buried away. But at the first moment the government economy relaxed and the society softened, gold jewelry hit the daylight of the marketplace, and then the government quickly stepped in to establish a state monopoly and a fixed price. In so much of new Cuba, regulation followed behavior.

In the case of gold, as was the case each time Fidel pushed another wedge into the old economy, some Cubans rushed in, busy and eager to wait in line to get the necessary licenses to buy or sell, to do something to make a dollar, to make a better life out of the "special period." But others stood back to look for the wiggle room in the margins, the not always legal opportunities that challenged the state for approval and profits.

"The government set up the Gold House; that's what we call it," said Paulo. "The Gold House. Anyone who wants to sell or buy something gold is supposed to go there and take what the government offers, or buy at the price it sets.

"I do this with a partner. We got together all the money we could. Sold things. Everything. Borrowed money. Did anything to get dollars. Now we hang out near the Gold House. We come and go, but spend a lot of time around there every day. When we see someone not from the neighborhood, we ask them if they are on their way to the Gold House. If they want to sell, we look at what they have; if we like it, we offer maybe ten percent more than the government will pay. Then we try to sell for another ten percent, or maybe more.

"I don't always shop around for the best prices. I just try to buy and sell quick. Sometimes we do really good, but mostly we don't make a lot on each piece. Ten dollars here, maybe twenty-five there. But we do okay. I have some very expensive pieces at my house. One chain worth a thousand dollars, we paid six hundred for. But that's unusual. Mostly we have small items. I will show you."

"What will happen if you get caught?"

"Peter, don't even say that. I don't want to think about it. Go to jail probably. At least a big fine. A friend of mine got fined a thousand pesos for selling an Italian gold necklace at the Malecón *feria*. That's a lot of money."

The government was cat's-pawing its way into a new national economy that defied precise characterization in the apocalypse of the post–Cold War world, and along the way it possessed little patience with those citizens who moved along the razor-sharp edge of commercial offense against the state. Without hesitation, without reservation, the government regulated, then clamped down to make certain it got its declared cut for the pinched-thin national treasury. It was in those slippery margins of economic change that Paulo had made his niche.

The business of gold filled Paulo's days. People telephoned the family apartment hoping to get together with him—rock stars, *jineteras*, *paladar* owners, anyone with dollars who wanted everyone else to know they had the cash to own gold, the time-honored, near-universal adornment that said *I've made it.* Some callers wanted to buy, others needed to sell, turning the four-room family quarters into a communications center and a drop-in business office that Paulo returned to several times a day to check messages patiently taken by his mother. Out on the street, people tooted their car horns or called out from the sidewalk for him to pull over so they could wheel and deal. For some customers, Paulo drifted the car over to the curb, got out to embrace or shake hands, to smile and chat, before getting down to it. Business. For others, he sat patiently, letting them make the approach, and then worked quickly. All business. We drove here and there through Havana's busy streets, to look, to buy, to sell—not a lot, and not for big sums of money. Paulo's activity was driven by his restless energy and enthusiasm, always on the move. Some days the police were so conspicuous near the Gold House that Paulo and his compatriots who made up this underground gold trade just didn't go around there, waiting for the cops to leave, waiting for a safer day. Then back to work, scouting the sidewalk for customers.

Paulo was one of the many Cubans building a life along the soft edges of the postrevolutionary society. He made his living off the new economics, dealing in gold, driving tourists, serving as a translator, finding foreigners rooms or apartments for a piece of the rent. When a millionaire from the Cayman Islands flew in to buy building materials, Paulo pocketed several hundred dollars for his services as translator and negotiator in the purchase of thousands of dollars' worth of Cuban marble. "It was a good business," said Paulo, "but not much fun. This guy complained about everything. Never had a meal that satisfied him. Left a lot of food on his plate even at the best *paladares*. I was glad when he was done here and went home. Good-bye," said Paulo, with a big smile and a wave of his hand, as if someone he knew had just lifted off the tarmac.

Over the next couple of days we cruised through Havana in the LADA, now so well used and well worn that Paulo had to stop each day to put in quarts of oil that left a smoky trail behind us, like a cartoon car sending signals to mark our progress. We made our way to familiar spots, checking things out, talking, drinking cold beer against the spring heat, and getting back into form.

The Malecón market looked much the same, a colorful sea of umbrellas shading sales tables manned by anticipating Cubans surrounded by a mix of tourists and *jineteros*. But Paulo said there were fewer sellers because the government regularly raised the price of licenses, trying to squeeze a few extra pesos out of merchants and craftsmen, but instead squeezing some of them out of business, eating the seed corn of Cuba's first harvest of capitalism. Others had to shut down because new regulations required them to sell only Cuban-made goods.

At the Plaza de Catedral I found Francisco and Raúl still busy selling their art under the Museum of Education overhang, surrounded by another twenty artists, and the courtyard in front of them was filled with tables of arts and crafts where tourists stood shoulder to shoulder, looking, handling the goods, and buying, all in dollars. A German woman walked over to an unsuspecting Cuban artist and threw her arm over his shoulder to strike a pose for her husband with his point-and-shoot camera. A group of five or six Americans walked past, looking like a couple of generations on a family vacation, trailed by several small Cuban children, all under ten years old. The patriarch of the group, a man in his fifties with untrimmed black and gray hair and beard, his stomach stretching tight an Oakland Raiders jersey and protruding over Umbro soccer shorts, had grown tired of the kids asking for handouts.

"Speak English?" he asked one of them, the obvious ringleader.

No, replied the kid with a shake of his head.

"French?"

Another shake of the head.

"German?"

Yet another passive confession of inability by the young Cuban.

"Speak anything?" asked the American, in English, as he had asked all his questions, with a scoffing snort of self-satisfaction.

Telltale signs flashed out a Morse message: *Dollars and tourism have a gripping hold on Havana, so breathe and go with it.* Small but signifying changes tugged at the reluctant city trying to pull itself out of its frayed, 1950s look and form a caravan heading for a more modern time. New information signs of industrial design, painted in aesthetically intrusive colors, pointed visitors to tourist attractions—purple for Castillo de San Carlos and Plaza de la Catedral, a bilious green for Plaza de las Armas, and on they went, leaving bright smudge marks on Havana's historic vista. Guitar and accordion players at the cafés still weaved their way between tables to entertain, to serenade, but many of them had forsaken traditional Cuban or mariachi music, relying instead on the drawing power of American pop sounds. Troubadours played "Blue Moon" for a group of French tourists at a café that looked across at Morro Castle. A cell phone rang at the next table, another Cuban first for me. A man wearing a red wool watch cap on his head and a plastic garbage bag over his body pressed close to me to chatter what sounded like an uncontrolled babble of several languages. No one even noticed. Leaving the café I tossed a crust of bread from my sandwich to one of the many dogs circling the place, at least a half dozen of them nervously watching each other in a competition to reach any charity thrown their way. A quick-footed, skin-and-ribs creature won the race to poke at my scrap with its nose, then turned its head to look at me and moved on, leaving the bread where it had landed on the sidewalk. A cab driver sitting nearby said, "We think he's a government dog. Won't eat just any scraps, only something with meat in it."

A walk down crowded Obispo Street took us past department stores well stocked with clothes and appliances, and specialty shops, big-city style, with one devoted exclusively to sheets and comforters. Consider it: a store in Havana trading only in bedding, housed behind a newly redone storefront of freshly varnished wood and plate glass windows, a decidedly upscale enterprise compared to the bleached-out appeal of Old Havana's historical neighborhood. Stores along that once-weary street now sold delicate jewelry, supple leather shoes, and expensive crafts. Busy pedestrians looked in shop windows, pointed at merchandise in appreciation, and carried packages down the sidewalk. At some shops, business was so good that doormen controlled the flow of customers at the entrance, allowing only a limited number inside at a time. A group of uniformed schoolgirls in yellow skirts and white blouses passed by laughing and joking; each carried a book bag slung over her shoulder, a couple of them were eating pizza slices, and one was carefully counting dollar bills, as if her right to possess dollars was commonplace in Cuba's experience, rather then a radical change that was younger than the schoolgirl doing the counting.

Down the street, the Ambos Mundos Hotel—Hemingway's hotel for a time, which had been boarded up in neglect the first time I saw it in 1991—was freshly reopened after a loving restoration that was the hallmark of the new Cuba, when everything worked right. Its spacious front opened onto the sidewalk, providing a direct view inside. Behind a brightly polished slab of mahogany the bartender stood ready to take orders in a starched white coat. In the frayed and yellowed physical culture of Old Havana, that hotel lobby was absolutely gorgeous, an architectural delight achieved by the artistic application of subdued ceramic tile, stark metalwork, and gray chipped masonry, a symbol of Cuba's hope for a restored future, without a doubt, like a shiny nickel in a tarnished landscape. The lobby was dominated by a waterfall and a polished-steel-and-glass elevator so aesthetically pleasing it was transformed into a stunning piece of modern sculpture each time it rose up slowly to the twenty-foot ceiling and disappeared. We sat for a while just watching it, and once, when it remained idle for too long, I walked over to press the button for the fifth floor just to see it move once again before we went on our way.

Rooms ranged from $65 for a single and $90 for a double, not bad for a well-appointed place in the heart of the city, and a rate that qualified as thrifty compared to Havana's nicest, newest hotel, the Meliá Cohiba, with 462 rooms spread out over 21 floors overlooking the sea, where an extra bed cost $65 a night in rooms that started at $155 and ran up to $450 for a suite. Dollars, lots of them, commanded the lobby, the twenty-four-hour restaurant, and the overall atmosphere of the prosperous place, where the standoffish manner of the uniformed staff would have the experienced traveler remembering Paris or New York, not a country that less than half a decade ago was trying to figure out how to do business properly, hoping to made capitalism work for it.

Back on the street, a growing number of brightly lit *El Rápido* signs in red-and-white plastic offered just what you might expect: an overly friendly clerk in a peaked paper hat stationed behind a Formica counter, ready to serve fried chicken or a ham-and-cheese sandwich (for $1.80) from stainless steel bins positioned under infrared heat lamps, bringing the trashy look and enormously popular appeal of fast food into Havana and other parts of Cuba as well. The *Rápido* on the Malecón was attached to a twenty-four-hour service station that sold tires and batteries and did minor repairs, where the last touches of construction were being applied to a drive-through car wash and a sign promised that a car rental agency would be opening in the near future. The *Rápidos* had competition from the *Rumbos* chain. Under the motto "For your imagination 24 hours a day," uniformed clerks measured out sandwich makings on a balance scale and rang up purchases on a finger-touch cash register. Perfect. The future is now—and moving fast.

Just down from my apartment the air was filled with the sound of pneumatic jackhammers and the smell of construction dust where the familiar, ugly concrete building that had housed the Sierra Maestra *tienda* was being torn down, already replaced across the street by a new *tienda,* a full-service *Rápido* made up of several open-front metal stalls and two walk-in stores. Each of the eight stalls had a different commercial emphasis—perfume, soap, and notions at one; women's and children's clothes at another; food and drink at a third; and on down the line. One of the small stores sold groceries and household appliances—TVs ($137 and up), refrigerators ($450), gas ranges, boom boxes, stereos—the works, all stamped with a variety of national origins, except for "Made in the U.S.A." Each morning a patient line of customers waited for the *tienda* to open, to start doing business with a flash of fifty- and hundred-dollar bills, Grants and Franklins everywhere in Havana, even at the lunch counter. I normally arrived at opening time to get something to eat at the food stall, where I was naturally befriended by the day man, Carlos, who told me that his parents, two brothers, and his sister were all in the States. I asked him why he stayed in Cuba, given that all his family was gone, living in velvet exile in Miami. "I have five daughters to raise in Cuba. They don't want to leave. What can I do? I won't even consider the idea of abandoning them," he said casually, without lifting his attention from preparing my breakfast, and without a hesitation or a concern, suggesting the commonplace quality of deliberations about staying or going, about Cuba or Miami, about *patria* or exile.

At 9 P.M., the metal fronts of the stalls were pulled down and locked, the store doors were closed and bolted, the gates to the security fence surrounding the compound were pushed together and padlocked. Security, a concept once reserved for foreign relations with the United States, had spread into everyday life since the arrival of the "special period," tourists, and the dollar economy.

Small signs of a low-grade apprehension festered here and there, and small though they were, they were unmistakable, like sores on the surface of a not altogether healthy society. Havana exhibited a newfound appreciation for chain link fences, around *tiendas,* construction sites, shops and stores, cars parked in front yards and around many of the nicer homes, presumably with dollar owners. Chain link, sometimes only four feet high, was more symbolic than practical, but the symbolism certainly carried weight. Acting like characters on a late-night infomercial on U.S. TV, Habaneros faithfully locked red-and-black Clubs to the steering wheels of their autos, even on the older, lesser models; and in every public parking area needy gentlemen would offer to watch your car for a few pesos, working throughout the city like geriatric protection squads. Paulo never failed to attach his Club, or to give the freelance watchmen a nod when we arrived and a few coins when we left. Ambitious Cubans could enroll in a new school set up to train rent-a-cops, who could be seen at appropriate spots in their signature gray uniforms and Sam Brown belts, looking out from behind the chain link of private building projects and pacing the parking lots of hotels, reassuring weary visitors that their cars were under twenty-four-hour protection. Watermarks on the clear parchment of a wobbly culture, changes that seemed a bit odd at first, they were so new for Cuba, but that soon seemed predictable given the new national economics.

In this matter of security and cultural change, in this matter of an evolving Cuba—an evolution that did not always point to a better place—other firsts jumped out here and there: a bribe demanded and paid before we could get the rental car we wanted; a clumsy attempt by a state cab driver to boost a fare; a cashier turned shortchange artist, whom I awarded high marks for creativity but no cash prize; and several warnings by well-meaning Cubans to be careful about snatch-and-grab bandits on the streets. In many cities in the world such circumstances would not have rated a second glance or a moment's worry, except in Cuba, and now, not even there, not any longer. Some days it felt as though Havana were changing her skin.

At the end of a hot day of talking, driving, looking around, and drinking Sterling beer (Paulo refused Hatuey, saying it was not as good as it once was), Paulo dropped me off at the apartment before he headed out for a late date, set late enough, he told me, to be certain I would be worn out and done for the day.

When I leaned through the passenger window to say good night, Paulo said, "Peter, this has been a fine day. I'm glad you are back in Havana. What time tomorrow?"

"Early," I told him with a smile, knowing, as he did, that such a suggestion was more apt to entertain him than inform our schedule.

A Good Life

Paulo and I spent most of one morning driving his LADA from one car rental agency to another, trying to find an economy model for me to rent, finally deciding a $30 bribe was not such an impossible request after all; then, with the paperwork completed and the three tens having changed hands, we headed out of Havana for another road trip. Paulo's LADA was too worn for travel beyond the city limits. He had the $300 for the necessary ring job, but he lacked the patience to wait for the work to be done. When Paulo and I first met in 1992 his ambitions had been modest, limited to hanging out, practicing his English, and learning something about the States. But like Cuba, my friend had grown restless and edgy, and he was too dependent on his car for his business and his style as a fast mover to be without it, even for a few days of necessary repairs.

Paulo was eager to see a part of Cuba that was new to him, and he always became more reflective the further we traveled from the city, his friends, and his fast-paced life, so off we went in a miniature Subaru with less than a thousand kilometers on it. Paulo had never traveled to Playa Girón and was better acquainted with its reputation for good fishing off the breakwater than its place as a centerpiece in Cuba's history, so he packed his rods and tackle along with a few clothes, and we agreed on Playa Girón as our destination that day, some 150 miles from Havana.

By midafternoon we turned south off the central highway onto a secondary road surrounded by a lush green mangrove swamp, filled with wiry roots and branches, razor-sharp palmetto bushes, standing water, and presumably a tropical variety of reptiles. Our narrow road was one of just two routes into or out of Playa Girón, situated at the very tip of the Zapata Peninsula, a fact that led us to wonder out loud what the CIA and the invading force of Cuban exiles could have been thinking when they landed there, setting such a trap for themselves, with their backs to sea and facing 20 miles of swampy land sliced through by only two narrow roads.

When we arrived in the small community Paulo instructed me to drive around, past the Playa Girón Museum, a *Rumbos* eatery, a pharmacy, and the motel with a main building and a series of white cottages with red roofs looking out to the sea. Finally he had me pull over next to a young woman in a black spandex body suit, who after a smiling conversation with Paulo got into the car—onto his lap, actually—and then directed us to the local black marketeer, where Paulo negotiated for a tank of gas. The fixer at work. We dropped the young woman at the *Rumbos*, as she told Paulo where he could find her later that evening, and then we checked into the motel, dropped our bags in our cabin, and got out the fishing gear.

For the rest of the afternoon we stood at various spots on the long, winding breakwater that follows the shoreline down as far as the eye can measure, looking toward the bright red of the lowering Caribbean sun. The stone and concrete structure was interrupted by an occasional section that had collapsed into the sea, leaving behind ragged edges and gaping holes of fallen rubble and twisted lengths of reinforcing steel. Salt spray flew into the air each time a wave tried to force its way through one of the jagged openings. The breakwater is anchored at one end by a stone and concrete tower that rises two stories and casts a watchful face out to the sea. Built after the invasion in 1961, and still manned, day and night, more than thirty-five years later by young Cubans in uniform, today it has an enduring presence that is presumably more symbolic than practical, though not all Cubans would share that assumption.

We cast spinning gear into the small blue surf, moved here and there to each new spot where Paulo predicted with absolute certainty we would find fish. "Don't worry, Peter. I know about fishing. We will catch something." And we did, or to be more faithful to the truth, Paulo did, a five- or six-pounder that met with the approval of the local fisherman who had come over to watch, standing barefooted on the barnacle-covered rocks. Paulo gave his catch to one of the locals who had shared his live bait with us, and then off we went, in the early Caribbean evening, back to the cottage, where Paulo periodically broke into a satisfied grin before poking me on the shoulder and declaring, "I told you I was a fisherman."

We fed our sea-air hunger with ham-and-cheese sandwiches at the *Rumbos*, then walked around the small community, strolling like tourists. As we approached the museum, I noticed that the oversized sign celebrating the "First Rout of Imperialism in Latin America" was missing, disappeared from the front of the museum where Bob and I had posed for smiling pictures with Roberto and Eric in 1991. My imagination immediately took me to the most cynical place, and I wondered aloud if Castro's courtship liturgy with foreign tourists and dollars could possibly include the decision to remove that sign; I quickly dismissed the idea as absurd, only to have it return, a suspicion caught in the ambiguity of Cuba's identity as she headed into an uncertain future. Annoyed with my obsession over the sign, Paulo stopped a local couple and learned that it was down only for paint and repairs, for a cosmetic restoration, not a political recantation.

Back at the motel we wandered into the bar, where the staff was busy preparing for the arrival of a busload of Canadian tourists later that night. They mopped the already clean floor, tidied the already neatly arranged tables, and laid out oversized trays of sandwiches and fresh fruit on the finely polished wooden bar, then stood around, tugging and straightening their brightly patterned uniform shirts. When the tour bus pulled into the circular drive to stop at the broad glass front of the motel, a line of mostly middle-aged North Americans in sensible travel clothes and fanny packs began pouring out.

As soon as the first guest passed through the tall glass door, the hotel employees, positioned across the back of the room, broke into an awkward dance routine accompanied by a song of greeting so forced in its merriment that Paulo blushed in embarrassment and refused to translate for me. He shook his head, mumbled an uncharitable comment about country people, and lifted his chair to turn his back to the gathering in the lobby.

The scene was a self-absorbed parody of a resort director's idea of clever tourism practices, something that Woody Allen might put on film to make an audience squirm. For their part, the Canadians either appreciated the show or were too well mannered to reveal another opinion. A few sets of clapping hands politely greeted the end of the routine.

Paulo and I remained in the bar long after the last, bus-weary Canadian trudged off to bed. We sat around drinking dollar shots of seven-year-old Havana Club rum, and for the first time since my arrival, after several days of nonstop activity in Havana, we slowed down, cruised into neutral and finally to rest, lounging in the bar, deserted except for the barman on a twenty-four-hour shift.

Paulo was always patient when he had something of substance to say. Not coy, just thoughtful about time and setting, seeking out the right moment and the appropriate spot—like the late-night bar of the Horizons Motel at the Bay of Pigs.

"Peter," he said, sitting there with sun-reddened face, in baggy tank top, shorts, and top-of-the-line Nikes, "you aren't going to believe what's happened. I don't sometimes myself, when I think about it. You remember the house we drove to where I took the food to the old lady, Tita? It's really a nice place, don't you think? Big, too. It needs a lot of work, but it's a great house. Well, it's supposed to be mine, but the government claims it."

The house, located on the northern edge of Havana and suffering from terrible neglect, had belonged to his grandfather, Frank's father, whose holdings in sugar lands and other property in Oriente Province had made him a rich man. He had been an early supporter of Castro's and a long-time friend as well, a friendship that had protected the family property even when the revolutionary government began wholesale confiscation of agricultural lands. "We have a lot of pictures of my grandfather with Fidel. They were really good friends. My father's family lost nothing after the Revolution. Frank had all you could ask for—a big house, car, motorcycle. But he was still unhappy."

Paulo explained that after a time his grandfather sold all his holdings in Oriente Province and bought the house in Havana. Family legend has it that he chose that house because it was close to Fidel's own residence.

"My father still had everything even after they moved, but he left for the United States anyway. Now I understand that he is just an unhappy person, but I don't know why.

"My grandfather stayed in Cuba. A couple of years ago before he left for a visit to Miami, he sold me the LADA, for $2,000. Really a lot of money for me. I sold everything I had. Clothes, my half of the fishing boat, my fishing equipment. I borrowed from friends. I did everything.

But that's okay. I love my car, really love it. But $2,000. That's a lot of money."

On another visit to Miami, Paulo's grandfather died. Both grandparents had agreed that the house would someday be Paulo's, but Grandfather never filled out the documents to make the transfer legal.

"Now," said Paulo, "the government claims that the death certificate we got from Miami is not valid under Cuban law, so they say the house belongs to them.

"I have spent a lot of money trying to get the house back, but I think I will get nothing.

"The only hope I have now is that the Catholic Church wants to buy the house for retired priests to live in. They are fighting with the government for me; they say they will do what they can even if I don't want to sell to them. But I don't think I will get the house. I can't fight the government. They do what they want.

"It's really a nice place. You were there. You saw it. The whole family could live there, easy. That would really be nice. You could have your own room when you visit."

Was there something to be done from the States, I asked, but he said everything had been tried or was being tried, and he did not seem to want to get into the details, so I let it drop, discouraged for him.

I asked him if the incident about the house had made him unhappy about Cuba, about the possibilities for his life, the way he had been when I visited in 1995. He seemed surprised at the question.

"No, I don't think so. I would love to have the house, for me and my family to live in. Anyone would. It's so much bigger and nicer than the apartment we have. But what more can I do? I'm doing everything I can. We'll see. But that doesn't make me unhappy about everything else."

"Paulo, the reason I asked is that Michelle—you remember, the person I sent to see you last year—came back to the States and told me she thought you had 'an unhappy and unfulfilled life.' Those were her exact words, 'an unhappy and unfulfilled life.'

"She made a big deal out of how miserable you were and how sad she found that. More than once she used you as an example of how difficult things were in Cuba, so I've been curious, and worried, wondering what was happening with you."

"Peter. That is crazy. I can't believe she told you that. She doesn't know me. She called me when she came to Havana, said she had talked to you, that you had given her my number and something you wanted her to give me. I got together with her to drive her around Havana for an afternoon and then we went to a couple of places one night, but that's all. I never told her anything.

"I don't know why she would say that to you. She came to Cuba to attend a conference outside Havana. Afterward, when she told me about it, she mostly talked about things she saw that made her sad about Cuba. I just listened. Didn't say anything about it because I think she's like Frank, never happy herself.

"I love my life. Love Cuba. I make my business, hang out with my friends. I party on the weekends with Cuban women. I love Cuban women. Never go with the tourists. Never.

"I have a good life. I don't know how Michelle could say what she did to you.

"I think some people come to Cuba to find our unhappiness. They can only see what we don't have. The things that make life in Cuba different from the States, as if there is only one way to make happiness. I think that's what Michelle did, like a lot of people do.

"That's not about my life. I know people who have much more than I do. Nice car, nice house, lots of dollars. But they make themselves unhappy. I chose not to. I chose to make a good life for myself.

"I've been lucky. No, really. I think so. I work hard. You've seen. You go with me, so you know. But I couldn't be happier. Sometimes I worry that it will all end. But if it does, okay. Okay. I will make another life."

Paulo revisited our conversations during the time when his father wanted him to move to the States, claiming that it would have been the worst decision of his life to go to Miami when Frank wanted him to. Then he told a story that was making the rounds in Havana, working its way up to the status of legend.

"I have one friend who went to Miami. He came back for a visit as soon as it was allowed, and once he got to Havana, he refused to leave. The government took him to jail when his visa expired, came after him and put him in the immigration jail. He told the officials the only way they could get him out of Cuba was to kill him first. It was talked about all over Havana. Many people thought he was nuts. But they also understood. That's what it's like in Cuba now for many people. Crazy to stay, crazy to go. It's not as easy as yes and no. Not as easy as that. Not as simple as what people in the States think.

"The government finally just gave up on that guy. After three weeks they let him out of jail and let him stay in Cuba. He's still in Havana. Kind of a celebrity for defying the immigration authorities and winning.

"He told me that in America he knew no one. No one spoke to him. No one looked him in the eyes when he walked on the sidewalk. He was really unhappy. Told me that drugs and violence and racism scared him, a lot."

Paulo reminded me again that he had seriously thought of going to the States.

"What stopped you?" I asked.

"Peter, you remember that when we talked I asked you about a car, a house, a boat for fishing? I kept thinking about those things, making myself unhappy.

"Later, I asked myself, What do I want my life to be? When I got that answer, I knew I could never leave Cuba, never leave my family, my country. I love Cuba. Cubans. The way we are with each other.

"It would have been a terrible mistake for me to go there. Things aren't great here, but you know things are better than when we met. Better even than when you were last here. A lot of people are unhappy; they just wait for something to happen. Many of my friends are like that. But I chose not to be. I chose to make my life. Make it in Cuba, with my friends, with my family.

"I am embarrassed now the way I felt about Cuba when we talked about leaving for the United States. I don't know that person. It's not me. Not now. You were a big help by being honest with me. I might have gone to Miami. It's possible, I think. What a mistake for me," he trailed off.

It was after 2:00 A.M. when I signaled to the dozing bartender for a tally so Paulo and I could quit the empty bar, leaving behind our depleted conversation. The next morning we headed for Trinidad, a colonial city with wonderfully preserved architecture that Paulo had only heard about. We headed north out of Playa Girón after a late start to the brilliant spring day.

As we headed up the gentle rise away from the marshy sea plains into the mountains, Paulo had me pull over to the side of the road next to three men sitting under a tree, apparently waiting for a ride. They came over to the car in response to Paulo's question about directions. We had earlier collected contradictory information about the condition of roads and bridges along the three possible routes to Trinidad. We wanted to get it right before we committed.

Bent low to the passenger's window of the small car, the three men jockeyed for best position and for Paulo's fullest attention while talking in an overlapping chorus of Cuban enthusiasm. One would begin, only to be interrupted by another, and then the third, unable to hold back, would jump into the discussion. They looked at us to measure our comprehension and at each other for agreement, but the discussion rambled on with rising volume and intensity. Paulo found an occasional small space to interject a question that only cranked everything up another notch. Suddenly one of the men pointed down the road to announce that the truck they had been waiting for to take them home was leaving. His alarm was properly given but ignored for some Cuban reason, perhaps because of an obligation to travelers, perhaps because they were having so much fun. Either way, none of them wanted to abandon their station or responsibility, they just kept at the nonstop discussion, which by now sounded like the start of a fierce argument or at least a passionate disagreement among friends.

With excited voices they all agreed, with great detail and animation, that of the three possible routes to Trinidad only one was a safe, sure highway in a Cuba characterized by a worn-out and potholed infrastructure. It was the longest route, heading north back to the central highway, east to Santa Clara, and then back south again to the coast, some 135 miles to cover a straight-line distance of less then 60 miles. A more direct route along the gentle coastline had been eliminated as a possibility some months back when a bridge collapsed, reduced to rubble, waiting patiently for repairs that no one thought would begin anytime soon. The remaining alternative arched in the shape of a soft quarter moon across the Escambray Mountains, a toss-up in distance between the other two, but not in safety according to our guides.

The mountain road was too dangerous. Their agreement was unanimous, and loud. They didn't travel it. Knew no one who traveled it. And they insisted that we not travel it. "*No, no, no. Muy peligroso.* Muy *peligroso,*" they exclaimed, one after another. Very dangerous.

For reassurance and clarity in the discussion that I knew would soon follow with Paulo, I asked the ringleader one more time, "Is the road too dangerous to drive under any conditions?"

His answer, a long, drawn-out, emphatic "*Sí,*" was punctuated by his tossing his hands in the air to indicate that he had already said as much, in as many ways as he could possibly imagine.

"Peter," said Paulo, having made up his mind, "we will take the mountain road. It will be fine. I don't think these guys drive very much. Probably don't really know the road at all. Trust me. We will go the mountain way," tracing his finger over the route on the map spread out before us.

I asked Paulo if maybe we shouldn't pay attention to what those guys had to say given that they lived and worked at the base of the mountain. I also confessed that I didn't like mountain roads that were well maintained and absolutely safe, particularly those characterized by steep drop-offs and sharp curves, which our guides had promised on that road—and more, much more.

"Peter, come on. Let's get going. We need to be in Trinidad"—which was of course a lie, Paulo's way of turning my own obsessive behavior against me. We didn't have to be anywhere, but off we went, heading up the gradual incline toward the misty peaks of the Escambray Mountains with me protesting that if I didn't like the road I was certainly going to turn around and head back, no question, to which Paulo smiled and shrugged, knowing, he later told me, that I was too much the compulsive American to waste time covering old ground, even when time wasn't an issue.

The narrow road offered a fine drive for a few miles, rising gradually through modest turns and leisurely switchbacks that carried us into the enveloping green of the mountain forests, the indescribable green of the tropics, past an occasional farm stamped into the side of the mountain, with thatch-roofed buildings, small patches of cleared fields, and grazing goats and cattle. A man with sun-blackened arms and a face hidden under a broad straw hat, with leather traces around his neck and heavy reins in his hands, walked behind a mule and a plow, etching dark brown chevrons in the green uniform of Cuba's landscape.

As we headed up a steep grade we came upon an oversized red sign, its size and color unmistakably chosen for emphasis, for a clearly thought out matter of local if not national concern: DANGEROUS ROAD NEXT 23 KILOMETERS.

I pulled over to the side of the road and parked next to the sign. But before I could say a word, Paulo got in a preemptive strike, "That sign is very faded, probably very old. I am certain the road has been repaired some since it was put up."

In what I knew to be a useless protest, I asked Paulo if he thought that our road was the only one in Cuba blessed with repairs in the past decade. And if so, if it was so safe and well maintained, why hadn't we seen another car or truck since we started up the mountain? There had been nothing moving, except for us.

"Probably means nothing, Peter. Let's go."

So we did, climbing into the mountains for the next two and a half hours, on a skinny blacktop road pockmarked with muddy brown potholes, some of a size that could easily have swallowed the tiny Subaru. More than once we rounded a turn to find half the road gone, disappeared, fallen away to reveal a steep incline of treetops and construction rubble that traced a path to the valley floor below.

Very scary, and not at all to my liking. At each such moment Paulo offered the same lighthearted remark: "Is this what those guys meant when they said the road was dangerous?"

Sometimes, though, we simply stopped in the middle of the forsaken roadway, one of the many constructed since the Revolution to connect the agricultural peasantry with the rest of the nation, to look out over stunningly gorgeous vistas of mountain peaks and foothills, magnificent emerald panoramas that Paulo had never seen before.

Then, as we arched the Subaru around a sharply angled downgrade switchback, the vista changed abruptly, with mountains transformed into flat farmlands again, and beyond that, on the horizon, a razor-thin blue strip of ocean, prefaced by the dotted rooftops of Trinidad. The sweat on my hands dried, the blood brought color back to my white knuckles, and as we hit the main road into the city a thoughtful Paulo commented how lovely his country was and how thankful he was for the day.

Our plan was to stay the night in Trinidad, to just look around the city I had visited in 1991 only long enough to add to the local lore by starting a balloon riot. That had been an unimaginable six years past, a fast-paced stretch of time during which Cuba had transformed herself beyond the possibilities of my imagination.

We pulled into town, drove around a bit, then found a sidewalk café. We were noticed. Glances. Then stares. Not unusual, particularly outside Havana. My meal was delivered and sampled—blood-red, raw chicken that smelled bad to boot, which I pushed away, which Paulo also tested and rejected, chicken so foul that I told the waiter-owner not to return it to the table no matter how long he cooked it, an instruction he accepted without apparent insult. "Paulo," I asked, "do you think it's possible we weren't the first customers to refuse that chicken?"

"Peter, it's Cuba. Anything is possible."

While Paulo and I joked about the food, four guys at a nearby table maintained a red-faced and steady curiosity over a nearly empty bottle of rum. They looked, they talked. They looked some more, they talked some more.

On they continued until one of them pushed back his chair to approach our table with a stub of pencil and a small piece of paper in his extended hand, to ask, "Will you draw the tattoo on your upper arm, explain to me please what it means, tell me where you got it, and will you be offended if I get one like it?"

I told him, "I can't draw a line; the tattoo represents the logo on my first Harley Davidson motorcycle, so has sentimental value for me, but if you wish, it's yours to copy and have as your own."

My new Cuban friend pulled a chair to my side and began to sketch the tattoo, praising it and touching it as he drew the lines, erased his mistakes, working with the thoughtful concentration of an artist. His three buddies, wearing an assortment of baggy pants and shorts, floppy shirts, and running shoes and sandals—the uniform of island life—drifted over to watch, as did a couple of other guys, and then a group passing by on the sidewalk stopped to join the expanding circle of curiosity. I admired an elaborately worked and finely shaded green dragon tattooed on a calf, which was drawn up for my closer inspection, and then one after another each of the young Cubans lifted up a pant leg, rolled up a sleeve, or pulled off a shirt to expose a forearm, a biceps, a calf, a thigh, an ankle, a back, or a chest to show off ink work—a dragon, a snake, a scorpion, a heart with a knife in it, and a barbed-wire ring around a biceps, the international male tribute to testosterone.

Several of the guys had pierced ears as well, and I realized that both tattoos and earrings had suddenly become common among men in Havana. But even so, plentiful or not, one change among the many, that was Havana, and here we were in Trinidad, far from Havana and Santiago, Cuba's two urban culture points.

A single local artist was responsible for every one of Trinidad's tattoos, a man of true art, I was told, who would do a wonderful job on any challenge to my inspiration for just two dollars, a tempting price, if not a tempting offer. Paulo was surprised to learn that a Cuban was responsible, and he reported that an Italian had a near monopoly in Havana, except for the homemade jobs, which were plentiful and easy to spot, he noted with disapproval.

Then he turned and said to me in very fast English behind a laugh, "Tattoos and earrings. What is Cuba coming to? I remember when someone their age could get into trouble for wearing a Beatles T-shirt." His remark of reminiscence, spoken by a twenty-five-year-old, suggested the nature of accelerated change in Cuba.

"Remember when we first met? I didn't think it was a good idea for you to come to our apartment and park the rental car out front. I was worried about that. Only five years ago. Hard to believe, don't you think?"

When I asked the young crowd how it could be possible that in the suddenness of a transforming flash they were so at ease with these changes, with the iconoclastic idea of men wearing earrings and having tattoos—to say nothing of accepting both as distinguishing features of their hip culture—they said, *TV, MTV,* the international franchise for what's cool and what's not, the universal operation of young ideas and affectations that separates one generation from another, that sets the standard for who's out front and who's dragging ass in the contest between cultures. And there in Trinidad, one of the oldest cities in the New World, a group of young Cubans, tattooed and pierced, inked up and punctured, demonstrated the power of raw culture, a force with sufficient might to corrupt the innocence of geography and language, more powerful than the competing ideologies of Cuba and the United States, proving once again that the cultural travel time to Miami's hip South Beach is pretty short. MTV—too big to miss.

One of the spokesmen asked why we were in Trinidad.

"No reason in particular. Just visiting," I said.

The group grew excited, hoping to persuade us to stay so we could see the place at night, to appreciate the new, revised Trinidad. With great dramatic affect one said, "It's changed a lot since you were here last. Come on, let us show you. It's great. A lot to do. Bars and clubs. Things to see that weren't here before. We can find you a room and a meal for eight dollars, then we can have a good time. Believe us. It's very different now. A lot of interesting things to do."

And by the looks of them standing there red faced with rum, with their earrings and tattoos, I was certain they were correct. At least correct that Trinidad was a changed society, a place revised and reconstituted by dollars, tourists, TV, and a restless generation. Of course it was, just as Cuba was a on the move, changing so fast it required a new appraisal each day to keep an accurate account. But we had changed our minds about staying the night.

Paulo was in a fidgety state, his natural condition heightened by a lack of faith that Trinidad's night life offered much, whatever the hopeful promises of its young citizens, so off we headed for Santa Clara.

An effortless country drive of some 60 miles ended in a maze of narrow, winding streets, many of which dead-ended at ugly concrete barricades that prevented cars from accessing a beautifully refurbished town square, characterized by smooth cobblestone streets, freshly painted stucco buildings, and fancy iron grillwork. All very nice, very clean. The stuff of postcards.

We parked illegally over the protest of a diligent local citizen then walked through the square for an inspection, which satisfied Paulo, who suggested I go back to sit with the car while he made arrangements for a room at the Santa Clara Libre, a small renovated hotel that sits on the edge of the open square. A good plan. We were tired, worn down by the day's driving with not enough food and too much rum the night before; we probably should have stopped for the day in Trinidad.

Paulo returned a few minutes later to say the hotel had empty rooms, at a rate of $27 a night for the two of us, which seemed reasonable. But we needed to go back together because the desk clerk was a bit hesitant about letting a Cuban register. So off we went, into the dark, wood-paneled lobby, empty except for a gray-haired woman behind the front desk, whose only greeting was her disapproving countenance.

Before Paulo could speak she took command of the situation with a set of prohibitions that were delivered from behind the heavy wooden registration desk that she leaned over, slightly bent at the waist, hands planted palm down and elbows locked tight, as if to announce that we should measure her determination by the contentiousness of her posture and then be on our way.

"Cubans are not allowed to stay here," she stated. "The rules are clear.

I have no authority in this matter. There was a notice just the other day about this. There is nothing I can do."

I fumed. Paulo just smiled. And then he assumed his most characteristic attitude, one that I much admired and had watched develop in the years since we first met, during the time he moved from his teens into young manhood—a belief that he could make things happen, his confidence that very little was beyond his capacity, that no problem was too grand, and in this instance, no restriction too severe. He charmed, he coaxed, he explained. He introduced me as a writer from the States, on my fifth visit to Cuba, a friend to their country with whom he traveled as guide and translator; then he flashed his plastic-laminated University of Havana card certifying his English proficiency as proof of his status. He explained that we had stayed in hotels across the island and back, and more than once, producing his guest card from the previous night's hotel at Playa Girón to certify that point. He made his case and documented it, but the woman was unbending, without a change in facial expression or a word spoken in her defense, until finally, just as Paulo asked to see the manager, I told him, "Fuck it, let's go. I don't like this. We don't have to put up with such shit."

Paulo tried to slow our descent into chaos by insisting that it would turn out fine, but I was out the door, muttering in protest, and he followed, telling me once again, "I could have handled it by talking to the manager. Everything would have turned out as we wanted." But by then I was in a pissy mood, tired and hungry and not inclined to watch Paulo charm his way into what should have been his by birthright and the common decency among citizens.

Back at the car and fumbling our way around the tensions I had caused, we found a courtly black gentleman smoking a big cigar who casually told Paulo he had seen me before in Cuba, who pointed our way to a motel outside of town, an accommodation he was certain accepted Cubans. We drove right to it, into a parking lot with four big tour buses unloading passengers, a parking lot ringed by glowing safety lights perched upon tall aluminum poles, a parking lot consecrated by a sign that promised security guards on duty twenty-four hours a day for our protection. The messy scene just set me off again: "Ah, tourism; ah, yes, the class struggle of petty theft from parked cars. Welcome to Cuba's future, which today looks a lot like her fuckin' past."

Paulo was uneasy, never having seen me act quite that way before, at least not without a bit of ironic humor mixed into my sardonic observations. We fell out of the car and made our way to the lobby, waited patiently for our turn at the front desk, only to be told by a dull-eyed clerk, "NO CUBANS."

Paulo shrunk ever so slightly before righting himself and asking to see the manager, a request delivered before I could get in a word. As the woman walked away, Paulo said simply, "Please let me handle this."

"Okay."

"Promise?"

"Jesus, yes. I promise."

A bright-faced, smiling manager who could have been a classmate of Paulo's entered the lobby, shook our hands, and listened attentively to Paulo, nodding his head in understanding and sympathy. But he insisted nonetheless that the decision was out of his control, that Fidel had given a speech just the previous day that restated the rules, actually expanded and tightened them. The rules were clear and unshakable. Paulo was not allowed in a room, not as visitor, not as paying guest, not as collaborator with the visiting writer from the States.

Paulo started in once again, showing his university card, pulling out the guest card from another hotel in the same chain, but the manager, still smiling, still pleasant, still terribly patient with my friend's pleas and protests, was unshakable.

I whispered to Paulo, "Tell him I'm doing a book. Ask him if this is the face he wants me to put on the Revolution, under his name in print as manager of this hellhole?"

"Peter, he knows about the book. You heard me tell him that already."

"Paulo, look at the big picture of Che in his office. Ask him if he thinks Che fought and died for such behavior as this."

"I don't think that will do us any good."

"Paulo, tell that motherfucker that if we're forced to leave, I'm taking that picture of Che with me, ripping it off his wall. He has no legitimate claim to it. None. Tell him that."

"Peter, *please*. Remember, I'm the fixer"—Paulo's good-natured way of telling me to shut up and let him do his work, which I finally did, still fuming as I waited for the two polite Cubans to find a secure spot on the cultural balance beam between Revolution and tourism, which at the moment seemed weighted at a dangerous tilt.

The manager left us to go into his office with an older man who had the look of authority, shutting the door behind them to cut off our view of Che's picture and any possibility of our overhearing their conversation. When the manager emerged, he came with a smile and a handshake for the both of us, welcomed us to the Horizontes Los Caneys Hotel, and without explanation guided us to the registration desk where he instructed the dull-eyed clerk to take care of us.

Once in the room and showered, once fed and soothed by a cold beer sipped at the outdoor disco, which was a couple of hours away from cranking up for the evening, I tried to figure out the best way to clean up the mess I had made. I felt terrible. I had taken from Paulo his contribution to our collaboration, to our etiquette of mutual responsibilities. I had done something that required restitution and forgiveness, I had violated the rules of the road and in so doing had corrupted our friendship.

"Paulo, I am really sorry for being such a jerk at the Santa Clara Libre, for not leaving you be. It really pissed me off that such elaborate explanations were necessary for such a small accommodation—for letting you stay in a hotel, for Christ's sake! It seemed so out of proportion.

"I should have listened to you. Take some small comfort from the fact that because I butted in the first time, we had to drive out here, put up with the same shit again, and then pay double the price for our room over the Santa Clara Libre, a penalty for my behavior." Paulo smiled.

Then I told Paulo about the scene with Bob in the Tuxpan Hotel in 1991, how Bob had lost patience when Roberto explained that since Cubans weren't allowed to stay in tourist hotels, he and Eric would leave us to find other accommodations for the night. How standing in the Tuxpan lobby I had censored Bob, accused him by implication if not exact language of being a self-righteous liberal for not considering the possibility that Roberto and Eric found leaving tourist hotels an acceptable sacrifice to make for the Cuban Revolution in crisis. I told Paulo that story, feeling a rush of embarrassment over the smug comments I had made to Bob and embarrassed too for having just done the same thing, under identical circumstances.

"I don't know exactly my point in telling you that story just now," I said. "Might be my hypocrisy in dealing with Bob, or it might be Fidel's hypocrisy in dealing with the Cuban people, and particularly you, my friend."

Acts of Public Scandal

While Paulo and I were out on the road, Fidel spoke to the nation about the post-Revolution wreckage in Cuba's gritty slipstream of capitalism, especially its messier side—the *jineteros* and *jineteras*, the black marketeering, the sex for barter, the acts and attitudes that mocked government regulations, the people's willful attempt to squeeze the golden egg for their own benefit, legal or not. People like Paulo, in their pilgrimage for dollars, trampling messy footprints all over the flat expanse of the state-run economy, diluting respect for authority as they trudged ahead.

Fidel's speech was driven by a checklist of cultural and dollar-related offenses against the state and the sensibility of the Revolution, offenses that were, said Castro, shaming Cuba before the world, corrupting Cuba and undermining the Revolution by hindering the flow of dollars into the national treasury. Prostitution, drugs, unlicensed business activities, and "other acts of public scandal," Castro told the people, could not be tolerated, must be changed or eliminated.

By the time we arrived in Santa Clara, our room—every hotel room in Cuba, presumably—had a neatly printed card placed conspicuously on the bureau, with the following printed in five languages:

INFORMATION FOR OUR GUESTS

In Cuba, child corruption, possession and trafficking of drugs, sexual soliciting, obscene acts, and other acts of public scandal are severely punished by law.

The card was printed on hefty, high-quality white paper, with black ink superimposed over a pinkish colored circle with a line drawn through it, the international symbol for prohibition, used in some cultures to tell people, *Don't smoke, Don't park, Don't litter,* but used in Cuba, in that instance, to tell visitors, *Don't fuck our women* and *Don't mess with drugs, or we'll mess with you.*

It was no longer a mystery why Paulo could find no room at the inn, why the no-Cubans-in-the-room policy was suddenly being enforced so rigorously when we had never encountered it during our trip across the island less than two years before. But that was then, a different time in Cuba.

"Peter, I need to show this to my mother," Paulo said, slipping the card into his suitcase. "It's the first time I've seen or heard of something like this. I wonder if they're in Havana, too." By the time we arrived back there, they were.

"It doesn't surprise me that Fidel made that speech. Things have been going that way for some time. I think we need to go to Varadero Beach on our way back to Havana. You'll see what I mean. There has already been a real crackdown there.

"Starting months ago, I think it was, the police began to stop every Cuban, the women for sure, asking for IDs, sending away anyone who did not live there, making them leave town.

"Before then the whole area was full of *jineteras*. People were going there from Havana to be with the foreign men. It had great discos, good food, lots of shops, and a lot of foreign guys who came just to be with Cuban women. Since the police crackdown to keep out Cubans, not so many foreign men visit Varadero Beach, I've been told. The place has changed. Not so many tourists, or at least not so many guys as before.

"We should go there to see. And fish some while we're at it," said Paulo with a smile at the prospect of more fishing. "What do you think? I know a couple of really good spots. Places I used to go all the time before, when I was a fisherman, not a fixer," he said, amused at his skill in describing his transformed life.

So we did, heading the next morning out of Santa Clara back toward Havana, angling off for a side trip to Varadero Beach, a place I had not seen for six years. We approached along the downtown main drag, where the business community spread out on both sides of the street and exhibited those characteristics common to beach towns everywhere. Shops and restaurants—places to eat and places to spend—ranged from pizza joints and T-shirt shops to upscale dining establishments and pima cotton resort wear boutiques. But the eateries and stores, the streets and sidewalks, looked anemic, depleted from the lack of a Cuban presence and energy. Tall, blond mothers and fathers pushed trams and trailed small children behind them, speaking French, German, and Canadian-accented English, but the streets offered up only the occasional sound of Spanish, the local language having left the community, along with those Cubans forced out, taking with them the quickened pulse that had carried each night through to the next day's new light. Clubs and discos were nearly empty, gone quiet, leaving the rest of the town in much the same condition.

Paulo directed me onto a side street, up to a small stall with two wobbly plastic tables out front, where an elderly man with a three-day growth of beard and a sweat-stained shirt moved behind the counter with a musical precision. At one work station he pounded long, thick slices of beef with a wooden mallet, trying to tenderize the cheap cuts from Cuba's ranchlands; then, moving down the line to an oversized metal bowl, he dunked the pieces of meat into a marinade colored dried-blood brown and dropped them onto a hot grill, actually a slab of sheet steel laid over a two-burner gas stove.

Paulo had tempted me even before we arrived at Varadero Beach with stories of delicious steak sandwiches, telling me how he had looked forward to having one each time he hitchhiked from Havana to Varadero to go fishing, which sometimes took twenty-four hours in the years when gas was severely rationed and rides few and far between. We ordered and ate, then ordered another round, congratulating the old man on how good his sandwiches were. We decided they were as good as any food we'd eaten in Cuba, and we told the old man so, but flattered or not he refused to surrender the secret of his marinade.

Back in the Subaru we headed out of town to the beach area, where several more outrageously large hotels had taken their place beside the Tuxpan, once the ace of trumps in the card game of tourism, now reduced to the status of a lower-level face card. The under-construction Las Americanas caused us to stop and gawk in near disbelief, a five-star offering intended to lure one-stop foreign tourists. From the highway, the vast stone structure seemed an endless array of massive gables, with dozens of oversized sash windows spread in neat rows along the front. Startling for its size and its design, it looked very much like an engorged version of a Stateside millionaire's dream house, one so oversized and architecturally elaborate that no one would attempt to challenge the vanity of its presentation. Feeling as though Cuba had exhausted my expressions of disbelief, I hit the gas to speed through Varadero's hotel row without word or comment, heading for the highway to Havana, where we arrived early in the morning.

Fidel's speech had offered no real news to anyone who stayed tuned in to what was happening behind the official policies, particularly the young people who played and worked in Havana's streets. To their savvy thinking, all Fidel had accomplished was a grand announcement to the public, to the international press, to Cuba's visitors, of something that had been known to them for some time—change was churning from the top and falling on them with a force unknown in the past few years. Fidel announced as a national policy what Havana's youths had already experienced as fact—cops were on the move and heading their way.

Fidel wanted the *jineteras* and *jineteros* gone from Havana, just as he had wanted them gone from Varadero Beach, and having succeeded once, he figured it could be done again. So the Havana cops suited up and went to work, looking for infractions real and imagined, large or small, anything from solicitation to having no ID, from selling illegal gold to having no proof of employment. With gray shirts and blue trousers, with formal hats and heavy leather belts that held night sticks and pistols, they swept through the Malecón, taking away or driving away young women in body-hugging skirts and tight-fitting shorts who stood patiently, waiting, hoping for a car with a rental tag to slow, to stop, to take them someplace, away from the boredom, into a doubtful opportunity. And then the police went to the tourist hotels, the Havana Libre, the Meliá Cohiba, where they had gone countless times before, on a regular basis, to mingle among the dozens of youths outside, sometimes a couple of hundred at the Cohiba on a Saturday night, only this time they checked IDs and took people to jail, though some of them stuck around, using their unsmiling presence to keep the kids away, the *jineteras* away, to sweep Havana clean like their uniformed brothers had swept Varadero Beach clean.

"The tourist police are everywhere now," said Carlos, a *jinetero* I had run into on several occasions, who approached me each time he saw me to make the offer of cheap cigars, acting as if we had never seen each other before, as if I had not refused him repeatedly until the ritual became a standing joke and a friendly connection between the two of us. "They are really out of control. They took a friend of mine to jail. She was doing nothing. Nothing! Just standing there with her boyfriend. But they took her anyway. She was just in the wrong place. Happens all the time.

"Part of the problem is that a lot of country people are coming to Havana. Too many of them. Groups of three or four girlfriends, girls with their boyfriends, wives with husbands. They come to Havana. A bunch of them rent a room, a house. They become *jineteras* and *jineteros*. They say they are going to stay for a time to make money. To buy clothes, jewelry; to get some dollars. Some go back home, but a lot of them don't, until finally they're everywhere. And they aren't as experienced with the cops as people from Havana. They act stupid sometimes, and make it bad for everyone.

"Now the police are ending that," said Carlos with a sardonic shake of his head. "The problem is that a lot of other people are getting into trouble too. People who are doing nothing wrong, really. Just trying to have some fun, a good time. The police don't care. They're treating everyone the same just to get them out of the way.

"Let me tell you how bad it's getting. This is a new problem. The government can't hire enough police in Havana. Nobody will take those jobs. So the government is hiring guys from the countryside to come here to be police. These country guys don't know Havana, don't know much of anything. Don't know what's okay and what's not. That makes it really bad. Hiring cops from the country to go after people in Havana! It's bad, very bad."

Fidel's police had not solved a problem, had only blurred the perception of it, the obvious look of it, when they emptied the Malecón and the sidewalks surrounding the hotels, rid them of kids on the make—even those whose plans stopped at an invitation into the disco. The *jineteras* no longer gathered together in unmistakably obvious groups, weren't conspicuous during a drive or a walk through Havana. But they had not quit their ambition for a good time or their need for a few dollars. They had simply moved out of plain sight.

On weekend nights, the out-and-out dollars-for-sex *jineteras* could be found among the party crowd at Havana's discos, where everyone danced and drank to loud, nonstop Latin music and a revolving disco ball that sent sharp slices of light reflecting down from the ceiling onto the pulsating talent of Cuba's supple dancers. At that moment the upscale crowd, identified by long black dresses and gold jewelry, by a clear and obvious ability to put together an outfit dictated more by good taste than budget, favored the Comodoro disco, where the door charge was $10, a beer cost $5, and nightlong companionship ran $100. But in the tradition of the hip urban elites everywhere, they were a fickle group, not burdened by an enduring loyalty and capable of drifting to another nightspot without notice.

At the discos where the everyday young people went to drink, to dance, to hang out in relative security, away from the threatening presence of the tourist police, the door charge was $3 or less and beers a standard $1, the *Rápido* price. Those late-night places were not plentiful or easy to find—some of the best operated on the edge of the city—but they were not impossible to get to, if you had the proper attitude. The doormen were polite, the music great, the bar crowded, the dancing a hip-swaying, body-rubbing, nonstop testimonial to rhythm and passion. The *jineteras* appeared in numbers, dancing, having a good time, like everyone, not necessarily on the make as the evening's first purpose, yet always casting about a watchful eye for an opportunity. They were not set apart from the rest of the crowd, from their friends, their neighbors, their schoolmates, by anything in the distinctiveness of their appearance or by a coercive social formality. What distinguished them from the others was their willingness to go with a foreigner for thirty or forty dollars, an act for which those who chose to stay and close the place made no judgment.

Chased off Havana's streets by the police, the *jineteras* made a mass movement to escape from harm's way, out of the city to East Beach. That small community, about a twenty-minute drive from Havana, all of a sudden found itself overrun by kids looking for a good time. They rented rooms and houses, partied in newly opened clubs and discos, and made an open-air beer garden along the main drag their center of social operations and a nightly hot spot, crowded and noisy, busy with beer and dancing and flirting eyes.

Leonarda had been in Havana no more than a few months when the crackdown came, lifting her off to jail one night, scaring her so badly all she could do was cry and pray to the Virgin of Charity, promising anything, everything, to get out of the frightening mess she was in, and wishing she had never left her hometown of Camagüey, where she had been born and raised, where her family still lived.

Leonarda told me her story at the beer garden, speaking softly and making eye contact only reluctantly, presenting herself as small and frightened. "I didn't want to leave home. I really didn't have a choice. For five years I had been teaching school, first grade. I loved it. I loved the children and did a good job. All the parents and the other teachers said so. But there were new people in the school, and when the new people found out I didn't have a university or a teaching degree, they took my job. I was educated at school and by my mother, who was a teacher and very strict with me. You wouldn't believe how strict," she said, without a smile to soften the statement. "But they didn't care how much I knew or how good I was at teaching the children. They just *took* my job.

"There is no work of any kind in Camagüey. Nothing at all. So I had to leave. My mother couldn't afford to take care of me. And how could I let her? I am twenty-four years old. So I came to Havana and found a job working in a hospital. I'm a clerk; I file papers all day. I used to be a teacher. I should be teaching. I can't live on what I make. I have a single room and don't eat enough. I always feel hungry.

"I come out here sometimes with my friends. There's nothing for us to do now in Havana, and I'm afraid of the police there. We don't go after foreign men, but we want something to do at night. Have some fun. But it's such a long way, it's hard for us to get here. I would rather be back in Camagüey. With my family. I want my old job.

"There are a lot of girls here like me. From other places, sometimes from smaller places than Camagüey. It's good for me to be around them, makes me feel better. But not all of them are as unhappy as I am. Most of them came here to have a good time, to go to the discos and clubs. Just to have a good time."

I asked Leonarda what it would take to make her life good, to make her happy.

"Just a house to live in," she said. "It doesn't have to be big. Just a house, someplace to live. Today I don't have twenty dollars to pay my room rent."

Her friend Tania did not act so small. When we began to talk, her commanding presence and tone of voice drew a small crowd to the table who dragged up chairs from here and there, and when space around the table filled, a standing circle formed behind the chairs, a group of curious people looking for something to do to pass the evening.

Tania was one of several Cubans I met who wanted to know about drugs and guns in the States, a recurring theme that left me wondering about its origin, a bit suspicious that it might be part of an information program designed to rub some of the gloss off the ideal of living in Miami.

I was told more than once, usually with a laugh, *No, there's no government campaign to convince people that life in Miami is dark and dangerous. It's just something we talk about, want to know about, because we see the TV and wonder.*

Their curiosity and confusion about guns and drugs, it turned out, was based in a clash of cultures that made it difficult for Cubans to imagine city streets as wicked as many in the States, where kids as young as ten or twelve used handguns, where crack cocaine was so cheap and available and potent it had the unthinkable power to addict on the first rock, the first smoke, and seize control of someone with such a potency that only five to eight percent of those trying to quit managed to stay clean for more than five years.

"How can it happen," asked a disbelieving young man at the edge of the group, "that the government doesn't care about those things. How can drugs and pistols be so cheap, so available to anyone, even schoolchildren? Doesn't the government care? And what about people living in their cars? Do they just park on the street and live in them? That doesn't seem possible. It doesn't make any sense to me. Don't the leaders care? Or can't they do anything about it? It really doesn't make sense to me," he repeated.

"I don't care about guns or drugs," said Tania. "I don't care how dangerous it is, I would prefer the United States over Cuba. I would gladly spend all my time locked inside my American house, with my American TV, my American air-conditioning, my American stove and refrigerator, and my American pantry full of food. I would watch TV and eat. I want to be someplace else. Not in Cuba. Let them call me *la gusana,* what would I care, so long as I have a nice TV and lots of food in my American house?"

Tania's story was the story of much of Cuba—like Neddie's and Hazel's—a surrender, a fatalism, a dreamy-dream of a better life without any idea of how to build it, how to make it happen, aside from going to the States. The notion of a proper life was made up of ill-fitting parts—from television fantasies, from need and want, but not from big ambitions or grand goals, which seemed to be in sorrowfully short supply in that culture where physicians drove cabs on their days off.

Tania's Cuba restated attachments to the United States, perhaps even devotions, represented by the day-to-day appeal of dollars and by the grander ambition of life in Miami, a city where the worry might be about guns and drugs but the goal was still tempted with dreams.

Neddie and Luisa

I don't think it's right for foreigners to take advantage of Cuba," said the cab driver taking me to visit Neddie. "I don't like to see it. And I don't approve of Cubans who take advantage of everything they can. Those who are out for themselves and break the law when they do it. It's not right, not when so many Cubans are unhappy about something as simple as food."

My driver and social observer was an engineer by profession, married to a doctor. He spent his off hours driving his own car as a taxi accompanied by his five-year-old son, who cruised Havana's streets with his father and strangers.

"The government was right to make the *jineteras* leave the area around the hotels. It looks terrible. That is not a proper first impression for the foreign visitor who comes to the front of one of our nice hotels. I didn't like to see them. They make Cuba look very bad. We are not that kind of people. Not at all. We are not that kind of people," he repeated.

"May I ask you a question?" he continued. "I don't want to offend you, and please believe me that this is a serious question. Very serious. Not a challenge. I would like to understand the answer. Why won't the United States lift the embargo so Cuba can have a fair chance of making a new start? Why does the United States hate Cubans so much? How can we be that important? The government of the United States must have *un corazón negro,* a black heart, to want to make the Cuban people suffer so much."

I said that the reasons were many and complicated. The defeat at the Bay of Pigs and the showdown over the missile crisis had a lot to do with it. So did the fact that Cuba tried hard to take care of its people with programs of health care and literacy that embarrassed the United States by comparison. And then there was the fact that Castro had rejected all U.S. influence after the Revolution, and survived repeated CIA attempts to oust and assassinate him. The United States, I told him, was unforgiving of a leader who refused to bend to the will of five presidents while going his own Marxist way without regard to or fear of U.S. wishes. Cuba under Fidel, I said, was an insult to America's notion of her own might, her destiny as the most powerful nation in the world, and the most moral and virtuous one as well.

"That is not reason enough for the suffering the United States causes in Cuba," he said, falling into silence for the rest of the ride to Neddie's part of Havana and then accepting the fare and tip without comment.

Neddie had a slightly different view of Fidel's new regulations and the present state of Cuban affairs. "The blockade gives the government in Cuba a chance to evade internal responsibility. If the blockade is broken, the government would have to accept a share of the blame for what is going on, would have to answer questions like 'Where is the rice crop? Where is the sugar crop?' The way things are, the government can control things, but without the blockade there is no excuse for Cuba not doing well. People in Cuba must accept responsibility, I tell you."

I asked Neddie what she thought about the unarmed Brothers to the Rescue planes that had been shot down by Cuban MIGS, referring to the two small planes dispatched by a Miami exile group whose purpose was to search for rafters but who often went deep inside Cuban airspace. That day, they had been positioned within international limits when the Cuban air force sent them into the sea with a rocket attack.

"I think they were shot down by Castro to protect the blockade," she responded quickly. "It was a plan. Castro knew that not many people in Cuba were sympathetic to those planes. They had been flying over Havana. Sent by the exiles in Miami. A very foolish thing for them to do.

"Many people in Havana worried that it was a plot by the exiles so the United States government could have an excuse to make an invasion," she commented, repeating a worry that I had heard more than once from anxious Cubans who believe their enemies in the States are capable of anything. "I never thought that, but many Cubans did. Can I tell you this, though? I think Castro knows that Clinton and his wife are intelligent, and they would want to stop the blockade, would say to Senators Helm and Burton, 'Forget the blockade.' But Clinton can't act now, not after what Castro did to those planes.

"Fidel is a very clever man. He uses the blockade. And we suffer.

"I will tell you this, although it may surprise you. I support Fidel's speech. I support what he said. People who rent out their house or rooms to foreigners don't pay taxes. That hurts us all. They don't register guests. How do we know who they are? They might be Mafia, might be drug dealers, might be pornographers. We can't allow such things."

I asked Neddie if she knew of drug traffickers or child pornographers in Havana, in Cuba.

"I don't know for myself," she said. "Not about such things as you ask. But remember, that was not all the speech. The *jineteras* and *jineteros*, they must be considered too. Castro was correct to speak about them, to ask for change. They have a fine life, a high life made by illegal activity. They have color TVs, stereos, CD players, air-conditioning, and new carpets. They go to *Rápidos* all the time, pay twenty dollars to go to a club to dance and hear a band. They are full of gold necklaces, watches, rings."

"Neddie, I understand what you say. But should everyone who has a gold necklace and has the dollars to go to a *Rápido* be placed under suspicion? Dollars and gold are legal now. The government encourages economic activity."

"Some of what you say is true, Peter, but not all of it. You know that. The black-market cigars, the girls—they're not legal. I hope you're careful in what you do. Very careful, particularly now, after the speech. 'Be careful' is all I can say to you. It would not be good for you to be in trouble in Cuba. Who would help you? Not me; not anyone I know.

"But Peter, I'm not talking about the legal people, the good people who work hard. Not them.

"Now a lot of people live beyond their means in Cuba. I am told that Cubans who live in Miami talk about keeping up with Havana! How is that possible? Some of the Miami Cubans rent gold jewelry when they come here to visit so they don't look like they are doing worse than us. That's what I was told. Relatives in Miami who hear about the fine life of some Cubans write to say, 'Please don't waste the money we send. Buy only important things. Just what you need.'

"Our *jineteros* know all the tricks to get that kind of life. A normal citizen can't do anything, but the *jineteros* can do everything. I have never been to a *Rápido*. My mother wants to go to have an ice cream. Just an ice cream, nothing more, a simple ice cream. But I can't take her. I just can't. I don't have the money to go there, not even a dollar for an ice cream. We are that poor.

"Let me tell you," said Neddie, hanging her head and swinging it from side to side, "decent people suffer a lot, but the *jineteros* have everything. Do everything. They have the dollars made by illegal activity. Everything is in dollars. If you want something done, tell someone you have dollars. That's all it takes. Tell them you have dollars."

Neddie had found work at a primary school where she earned 226 pesos a month—about $10 or $12. And at that time Cuban coffee cost 30 pesos a pound, fish 25 pesos, and pork 28 pesos. Neddie was trying to get into the swing of the new Cuba, trying to buy and sell, but without much success. She sometimes made fifty cents or a dollar selling a dress for a friend or some fabric, but the mechanics of the process, the finesse of modern Cuban life, seemed to elude Neddie.

"It's extremely difficult," she confided. "Extremely difficult.

"If your friends come to Cuba, please have them see me. I will cook food for them. I will wash clothes. I will do anything to save money, to make dollars.

"I am just working to get by, and sometimes I can't even do that. I am exhausted, Peter. Exhausted. Life is very, very difficult. I get so tired. So tired. Like now."

Everything seemed to be tumbling down around Neddie, out of control and leaving her short on hope, and I couldn't help but think of her life in comparison to the lives of others I had met and talked with, had conversation with over the years on my trips to Cuba. Gracus, the actor from the park in Santiago, was most likely lost as well, doomed to sit, to wait, to drink rum before lunch, and describe himself as too close to the moon, driven half mad by his despair. And there were so many others like him and Neddie, weary people unable to get a clear view or small handhold in this society in transition, people who waited patiently, if sadly, for what they had grown accustomed to, had been taught to expect—salvation, provided by a government that could no longer provide what was needed, not direction, not even hope in their cases.

Others, even the angry Hazel—who sat in the café drinking coffee and waiting to do "business" that was never fully described to me, who had planned to leave Santiago by boat because she wanted a new life so badly—would be okay, would make her way if not her peace with Cuba. She was smart, tough, and determined. Hazel would be fine, if not altogether happy.

I was less certain about the street-level, fiercely loyal *Fidelistas* I had met. I worried about them the most. Like the medical student María, whose introductory comment to me was a pledge of trust in the Revolution and in Castro, María who refused to believe that most of Havana's youth did not share her confidence in the revolutionary tradition, in a Cuban tomorrow guided by a revolutionary past. I suspected, worried, that a crisis of faith and a broken heart would be part of Maria's transition into modern Cuban society.

It seemed likely that the street-smart, cigar-selling, wisecracking, sweet-talking *jineteros* would slide forward in Cuban life easier than María, though I hoped I was wrong.

Roberto and Eric had plugged into the future early, a circumstance of good fortune. Both had enviable state jobs, Eric had a military pension, and Roberto had his charm, his hustle. Roberto had cracked the code before I ever met him, knew how to watch closely and adjust to what was going on, working along the edges of government policies, guiding tourists from hotel to hotel, often into the foreigners-only shops to buy cosmetics for his girlfriends.

Paulo was committed to making a life for himself in a Cuba that he loved, crazy-loved, for all her best qualities. He paid attention, worked hard, and glided smoothly with each shift in Cuba's evolution into the postrevolutionary age. Paulo with the LADA, the gold, the quick English; the fixer, with an uncommon faithfulness to responsibility and friendship. Plus he had come to respect Cuba's revolutionary heritage while getting ready for her tomorrows. Paulo would most likely be fine, because he could adjust with the changes.

I was less certain about the many workaday Cubans. I supposed that life would be difficult for them, perhaps for some slow time to come, but it would be reckless for me to drift into further prophesy. The Cuban future might take care of itself, as Roberto had been so fond of predicting; fine, but the polite yet stern-faced cab driver Eduardo had predicted blood in a world of power blackouts and not enough milk for his babies. And Neddie's story was so pressing in the moment it was difficult to be hopeful for her or the many like her, the people who just could not keep up. And that was the key, keeping pace in a nation being squeezed by the process of ferocious change.

"I have the important goal of going to the United States," continued Neddie, with a noticeable shift in her tone.

"Luisa has been in Cancún for seven months. She has tried to call you, but we must not have your correct phone number. She has tried to call to ask you to visit her there. She would like to see you so she could have a talk with you. A serious talk."

Neddie claimed not to know Luisa's intentions, but I didn't believe her. The purpose was clear enough to me, and I became uneasy, a reaction I must have betrayed, so Neddie let the conversation drift for a time.

"She will stay in Mexico trying to make money. She makes twelve dollars a day plus room and board. We survive on what she sends from Mexico, fifteen to twenty dollars a month. The first place she worked was the Party Center, then a hotel, and now the Presidential Cabaret, not such a good place. She had to make a special arrangement with the manager to get that job or she would have needed to return to Cuba, even though her visa is good until September. She has a status called 'outside resident' that allows her to come and go and to send money.

"She and Paul are no longer together. He turned out not to be a good man. She would like to find someone nice.

"Luisa is very anxious to speak to you. She hopes you will visit her in Cancún. Do you think it possible you will go?"

I told Neddie that it was unlikely I would go to Cancún and left it at that, feeling a bit embarrassed for the both of us, particularly for Neddie, seeing where life had taken her in the few short years since we'd first met.

As I said good-bye standing at the front door about to leave the apartment for the night, and Cuba for the States in the morning, Neddie remarked, "My family thinks that Cuba has no future for us, but we know you are our friend." I turned down the narrow staircase with the single comment that I would see her the next time I visited Havana.

I left Cuba the next day with one additional bit of uneasy business to conclude before I reached home—getting through U.S. customs in the Nassau Airport. Traveling to Cuba without a Treasury Department license was a breach of the embargo that left me with two unattractive choices: either leave empty the line in the customs declaration card that asks, *What other countries have you visited?*, hoping that no one searched my bags to discover Cuban paintings or gifts stamped *Hecho en Cuba*, or my journals and film, to say nothing of the unforgivable trespass of Cohiba cigars and the seven-year-old Havana Club rum I had so cleverly wrapped in dirty laundry; or I could write *CUBA* in the appropriate space on the declaration card, list everything Cuban I was bringing home, and hope for the best, despite such a boldfaced challenge to the U.S. embargo of Cuba.

I made my decision at the last minute as I followed a crowd of laughing tourists as they headed down the corridor toward a series of stalls marked "United States Customs." I lurked behind for a time, trying to be inconspicuous, letting everyone else go ahead while I surveyed the agents, searching for just the right one, a pleasant one with a kindly disposition, I could only hope. I took a position at the end of a line moving rapidly thanks to the smiling goodwill of the large black woman in charge.

When my time came, she took my customs card and passport, looked at me, looked at my card, and said with an island accent, "Been to Cuba, huh? I *know* my man's got a Treasury Department license."

"Well, I've got one, but it expired last February. I probably have another one waiting for me at home. I made the proper application. The Treasury official I spoke with said it would take four weeks to get it to me. I left for Cuba after seven weeks, and it hadn't arrived."

"That's a sad story for certain, but I think it means you *don't* have a license. Right?"

"Yes, no license."

Examining the card, she turned to the agent in the next lane and said, "Julienne, *my man* here has listed, 'religious painting'; I think he knows what he's doing," making reference to the fact that such items could be brought from Cuba into the United States without penalty or limit, if you had a license.

"Religious paintings," she said again with a laugh and a shake of her head.

"You've got cigars listed. Only one box?"

"Yes. Just one."

"You wouldn't lie to me about that, would you?"

"No. If I was going to lie to you about that, I probably would have lied about everything," I said with a toss of my hands. "But I figured, I'd rather take my chances than let the likes of Jesse Helms and those mean-spirited bastards who made that embargo turn me into a liar and a sneak."

She looked me over for a second, judging, I suppose, whether or not she was being hustled, then she reached for her stamp and said, "I don't feel like doing all that paperwork on you just because those boys in Washington can't do their job right. Why don't you just go on through? Take yourself on home."

Epilogue: July 1999

At the new José Martí International Airport my first bag came off the carousel with the zipper ripped open and several items missing. I wheeled over to a customs official demanding to know *what the fuck is going on, who's in charge, is this another new Cuba or just the old one with a meaner spirit?*

"Wait five minutes, señor, five minutes I ask."

"What does that mean?"

"You will know in five minutes," he repeated, holding up his hands in surrender and turning back to his companion in conversation.

Fine. Okay. I went to wait for my other bag, wondering if it too would come off damaged, like my mood, but it did not. I gathered up everything, walked past green-uniformed officers with drug dogs on short leashes, past a fellow American traveler whose bags were systematically being emptied item by item onto a large table, to return to the immigration official who watched me approach, then politely directed me to a set of double doors, where I presumed I would find someone in charge to explain why my bags had been crudely vandalized and items of various importance had been plundered from my luggage, including a quantity of expired prescription drugs destined for Havana's hospital. I was pumped and ready for that discussion as I passed through the automatic doors, which shut behind me, leaving me staring *not* at the complex of an indifferent government bureaucracy, but at the airport's main lobby, with no reasonable way to return to the immigration station. I had been beaten, and cleverly so. I smiled as I walked outside to get a cab, charmed once again by Cuba.

A cab was necessary, Paulo had instructed me over the phone before I left Florida, because "things aren't like before, Peter. Not like it's been. It wouldn't be safe for me to pick you up at the airport. I'm really sorry, but the police . . . It's just not possible." An introductory caution from

Paulo—the fixer, the guy who knew Havana's streets—I accepted as a proper alert and a confirmation that another firsthand look around Cuba had been a good decision. My last visit had been more than two years before, and current State-side rumors included worrisome stories about dramatic changes.

The cab dropped me at Paulo's new apartment, filled with the scents and sounds of restoration—a newly tiled bath and kitchen, fresh plaster and paint throughout, the front entrance defined by a wall of professionally finished stucco and artistic metal gates that opened into a secure parking place for the refurbished LADA. Very nice. Very protected. Very New Cuba. Very like Paulo, who was spending the cash he had obsessively saved over years from driving, fixing, trading, fishing, anything, everything, putting thousands—every dollar he had—into house and car, into meeting the ambitions he had spoken of in 1993. But his worry was apparent as he rushed about getting black-market building materials, directing workers, fending off his girlfriend's complaints that he was ignoring her, while trying to accommodate the complication of my visit.

Paulo's greeting was a repeated apology for not meeting me at the airport. "Peter, police are everywhere. They stop us for nothing on the street to ask for an ID. Will stop a car with a foreigner and Cuban together. A foreign man and a Cuban woman for sure, every time. You and I and my lady friend can't go in the car together the way we used to; the police will think she's with you and I made the arrangement. You're going to see. It's really bad.

"These aren't the tourist cops; they're a pain in the ass. But the new cops, the national police, the ones with berets, they can be mean. They don't fuck around, just take you off to jail to spend the night if you do *nothing,* longer if you do something. They're everywhere. Every street, two or three walking along, standing, watching, riding new Italian motorcycles, riding in new police cars. Hundreds. And, Peter, get this—they make 800 pesos a month, 800, that's more than a doctor earns," he concluded before interrupting our conversation to discuss details with a carpenter working on the windows of his house.

"There's so much that's happened," he sighed when he came back. "I don't know what to tell you first. It's bad for everyone, but worse for the *jineteras.* If you look like you might be a *jinetera* you better be with a Cuban man. Best if he's your husband. Getting rid of the *jineteras,* that's what this is about. And it's worked, too; they're gone, from around the hotels, the Malecón, the clubs. Disappeared. Not like before, off to East Beach or someplace else. This time, just gone. Driven indoors, I guess.

"If a girl is arrested a third time, she goes to jail. A real jail, with real criminals, for three, four years, I'm not certain. If a guy is pimping, he gets twenty. Twenty years in a Cuban jail. Think about that," said Paulo, pulling a folded handkerchief from his pocket to wipe summer sweat and construction dust from his brow.

"Peter, I don't know exactly what to think about this. I don't want people in other countries to think Cuban women are whores, so in some ways I know Fidel has done the correct thing. My mother and sister are Cuban women.

"But here's the big thing. Everyone is more worried than ever. Before, the crackdowns came, but in a few weeks, maybe a little more, they faded. You know how it is. It's Cuba. But this one, it goes on a long time, January to July, so we start to ask, Is Fidel serious this time, is this the new way for us? The new Cuba? You know that I'm not someone who worries. I can make do for myself, but this worries me, Peter, a lot."

Castro had apparently determined it was time to adjust the tolerance level of Cuba's economic program tied to tourism. The number of crimes against foreigners was growing, including violent robbery and even murder, although not at a rate that would alarm most nations; countless visitors had lost cameras or purses to petty thieves; and every time a tourist bought cigars or a souvenir from a black marketeer or rented an illegal room, the government was cut out of its share of the revenue. Having decided that crime, sex, and illegal commerce should not control the balance sheet for Cuba's future, Castro ordered a crackdown, this one in a style not experienced for a long time.

The stern decision concerning *jineteras* was only one step in a government program driven by a crippled economy as much as by the need for social control; a pinched-thin national treasury was as worrisome as Cuba's developing reputation as the whorehouse of the Caribbean. And, in truth, what felt new was the fierce application of laws, the inability to skirt them. The laws themselves were well established, some old, like those prohibiting prostitution, some newer, such as government regulations that allowed Cubans to make dollars by selling things, renting rooms, serving food, and providing services. What felt harsh was the elimination of the elastic quality that had helped comfort a crisis-ridden society in transition.

The fee to operate a *paladar* cost $1,200 a month, said one owner. Since January, licensed operators were required to show receipts to officials to prove they bought food from government suppliers. That regulation had been on the books for some time, but now that it was being enforced, money-saving deals on the black market were difficult to mask, and the law was blamed as one reason for so many *paladares* going out of business. Homeowners taking in foreign guests paid a government fee of $300 a month per room, rented or not, explained the man who accepted my $30 per night for an air-conditioned room with a private bath and maid service; but the fee kept creeping up, and the room sat vacant more often than in the past. Unlicensed *paladares* and boarding houses were nearly gone from Havana, shut down by government regulators on the hunt for state revenue. Outdoor vendors at the *ferias* along the Malecón and near the Plaza de la Catedral needed a state license to set up shop (one artist paid $169 per month) and then paid $3 a day for a space big enough to accommodate a card table, an umbrella, and a chair. Too expensive, they all insisted, with declining tourism making business bad, leaving them scrambling to survive and sharing a feeling of resentment toward a government that made everything "too difficult." A man sold me a painting he carefully wrapped in that day's edition of *Granma,* the government newspaper; when I asked what he thought Fidel might say about such a thing, he replied good-naturedly, "Take Fidel back to the States with you and ask him."

Paulo was correct. The squeeze was on, the changes dramatic and perhaps enduring, too—which was the most terrible worry among many Cubans, *that it might last.* The crackdown worked its way through Cuban society, mustering a force that rid the city of familiar, postrevolutionary Cuban sights and sounds and opportunities, then reached far beyond what its designers might have considered. News of the tough cops positioned everywhere day and night and of *jineteras,* cheap rooms, and illegal cigars disappearing from the streets spread to foreign males, whose arrival numbers dropped, then dropped even more, and kept dropping until so many of them abandoned vacation plans of Cuban sun and sex that their absence shocked Cuban's tourist economy.

To trust Havana street wisdom is to accept one black marketeer's explanation: "The *jineteras* and black marketeers got the foreign dollar first, then it went to the guy who sold gold, ran a *paladar,* operated a disco, or sold oranges on the street. Now, because of the cops and the crackdown, foreign men don't come, and that dollar is gone. Discos have disappeared; *paladares* are closing; no one buys gold. Even the man who sold oranges isn't where he used to be every day; I don't know where he is, and I don't know if he'll be back."

Víctor, Paulo's stepfather and the son of Fidel's spy in Miami, had a bigger view. Yes, he acknowledged, the *jineteros* and *jineteras* were off the streets and the sex-seeking men were forsaking Cuba, and all to the good, was his opinion. But more traditional tourists were also avoiding Havana, apprehensive about being stopped by ever-present cops who asked for IDs and certification of registration at approved hotels and guest houses, and some tourists stayed away for the pure natural fact that cops in such numbers can cause any reasonable visitor to wonder, *What's going on here?* Víctor, whose profession made him a candidate for respected predictions, hinted at a drop in tourism revenues that could cause a further national crisis—the remedy compounding the problem.

After several days of walking around, looking, and talking, I determined that Paulo's dramatic observations were as reliable as his friendship. Always-polite Habaneros passed by on the sidewalk without acknowledging my greeting, kept their eyes locked straight ahead, failed to approach me with a common "*¡hola!*" or with an offer of cigars, companionship, gold, or anything else. After lingering at familiar places throughout Havana, I concluded, for the first time in my visits there, that Cuba felt like a regulated society, felt like the sort of place many Americans always presumed it to be, where people acted as though they were being watched, a Cuba that seemed to confirm that Fidel could exert his will only by casting a shadow large, firm, and threatening. Even as I stood alone, leaning against the Malecón seawall one late night surrounded by young people dancing and drinking Sterling beer, not one of them came to me with the curiosity I had come to expect and normally welcomed, not a single one. Havana had become a city with downcast eyes and a cop on every corner.

But the next night, sitting on a bench in Central Park across the busy street from the Hotel Inglaterra, I found something else, the flip side, a different look of things, a look at the bedrock just below a roughed-up surface. The park area was busy, percolating with people. At 9:00 on a summer evening Cubans chatted casually, strolled the sidewalk, held hands and spoke softly, greeted each other with an embrace, guided small children across four lanes of traffic that separated the park from the hotel. What was set before me that warm night were the everyday happenings of an ordinary community, moving through their lives in the customs so common to honorable citizens of the workaday world.

And on another day, in another park, in one of the several towns I visited outside Havana, I spent a long time with a young man who spoke easily about his life and what was happening in that moment in Cuba. He had no complaints other than those expected of a sixteen-year-old, not even about police or a crackdown that apparently had not reached his neighborhood. We talked for perhaps a couple of hours, moving from bench to bench to escape the awful heat of the July sun. Then he offered to help me find a metal artist I had met during a previous visit but for whom I had only a partial local address. We must have spent another two hours walking the streets, with him stopping strangers, asking questions, knocking on doors, directing us to the next possibility until we learned that the artist had moved away. We returned to the park with sweat-stained clothes, cold drinks in hand, and a running joke about our futile search for the missing artist. After spending so much of the afternoon together, when I rose to leave, I thanked him for his help and pressed a folded dollar bill into his hand. He accepted my thanks but turned back the dollar with the statement that he and I were friends, and he couldn't accept it.

That Cuban community of fellowship took Paulo and me to the U.S. Interests Section in Havana one afternoon after I got back in town. We had spoken repeatedly over the years about him visiting the States, and Paulo was confident, as he never had been in the past, that conditions were right for us to start the process. And he was clearly attentive to the details of such matters.

"There have been a lot of changes in the immigration program, Peter. A set number of visas are issued each year, and the rafters are being sent back if they are found at sea by the U.S. Coast Guard, not taken to the States. Things for Cubans are more like with other countries than they used to be. I think it's going to be easy. We fill out the papers, you write a letter inviting me, the U.S. Consul in Havana calls me for an interview, and then we have Christmas together in the States. Come on, let's go, my friend."

So off we went, to take our place on the shaded sidewalk across the street from the U.S. Interests Section, where a very large, very loud

Cuban-American assumed responsibility for keeping everyone informed about their proper place in line as he stood impatiently with the rest of us. Paulo and I talked strategy while we waited our turn to cross the street to speak with a Cuban policeman stationed in a booth, our first stop in the day's bureaucratic chain.

"Peter, keep it simple. Just tell them we're friends, and you want me to visit. The more you tell them, the more questions they can ask. Say nothing unnecessary, that's my rule when dealing with the government."

I had a different view, one that involved playing a couple of crass power cards from American culture: my status as a university professor and author of a forthcoming book about Cuba. Paulo was unconvinced, and the discussion continued as we presented papers and passport before the Cuban cop at the booth, waited for him to fill in forms with a pencil stub almost too small to hold, then made our way through a heavy gate, through a metal detector, and through another gate to the door of the U.S. Interests Section and into air-conditioned comfort.

Our strategy debate was arbitrated by a wonderful Cuban-American woman who sat behind us in a near-empty room full of folding metal chairs and interview booths along a side wall, only one of which was active. She was there with her nephew, who had won the lottery for one of the 20,000 immigration visas the U.S. government issued to Cubans every year.

"Everyone thinks winning one of the lottery places is the goal, but it's only the start. Then you have to satisfy the U.S. immigration standards, which are interpreted by the consul here in Havana. My nephew," she said, switching to English, presumably to cut him out of the conversation for a crucial moment, "will most likely not be allowed to go. The reason? He has what in the States we would call a GED, not a real high-school diploma. They're that tough," she said, waving her hand back and forth in exasperation.

"I've gone through this many times with many relatives, and my experience tells me they won't accept him for that reason. I have my own business; I'm his sponsor; he has a guaranteed job. But that won't be enough. They look for the reason to say 'no.'"

As the woman spoke, the enthusiasm fell from Paulo's face; he and I turned away from the woman to confer. "Paulo," I said, "this is only the first step of plan A. If this doesn't work, we'll try something else until we have a Cuban sandwich in my hometown," making reference to my ongoing commentary that the Cuban food was better at my local restaurant than in Havana, except at his mother's house.

"That's right," said the helpful woman. "You've got to try everything and keep at it. My advice to you," she said, turning directly to me, "is to give them as many reasons as possible to say 'yes,' everything you've mentioned—your book, letters of invitation from your publisher, from your university president, anything, everything."

Paulo didn't respond, drifted away from the conversation to walk around the room, getting a drink of water, washing his face in the men's room, waiting for my name to be called so we could make our case before the glass partition of state bureaucracy.

Our time finally came and we took seats before an assistant consul, who was terrific. She accepted the completed government forms, my passport, my faculty ID, and the publisher's advertisement for *Conversations with Cuba,* all of which I slipped through a slot in the glass window. She listened to everything I said through the microphone system, commenting how wonderful an opportunity it would be for Paulo to give lectures at the university, and how wonderful it would be for the students to be able to meet him. She said she would be in the States when the book came out and hoped to see it. She could not have been nicer.

But when I asked her what effect the book, the invitation, and the letters would have on the process, she paused and said, "Not much."

"What about contacting my senator?" I asked.

"He will send us a polite form letter, and we will send one back to him."

"What's important here?"

"All the consul will care about is whether or not Paulo has enough at stake in Cuba to return home. Understand, we treat Cubans like people from no other country. If a Cuban arrives in the United States with a travel visa and decides to stay, we won't do a thing. We can't. They get to stay. So when we make a decision here, we have to be 100 percent confident that it's sound."

"Why are Cubans treated so differently?" I asked.

"If you just wrote a book about Cuba, you know the answer to that question," she said through a smile. "You know what group has that sort of power in the States."

"Look, my friend loves Cuba and doesn't want to leave. His father lives in Miami and has asked him to move there, but he doesn't want to. He has a house and a car, a mother and sister here. He doesn't want to give up everything."

"I understand," she said. "But our belief is that a house and a car are easy to replace in the States and may not be enough to guarantee a return to Cuba."

"What I'm hearing is, our chances aren't very good."

"I encourage you to make the application, but I'm trying to be candid," she said, returning my stare with kindness.

Paulo and I scraped back our chairs, and as we turned to leave, the wonderful Cuban-American woman from Miami who had been sitting nearby gave us a big smile and a thumbs-up, but both Paulo and I knew it was for the quality of the presentation, not for his chances of getting a visa to the States.

We left the embassy with Paulo quiet and me trying to talk down my barely controlled rage at the absolute cravenness of U.S. policy toward Cuba, telling Paulo that we would try this and then that. I would need a picture for forged documents that would get him in through Mexico, and if that failed I knew little-used back roads across the Canadian border into Maine; we would try it all until we ate a Cuban sandwich together in the States, I told him. But it was all talk.

We piled into his sweltering car, and the engine wouldn't even turn over. Dead, and not for the first time over the past couple of days. Another afternoon insult, as if El Cobre had forsaken us.

We got out to push the LADA for a sweaty jump-start. Two guys trotted over to give us a hand. We got it rolling and running. Then Paulo backed up the car until we were beside the helpful pair.

Paulo thanked them; the larger of the two responded with, "Americano."

"Was he referring to me?" I asked, thinking the man might be someone I had met during an earlier trip to Cuba.

"No, Peter," said Paulo. "He was just saying, 'American.'"

"I don't get it," I said.

"*Americano, Americano,*" said Paulo. "It's a word used in Cuba as a praise, as a compliment. *Americano.*"